A Survey of Arab History

A Survey of Arab History

Revised Edition

Bernard G. Weiss
and
Arnold H. Green

THE AMERICAN UNIVERSITY IN CAIRO PRESS

113 Sharia Kasr el Aini
Cairo, Egypt

This edition first published in 1987 by The American University in Cairo Press

Third printing 1990

Dar el Kutub No. 4631/87
ISBN 977 424 180 0

Printed in Egypt by The American University in Cairo Press

Contents

Illustrations

PREFACE TO THE REVISED EDITION

This book's 'first edition' exhibited signs both of its hasty composition and of its do-it-yourself production. Written under the pressure of deadlines, the typescript was prepared by two different typists on three different machines and then printed by photo offset at the AUC Printshop. The AUC Press as such had nothing to do with it until the 'third printing' in 1985, when the cover alone received a facelift. Although its virtues included a very inexpensive price, not an insignificant consideration in an era when students routinely spend $50 and up on a single textbook, it contained many errors and lacked some of the standard features of a book. The present edition is therefore styled 'revised' rather than 'second' in large part because, although previously reprinted three times during seven years of limited circulation, this is the first time the volume is being at once prepared by a bona fide publisher and made available to a wider audience.

Among the symbols of its newfound authenticity are such features as a uniform typeface throughout and a table of contents. Substantive changes were also made. The introduction was condensed rather radically in order to bring into greater relief the argument that history, although in several respects a social science, has its own peculiar disciplinary assumptions, techniques for gathering data, methods for evaluating evidence, and genres for packaging conclusions. Several other chapters were subjected to considerable rewriting, in part to establish common themes running throughout the entire work. In the process, a large number of errors, both typographical and factual, were eliminated. Also, several new maps and illustrations were added. While still intended primarily for use as a textbook for The American University in Cairo's history requirement (History 246: Survey of Arab History), *A Survey of Arab History* now presents itself to readers outside AUC.

For bringing to our attention the mistakes in the 'first edition' and for suggesting some of the ideas incorporated into the revision, we are indebted particularly to fellow instructors of History 246 but also to the many students whose complaints sprang from reflection and insight and to a few colleagues kind enough to read and to offer counsel. The resultant modifications in the revised edition by no means render the work perfect -- in neither the Greek (without flaw) nor the Hebrew (having attained its final or most mature form) understanding of 'perfection'. This is said not only as prelude to the standard acknowledgment that the authors assume full responsibility for the errors and faults still present in the book. It is said also in anticipation that, in light of the next round of criticisms and comments, further corrections and changes will be made in a future 'second revised edition'.

BGW & AHG
June 1987

INTRODUCTION

WHAT IS HISTORY?

Since this textbook was written mainly for undergraduates enrolled in their first college-level history course, it is appropriate that its opening pages be devoted to a consideration of what 'history' is. At first glance, the question 'what is history?' seems to invite a straightforward answer. Since 'history' is a common word, anyone might presume to know what it means without reflection. When pausing to think about it, however, it becomes evident that this word can convey more than one definition. E.g., three different senses of 'history' may be detected in the following statements: "A nation is shaped by its history"; "Professor Hitti wrote a history of the Arabs"; and "My friend is majoring in history." In the first statement, 'history' could be replaced by 'past' ("a nation is shaped by its past"), a substitution which would not work well in the other two statements, however. It would be proper to say neither that "Prof. Hitti wrote a past of the Arabs" (rather, he wrote <u>about</u> the past of the Arabs) nor that "my friend is majoring in the past" (rather, one is majoring in the field which devotes itself to studying the past). Noting that the concept of the 'past' is central to each of the statements, we can distinguish three usages of 'history' by saying that it may refer to (1) the past itself, (2) a written account of the past, or (3) the academic study of the past.

While it is the first of the three meanings that is suggested by this book's title, this chapter is concerned with the last one--i.e., with 'history' as a field of study. In this sense, 'history' is a branch of learning or an academic discipline. Because it is a field of study and of specialization, 'history' has a formal place within an academic institution. There is ordinarily a 'history department' in a university's administrative structure, 'history courses' and a 'history major' in its curriculum, and a 'history section' in its library. What is 'history,' then, considered in this sense? "The study of the past" may seem to be an adequate definition; yet, under scrutiny, that definition is still too vague. The historian's concern is not with the past of everything in the universe; rather, it is confined to <u>man's</u> past. So, as a subject field, history can be delimited to 'the <u>study of</u> the human past.' But even this does not reveal much about what the discipline of history is and does. In a sense, every subject field dealing with human beings is concerned with the human past, which is the sum total of what is known about humans; many academic disciplines study the human past in quest of information about various aspects of human life and behavior.

What, then, are the particular assumptions and methods which make history different from other fields dealing with the human past? An answer to this question necessitates a consideration of history's relationship with the other social sciences and with the humanities. By speaking of history's relationship with the <u>other</u> social sciences, we have already implied something fundamental--<u>that</u>, because it shares a general subject matter (human activity) and certain methods of analysis, history is itself a social science. Yet history is unique among the social sciences in several respects: it considers the human past as such to be specifically its subject matter; it is concerned mainly with specific past events rather than with recurring phenomena; it often explains aspects of the human past through the medium of the narrative; and it learns about the human past primarily by studying archival documents and other primary sources. By exploring these and other ways in which history's method of dealing with the human past differs from that of the other social sciences, we will be in a better position to understand what is distinctive about history as a subject field.

The human past as such is essentially the subject matter of history, whereas it is not essentially the subject matter of any of the other social sciences, even though they also investigate it regularly. E.g., the subject matter of economics is human economic activity. So economists study the human past in order to accumulate data about the ways in which men produce, distribute and consume wealth; and political sceintists often study the past in order to accumulate data about human political activity. While the other social sciences fully appreciate the importance of mankind's 'historical dimension' reaching backwards through time, history is the only discipline which takes that dimension as such for its essential subject matter.

History's way of dealing with the past may also be distinguished by the quality of 'specificity.' By this we mean that the main focus in history is upon specific past events or situations. As a rule, the other social sciences--and, in fact, most natural or physical sciences too--make use of specific events or situations as a means to the end of generalizing about recurrent 'patterns' or 'types' of phenomena. For the historian, the specific event or 'case' is something to be understood for its own sake. The interest of the social scientist in recurrent patterns leads him to place specific events in a 'comparative context'; i.e., he groups a particular event with others exhibiting similar features. The historian, on the other hand, seeks to understand and to explain a particular event or situation in its original or 'historical context'--the actual context of time and place in which it took place. Although he may take into account typical aspects of certain kinds of events, he assumes that history 'repeats itself' only approximately but not exactly and consequently considers every event or situation to possess certain unique features. It would be pointless to insist upon this quality of specificity or uniqueness with regard to such things as the falling of a raindrop or the blooming of a flower. But the career of Saladin, the Mongol destruction of Baghdad, the construction of the Suez Canal--these are events which truly occurred only once and which therefore deserve to be investigated and reconstructed in all their unique detail. As one historian put it, "each phenomenon is embedded in its own circumstances, never to be repeated, from which it cannot be completely detached."

It is because the historian deals with past events and situations within their historical contexts that he is especially conscious of 'continuity.' Thus a historian pays closer attention than other social scientists to the 'before' and 'after' of particular events and situations;

he therefore deals with whole series of events, each following from what precedes and leading to what ensues. In other words, the historian is interested in telling a story--the human story--and is, in a sense, a narrator. The very word 'history' derives from the Latin word 'historia,' meaning 'story.' To tell a story is to relate a series of events or situations in their correct order and to show their interconnectedness. A story is by its very nature a continuum; it is built around a plot, which unfolds stage by stage. Another distinguishing feature of history as a discipline is thus that it frequently uses the genre of the 'narrative' as a means of presenting the results of its research into the human past.

The fact that there are differences between history and the other social sciences does not mean that the two are at cross purposes with each other. There has simply occurred a division of labor among scholars whose common subject, ultimately, is mankind. Social scientists do not develop theories concerning patterns of human activity so that these may be stored away in the deep freezes of academia. From a comparative study of particulars they develop theories the ultimate value of which depends on their applicability to other particulars. And historians, whose main concern is with the specific events of the human past, cannot expect to understand these particulars fully without some reference to the social scientists' patterns and theories. The historian-social scientist relationship is similar to that of the police detective and the criminologist; the latter draws upon the detectives's specific cases in order to generalize about 'patterns' of criminal behavior and 'rules' of police detection, while the former draws upon the criminologist's patterns and rules in order to solve his specific case. A similar relationship obtains between the physician and the pathologist.

Since historians assume the task of telling the story of the past, of narrating the sequence of particular events and situations that make up the past, they are responsible for discovering the incidents belonging to the story and of putting the story together. I.e., they must carry out the research necessary to produce an accurate and explanatory account of memorable past events and situations. This research consists essentially of investigation into source materials. What are history's source materials? To answer this question, let us imagine outselves to be engaged in writing an account of the history of Egypt during the Ottoman period. How would we put together such a story? Our first inclination perhaps might be to go to the library where we would discover, by looking in the card catalog or on the shelves, that a number of history books have already been written about Egypt during the Ottoman period, including <u>Egypt and the Fertile Crescent 1516-1922</u> (London, 1966) by P. M. Holt. Is this an 'historical source?' Yes, of course; it is a certain kind of source. History books are sometimes called 'secondary sources'; i.e., they are sources 'derived' from others considered to be 'primary' or 'original.' Should our investigations result in the writing of a book, this book would itself become a secondary source on Ottoman Egypt; and since it would be foolish of us to attempt to say something meaningful about this subject without first reading what earlier historians have said about it, it is essential that we consult the existing secondary sources. If we look at the footnotes and bibliography in Holt's book, we find that he duly read a large number of history books written by previous historians. We may thus trace the secondary source back to the very earliest historians--perhaps to such native Egyptian historians as al-Jabarti (d. 1825), who completed his Aja'ib al-athar fi'l-tarajim wa'l-akhbar about 1802.

But this is just the beginning of our search for historical sources. For we must proceed to locate and to investigate the 'primary sources' or the 'original documents.' Documents containing information about Ottoman Egypt may be of may be of many kinds: decrees by Ottoman sultans, lists of soldiers in the Turkish regiments, tax records, legal decisions by religious judges, receipts for goods received by local merchants, reports written by foreign diplomats temporarily living in Egypt, diaries kept by educated Egyptians or by European travelers, local scholarship or poetry from the period and, if we're lucky, contemporary Turkish or Egyptian historical works (such as al-Jabarti's book, which was published in four volumes in 1879-80). Except for such 'published sources,' however, 'unpublished historical documents' are ordinarily not collected into libraries but rather into 'archives' which are usually established and maintained by governments. For a long time, historians relied mainly on such secondary sources as might be readily available in the personal library of an educated gentleman. It was the German historian Leopold von Ranke (d. 1886), among others, who insisted that historians must use strictly contemporary sources of information and who personally exploited archival documents systematically and effectively for the first time, thereby poineering the technique of 'archival historical research.'*

Since the historian, in carrying out research in documentary sources, is mainly concerned with the particulars of the human past rather than with general patterns of human activity, it may be argued that history does not engage in inductive inquiry and therefore is not a true social science, that it is at best a helpmate to the other social sciences. History is undoubtedly a helpmate to the other social sciences, just as mathematics is a helpmate to the physical sciences, but there are good reasons for considering history to be a social science in its own right. Even some natural sciences have an historical dimension and are concerned to some extent with particulars. E.g., geology investigates, among other things, the history of the earth--i.e., its origin and development through time and the formation of its main features. In a sense, a geologist is an historian of the earth; he studies features of the earth's development whether or not they conform to general patterns. The non-recurrent, atypical aspects of the earth's development interest him as much as those aspects which recur elsewhere in the universe. Another science having an essentially historical character is natural history, which deals with the origin and

*With regard to historians' heavy reliance on "historical documents," it might be useful at this point to distinguish between the discipline of history proper and a branch of history called PRE-HISTORY. Of course the prefix "pre" means "before" or "prior to," and we have said that history is the study of the human past. But pre-history does not entail studying what was prior to the human

past; rather, it entails development of the various forms of plant and animal life on the earth. Natural history is a branch of biology, which concerns itself with the evolution, characteristics and behavior of the many species of plant and animal life. There is also in natural history, as in geology, much that is non-recurrent (as far as the biologist knows). History, geology, natural history, archeology and certain other disciplines may be called the 'historical sciences.'

Broadly speaking, science is a systematic attempt to acquire knowledge about anything that is in principle knowable; i.e., it is an assault on the unknown. By extension, science is also the body of knowledge thus acquired. Since science in its totality is too vast for any one individual to master, it has traditionally been divided into various separate sciences on the basis of a differentiation between distinct subject matters. All sciences share at least three basic characteristics: (1) they all entail a systematic collection of data, (2) they all seek to formulate hypotheses on the basis of the data collected, and (3) they all go on to test or verify these hypotheses on the basis of further data collected, producing in the end theses or even 'laws.' The theses may have to do with general patterns observable in particular data about recurrent phenomena, or they may (as in the case of the historical sciences) have to do with particular events, developments or situations.

History has a clearly defined subject matter: the human past viewed in specific terms as a continuity of particular events and situations. History also exhibits the other three characteristics mentioned above. The data which the historian collects is that found in documents and other primary sources. On the basis of this data, the historian constructs hypotheses about past events and situations. A hypothesis in history may relate to <u>what</u> happened, or it may relate to <u>why</u> something happened as it did. Finally, the historian gathers additional data from the sources to see whether the hypothesis is

---

past; rather, it entails studying the human past during certain (usually very early) periods for which written sources do not exist--either because writing was not practiced then or else because writing was done on materials which have not survived for one reason or another. Instead of relying on documents, pre-historians exploit such non-written sources as ruins, tools, pottery fragments, coins, etc. "Pre-history" thus actually means "pre-literary history." This distinction implies that history proper is the discipline which attempts to reconstruct and to interpret the human past in its original context primarily from the evidence contained in written documents. The central role of documents in historical research does not mean that historians never take non-literary sources into consideration, for the best historical accounts have always been based on the available archaeological evidence as well as on the evidence contained in literary sources. In recent years, historians have also begun increasingly to tap sources of information used extensively by social scientists, including personal interviews and the recording of "oral history." But historians usually regard these other kinds of sources as supplements to, not substitutes for, the available written documents.

confirmed or contradicted. It it continues to be confirmed, the historian will try to convince other historians of the validity of the hypotheses, which may become a widely accepted 'historical thesis.' Every history book, even if the author never actually says so, is a thesis about its particular historical subject.

It is true that history and the other social sciences, unlike some physical sciences, cannot engage at will in experimentation with their subject matters in laboratories under controlled conditions. It is also true that history, unlike most other social sciences, as a rule cannot even engage directly in the empirical observation of its subject matter. But this is a surmountable problem which, incidentally, is shared by all the historical sciences and even by some physical sciences. E.g., no biologist ever saw a dinosaur; no geologist witnessed the drifting of a continent or the Red Sea materializing from the widening of the great Rift Valley; no physicist has ever even seen an atom. Yet empirical observation does play a role in all sciences--even in the historical sciences. The biologist <u>reconstructs</u> the form of the dinosaur on the basis of evidence (e.g., skeletel remains, fossils) which is empirically available. The same is true of the physicist in the construction of the atom. In each case the scientist constructs or reconstructs, on the basis of evidence observed empirically, some reality which is not unobservable. In using evidence, scientists proceed somewhat in the manner of police detectives, who 'reconstruct' crimes on the basis of observable evidence left behind.

The evidence used in history is the data collected from archival documents and other primary sources. The historian of course must use such data with skill and discretion. The many statements about a given past event are sometimes mutually contradictory; and the historian will often detect inaccuracies or biases in them. It is of course not by virtue of being able to check the data against direct observation of the event itself that the historian considers a particular statement to be inaccurate or biased. The critical evaluation of data or evidence is thus based on considerations which emerge from the data itself. Indeed, the suggestion of error or prejudice in a source is itself a hypothesis based on the comparative analysis of the available evidence.

Nor is it an insurmountable problem that historians do not employ the inductive method of reasoning in the same way that most scientists do: to induce generalizations about recurrent phenomena. Historians do generalize but mainly about specific events or situations. I.e., after examining many pieces of evidence about the various aspects of an event, in the reconstructed account of the event the historian tends to omit unessential details and to emphasize major factors, developments, figures and issues; the story is thus usually presented in summary rather than in exhaustive detail. The process of moving from the specific data contained in the primary sources to the narrative summary represents a process of generalization, a particularly historical use of the inductive method. In other words, the historian generalizes about the pattern perceived in a specific event rather than that perceived in recurrent phenomena. Here, the term 'pattern' has a slightly different meaning with special applicability to history. Any event or situation can have an observable pattern, which need not reoccur in any other event or situation. As in the case of snowflakes, a pattern need not be recurrent in order to be a pattern. A work or art, for example, may have a pattern (a unique combination of form, color, texture, etc.) found in no other work of art. Each segment of the past has a pattern in this sense. By investigating primary sources the historian thus first tries to discover this pattern in particular events or situations and then, by describing the main causes and trends, to provide an explanatory reconstruction. To the extent that he does so, the historian is engaging in inductive inquiry.

History also has important links with another main branch of scholarship which, in the Western curriculum, is usually placed alongside the sciences: the humanities. In the curricula of most universities, the humanities include some of the following subjects: languages, literature, the fine arts (art, music, theatre, dance), and philosophy. Although classified as a social science by most universities, history is often included among the humanities in other contexts. E.g., the U.S. National Endowment for the Humanities lists the following subjects as humanities: history, philosophy, literature, ethics and comparative religion, language, jurisprudence, archeology, art history and theory, and the humanistic social sciences. Historically, the humanities originated with the study of Greek and Latin classics during the European Renaissance. Whereas medieval learning in Europe had been concerned principally with theology, Renaissance learning became interested in the cultural achievements of the ancient Greeks and Romans as a subject to be explored for its own sake. The emphasis shifted from God to man. The interest in man and his cultural achievements came to be called 'humanism.' The slogan associated with humanism was "man is the measure of all things." Most of the first humanists were committed Christians; in time, however, as did scholars in various fields, many humanists began to abandon Christian concepts for a secular approach to life. Whatever the religious position of the humanists, they all shared a common point of view: whatever was humanly significant was worthy of man's serious attention. This point of view pervades all the humanities as we know them today.

The humanistic interest in man's cultural achievements and in the aesthetic and moral values which he creates is very pronounced in the discipline of history. The historian is interested not just in developments related to social institutions or trends but also in the creative activity of individuals. One has only to browse through general works of history to discover that historians are greatly concerned about literature, music, art, and philosophical or religious thought--about all facets of man's cultural and spiritual life. General works of history (or general university courses) often bear the title 'history of civilization' or even just 'civilization.' History's story-telling function links it to literature. Indeed, prior to von Ranke and the rise of a rigorous archival method of historical research, history was widely considered to be mainly a branch of literature. The best historians have often been listed among the great writers of their time, along with novelists, poets and essayists. This is so not just because those historians pay attention to the style of their prose but

THE PLACE OF HISTORY

AMONG MODERN ACADEMIC DISCIPLINES

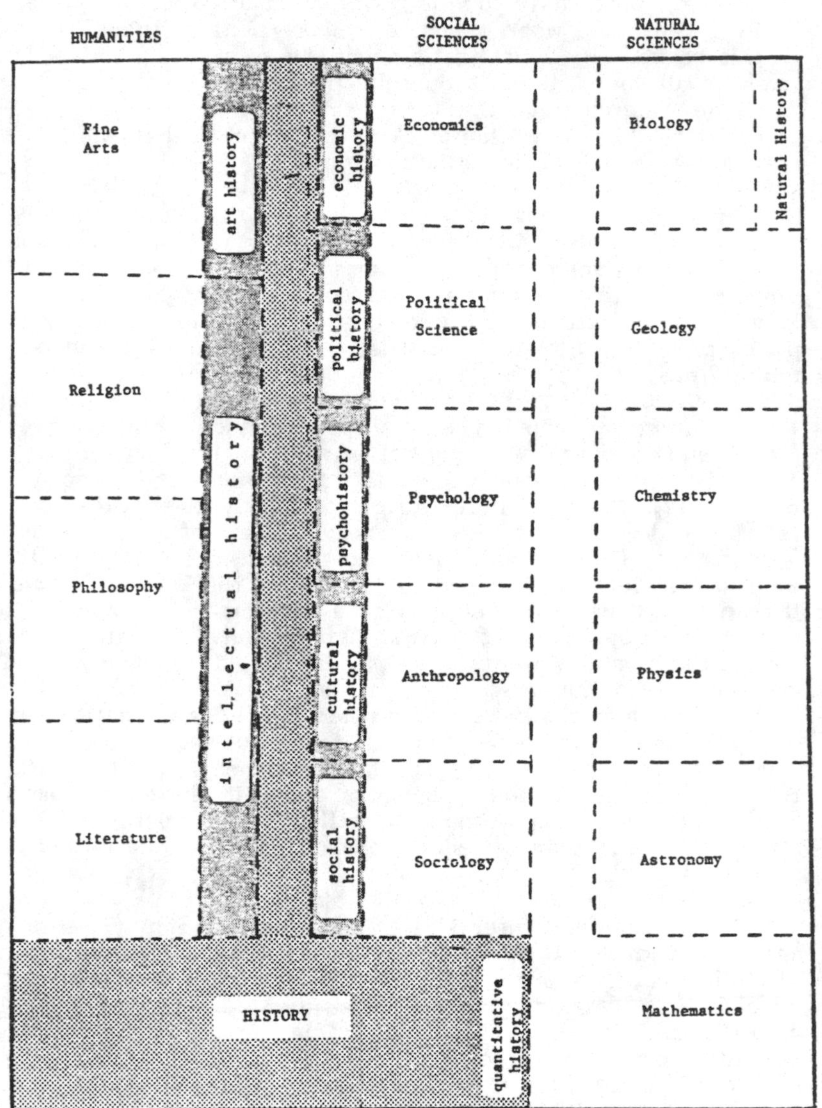

also because they share with other literateurs the goal of arousing in their readers certain feelings and appreciations.

The dual social scientific-humanistic character of history may be seen by considering the various subfields into which history is divided: economic history, social history, political history, cultural history, intellectual history/the history of ideas, art history, the history of science, etc. The fact that historians specializing in such subfields can all work together in a single university department indicates that these specializations are all of a piece. Of course, some historians lean further toward the humanities. It can perhaps be said in conclusion that history, taken in its entirety, is one of the most comprehensive and synthetic of all the subject fields. In history the social sciences and the humanities converge in an effort to preserve, to understand and to appreciate the heritage of mankind.

THE CONCEPT OF ARAB HISTORY

Having considered the nature of history as a discipline, we may now consider what is meant by the phrase "Arab history." We have deliberately chosen this phrase to designate this book's subject matter rather than such alternatives as "history of the Arabs" or "history of the Arab lands," since the phrase "Arab history" avoids certain problems encountered in the other phrases.

The problem with the phrase "history of the Arabs" is that throughout the larger part of the history that we shall be dealing with we shall not be *primarily* concerned with people who considered themselves to be Arabs or were considered by their contemporaries to be Arabs. In fact, only in dealing with that part of our history which ends around 750 A.D. and with a much later part which begins around the middle of the nineteenth century will it be possible for us to speak of Arabs as our primary concern. This leaves an intermediate period of approximately eleven centuries during which Arabs as such will not be our primary concern. They will, of course, be present in our history during those centuries, but they will represent only *part* of the total picture that we shall be dealing with--and in some periods a rather small part.

This rather startling statement can be explained in the light of certain observations about the word "Arab." Nowadays an Arab can be anyone who speaks the Arabic language as his native tongue and considers his real home or roots to lie within the "Arab world." Thus the major part of the population inhabiting the region from Iraq to Morocco are called Arabs. However, this rather broad sense of the word "Arab" is of relatively recent origin. It is essentially the product of Arab nationalism, a movement which first emerged during the latter part of the nineteenth century but did not spread to all the countries of the present-day Arab world until the present century. In fact, only since the 1950s has it been possible to speak meaningfully (and without anachronism) of the area from Iraq to Morocco as a unified Arab world (or Arab nation, *ummat al-ᶜarab*) and the greater part of its inhabitants as Arabs. Earlier in the century it was primarily people living in the Fertile Crescent and Arabia who thought of themselves as Arabs.

This modern meaning of the word "Arab" must be distinguished from an earlier one, which may best be described (in contrast to the modern meaning) as the classical meaning. Originally, in pre-Islamic times, the Arabic collective noun ^{c}*arab* referred exclusively to the bedouin population of Arabia and thus did not include the agriculture-based population of the southern part of the peninsula. (Since Arabic was originally the language of this bedouin population, ^{c}*arab* was a self-designation of the bedouins themselves.) Typically the *bedouin* was a nomad distinguished from other nomads by his use and breeding of the camel. However, the bedouin population also included communities which had settled around oases in order to carry on a modest agriculture. Both the nomadic and oasis-based bedouin were subsumed under the word ^{c}*arab*. Both spoke dialects of the same language, were tribally organized and possessed camels. A variant of ^{c}*arab*, viz. *a*^{c}*rāb*, seems to have been restricted to the nomadic bedouin, and indeed he was regarded by all as the truer bedouin type.

The classical meaning of "Arab" is an extension of the original meaning of ^{c}*arab* resulting from the conquests of early Islamic times. The great majority of the participants in these conquests were bedouin, led by prominent men of the Arab town of Mecca. During the course of the conquests, inhabitants of South Arabia were absorbed in great numbers into the Arab movement and therefore came themselves to be regarded as Arabs. Although in remote pre-Islamic times the South Arabians had been distinguished from the bedouin Arabs, they had in the period just before the rise of Islam adopted the Arabic language and were therefore at the time of the conquests tied to the bedouin population by this common bond and thus more easily absorbed into the bedouin movement. The Arab genealogical tradition, however, posited a separate original ancestor for the southern "Arabs," thus setting them apart from the main body of bedouin Arabs as a distinct family.

As the South Arabians became absorbed into the Arab movement, the word "Arab" came to have the broad sense of native Arabian, inclusive of both bedouin and South Arabians. However, the bedouin Arab continued to be regarded as the true prototype of the Arab. The language of the Arabs was, after all, his language, and the poetry and lore which constituted the core of Arab culture reflected his values and customs.

In the aftermath of the first conquests, great numbers of native Arabians, the majority of them bedouin, found themselves stationed in military encampments in various parts of the conquered territories. Here they were compelled to work out for themselves a new way of life very different from that of their bedouin homeland, which was now far behind them. Their descendants had not even the memory of a bedouin past, yet among them an Arab identity persisted, nurtured by the continuing use of the Arabic language and the perpetuation of tribal affiliations and Arab oral traditions. Thus among new generations of Arabs born in the conquered territories Arabness came to depend, not upon adherence to the bedouin way of life, nor upon inclusion among the native population of greater Arabia, but upon descent from earlier generations of native Arabians.

With the emergence of this new type of Arab, the evolution of the classical meaning of "Arab" was complete. An Arab, in classical usage, was either a native Arabian or the descendant of native Arabians. His true prototype continued to be, always, the bedouin Arab, and preeminently the camel-breeding nomad.

In the history that we shall be studying in this book Arabs, in the classical sense of the term, will occupy the center of the stage only up to around the year 750 A.D. From that point onward they will play a subordinate role; as we suggested earlier, they will be simply part of the overall picture, and at some points will be out of sight altogether. When we approach the later part of the nineteenth century, we will again become increasingly preoccupied with Arabs, but at this point it will be the modern rather than the classical sense that will predominate.

Clearly a history the better part of which does not have Arabs as its primary subject matter is best not described as a history of the Arabs.

As for the phrase "history of the Arab lands," this too entails certain problems. To begin with, most modern readers would undoubtedly tend to take the term "Arab lands" to refer to the Arab world as now constituted; that is, they would tend to identify the Arab lands with the modern Arab countries, among whose citizens there is a strong sense of Arab identity. On this understanding of the term "Arab lands," the history of the Arab lands would have to begin properly with the rise of modern Arab nationalism in the nineteenth century, with perhaps a prologue on the historical setting within which that nationalism arose. Our history will begin much earlier.

There is, of course, no reason why Arab nationalist consciousness has to enter into the definition of the Arab lands. One can quite legitimately set aside the understanding of "Arab lands" just described and take this term to refer simply to lands which have an Arab character. If the widespread use of the Arabic language, both at the spoken and literary levels, be taken as indicative of an Arab character, then it is possible to speak of Arab lands as existing even in a time when the inhabitants of those lands did not generally speaking consciously identify themselves as Arabs. Our primary criterion in this case is language and, to a certain extent, culture; whether or not the people themselves regard themselves as Arabs is immaterial. With this broader understanding of "Arab lands," it is possible to begin the history of the Arab lands at that point in time when these lands first acquired an Arab character (that is to say, when they were first arabized). The result is a history extending back many centuries before the nineteenth century.

There is, however, still a problem with this approach. The process of arabization, which gave rise to lands having an Arab character, was a gradual and uneven process. The Arabian peninsula has had an Arab character since time immemorial. Outside the peninsula, the lower plains of the Fertile Crescent were more or less arabized within a century after the Arab conquests of the seventh century (some parts of Syria were arabized even before the conquests), whereas the Maghrib (Muslim North Africa,, owing to the lingering hold of Berber languages on a large part of the population, was not genuinely arabized until after the Hilalian bedouin invasions, which began in the eleventh century. Thus the Arab lands are, on this understanding, an evolving entity, and one cannot include certain parts of the present-day Arab world in the earlier chapters of the history of the Arab lands. The Arab lands are, in other words, not a fixed geographical entity, as is, for example, the Middle East or Europe. On top of this there is a further difficulty. In some parts of the Arab world--Egypt is a good example of this--the process of arabization is very difficult to trace, and it is very difficult therefore to say precisely at what point the area in question became part of the Arab lands and should be included in the history of those lands. This problem increases the geographical haziness of the Arab lands.

But, it may be asked, is it not possible to take the Arab lands (or Arab world) as now constituted geographically and to make the history of that geographical area our object of study? The present-day Arab lands have geographical boundaries that are relatively well defined politically. (Certain countries which have obtained membership in the Arab league, Somalia for example, may be excluded.) Given these boundaries, is it not possible to say that we are going to deal with the history of this area from the rise of Islam to the present day (which, for purposes of background, might reasonably include an introductory chapter on pre-Islamic Arabia).

As attractive as this last approach might seem, it still is not free of complications. It would be very well and good to deal exclusively with the history of that geographical area now called the Arab world if that history were a relatively self-contained history. But it is not, at least not so far as the earlier centuries of the Islamic era (not to mention the pre-Islamic period!) are concerned; for the history of the area in question was for a considerable stretch of time after the emergence of the Arab empire inseparably bound up with the history of the Iranian lands to the east of the Tigris-Euphrates valley. In fact, after 750 A.D. the Iranian people exercised, for several centuries, a large measure of influence upon the affairs of the eastern part of what is now called the Arab world. So inextricable is the tie between the latter area and the Iranian lands during these centuries that historians of Islam commonly regard the two areas together as constituting the "central lands" of Islam, in contrast to the "peripheral lands," prominent among which is the western part of the region now called the Arab world, the Maghrib. While the present-day Arab world may seem to us to be, clearly enough, a unity worthy to be an object of historical study, this unity owes its existence more to linguistic, cultural, and political variables than to any strictly geographical or natural integrity the area may possess.

What our discussion thus far leads to is this: neither the phrase "history of the Arabs" nor the phrase "history of the Arab lands" is quite adequate as a designation for the history we shall be studying because neither is sufficiently broad to cover that history in its entirety. A certain part of our history, namely the part which begins in pre-Islamic times and ends with the fall of the Arab empire in 750 A.D., can no doubt be appropriately called "history of the Arabs," and a certain part, namely that which begins at the point where the area now known as the Arab world emerges as a distinct entity worthy in its own right to be an object of historical study and which extends to the present time, can clearly be called "history of the Arab lands," but our history as a whole can be called neither. Hence the need for a more comprehensive designation, and it is in order to meet this need that we have chosen the phrase "Arab history."

As the preceding remarks imply, Arab history is a composite of an earlier "history of the Arabs" (pre-Islamic times to 750 A.D.) and a later "history of the Arab lands," together with an intermediate period which lies in between. In the earlier period, our attention is clearly focused on Arabs as such (in the classical sense), and not upon any geographically and stable entity. Throughout the long pre-Islamic period the activities of the Arabs, of course, take place within the relatively fixed boundaries of the Arabian peninsula and Syrian desert. But the attention which we shall give to the pre-Islamic period will be somewhat cursory as compared to the more sustained attention that we shall be giving to the period from the rise of Islam to the fall of the Arab empire. In this important period of a century and a half, the Arabs undergo phenomenal expansion and make an enormous impact upon the world at large; the boundaries of their domain are continually changing as a fixed geographical entity has not emerged. In the later "history of the Arab lands," we are patently area-oriented. The area which we now feel free to call the Arab lands can be treated apart from other areas to a degree that was not possible before. The history of this area has become relatively self-contained.

A problem seems to arise with respect to the intermediate period of Arab history. If in the earlier period our attention is focused on the Arabs (in the classical sense) and in the later period it is focused on the Arab lands, then what is it focused on in this intermediate period? What is our history in this period the history of? Surely all history, and therefore all Arab history, must be the history of something. If this something in the intermediate period is neither the Arabs, as such, nor the Arab lands (however much these may enter into our thinking in dealing with this period), then what is it? To be truthful, it is not easy to give a precise answer to this question. What must be kept in mind is that this intermediate period is, within the broad stream of Arab history, a transitional period: a transition is taking place from an earlier history of the Arabs to a later (and in a sense ultimate) history of the Arab lands. The historian's attention is, accordingly, shifting from the Arabs to the Arab lands. But since it is as yet not possible for him to deal with the Arab lands as a more or less self-contained and stable entity, he will tend to concentrate on developments which will have a bearing on the later history of the Arab lands toward which he is moving. In this way, the historian will, in dealing with this intermediate period, keep his subject matter within the province of a truly Arab history.

While the point at which the "history of the Arabs" ends is fairly easy to determine, the point at which the intermediate period ends and the "history of the Arab lands" begins is somewhat elusive. We suggest 1250 A.D. for three reasons. First, it was around that time that the Mongols overran the Iranian lands, creating an unprecedented barrier between those lands and the eastern Arab lands and thus isolating the latter from the former to a degree that permits us to deal, as never before, with the history of the Arab lands apart from developments occurring further east. The exception to this general isolation is Iraq, which continues to fall within the Iranian orbit until Ottoman times. As for the rest of the Arab East (Greater Syria and Egypt), it now embarks, to an extent unknown previously, upon a history of its own. This is not to say that the detachment of this region from the Iranian lands is entirely the result of the Mongol conquests. There is good reason to see the process of detachment as a gradual one beginning with the collapse of the Great Seljuk empire around 1100 A.D. and only culminating with the coming of the Mongols. It is the culmination that we are taking as one of the factors permitting us to speak of A.D. 1250 as the beginning of a bona fide "history of the Arab lands."

Secondly, with the coming of the Mamluks to power in Greater Syria and Egypt in A.D. 1250, the population of these lands, especially of Egypt, begins to acquire a new consciousness of having an Arab character. We have noted earlier that while the arabization of the Fertile Crescent seems to have proceeded with relative rapidity in the aftermath of the Arab conquests the arabization of Egypt is much more difficult to trace. Arabic was, of course, the language of government and, among Muslims, of worship and pious discourse. However, the Coptic population continued to cling steadfastly to its own indigenous language. Even with the population which embraced Islam it is virtually impossible to trace the process of adoption of a colloquial Arabic dialect as the language of daily use. We can only assume that this process must have occurred more rapidly among Muslims than among Copts. The process of conversion to Islam is itself beyond reach of quantitative investigation. It may have been centuries before Arabic penetrated everyday life within the country at large, however much preeminence it enjoyed in the major urban areas. By 1250, however, this penetration seems to have taken place. That this is so is betokened by the appearance in the thirteenth century of the first Coptic writings in Arabic. This rootedness of Arabic within the general population worked together with a growing sense, on the part of that population, of being different linguistically and culturally from the Turkish ruling class which implanted itself in Egypt in 1250 to foster the consciousness of possessing an Arab character just mentioned. This is not to say that people became willing to call themselves Arabs. The term "Arab" continued to retain for the most part its classical sense. On the other hand, we do encounter here and there in literary sources the use of the expressions abna al-ᶜarab and awlad al-ᶜarab (both meaning "sons of Arabs") as a designation for the general population in contradistinction to the ruling elite.

Finally, it is around A.D. 1250 or at least soon thereafter that the arabization of North Africa, as a result of the impact of bedouin migrations into that area which had been going on since the late eleventh century, reaches its completion. With these developments a vast arabized zone corresponding to the Arab lands as constituted at the present time may be said to have emerged, and the study of the "history of the Arab lands" may properly begin. It must be emphasized that this periodization of our history is not meant to suggest that there were no areas qualified to be called Arab lands before 1250. After all, Arabia was an "Arab land" from time immemorial, and much of the Fertile Cresent and perhaps part of Egypt became an "Arab land" in the period following the Arab conquests. What we have been searching for is the point at which the territorial entity known to us today as the "Arab lands" or "Arab world" and believed by us to have existed as a constant over a relatively long stretch of time may reasonably be considered to have become fully formed.

The Arab history to be surveyed in the following chapters should be viewed as a continuum which runs from the Arabs of the earlier period (pre-Islamic to A.D. 750) to the Arab lands of the later period (A.D. 1250 to the present), including, as a component no less important than these flanking periods, an intermediate period of some five centuries (A.D. 750-1250). The subject matter of the intermediate period consists of all those things that link the two end sections of the continuum together. That the Arabs of the earlier period are to be linked with the Arab lands of the later period in a continuous history makes perfect sense. The Arab lands are what they are by virtue of a language (spoken and literary) and a literary culture which were originally the possession of Arabs from Arabia. Since Arabic in its various dialects became the spoken language of the Arab lands, the literary language and culture of the original Arabs acquired deep roots in the Arab lands, the likes of which were not to be found in other areas where Arabic was used in a rather esoteric manner (much like medieval Latin) for scholarship alone. It is this combination of the vernacular use of Arabic dialects together with the consequent deep-rootedness of the Arabic literary culture that gives the Arab lands their Arab character and creates a special link between the inhabitants of these lands and the original Arabs, a link which is not only linguistic and cultural but to a certain extent psychological as well. Already in pre-Islamic times the inhabitants of South Arabia had "become Arabs" by virtue of their linguistic assimilation to the main Arab stock living to the north of them. It was the same sort of process of assimilation that was to give rise to the Arab lands. Although an Arab identity expressible by means of the word ^{c}arab was not to emerge among the larger population of the Arab lands until modern times, it was certainly latent in the psyche of that population from the very time that the process of arabization had been completed.

Three moments of special importance in the history we shall be studying determine the shape of that history. These are (1) the rapid expansion of the original Arabs into lands beyond the Arabian peninsula, (2) the gradual arabization of the population of certain of these lands producing in time what we have described as the Arab lands, and (3) the articulation of a new sense of Arab identity among the inhabitants of the Arab lands in modern times as a result of the impact of nationalism. In a sense, the third moment is the culmination of Arab history seen as a total continuous process, in spite of the fact that the catalyst in the third moment is an ideological force external to the Arab lands (i.e., nationalism). Accordingly, this history will be viewed as forward-moving, as moving toward the emergence of a new Arab identity in modern times. To use a philosophical term, our history will have a teleological character. To an extent, the very idea of Arab history as a continuous process extending from pre-Islamic to modern times is a product of modern nationalism. This is not to say it is a pure fiction. Rather, what we mean to say is that it is the birth of Arab consciousness throughout the Arab lands that makes the idea of Arab history feasible. To be an Arab in modern times means, almost by definition, to have roots in an Arab past. Arab consciousness has, in other words, been retrospective (and perhaps also to a degree retroactive); it has emphasized the Arabness of the Arab lands and its population in the past as well as in the present, and it has also emphasized the special links which tie the inhabitants of the Arab lands to the original Arabs, who are the true forebearers of Arab history. Thus, while modern Arab nationalism cannot be said to have invented Arab history, it can be said to have brought it to light and even to have shaped it, while at the same time making its own very important contribution to it as itself a part of that history--and in fact its culmination (or *telos*). Arab history, in the eighteenth century or earlier, would hardly have made sense (except perhaps as the history of Arabs in the strictly classical sense, in which case the only Arab history of any great interest would have been that of the first century and a half of the Islamic era). It required the rise of a history-conscious nationalist movement to give it credibility and relevance.

CHAPTER ONE

THE ARABS BEFORE ISLAM

Arab history begins, necessarily, in Arabia, the original homeland of the Arabs. Before the conquests of the seventh and eighth centuries made the Arabs masters of a great world empire, their activities were limited almost entirely to this homeland and the borderlands adjacent to it. This earlier history of the Arabs in Arabia is a long one which can be traced back at least to 1000 B.C., although the ultimate origins of the Arabs remain obscure. During this long period the Arabs developed social and cultural traditions which were to become an important ingredient in their history after the rise of Islam and in the subsequent history of the Arab lands. The period is thus important not merely for its own sake as the initial segment of Arab history but also as a prologue to later times.

In earliest usage the Arabic term ^{c}*arab* (Arabs) referred to the camel-breeding pastoralists who inhabited the central, western, and northern parts of the peninsula. "Arab" was in effect synonymous with "bedouin," and the use of camels was a distinctive mark of the Arab. The typical Arab was a nomad whose livelihood depended entirely on herding and who traveled great distances in search of pasturage, except during the harsh summer months when it was expedient to remain close to a well. Many Arabs, however, lived a permanently sedentary life in oases, where they were able to combine a degree of animal-raising with a simple agriculture consisting mainly of date cultivation. Though sedentary, these oasis-dwellers remained essentially a part of the bedouin milieu and were sometimes tribally related to the nomads. It was the nomadic Arab who was the ultimate source of Arab values and traditions.

The Arabs stood in sharp contrast to the fully sedentarized inhabitants of the southern part of the peninsula, who should not, properly speaking, be called Arabs (except after their arabization in the period just before Islam) but rather South Arabians (the term Arabian being a general designation for all the inhabitants of the peninsula). The population of Arabia was thus divided into two main types: the Arabs proper, who inhabited the steppe and desert regions of the peninsula punctuated with oases, and the South Arabians, who were concentrated mainly in the rich monsoon-watered agricultural lands of the Yemen. This bifurcation is reflected in the Arab genealogical tradition which acquired its classical form in early Islamic times. According to that tradition, the population of Arabia comprised two distinct families, the descendants of Q̣ahtan, who hailed from the South, and the descendants of Adnan, who inhabited the rest of the peninsula.

The Arabs differed from the South Arabians not only by virtue of their predominant pastoralism but also by virtue of their language and culture. Their language was Arabic, which though varied in its dialects was nonetheless quite distinct from the language of the South Arabians (Sabaic), notwithstanding the fact that the latter was closely related to it within the larger family of Semitic languages. In respect to culture (and especially to religion) the Arabs were a great distance removed from their South Arabian neighbors, whose culture and religion were derivatives of the more advanced Semitic civilization of the Fertile Crescent.

For our purposes it is the Arab population of ancient Arabia that is most important, since it is primarily within that population that cultural and social institutions are to be found which were to enter into the shaping of later Arab history. It is, indeed, best to consider our proper subject matter in this chapter to be the "Arab part" of Arabia and to view South Arabia as external to it. By adopting this conception, we will be able to picture in our minds an Arab heartland flanked by two flourishing centers of civilization, the Fertile Crescent to the North and South Arabia (or the Yemen) to the South. Both of these neighboring areas impinged on the Arab heartland to varying degrees. For about a thousand years prior to the beginning of the Christian era it was influences from South Arabia which predominated. Thereafter the great empires in the lands to the North (especially the Roman-Byzantine and Sasanian) began to play an increasingly large role in the affairs of the Arabs. With the decline of South Arabian civilization in the period just before Islam and its subsequent arabization, South Arabia became absorbed into the Arab milieu and its inhabitants came to be regarded as Arabs, albeit of separate ancestry (as descendants of Qahtan) from the older Arab stock. Consequently, by the time of the rise of Islam, South Arabia had lost much of its peripheral standing in relation to the rest of Arabia.

Since it is with the Arab heartland that we shall be primarily concerned in this chapter, we will devote the next section of this chapter to a consideration of the principal social and cultural institutions which prevailed in that area. Our approach will be cross-sectional; that is, we will attempt to provide a "still-life" construction of the institutions in question, with little regard for historical development. In the concluding section a chronological perspective will be adopted, as we attempt to look at broad historical changes that took place in the pre-Islamic times, largely as the result of interaction between the Arab heartland and the centers of civilization on its northern and southern flanks.

Values and Institutions of the Ancient Arabs

Socio-economic Institutions

No doubt the most important social unit of bedouin society was the tribe (qabīla), which was customarily subdivided into clans (qawm-s). The clan consisted in turn of a number of nuclear families each inhabiting a separate tent. While many basic human needs were satisfied at the level of the nuclear family, the tribe was the main focus of the bedouin's ultimate loyalty. The individual acquired and maintained an identity through his membership in a tribe, which protected him against hostile outsiders as well as against the harsh elements. Although the Arab nomads' standard of living was very modest, they were vulnerable less because of their incessant poverty than because of their helplessness in the face of sudden catastrophes--floods, draughts, or invasions. Thus tribesmen survived individually and collectively by adhering to the ideal of "all for one and one for all." Certainly the ancient bedouin didn't practice socialism in the modern sense of the word, but the cornerstone of their "code of the desert" was the principle of group solidarity (*^{c}asabiyya*), which tended to foster a certain degree of material equality. Tribal solidarity, along with the other bedouin ideals--such as generosity (*karam*), hospitality (*ḍayf*) and honor (*^{c}ird*)--obliged the comparatively rich and strong individuals within a tribe to feel a sense of responsibility toward the comparatively poor and weak.

The ecology of pastoral nomadism in a desert environment dictated that tribes functioned most efficiently at the optimum size of about 600 individuals. Notwithstanding the powerful sense of tribal solidarity, when bedouin tribes became too large they therefore tended to fragment into their component parts--the clans. The old tribe would dissolve at the top, and each major clan (or group of clans) would become a separate, new tribe. Inasmuch as genealogy represented the main form of history--and an important genre of poetry--among the bedouins, each tribe remembered the identity of its "brother tribes" and "cousin tribes." In this regard, the bedouin concerned themselves a great deal with the nobility of their descent. The custom was thus for marriage to be endogamous (i.e., to occur within the tribe or at least within a group of closely related tribes) in order to maintain the purity of the tribal bloodlines. In accordance with the ideals of hospitality and generosity, outsiders sometimes were accorded refuge and protection from a tribe other than their own. But these "clients" (*mawalī*), who were ordinarily treated as second-class citizens, were often barred from marrying into the tribe itself.

The principal economic activity of the Arab bedouin, like other pastoral nomads, consisted of breeding and herding certain kinds of animals--mainly sheep, goats, donkeys, horses, and camels--that could be exploited for food, clothing, shelter, fuel, and transportation. In herding their flocks the bedouin did not wander about aimlessly; rather, their movements were characterized by a high degree of regularity and purposiveness. In May or June of each year the tribe would habitually return to its summer quarters, invariably located near a well or a spring, where it would remain throughout the hot, summer months. If a particular tribe was not fortunate enough to possess a well of its own, necessity and custom obliged it to become the client of a stronger tribe that controlled a year-round water supply. Water was scarce and therefore precious in the Arabian peninsula, an area which received very little annual rainfall. Mountainous Yemen and Oman received generous amounts of monsoon rains from the climatological system of the Indian Ocean, but flat North-central Arabia had to depend on the Mediterranean system which brought only scattered showers in the Winter and Spring. So in September or October of each year the bedouin tribe would leave its summer quarters, taking its flocks in search of the pasturage brought forth by the first of the seasonal showers. Depending on the amounts and sites of the rainfall, the tribe might change locations several times during the Winter and Spring. However, it usually remained within a general area, considered its own pasturing territory, and almost always returned by mid-June to its tribal well. It was because of this annual pattern that bedouins were called "prisoners of the seasonal cycle."

Among the animals herded by the bedouins, the camel deserves special mention. It is likely that, in remote antiquity, pastoralists in the Arabian peninsula relied for transportation mainly on the donkey and therefore restricted their movements to the fringes of the steppes, avoiding the hitherto impassable desert. The domestication or introduction of the dromedary or one-humped camel, in about 1000 B.C., led to a socio-economic revolution of sorts. The camel proved to be a superb riding animal; its speed over long distances was three times as fast as a horse. It thus greatly increased the bedouin's mobility, enabling them to traverse the deserts at will and to raid anywhere in the peninsula. A splendid beast of burden, the camel also facilitated the rise of long-distance trade. Carrying up to 160 kilograms, a camel could travel 40 kilometers daily for eight days without water in temperatures of 57 degrees centigrade. Tribesmen obtained other benefits from the camel: they drank its milk and ate its flesh; they used its hair for tent-cloth and its dung for fuel. In the centuries just prior to the rise of Islam, Arab nomads became increasingly devoted to camel-breeding, and they have consequently been described as "parasites of the camel."

Since wealth and power were measured among the bedouin in terms of numbers of animals, possession of summer wells, and access to winter pasturage, there occurred intense and almost constant rivalry among tribes for control of the Arabian peninsula's limited resources. One consequence of this rivalry, particularly during cycles of draught and famine or of overpopulation, was the tendency for certain tribes to emigrate outside the nomadic zone to such regions as South Arabia or the Fertile Crescent where sedentary agriculture was possible. Another consequence was endemic warfare among those tribes remaining in the central peninsula. This intertribal conflict over livestock and natural resources expressed itself not so much in all-out warfare as in raiding (ghazw/razzia), which aimed at carrying off animals, goods, or prisoners. In this regard, because each tribe was a more or less self-contained social unit, raiding was not considered "illegal" or even immoral; rather, raiding for booty and for the capture followed by the ransom of prisoners was a legitimate form of economic enterprise. Indeed, to exhibit daring and bravery when conducting a raid or when engaging in a skirmish was another important bedouin ideal, part of the "code of the desert." Raids were carried out not only against rival tribes but also against sedentary villagers or against the camel caravans which transported goods from South Arabia to the Fertile Crescent. Indeed, some of the stronger tribes were able to levy tolls on the South Arabian merchants; in return for payments in kind, a tribe would guarantee the caravan's safe passage through their territory.

Although self-sufficiency was an ideal and raiding a common practice among bedouin, they did not abstain from peaceful economic intercourse with persons outside their own tribe. Indeed, the custom was for each tribe to hold a weekly market (sūq), to which members of other tribes could come and exchange goods, usually by barter although money was not unknown in certain areas. Market days were customarily designated as truce periods, so that exchange between tribes could take place without danger of conflict and bloodshed. During the winter, the market would be held wherever the tribe's camp happened to be located; during the summer, it would occur at the tribal well, where a fraction of the tribe would sometimes remain behind even during the pasturage season in order to engage in commerce year-round. In this way a summer tribal weekly market could evolve into a permanent village market. Occasionally, village markets also served as sites for annual trade fairs, which were attended by all the tribes within a given region and for which longer truce periods were declared in order to facilitate the gathering. It was thus not unusual for the economic patterns of Arab nomads to include regular and peaceful intercourse with quasi-sedentary merchants.

In this regard, the Arab bedouin also lived on the margins of an important pattern of international trade: the network of camel caravan routes from Yemen through North Arabia to the Fertile Crescent (see map on p. 31). While some bedouin tribes were drawn into association with the caravan traffic through quasi-military roles as guards, others became involved in it through service roles by providing water, food and shelter to the caravaneers and their camels. These "way stations" along the caravan routes were ideal sites for local town markets, for they had access to the wider variety of goods carried by the South Arabian merchants. A way station/town market thus enjoyed the possibility of developing into a relatively important commercial center; and from among the inhabitants of such a center could evolve a group of local retailers, who would purchase commodities from the caravaneers for resale to the villagers and tribesmen of the surrounding region. If draught and overpopulation in North-central Arabia represented "push factors" which periodically drove tribes out of the desert, the agriculture and the caravan trade represented "pull factors" which induced tribes at times to abandon pastoral nomadism for a more sedentary existence.

Political Institutions

Among the bedouin, the tribe represented the most important unit not just with respect to socio-economic institutions but also with respect to political ones. According to the ideal that we may call "tribal autonomy" (if not "sovereignty"), in theory the tribe neither acknowledged nor obeyed any political authority above or beyond itself. Arab nomads were instinctively wary of entering into close relations with other, more powerful tribes or with governments of centralized states, lest their independence of action be partially limited or curtailed altogether. In this regard, even though most bedouin had dependent economic relations with town markets, they considered themselves superior to sedentary farmers and merchants who permitted themselves to be taxed and in various other ways to be exploited by kings and their agents. Complete autonomy from any political authority outside their own tribe thus constituted an important value to the bedouin, as indeed it did to most pastoral nomads, who habitually claimed to prefer a life of austere freedom over one of subjugated comfort.

With regard to the internal dynamics of bedouin political institutions, there also existed an element of egalitarianism--some scholars have called it "tribal democracy." Tribes characteristically lacked authoritative leadership. Decision-making powers within a tribe were vested in a council or majlis, composed of the tribal elders. It was customary for each clan--or at least each important clan--to be represented on the majlis by one of its leading men. The members of the majlis elected one of themselves, customarily the most respected man of the tribe, to be their spokesman or shaykh. The shaykh needed to possess certain clearly defined qualities of leadership--experience, wisdom, bravery, eloquence, honor, generosity, etc.--those bedouin virtues which made up the "code of the desert." Yet there was a significant difference between the office of "king" and that of "shaykh." The latter was less of a "ruler" than a "spokesman"; for he enjoyed a very limited scope of authority. The shaykh's influence was derived from personal dignity rather than from institutionalized power and was expressed through persuasion rather than through force. He was, in a sense, merely primus inter pares ("first among equals"), since an important decision--moving to new pastures, undertaking a raiding expedition, or joining other tribes in a confederation--would be made collectively by the entire majlis. The shaykh's leadership was thus in large part ceremonial. He represented the tribe in its dealings with outsiders. He was often, but not necessarily, the tribal leader in war. A percentage (20 to 25 percent) of booty from raids went to him, but mainly so that he could fulfill such official obligations as showing hospitality to guests on behalf of the tribe.

Sometimes it became expedient for a bedouin tribe to join a confederation, thereby giving up full sovereignty in the short run in order to assure its survival in the long run. The kind of condition that would render such a step desirable or necessary usually entailed a serious external danger--for example, the attempt by a very powerful tribe to subjugate its weaker neighbors or perhaps the incursion into Arabia of a Roman or a Persian army. In the face of such a threat, a given tribe would be obliged to join forces with neighboring and/or related tribes which could defend themselves collectively against a common enemy too powerful to resist on an individual basis. Extreme caution was of course exercised when selecting the temporary confederation's leader, who was expected to possess the same personal qualities as a tribal shaykh but who was customarily chosen from a weak tribe. This custom was observed so that strong tribes could not easily assert permanent control over the other partners in the confederation. To an even greater degree than in the case of the tribal shaykh, therefore, the confederation leader's scope of authority was very limited. Major decisions had to be ratified by the majlis of every participating tribe. Also, each warrior fought in the ranks of his own tribe and under his own tribal leadership. Then, as soon as the external danger receded, the confederation would dissolve, and every participating tribe would resume its independent status.

The bedouin tribe was not a "state." That is, it performed none of the essential functions that a state does. For example, tribes did not collect taxes; they had no police force; they possessed no formal "judicial system" composed of judges, courts, and legal codes. There even seems to have existed no word for "state" in the ancient Arabic language. The term dawla did not acquire the meaning of "regime" or "state" until Abbasi times (i.e., after A.D. 750); its original meaning was "turning" or "revolution." Of course the bedouins had a legal tradition--ᶜurf or customary law--which guided them in such matters as inheritance, divorce, and orphanage. But these questions were ordinarily resolved on an ad hoc basis among individuals without recourse even to the majlis. Similarly, when a crime was committed against an Arab tribesman, he or his nearest kinsman assumed, on a unilateral basis, the responsibility for seeing that "justice" or vengeance was done. Serious crimes like murder, when committed against either a relative or a stranger, could entail a cycle of vengeance and counter-vengeance leading ultimately to a "blood feud" lasting many generations. If a blood feud developed and began seriously to hinder normal economic activities to the detriment of both sides, one custom was jointly to choose a respected neutral arbiter who would act as a temporary judge to settle the conflict once and for all. Occasionally, the clan or tribe of someone who had committed a serious crime would decide that he no longer deserved the protection of his kinsmen. Since such a decision was tantamount to expulsion from the clan or tribe, which rendered unprotected tribesmen extremely vulnerable, as a rule they immediately sought the patronage of another tribe within which they assumed the status of clients or mawālī.

Cultural Institutions

Some may think it inappropriate to speak of "cultural institutions" among the pre-Islamic Arabs. After the rise of Islam, Muslim Arabs began to refer to their pre-Islamic history as the "period of the Jāhiliyya," meaning the time of ignorance and implying an age of barbarism as well as of paganism. Ibn Khaldun (d. 1406) explained that the principal difference between settled and nomadic populations was that the former, while lacking "solidarity" (ᶜasabiyya), developed states and possessed "civilization," whereas the latter possessed solidarity but lacked any real civilization. This tendency to depict the pre-Islamic bedouin as being devoid of cultural institutions perhaps is justified when considering certain aspects of culture--science, for example, or architecture and the visual arts. According to K. A. C. Cresswell, the pioneering scholar of the history of Islamic architecture: "Arabia, at the rise of Islam, does not appear to have possessed anything worthy of the name of architecture. Only a small portion of the population was settled, and these lived in dwellings which were scarcely more than hovels" (p. 1).

But the charge of crude barbarity seems incorrect and unjust when considering other aspects of ancient Arab culture--for example, language and literature. It is probably true that there existed no standard written language among the the various North Arabian tribal dialects, so that stories and poems as well as genealogy had to be transmitted orally by narrators. There may even be a grain of truth in what Taha Husayn and others said to the effect that pre-Islamic poetry may have been modified or even fabricated by Muslims seeking to document the barbarity of the Jāhiliyya period. Yet the bulk of the

Jāhilī poetry is now generally considered to be authentic by most scholars, whether they be Muslim or non-Muslim. It is also widely recognized that oral literature--stories and especially poetry--had developed into a sophisticated art form among the ancient bedouin. The principal medium of intellect and of culture among them, their poetry, was a genuine classical tradition expressed in a variety of forms but possessing more or less standardized rules for enunciation and evaluation.

Eloquence or skill in language was another of the bedouin ideals. A poet capable of extemporizing elegant or satiric verse could always command an audience and was usually honored and admired by his fellow tribesmen. The ancient Arabs even regularly held poetry competitions, sometimes in conjunction with annual trade fairs--like the fair of ᶜUkāz near Mecca. According to Arab traditions, seven winning poems from one competitive series were gathered into an anthology known as the muᶜallaqāt ("the suspended ones" or "the seven golden odes"), so called because they were eventually written down in letters of gold and then suspended in the shrine at Mecca as models of poetic excellence. Among the preferred forms of Arabic verse was the qasīda or long ode, which required complicated metric patterns, rhyming schemes and thematic descriptions of desert scenery: night, a clear moon, the artistic formation of sand dunes, camels grazing, etc. Other themes seem to have eulogized certain of the Arabs' customs and ideals later criticized by Islam: love affairs, tribal politics, and blood feuds. Nor was it uncommon for poets to indulge in self-glorification, attributing to themselves liberal portions of such personal qualities as generosity, bravery, and cleverness.

Religious Institutions

A number of different terms have been used to describe the religious ideas and institutions of the ancient bedouins, including such terms as "paganism," "polytheism," "fatalism," and "tribal humanism." To the extent that the Arab nomads possessed a religious ethic or a moral code, it was their "code of the desert" which was dominated by the ideal of honor. As W. M. Watt observed, "The effective religion of the nomads of Arabia--that whereby they lived--was what may be called 'tribal humanism.' Their thoughts were dominated by the conception of honour, the honour of the tribe and of the members of it." In their outlook, in religion and in general, the Arabs were also fatalistic. That is, they accepted what happened to them as being inevitable. In some ways this was not strictly a "religious" belief, for fate as such was conceived of neither as a celestial power to be worshipped nor as a formal dogma to be taught and professed. Rather, as Watt put it, "it was simply a fact of experience that in certain matters, however hard men tried to achieve a thing, their plans went wrong . . . that there are certain limits to human life." Fatalism, therefore, consisted largely of "a recognition of man's dependence on the erratic climatic conditions of the Arabian desert and the unforeseeable chances of desert life." The bedouin's "religious" ethic and "religious" world view therefore seem to have been shaped to a considerable extent by his socio-economic and geographical circumstances.

With regard to the nature and the role of the divine, the bedouin's religion can, on the one hand, be contrasted with the monotheistic faiths--Islam, Christianity, and Judaism--and can therefore be classified among the various "pagan" system of the ancient world. Indeed, the Muslims would later refer specifically to the Arabs of the Jāhiliyya as mushrikūn (polytheists). Polytheism (belief in many gods), as opposed to monotheism (belief in one god), would also describe the religious systems of many other ancient Mediterranean and Near Eastern peoples, including the Egyptians, the Babylonians, the Phoenicians, the Greeks, and the Romans. When contrasted with the rather elaborate and sophisticated religious systems of Pharaonic Egypt or of ancient Greece, however, the paganism of the Arabs appears to have been quite rudimentary. For example, much of the Arabs' awe of the supernatural was expressed as concern for the spitefulness of the numerous invisible jinn (demons or "genies"), who capriciously inflicted misfortune, illness or even death on those who unknowingly offended them. On the other hand the bedouin acknowledged the existence of dieties whose jurisdiction was conceived of as being somewhat local, even tribal, in character. Moreover, the dwelling places of these non-universal deities were as a rule located in such natural formations as caves or stones. The religion of the bedouin thus produced no monumental places of worship, nothing at least that could even begin to compare with the temples of Thebes, Baalbek, or Delphi. Nor did it require an hereditary class of fulltime priests to burn incense, to perform ritual sacrifices, or to admonish and bless ordinary people on the gods' behalf. Occasionally, in a given Arab tribe an individual would acquire a reputation for possessing the gifts of a soothsayer (kāhin); and poets were also at times regarded as having spiritual insight. But such religious functions as were sporadically exercised by kāhin-s or poets became neither institutionalized nor hereditary among the Arab nomads.

In locations where year-round tribal markets had grown up around a well or some other water supply, permanent albeit rudimentary shrines occasionally were erected. Usually consisting of a simple cube-like structure (kaᶜba) to house the stone and/or the idols representing the tribal god(s), such kaᶜba shrines could be found in Sana'a and Najrān as well as in and near Mecca. Frequently the cult associated with a given shrine would not be confined to the tribe which controlled the well and the town market but would spread beyond it among the other tribes in the region. In that event, a pilgrimage ritual might develop around the shrine as it did around the Kaᶜba at Mecca. A pilgrimage ceremony would normally require the wearing of special clothing and the performance of such rites as circumambulating the shrine (tawāf), standing in worship (wuqūf), and slaughtering a sheep. Pilgrimage ceremonies were usually timed to coincide with a local trade fair, so that truce months had a religious as well as an economic purpose and character. The idea of truce could be extended not just to the time of the pilgrimage but also to the place of it. The shrine itself and the area immediately around it were often considered to be a holy and inviolable zone (ḥarām) where all living things would have the right of asylum.

Historical Developments Among the Arabs Before Islam

It may be said that bedouin, left entirely to themselves, do not engender a real history, for the life which they live in their natural habitat of steppe and desert follows a pattern determined wholely by the seasons, making it repetitious almost to the point of monotony. Because a bedouin is so much a product of the seasonal cycle, his institutions and customs are highly conservative, allowing little or no scope for fundamental change. When change does occur on a scale sufficient to arouse genuine historical interest, it is inevitably related to conditions existing in the world outside the Arab heartland. Two primary conditions invite change. First, the populated areas flanking the Arab heartland may suffer from political breakdown, resulting in weakened frontiers and increased vulnerability to bedouin infiltration. In this case, large scale bedouin movements into the neighboring areas deeply affect the pattern of events in the Arab interior. This was the state of affairs which transpired at the time of the rise of Islam. Secondly, the neighboring areas may experience moments of great political strength, resulting in an impingement of alien elements on the Arab interior and perhaps even a penetration by these elements of the interior. This situation can also deeply affect the lives of the bedouin. At times we may see both situations occurring simultaneously.

Since camel-breeding, which was to become a distinctive mark of the Arab bedouin, appears to have been introduced into Arabia around 1000 B.C., we may take that date as a convenient approximate starting point of Arab history. The ultimate origin of the Arabs (even if the term itself came to be associated with camel-breeding) cannot, of course, be connected with the camel as such, but lies in the earlier history of Arabia. This earlier history, however, eludes the historian almost entirely. The question of the origins of the Arabs merges ultimately with that of the origins of the Semites. The term Semite covers all those peoples who speak languages belonging to an interrelated group known as the Semitic family of languages. These languages are believed to be derived from a common parent language known to scholars as proto-Semitic. The speakers of this parent language are presumed to be the original Semites. Although the Semitic family of languages includes a number of prominent ancient languages, such as Akkadian, Hebrew, Aramaic (or Syriac) and Sabaic, Arabic holds a special place among them. Many scholars specializing in Semitics (the study of Semitic languages and literatures) have regarded classical Arabic as the closest of all the extant Semitic languages to the original proto-Semitic. It is believed that because Arabic in the form in which it is preserved in its earliest literature (including the Koran) was spoken in the conservative environment of Arabia it deviated less from the parent language than the other Semitic languages, all of which were spoken in the Fertile Crescent (or South Arabia) where greater corrupting influences were at work.

As to the origins of the Semites, there are at least two major theories, which relate also to the origins of nomadism in Arabia. According to one theory, which may be called either the Winckler-Caetani theory (after its formulators) or the "eternal bedouin" theory, the ancient homeland of the Semites was the Arabian peninsula and the first Semites were nomads, or bedouin. These nomads, it is believed, were in fact among the very first human inhabitants of the Near East as a whole. They constituted a kind of reservoir for periodic migration (or even invasion) into the Fertile Crescent. These migrations were caused by cycles of famine and/or overpopulation in the peninsula. Those nomads who thus migrated abandoned their nomadism in favor of a sedentary way of life. The second theory, which we may call the "drop-out" theory, is essentially the opposite of the first. It suggests that a purely nomadic life style represents a comparatively late phenomenon in the Arabian peninsula. The first nomads of Araba were, according to this theory, drop-outs from the settled population of the Fertile Crescent; they were forced by overpopulation in the Fertile Crescent to seek a life for themselves in the steppe areas. At first they depended on the donkey as a beast of burden and means of transportation, but then later the camel was introduced making the interior regions of the desert more accessible and producing in time the nomad of the Arab type.

Whatever may be the final answer to the question of the origins of the Semites, Arab history may safely be said to begin with the first appearance of camel-breeding nomads around 1000 B.C. The appearance of these camel-breeders coincided roughly with the rise of a flourishing civilization in South Arabia. The two events were, in fact, connected. Although South Arabian civilization was built to a large extent on agriculture, a second important mainstay of that civilization was international commerce, which depended on the camel for transportation along the Arabian trade routes.

In terms of relationships between the Arab heartland and the neighboring areas to the North and South, three major periods in the history of the Arabs before Islam may be discerned. The first, extending from around 1000 B.C. to around 300 B.C., is characterized by South Arabian predominance. The Fertile Crescent during this period comes under the political control of a series of powerful empires, which impinge upon the Arabs to some degree and at the same time prevent any major penetration of Arabs into the Fertile Crescent. But it is South Arabia, unquestionably, that has the lion's share of involvement in Arab affairs. During the second period, which extends from around 300 B.C. to around A.D. 300, the area to the North begins to assume a much greater importance in Arab affairs, as the role of the South gradually decreases. The political unity of the Fertile Crescent is broken as the area becomes divided between contending powers based in the eastern Mediterranean (first the Hellenistic states, then the Roman empire) and the Iranian plateau (first the Parthain empire, then the Sassanian). At the same time, an increasing number of sedentary Arab communities emerge at oases or commercially strategic locations on the periphery of the Arab heartland. Two of these communities, which have the character of caravan city-states and are located on the fringes of the Fertile Crescent, achieve a high degree of political power, which remains for a time unchallenged by the larger empires. These are the Arab kingdoms of Petra and Palmyra (Tadmur). Through them and other similar establishments the Arab presence in the Fertile Crescent increases greatly. The third period (roughly A.D. 300 to 600) sees the final decline and collapse of south Arabia and its absorption into the Arab milieu, the tightening of control by the two great empires (Roman, or Byzantine, and Sassanian) over their respective spheres of influence within the Fertile Crescent, largely through the creation of client Arab kingdoms, the ascendancy of monotheistic religion throughout the Near East, and the inauguration of a heroic age (Jahiliyya) among the Arabs due in large part to the increasing militancy of the bedouin and perhaps also to a sheer growth of bedouin population.

The Period of South Arabian Predominance c. 1000-300 B.C.

The Old Testament tells of a "queen of Sheba" who visited King Solomon (962-922 B.C.) to see whether the latter lived up to the fame which had reached her country. This queen, we are told, "came to Jerusalem with a very great train, with camels that bare spices, and very much gold and precious stones" (I Kings 10:2). There is little doubt that Sheba is the Hebrew form of Saba, the name of one of the earliest kingdoms that flourished in South Arabia. This Old Testament story thus bears witness to the existence of a flourishing civilization in South Arabia in the tenth century B.C., and it also alludes to the importance which the camel had for that civilization. From at least 1000 B.C. South Arabia enjoyed a remarkable degree of material prosperity and political strength, which gave to the area a dominant position within the peninsula at large that was to last for about seven centuries. Throughout these centuries the Arab heartland was, therefore, subject to strong South Arabian influences.

The Kingdom of Saba was but one of a number of kingdoms which flourished in South Arabia in the period in question. Among others, the three most important were the kingdoms of Maʿin, Qatabān and Hadramawt. These kingdoms had the character of city-states, each encompassing a major city and the surrounding cultivated lands. This political fragmentation of South Arabia was due to some extent to geography: the mountainous character of the area made difficult the degree of regional unification that was possible in the great river valleys of Egypt and the Fertile Crescent. (South Arabia may in this respect be compared to Lebanon and Palestine, which in ancient times were often divided among city-states.) On the other hand, South Arabia was not without a certain degree of political unity. The Kingdom of Saba clearly exercised a dominant role in South Arabian affairs, being unquestionably the strongest of all the city-states and most able to impose its will on its neighbors and thus on the area as a whole. It is this political primacy of Saba that explains why scholars usually refer to the civilization of ancient South Arabia as a whole as Sabaean and the language of the area as Sabaic.

The rise of a flourishing civilization in South Arabia was due to two primary factors: agriculture and trade. A rich agriculture was made possible by South Arabia's geography and climate. A land of high mountains located next to the Indian Ocean, it received regular and generous rainfall. Cultivation of the mountainous terrain was carried on mainly through an elaborate network of terraces that were painstakingly built and maintained. At the Sabaean city of Ma'rib a stone dam was constructed to distribute the waters of the Wādī Dhana. The productive terraces, watered by the monsoon rains and by irrigation from the Ma'rib dam, guaranteed the Kingdom of Saba a consistently abundant food supply. The large number of mountain peasants could be taxed by the kings and thus made into an important source of revenue. From time to time agricultural prosperity induced neighboring nomadic tribes to take up the life of cultivators.

The other main basis of South Arabian civilization, namely trade, was facilitated by South Arabia's advantageous position vis-à-vis the great international trade routes running between the Mediterranean and the Far East (and India) via the Indian Ocean and the Arabian peninsula. Once partially controlled by ancient Egypt, this East-West trade fell under the control of the South Arabians after the decline of the New Kingdom (1570-1075 B.C.). As the most powerful of the South Arabian kingdoms, the Kingdom of Saba played a dominant role in this lucrative trade. Sabaean commercial activities fell into two spheres: maritime and caravan. Called "the Phoenicians of the South," the Sabaean ships followed the trade winds to India and beyond, bringing back spices and silks. These commodities from the maritime trade, together with the locally grown frankincense (an aromatic wood that was burned as incense in religious ceremonies by the Babylonians, the Phoenicians and the Egyptians), were then transported by camel caravans northward to markets in the Nile Valley and the Fertile Crescent. The kingdom of Solomon, visited by the Queen of Sheba, would no doubt have constituted such a market.

It was in order to facilitate the caravan trade that the Sabaeans sought to extend their influence and even control over the Arab heartland. This they did by establishing way stations along the main caravan routes and by subjugating or forming treaties with bedouin tribes through whose territories these routes passed, especially those tribes owning the wells at which the way stations were located. Thus a large part of the population of the Arab heartland was incorporated into a commercial network dominated by and designed to serve the interests of South Arabia. This development deeply affected the lives of the Arabs. For one thing, the Arabs were, in varying degrees, drawn out of the isolation of the steppe and desert and placed in contact with the larger world outside their traditional habitat. The Arab area had become a vital link in a world-wide commercial enterprise. Furthermore, the way stations gave impetus to increased sedentarization of nomadic Arabs, as they expanded in many cases into rather sizeable settlements. In the way stations an Arab might find a new means of gaining a livelihood by servicing caravans or perhaps even by becoming involved to some extent in the trade itself. Those who remained nomads could also perform vital roles as guards or guides for South Arabian caravans and as auxiliaries in the South Arabian armies.

The Period of the Great Caravan Cities of the North, c. 300 B.C.-300 A.D.

The death of Alexander the Great in 323 B.C. brought to an end a long period of relative unity in the Fertile Crescent. Up to that time, a series of great empires, beginning with the Assyrian and ending with that of Alexander, had imposed a large measure of political hegemony over the area, notwithstanding intermittent periods of instability. After the division of Alexander's empire (which included also vast territories beyond the Fertile Crescent) among his generals, the Fertile Crescent was never again to enjoy political unity until the Arabs conquered the area in the A.D. seventh century. The Fertile Crescent at first became a bone of contention between Mediterranean-based Hellenistic dynasties (the Ptolemies of Egypt and the Seleucids of Syria), after which a new Iranian empire, that of the Parthians, imposed its rule over the eastern part. In the period just before the birth of Christ, the Romans put an end to the Hellenistic states and integrated the western and central parts of the Fertile Crescent (Palestine and Syria) under their rule, but the Parthians remained in control of the eastern part. Parthian rule, in A.D. 226, was replaced by that of the Sasanians. Relations between the Romans and the Sasanians varied between peace and war, until the Arabs put an end to the rule of both empires and reestablished the political integrity of the Fertile Crescent, which became part of a much larger world empire.

During this long period of political rivalry within the Fertile Crescent, commercial opportunities made possible the expansion of Arab influence in the area. A number of caravan cities arose on the southern fringes of the Fertile Crescent which functioned as middle-men in the great East-West trade. Despite political rivalries, the Middle East continued to be a vital crossroads for international trade, and the empires themselves were anxious to benefit from this trade as much as possible. Two of the caravan cities were able, in succession, to establish a dominant position over the caravan routes and to control or at least influence the other cities which lay along these routes. These city-states were Petra (c. 300 B.C.-A.D. 105) and Palmyra (c. A.D. 1-272).

As the influence of these caravan cities over the international trade increased, that of the South Arabians decreased. The fortunes of the Kingdom of Saba had begun to wane soon after 300 B.C., when the Ptolemaic dynasty in Egypt began to expand its influence in the Red Sea and Indian Ocean. In 115 B.C., the Himyarites (Banū Himyar), a tribe in Hadramawt which became associated with the sedentary life of agriculture and commerce as cultivators of the frankincense tree, overthrew the Sabaeans. Although they ruled South Arabia independently for nearly seven centuries (115 B.C. - A.D. 570), the Himyarites never recovered the degree of power and prosperity once enjoyed by the Sabaeans.

The shift of the major commercial activities to the caravan cities of the Fertile Crescent gave the North an increasingly important place in Arab affairs. The map shows the most important of the trade routes which ran through the Arabian Peninsula and the Fertile Crescent.

Petra's development into a commercial center took place under the rule of the Nabataeans (al-Anbāt), who had come to the settlement originally as nomads in the sixth century B.C. Although the earliest

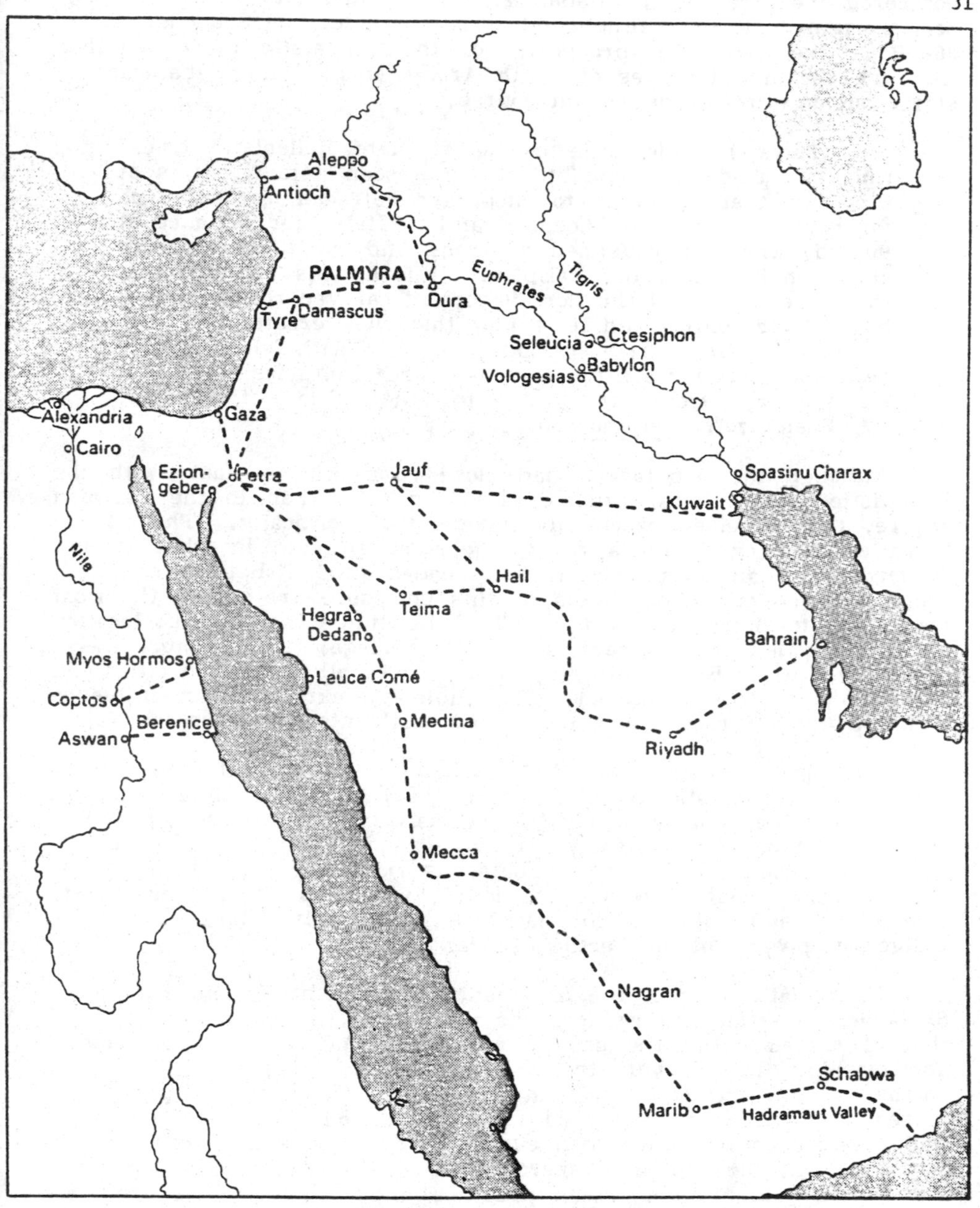

Trade routes of the ancient Middle East.

from I. Browning, <u>Palmyra</u>

commercial ventures of the Nabataeans lie in obscurity, the settlement seems originally to have functioned as a colony for the Sabeans. After 300 B.C. the commercial prosperity of the Hellenistic world together with the declining fortunes of South Arabia enabled the Nabataeans to strike out on a more independent course.

> (Petra's) golden age dawned in late Hellenistic times, when her trade developed to an unforeseen extent. It is at this date that we begin to encounter Petraean merchants as far north as Sidon in Phoenicia and in Italy, for instance at Puteoli, where they formed a strong and wealthy community and even had their own temples. It is at this time too that the protection of all the more important caravan roads seem to be in their control and it is now that they create their own caravan empire. This period, perhaps with short interruptions, lasts for a little less than three centuries . . . that is to say from 164 B.C. to the time of Trajan. (M. Rostovtzeff, Caravan Cities, p. 50)

Although the Nabataeans had close commercial contacts with the Hellenistic states, being situated closer to them than to the Parthian empire, they remained essentially independent politically. The city of Petra was located within a rocky enclosure situated in what is now Jordan. (The gorgeous Greco-Roman facades which Nabataean sculptors literally hewed out of the walls of this enclosure are among the most fascinating touristic attractions in all of the Middle East.) This location made the settlement extremely difficult to besiege; the enclosure was a natural fortress. By establishing primacy over other caravan cities and way stations, the Nabataeans were able to extend their influence throughout the Syrian desert and as far south into Arabia as the Najd.

Although Aramaic was the dominant language of the Fertile Crescent in Hellenistic times (in spite of the use of Greek in high circles) and the Nabataeans used it extensively, the native language of Petra was nonetheless clearly Arabic. Since there was as yet no distinctive Arabic script, the Nabataeans made use of a form of the Aramaic script, out of which was later to develop the Arabic script. The religion and culture of the Nabataeans was derived largely from the indigenous peoples of the Fertile Crescent.

In the latter half of the first century B.C. the Romans conquered Syria and Palestine and reduced the position of the Nabataean kings to that of vassals. But the change was purely political. Under Roman sponsorship, the caravan trade continued to prosper, and Petra's commercial influence remained undiminished. If anything, prosperity increased, thanks to Roman administration which rendered the roads under Roman control safer than ever. Petra's real eclipse came in 105 A.D., when the Roman emperor Trajan transformed it and the surrounding area into a Roman province under the name of Provincia Arabia. The Nabataean caravan city disappeared completely during the following century.

Petra's decline coincided with the blossoming of the second great Arab caravan city of pre-Islamic times, Palmyra. Palmyra's emergence in the A.D. first century as an important commercial center was due largely to rivalry between the Romans and Parthians. Situated more or less half-way between these two powers, Palmyra provided a vital link in the trade flowing between the eastern and western halves of the Fertile Crescent. Unlike Petra, which gravitated toward the Hellenistic and Roman world to which it was adjacent, Palmyra at first maintained a larger measure of neutrality vis-à-vis the two powers.

Palmyra's period of splendor came in the late second and early and middle third centuries. Like Petra, the city was strongly influenced by the Aramaic language and culture of the Fertile Crescent, while retaining Arabic as a spoken language. Like Petra also, Palmyra became, in the second century, a Roman vassal, thus ending its former neutrality. The civil wars which plagued the Roman empire in the third century gave Palmyra opportunity for a spectacular but brief political and military adventure. The preoccupation of the Roman army with internal struggles enabled the rulers of Palmyra to strengthen their own forces. In A.D. 262 the Palmyrene king, Udhayna, was appointed by the Romans dux orientis (ruler of the East), with authority over Syria, Egypt, Asia Minor, and North Arabia. After his death in 266 (or 267) his wife and successor Zenobia (or Zaynab) undertook a daring enterprise. Adopting the title of Queen of the East, she defied the Roman empire by sending her own armies into Egypt and Asia Minor and managed to defeat a Roman army at Ankara in 270. For a brief moment Zenobia was, nominally at least, ruler of all the eastern Mediterranean lands. However, in 272 the Roman armies gathered their strength and completely destroyed the caravan city, putting a sudden end to both its political and commercial power.

The Pre-Islamic Period, A.D. 300-600

Although the term "pre-Islamic" (like pre-anything else) has no definite time reference and can be applied to as long a period pre-dating the rise of Islam as one chooses, it is most meaningfully applied to the period during which the most prominent features of the setting within which Islam appeared began to emerge. There is good reason to regard the three centuries prior to the rise of Islam as such a period, even though certain important features of the setting within which Islam appeared did not emerge until the latter part of this period.

Throughout this period the Middle East, and the Fertile Crescent in particular, was divided between the two powers that were later to confront the expanding force of Islam: the Roman (or Byzantine) and Sasanian empires. Relations between these powers vacillated between war and peace, although even in peace intense rivalry prevailed. As both empires remained relatively strong throughout the period, the Arabs who lived on the fringes of the Fertile Crescent were no longer able to create relatively independent establishments, much less embark on a path of conquest as did Palmyra. The fall of Palmyra in the latter part of the third century had marked the end of an era. The great caravan cities of the earlier period were now a thing of the past, and those Arab communities that now emerged between the desert and the cultivated lands lived in much closer relationship with the great powers.

Two such communities in particular deserve our attention, the Ghassānids (Banū Ghassān) and the Lakhmids (Banū Lakhm), clients of the Romans and Sasanians respectively. These communities amounted to tribal kingdoms. That of the Lakhmids was fully sedentary, having as a permanent base al-Ḥīra, a town located on the edge of the lower Euphrates valley. The Ghassānids, on the other hand, seem to have been only partially sedentarized, as there is no evidence of their having established a permanent capital similar to al-Ḥīra. The primary function of both of these tribal kingdoms was a military one--to defend the frontiers of the empires which they served. Two forces threatened these frontiers: bedouin tribes from the Arab heartland intent on raiding and the armies of the opposing empire. Frequently the two tribal kingdoms fought each other. These battles were to become a favorite subject of Arab lore. The heyday of the military exploits of the two kingdoms occurred in the A.D. sixth century.

The period from A.D. 300 to 600 witnessed momentous changes in South Arabia. At the beginning of the period a Himyarite king, Shammar Yuharᶜish (or Yarᶜash), made use of Arab warriors to undertake raids on the Sasanian border in the far north. Though short-lived, this event testifies to the increasing importance which Arabs were to have from this point on in the military affairs of South Arabia. During the three centuries in question this Arab influence gradually increased, resulting in the arabization of the south and the blurring of the distinction between Arab and South Arabian. Another similar expedition in the North was attempted in the early fifth century by Abū Karib Asᶜad, again with the help of Arab warriors.

Just as the great powers of the North had client kingdoms to defend their interests vis-à-vis the Arab heartland, so also did the Himyarite state in the late fifth and early sixth century. The client kingdom in this case was that of the Kindites (Banū Kinda), a tribe of south Arabian origin. The Kindites seem originally to have been part of a larger tribal confederation formed to resist Sasanian penetration into Arabia. Somehow the tribe was able to assert its control over the other tribes in the confederation thereby creating a desert kingdom in Central Arabia with ties of loyalty to the Himyarite state. This Kindite kingdom lasted from about A.D. 480 to 550.

From the beginning of the period in question the Himyarite state was threatened by a rising new power located across the Bab al-Mandab in Ethiopia. There, around the beginning of the Christian era, colonists from South Arabia had established a state called Aksūm. Around the middle of the fourth century the Aksūmites had invaded and, for a brief period, ruled South Arabia, at least nominally. Thereafter the threat of another invasion hung heavy over the heads of the Himyarite rulers. After adopting Christianity, the Aksūmites formed an alliance with the Roman, or Byzantine, Empire, which, itself Christian since the early fourth century, posed as patron of all Christians. When, as an act of hostility toward the Aksūmites, the Himyarite king, Dhu'l-Nuwās, adopted Judaism and began to persecute

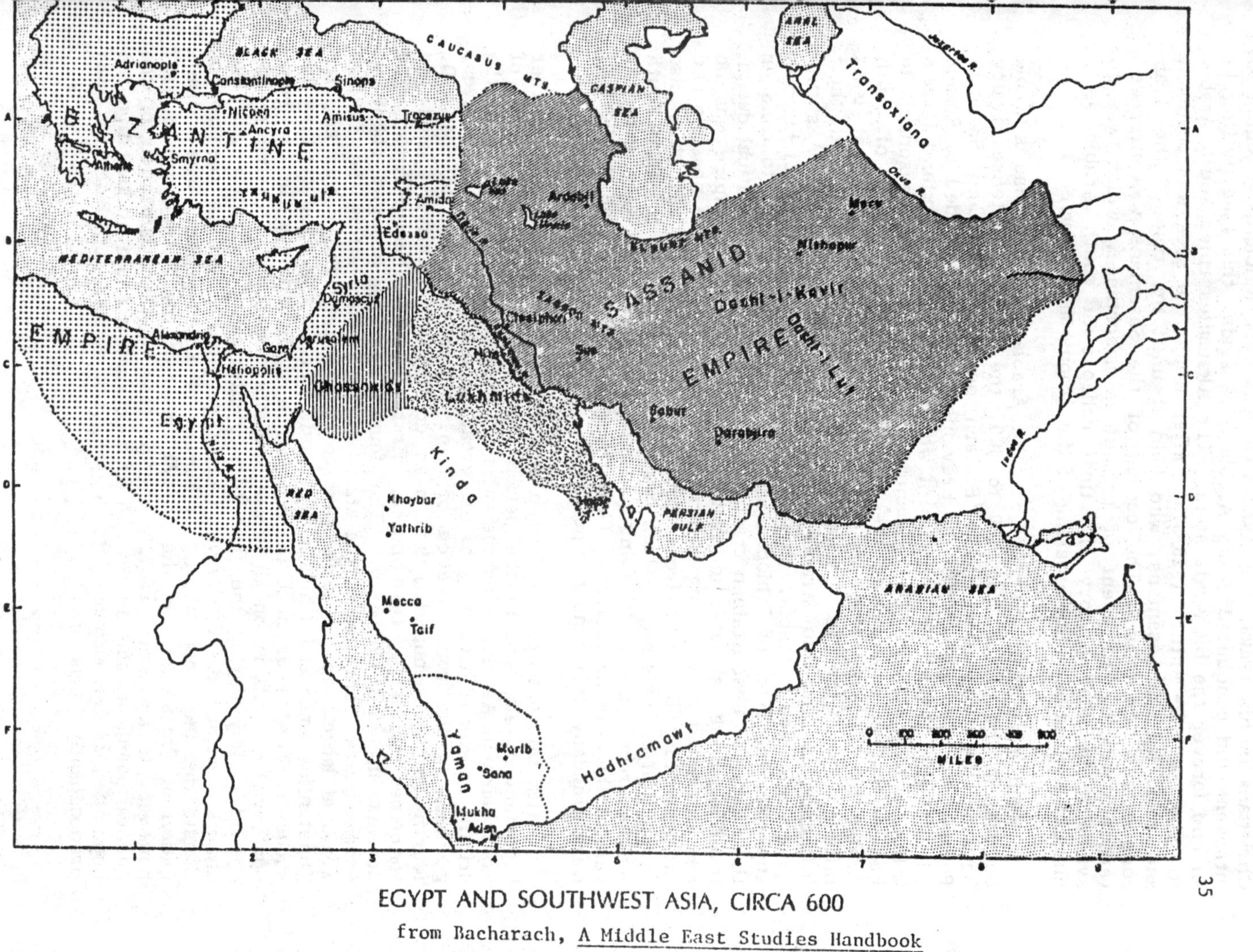

EGYPT AND SOUTHWEST ASIA, CIRCA 600

from Bacharach, A Middle East Studies Handbook

Christians in his realm, the Aksūmites took this action as a signal to intervene and conquered South Arabia once again, this time putting to an end forever the Himyarite state. The Aksumites ruled south Arabia for about a half-century (525-575), after which the area was occupied and ruled by the Sasanians, who held it until the time of the Arab conquests under Islam. The coming of the Sasanians was preceded (around 570) by an event of momentous importance, which was to symbolize in later memory the final collapse of south Arabia as a distinct civilization: the breaking of the famous Ma'rib dam.

Much more than ever before, the Arabian peninsula as a whole became, in the period from 300 to 600, the scene of intense rivalry between the two major Middle Eastern powers, Rome and Sasanian Persia. We have already (in the previous paragraph) alluded to Rome's alliance with Aksūm, the purpose of which was clearly to extend Rome's influence to the South (Ethiopia and South Arabia). It is reasonable to believe that in encouraging the Aksūmites in their invasion of South Arabia in A.D. 525, the Romans hoped to gain control or at least influence over the West Arabian trade routes and to extend their influence as far into Arabia as possible. Although the Aksumite governor of South Arabia, Abraha, made himself independent of his own superior, the ruler of Ethiopia, we may see in his attempt to conquer the Hijāz (the West Arabian coastal region) a broader geopolitical design involving Rome, at least indirectly. But the Sasanian empire was no less interested in acquiring as much influence in Arabia as possible and in preventing its rival from acquiring influence. It was thus also geopolitical considerations which prompted the Sasanians to assist South Arabian rebels in overthrowing Aksūmite rule and then take over the rule of the area themselves. Thus the great powers of the Middle East were gradually encircling the peninsula.

With this extension of Roman and Sasanian influence came another important development in the period from 300 to 600: the spread of monotheism in Arabia. Monotheism is an ancient religious tradition, the origins of which, according to the great monotheistic faiths themselves, go back to the very creation of man. However, prior to the A.D. fourth century monotheism had been confined to relatively small and sometimes scattered communities, first Jewish, then Mazdean (or Zoroastrian) and Christian. The fourth century brought about an enormous transformation in the status of monotheism within the civilized world at large. In the early part of that century the Roman emperor Constantine embraced Christianity, and later in the same century his successor Theodosius made the acceptance of Christianity (in its orthodox form) compulsory on all Roman subjects. Although Christianity had spread rapidly during the first three centuries of its history, it had always remained essentially a minority religion. Even in the time of Constantine the great majority of Romans remained pagan. The promulgation of Christianity as the official creed of the Roman empire was, however, to accelerate rapidly the process of Christianization of the general populace, and by the mid-fifth century it could be said that the population of the empire, including Egypt, Syria, and Palestine, was predominantly Christian.

In the Sasanian empire another monotheistic tradition, that of the Mazdeans, was established as the official creed, even before Constantine had espoused Christianity. However, unlike Christianity, Mazdaism (from the old Iranian name for God, Ahura-Mazda) never struck deep roots among the populace. Instead, it took its place alongside other allegiances, including Christianity, thus producing a more pluralistic (and somewhat more tolerant) religious climate than existed in the Roman empire. The form of Christianity which was sanctioned by the Sasanian state was, however, not the orthodoxy of the Roman empire, but a "heretical" creed known as Nestorianism.

Wherever the Romans and Sasanians were able to extend their influence, allegiance to one of the prevailing monotheistic traditions usually came as well. Thus the Ghassānids, clients of the Romans, embraced Christianity. So too did a part of the Lakhmid tribe, but in keeping with their affiliation with the Sasanians it was the Nestorian creed which the Lakhmids adopted. The monotheistic traditions also penetrated the southern, and to a limited extent the west-central, part of the peninsula. In the South, the inhabitants of the town of Najrān embraced Christianity around 500 B.C. We have already noted that Dhu'l-Nuwās, the last Himyarite king, adopted Judaism in defiance of the Aksūmites of Ethiopia, who had embraced Christianity a century or so earlier. It was the Christians of Najrān who were subjected to persecution under his rule. Jews existed in South Arabia since the A.D. first century, though they had always been, and continued to be, a minority. In West-Central Arabia, Judaism was established at the oasis-settlement of Yathrib (later called Medina).

Within the central and western parts of the peninsula, where the real heart of Arabism lay, a rather different world was to be found. By virtue of its relative distance from the great powers and their allies, this area was not as much influenced by the major political and religious currents of the time as were the areas on the periphery. Judaism was implanted in Yathrib; Christians were to be found here and there. But by and large the inhabitants of this inner part of the Arab heartland remained faithful to their ancestral traditions.

It was, despite the prevailing conservatism, a time of intense cultural activity for the Arabs. As was noted earlier in this chapter, the principal cultural contribution of the ancient Arabs was their literature, and especially their poetry. While the ultimate origin of Arab poetry is extremely difficult to trace, owing to the lack of documentation, it can be reasonably conjectured that some sort of poetry, or at least rhymed utterance, must have developed among the Arabs over a very long period of time. Nonetheless, even if we make allowance for a long period of undocumented gestation of the poetic art, literary evidence available to us makes it undeniable that in the century or century and a half before Islam the Arabs reached an all-time peak of finesse in their poetry. The emergence of a great wealth of poetry in sixth century Arabia, seemingly out of a void (the void being due, of course, largely to our lack of documentation), is one of the more notable surprises of history. To a large extent, this copious poetic production was nurtured by the patronage of the Ghassanid, Lakhmid, and Kindite courts. But the spirit of the poetry clearly does not spring from the semi-Christianized, highly aramaicized courts of the North, or even for that matter from the more indigenous court of the Kindites; its source is the soul of the bedouin inspired by the challenges and even the adversities of the desert life. This is clear from the principal themes, values, and sentiments of this poetry. By keeping poets at their courts, the tribal magnates of the North were keeping in touch with an Arabism whose true habitat was the open desert.

Because the literary language of the poets was a standard one used throughout Arabia it, together with the poetry composed in it, fostered a vague sense of cultural unity among the Arabs which could not have existed at the level of everyday tribal life. Although this sense of unity would become much more focused and consciously expressed under the banner of Islam, it could scarcely have existed at all without a strictly Arab cultural heritage such as took shape in the epoch just before Islam. The poetry was the repository of all those values and ideals that gave meaning to the life of the Arab and formed the basis of manhood (muruwwa) and cultural identity. It was, in other words, the repository of ᶜuruba, of Arabism. Despite his intense tribal parochialism, his constant tendency to feuding, the pre-Islamic Arab could recognize even in his enemy an Arabness that was the basis of a common identity and common cultural commitment. After the coming of Islam and the co-mingling of peoples under its aegis, Arabism was to linger on, modified of course by Islam but continuing to foster an Arab identity within the larger cosmopolitan world that Islam created. It was to be the most important cultural component in the shaping of Arab history, apart from Islam itself.

The era reflected in the enchanting lines of the great pre-Islamic poets was to become in later memory a heroic age. Muslim religious usage would call it the Jāhiliyya, a term that suggests disavowal. But not all that belonged to this age was rejected. Much indeed was admired. The pre-Islamic Arabs had, it is true, been deprived of divine revelation and guidance and had thus been wayward, arrogant, and given to excess. But they had also been brave, loyal, generous, honorable, and strong, and these were qualities to be emulated in any age, even under Islam. However pagan, the world which came alive in the poetry of the pre-Islamic bards could not but capture the imagination of generations to come.

One cannot leave aside this heroic age of the Arabs without mentioning an animal without which the heroic ethos would hardly have been possible: the horse. Although the camel was by far more vital to the Arab, it was the horse that made possible his transformation from a mere cameleer and caravaneer into an armed cavalryman. The Himyarite rulers, who, as noted earlier, had employed Arabs as warriors, had equipped them to fight in cavalry units. For military purposes the horse is far more effective than the camel, being faster and capable of charging. The increasing use of the horse after A.D. 300 helped to produce the militant warrior-type, which is so prominent a feature of the heroic age. Militancy found expression in the chivalrous ideals associated with manliness in the ethos of the Jāhiliyya.

Institutional Change Among the Arabs in Pre-Islamic Times

In reviewing the major historical developments that took place among the Arabs in the sixteen centuries or so that preceded Islam, we have taken note of a number of settled communities which were formed on the periphery of the Arab heartland, such as the Nabataeans, Palmyrenes, Ghassānids, and Lakhmids, all of which developed into states or kingdoms. We also noted, earlier in the chapter, that throughout the peninsula there were communities of sedentary Arabs clustered around wells or oases; and at least one tribal kingdom emerged in Central Arabia, that of the Kindites. Generally speaking, such communities had nomadic origins, which means that at some point in their past they had undergone a transition from nomadism to sedentary life. Even in South Arabia this transition occurred from time to time. The Himyarites, for example, seem to have been originally a nomadic tribe that had become sedentarized as a result of their attraction to the profitable cultivation of the frankincense tree. Either the benefits of agriculture or of trade could induce nomads to seek the sedentary life.

Thus the transition from nomadism to sedentary life forms an important theme in the history of the pre-Islamic Arabs which is worth exploring in general terms, as we shall attempt to do briefly in this section. Of course, the opposite transition--sedentary life to nomadism--was not unknown. The collapse of the Ma'rib dam in A.D. 570, for example, brought about a sudden displacement of a population of cultivators. One theory has it that the original migration of the Ghassānids and Lakhmids (both of whom are said to have been of southern origin) into the North is to be attributed to this event. The great bulk of the displaced population, however, simply reverted to nomadism. On the whole, however, this sedentary-to-nomad transition is of less interest to us than the nomad-to-sedentary transition, since it was the latter process that <u>produced</u> those settled communities around which the history of pre-Islamic Arabia so largely turns. Further, an understanding in general terms of the nomad-to-sedentary transition will help us better to understand the social background of events that were to take place in a settlement to be discussed in the next section as well as in the following chapter, whose importance for the subsequent course of Arab history was to far outshadow that of the other Arab settlements of pre-Islamic times.

It is the larger settlements which acquired the character of states that interest us most, since here the nomad-to-sedentary transition was carried to its furthest extent. Sedentarization in these cases led not only to the adoption of the sedentary life style; more importantly, it led to contact with powerful and advanced civilizations, under the influence of which sedentary institutions were developed.

Many of the most important changes that take place in the transition from nomadism to sedentary life relate to economic and political institutions. An economic division of labor invariably begins to occur. Raiding is abandoned as an economic enterprise; while the role of stock-breeding diminishes, those of agriculture, handicraft, and trade expand. In addition, farmers and artisans labor not just to sustain themselves from year to year but also to produce an annual surplus that can be sold in this marketplace, which therefore assumes a more important role in the life of the individual and of the community. The tribal democracy of the majlis and the shaykh are usually abandoned in favor of a monarchical system which more often than not becomes hereditary. The king heads a state which taxes the "surplus" of its subjects and which develops formal judicial institutions for judging the legality of their behavior according to official codes. Not all of the Arab states mentioned above underwent each of these institutional changes to the same degree. The tribal majlis, for example, continued to function in most of them, at least for the first few generations. Such kingdoms as those of the Ghassānids and Kindites even remained to some degree nomadic in that neither had a permanent capital. But the enhanced role of agriculture and/or trade and the emergence of hereditary kingship are indicative of the economic and political changes that could and did occur among them.

Nomadic tribes, upon becoming sedentary, also found that their social institutions became subject to change. The tribe and the clan remained functional as social units, but their importance diminished somewhat. Sedentary tribesmen no longer had to be so mindful of the precarious desert ecology; there was no need for them to fragment into smaller, more intimate tribes of less than 600. Sedentary tribes consequently tended to grow larger and more amorphous. As they did so, individuals tended to acquire new dimensions to their self-identity. For example, they began to identify themselves in terms of their vocations as well as in terms of their tribe and clan. Since property holdings varied in size and in quality and since certain vocations proved more lucrative than others, social status and political power came to be determined by wealth as well as by such personal qualities as bravery, honor, eloquence, and wisdom. In other words, although the tribe remained an important social unit, sedentary life put strains upon it just as modern industrial society puts strains on the nuclear family.

The cultural and religious institutions of nomadic Arabs also changed when they took up a sedentary existence and (in some cases) associated themselves with a great power. The Nabataeans, for example, adopted the Aramaic language, the lingua franca of the Fertile Crescent, which they used alongside Arabic, as well as certain features of the Semitic religion of the Fertile Crescent, to which Greco-Roman features were later added. Among the Himyarites there developed a sort of sophisticated paganism resembling that of the Sabaeans, whom they overthrew, and traceable ultimately to the religious systems of the Fertile Crescent. After the A.D. fourth century, the Arab states, as we noted earlier, tended also to be influenced by varieties of monotheism. Monotheism became so pervasive that even in Central Arabia, where the old bedouin paganism still predominated, individuals called _hanīfs_ began to appear who criticized idols and espoused a vaguely conceived monotheism of their own.

Mecca in the Pre-Islamic Period

Within the central and western part of the Arabian peninsula, where Arabism and paganism reigned and influences from the outside world were marginal, a city named Mecca arose to great prominence during the sixth century and drew a large part of the bedouin population of the area into its orbit. Mecca is a unique phenomenon in the history of Arabia in that never before had a settlement located so far from the great centers of power and civilization in the North and South arisen to such prominence. Hitherto the settled communities located along the West Arabian trade route had functioned as way stations in a commercial network dominated by outside powers. Now one such community was to become a center of great wealth and influence in its own right and to maintain a commanding position vis-à-vis other communities and tribes in the area. Mecca's leadership provided an important rallying point for the Arabs in general, whether included directly in the city's orbit of influence as allies or not. Like the Palmyrenes of earlier times, the Meccans maintained a careful neutrality vis-à-vis the great powers, a policy facilitated by the city's remoteness.

There were two principal reasons for the emergence of Mecca as a town, one religious and the other economic. We have already mentioned the existence of the cube-shaped shrine (ka^{c}ba) which was located at Mecca and which had become the object of a relatively important pilgrimage tradition among the tribes of West-Central Arabia. Thus, by the end of the sixth century, Mecca had developed into a center and symbol of Arab paganism; and certain of its inhabitants--notably among the dominant Quraysh tribe--were involved with the pilgrimage traffic in various ways: by acting as custodians of the ka^{c}ba, by making and selling the special clothing to the worshippers, or by vending food, lodging, and sheep to the pilgrims. Thus even the religious raison d'etre of Mecca had an economic dimension.

But the economic factor in the strict sense was probably the more important reason for Mecca's emergence as a major town in Arabia. The site of a well (Zamzam), Mecca had undoubtedly long been the object of intertribal rivalry. The powerful Quraysh tribe seized the well before the sixth century and retained it thereafter. Mecca became not just a permanent tribal market but also, because of its water supply and its strategic location, a way station on the caravan route. Mecca's town market thus grew larger and more attractive than many others in West-Central Arabia because of its connection with the international trade and its access to a greater variety of goods. There consequently developed in Mecca a class of local retailers who purchased from the South Arabian caravaneers items that could be resold at a profit to the local tribesmen. During the sixth century, as the Himyarite kingdom continued to decline and to lose its grip on the international caravan trade, some of the Meccan retailers took up the slack. That is, they began to send out their own caravans, summer and winter expeditions to both the South and the North; they thereby transformed themselves from local retailers into entrepreneurs having farflung connections. By the end of the sixth century, Mecca had established itself not just as a center of Arab paganism but also as a center of international commerce.

The increased religious and economic stature of Mecca is suggested, among other things, by the hostile attitude exhibited toward it by an Aksumite regime in South Arabia. When the Himyarite king Dhu'l-Nuwas converted to Judaism and destroyed the Christian cathedral at Najran, an army of Christian Aksumites (Ethiopians) under General Abraha invaded and occupied South Arabia in about A.D. 535. Abraha subsequently declared himself to be the independent ruler of South Arabia, which he hoped to revive economically and to use as a base of operations for spreading Christianity throughout the Arabian peninsula. Attaining these two objectives, he felt, would be facilitated by the destruction of Mecca, a stronghold of Arab paganism and a dynamic new center of the caravan trade. So Abraha led a military expedition (which included an elephant) against Mecca in about A.D. 570, a season remembered by Meccans as "the year of the elephant" (reportedly the year of Muhammad's birth). The expedition failed, owing in part to an epidemic which weakened the Aksumite troops, and Abraha returned to South Arabia where he was overthrown by a popular uprising just about the time the Ma'rib dam burst. The old pagan religion and the new economic system of Mecca were spared and consequently continued to flourish. They would not seriously be threatened again until attacked by Muhammad himself.

The emerging power of Mecca meant the emerging power of the Quraysh tribe which inhabited it. This tribe, probably long considered one of the dominant tribes in the central Hijaz, presumably consisted of the descendants of someone named Quraysh, of whom we know very little. A sixth-century tribal leader--perhaps even the Shaykh--of Quraysh about whom we know somewhat more was a man named Qusayy, who apparently played a key role in Mecca's transition from being a mere way station/tribal market into being a center of international trade. Qusayy reportedly sent out his four grandsons (Hashim, ᶜAbd Shams, Nawfal, and al-Muttalib) to establish commercial contacts in such places as Ethiopia, South Arabia, Syria, and Iraq. Under Qusayy's leadership, the Quraysh merchants also built up a network of allies or clients among bedouin tribes so that their caravans, like the earlier South Arabian caravans, would have regular way stations and guards. In some of the first biographies of Muhammad, the group of bedouin tribes affiliated with the Meccan caravans is called the Hums alliance. It is sometimes mentioned in connection with the conflict between Quraysh and its main rival in the caravan trade, the Thaqif tribe of al-Ta'if, which had its own network of bedouin allies. When a tribe allied with Thaqif attacked a tribe allied with Quraysh, the two confederations clashed in a battle known as the war of Fijar, in which the youthful Muhammad reportedly fought alongside his uncles. The victory of Mecca over al-Ta'if in the war of Fijar consolidated the position of Quraysh as one of the most powerful tribes in West-central Arabia.

Thus all tribes were not equally strong in six-century Arabia; and the Quraysh tribe, even though (or perhaps because) it had become almost wholly sedentary, was the strongest of a rather large region. Yet the strength of Quraysh lay not in its will and capacity to conduct daring raids but rather in its will and capacity to engage in lucrative commerce. While renouncing neither military preparedness nor the ideal of bravery, Quraysh simply became more prosperous than its fellows. In this regard, just as the control by Quraysh of the caravan trade created distinctions of wealth and power between it and other tribes, the same factor created the same distinctions between various elements within Quraysh itself. In other words, during the sixth century Meccan society became rather stratified internally as it reflected increasingly unequal divisions of wealth, power, and status. The pressures which sedentary life and commercial activities exerted on traditional bedouin institutions weakened the tribal solidarity of Quraysh and encouraged in Mecca the emergence of such tendencies as individualism and cupidity.

By the time of Qusayy in about the mid-sixth century, there reportedly existed within Quraysh two general groupings: Quraysh al-zawahir ("Quraysh of the outside") and Quraysh al-bitah ("Quraysh of the inside"). Quraysh al-zawahir consisted of the poorer and weaker clans whose places of residence were located on the outskirts of town, farthest from the well, the kaᶜba, and the market and also in the position most exposed to desert storms and to bedouin raids.* Quraysh al-bitah consisted of the wealthier and more powerful clans whose places of residence were prestigious as well as protected in being located at the center of town and therefore near to the well, the kaᶜba, and the market. The wealth of the "inside clans" derived from their control of the shrine and the pilgrimage traffic and especially from their domination of the trade, both retail and long-distance. As indicated on the geneaological chart, Quraysh al-bitah included the clans descended from Qusayy (Hashim, ᶜAbd Shams, etc.) along with the clan of Makhzum.

In the years between the death of Qusayy and the end of the sixth century, however, there seems to have occurred some readjustments in Mecca's internal political and economic power structure. Certain clans, once numbered among the most prosperous and powerful families, appear to have slipped to a middle position. What happened to the clan of Hashim is a good example of this process of readjustment. It is likely that this clan was at one period, during the last years of Hashim's own lifetime, quite prosperous and influential. It apparently had a significant role in the custodianship of the kaᶜba as well as a lucrative share in the caravan trade to Syria. In this regard, it had reportedly been Hashim himself, one of the four grandsons of Qusayy, who was sent to Syria in order to request the Byzantine governor's permission to sell Meccan goods there. Hashim seems to have been an important political figure too. He may even have been the shaykh of Quraysh, for according to some reports it was he who negotiated with Abraha on behalf of the inhabitants of Mecca. Yet the early deaths of Hashim and of ᶜAbd Allah (Muhammad's father) were probably among the factors which led to the decline in the clan's prosperity and influence. It apparently retained a role in the custodianship of the kaᶜba; there exists an account of Muhammad himself, as a teenager, taking an active part in the resetting of the black stone in the structure's wall. But by that time the clan of Hashim seems to have

*Presumably, those residents of Mecca who were not full members of the Quraysh tribe (e.g., mawali, slaves, etc.) could either be included in this category or put into another one below it.

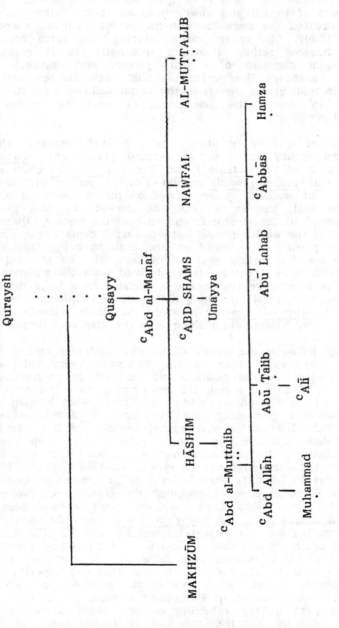

Some Dominant Clans in Sixth-Century Mecca

- Quraysh
  - MAKHZŪM
  - Quṣayy
    - ʿAbd al-Manāf
      - HĀSHIM
        - ʿAbd al-Muṭṭalib
          - ʿAbd Allāh
            - Muḥammad
          - Abū Ṭālib
            - ʿAlī
          - Abū Lahab
          - ʿAbbās
          - Ḥamza
      - ʿABD SHAMS
        - Umayya
      - NAWFAL
      - AL-MUṬṬALIB

lost its former significant share in the Syrian trade as well as its political preeminence. Thus by A.D. 600, Hashim, along with certain other once important clans, had moved downward in Meccan society.

Indeed, by the end of the sixth century much of Mecca's long-distance trade, along with the wealth, power and status derived from it, had essentially become concentrated in the hands of the Banu Makhzum and the Banu Umayya, the two wealthiest and most powerful clans. A majlis still functioned within Quraysh, but the leading man or shaykh seems consistently to have been chosen from the two dominant clans. During the lifetime of Muhammad, for example, the shaykhs of Mecca were Abu Jahl of the Banu Makhzum and then Abu Sufyan of the Banu Umayya. This suggests that a merchant oligarchy was emerging to control Mecca's political affairs and to monopolize further the major source of wealth. In this regard, shortly before the birth of Muhammad there occurred in Mecca a very interesting phenomenon: the formation of an intratribal confederation. That is, some of the poorer and middle clans, including Hashim, banded together against the increasing power of Makhzum and Umayya. This confederation, referred to in the sources as hilf al-fudul, seems to have expressed two major concerns. With regard to the economic issue, the poorer and middle clans apparently feared that the two most powerful clans would soon completely monopolize the caravan trade. They consequently pooled their resources in an attempt to retain and to expand their share in the commercial activities. Secondly, hilf al-fudul seems also to have expressed what amounts to an ethical concern: that the two dominant clans were exhibiting greed and materialism and that, in pursuing excessive wealth, they were neglecting their poor relations. In effect, the poorer and middle clans accused the Banu Makhzum and the Banu Umayya of violating the "code of the desert," which included the bedouin ideals of tribal solidarity and generosity.

The new commercial relations which Mecca established during the sixth century with South Arabia, Abyssinia, Syria, and Mesopotamia entailed new cultural and intellectual contacts as well. As a result of these increasingly strong and increasingly frequent contacts, there began to seep into Meccan society new ideas, including religious ones. Each of Mecca's trading partners had a large and growing Christian population. The Nestorians of Iraq and the Jacobites of Syria as well as the Abyssinians actively sought converts among the Arabic-speaking tribesmen. Communities of Jews in South Arabia, Yathrib, and Khaybar, while not so aggressive in terms of proselyting, nevertheless served as examples in such religious beliefs as monotheism and in such religious practices as fasting and dietary laws. Arabia had become a pagan island in a rising sea of monotheism and Mecca was on low ground at the water's edge. Perhaps bedouin institutions were still very deeply rooted in the interior of central Arabia, but Mecca, gradually relinquishing the desert life style which served as the well spring of the old paganism, was on the threshold of a revolution.

CHAPTER TWO

THE RISE OF ISLAM AND THE ASCENDANCY OF THE ARABS

600-750 A.D.

The appearance of Islam in Arabia in the first half of the seventh century was an event of inestimable importance, not only from the point of view of Arab history, but from the point of view of general world history as well. From the point of view of Arab history, the event was important in that it endowed the Arabs with a degree of unity and political consciousness unknown in their previous history; from the point of view of general world history its importance lay in the fact that it projected the Arabs into the mainstream of world history as empire-builders in their own right and as bearers of a freshly revealed universal religion. The ultimate consequences of their intrusion into world history were to be felt throughout the globe.

As an event within Arab history, the coming of Islam opened up an exciting new chapter. In the previous centuries, even though the Arabism expressed in Jāhiliyya poetry had fostered a vague sense of cultural unity among the Arabs, the Arabs were still far from being a people in the true sense of the word. Since the time of the great caravan cities of the North, the life of the most flourishing sedentary centers among the Arabs had been far removed from that of the bedouin living in the interior. Even in the period of the client kingdoms, when Arabism strengthened psychological and cultural ties with the interior, this remoteness from the bedouin world persisted. As for South Arabia, it had for centuries remained essentially outside the world of Arabs and had only in the period just before Islam begun to be absorbed into that world. Among the bedouin themselves, ancestral tribal loyalties had fostered an intense parochialism, commonly expressed in feuding. It was against this background of parochialism and regional variation that Islam appeared as a higher loyalty able to draw all the inhabitants of the Arabian Peninsula together in a common enterprise. By putting before the Arabs a monotheistic vision of life contained in an authentically Arabic scripture, Islam strengthened the vague self-identity of the Arabs and transformed them into a true people. Genealogical traditions emphasizing the racial unity of the Arabs were strengthened, and agriculturalists, merchants and bedouin joined hands in the pursuit of common interests that hitherto would have been unthinkable.

But Islam as a social force was not to be content with the creation of an Arab people. As an essentially universal religion, it offered itself to all men and not just to the Arabs. As a result, the community which it brought into being soon broke through the confines of the Arab milieu in which it had arisen and incorporated vast numbers of non-Arabs. When this happened, it became apparent that the community of Islam was not to be identical with the community of Arabs.

In the meantime, however, the Arabs had erected a vast empire within which they tried to maintain themselves as a ruling elite distinct both in race and in religion from the subject population. As one historian has put it, Islam became for the ruling Arabs a badge of their Arabism, a national religion, a basis of racial identity. This attitude soon showed itself to be in conflict with the universalism of the Koran and the Prophet Muhammad. That universalism in time undermined the exclusivism and elitism of the ruling Arabs. Thus the very religious movement that had brought the Arabs together in the first place, making possible the creation of an Arab empire, now persisted in bringing Arabs and non-Arab together as equal partners in a common faith, thus contributing to the ultimate downfall of the Arab empire.

In this chapter we will consider first how the Arabs were united under Islam through the leadership of the Prophet Muhammad. Then we will trace the history of the empire which the Arabs, thus united, brought into being, giving special attention to certain problems which were eventually to result in the undoing of the empire.

Unification of the Arabs Under the Prophet Muḥammad

The Proclamation of Islam in Mecca

The religion of Islam, which we now think of as a vast historical phenomenon embracing large populations throughout the world and comprising a variety of long-established institutions and traditions, first appeared as an urgent message from God delivered by a prophet named Muhammad to his contemporaries in the West Arabian town of Mecca. Although the message was at the outset addressed primarily to the people of Mecca, it was offered implicitly to all who would listen, whether inside or outside of Mecca.

The situation in Mecca at the time the message was first proclaimed has been described in the previous chapter. There it was noted that the high level of material prosperity of the town had resulted in a concentration of wealth in the hands of certain powerful clans, especially the Banū Umayya and the Banū Makhzūm, who had a virtual monopoly on the town's most lucrative commercial operations. As a result, a notable gap had arisen between powerful and rich clans on the one hand and the less fortunate clans on the other, the latter group including poor clans as well as other clans, like the Banū Hashim, which had been forced out of the wealthier circles into an "in-between" status. This gap militated against the solidarity of the Quraysh tribe. Furthermore, the intensely capitalistic atmosphere of Mecca had produced a spirit of individualism, which also militated against tribal solidarity. Wealth was viewed as a means of acquiring more wealth--hence the tendency to hoard rather than to distribute wealth, as called for by the tribal ethic.

The message which the Prophet Muhammad delivered to his fellow townsmen addressed itself to this situation of social malaise. It was an essentially moral message. It proclaimed not merely that there is one and only one God but that this One God demands justice and mercy of his creatures. Thus it upheld the ethical concern which had been implicit in the hilf al-fudul (see previous chapter) and in the traditional tribal ethic; it upheld the cause of the poorer and weaker members of the community and affirmed the responsibility of the fortunate toward them. While there is no evidence that the revelation of which the Prophet Muhammad was bearer forbade the acquisition of wealth as such, it is abundantly clear that it demanded a responsible use of wealth. But the message of the Prophet went beyond the tribal outlook in one very important respect. It affirmed an essentially individualistic ethic. Whereas the tribal code had placed the emphasis on the responsibility of the group as a whole toward its own weaker members (or toward persons coming from outside the tribe), the message borne by Muhammad proclaimed the responsibility of each individual under God to act rightly and fairly. In an environment in which the acquisition of wealth had become an intensely individualistic pursuit, it was to individuals as individuals that the message of justice and mercy was addressed. This individualism found ultimate expression in the doctrine of the impending Judgment. At the Day of Resurrection each man would be judged individually for his deeds.

The Prophet's preaching was soon regarded by the leading Meccan merchants as a threat to the town's status quo and to their economic interests, which were linked to the status quo. The summons to worship a single, universal deity was in effect a call for a break with the existing cult with its plurality of deities. The commandments of the One God were ethically rigorous, demanding generosity toward the less fortunate, compassion for the weak, and humility before God. The wealthy merchants had been accustomed to managing their own affairs without regard for a higher power. Now such a Power was addressing them through one of their own townsmen. As the Prophet's following increased, their position of leadership became more and more tenuous and their control of the town far from secure.

Owing to the increasing opposition of the leading merchants, the Prophet soon found Mecca unsuitable as a place in which to continue his mission. Unable to harm him physically because of the customary law of retaliation, the Prophet's opponents attempted to pressure his kinsmen among the Banū Hashim into curtailing his activities by imposing an economic boycott on that clan. Though the boycott itself proved unsuccessful, the climate of hostility to the Prophet which it engendered remained in force as the opponents turned to verbal abuse, belittling the Prophet's person and ridiculing his claims. Furthermore, they were able to impose economic penalties on individuals who openly supported the Prophet. In 619 the Prophet's situation reached its lowest point with the death of his uncle Abū Ṭālib who, as head of the Banū Hāshim, had assured the Prophet of the clan's protection. Abū Ṭālib's successor, Abū Lahab, also an uncle of the Prophet, was a friend of some of the wealthy merchants and threatened to withdraw protection from the Prophet.

Desiring a new base of operations where he could carry on his mission freely, the Prophet made a number of contacts with parties outside Mecca, including some bedouin tribes and a group in the nearby settlement of al-Ṭā'if. His most fruitful contact proved to be with a small group of men from Yathrib, a town located about 200 miles north of Mecca, soon to be renamed Medina. This first contact took place in 620. It was followed by further contacts in the two following years in the course of which the stage was set for the transfer of the Prophet and his followers to Medina in 622, an event known usually by its Arabic name *hijra*. Many scholars have seen this event as the outworking of a plan which had been taking shape in the mind of the Prophet for some time. On this view, the Prophet had wished, while carrying on his mission in Mecca, not only to proclaim the message of Islam but also to implement that message. For this he needed to create a community over which he could exercise moral and political leadership. In such a community the principles contained within his message would not only be acknowledged but also carried out: the new social order under the One God called for in the message would become a reality.

The Establishment of the Umma in Medina

Prior to the Prophet's arrival in Medina, the town had been suffering from severe internal dissension, owing to a longstanding feud which had originally involved two clans but, as other clans took sides, had come to engulf the entire population. Just two years before the first contact between the Prophet and the men from Medina was made, a great battle had taken place in which there had been much loss of life. As a result of this disaster, the people of Medina had come to the realization that their town could not sustain a continuation of the feud and consequently began looking for an arbiter capable of settling their differences for them. The Prophet appeared in the eyes of the leading men of Medina ideally suited for this role. Not only as a Meccan was he a neutral outsider to the conflict, but as a Prophet he possessed an authority based on religious claims.

In the course of his contacts with the delegates from Medina prior to the *hijra*, the Prophet concluded two agreements with the delegates, which are known, after the place where the meetings took place, as the First and Second Pledges of ^{c}Aqaba. Since the delegates represented the most important clans of Medina, these agreements were regarded as binding on the entire town. In the First Pledge of ^{c}Aqaba (621) the Medinans declared their acceptance of Muhammad as Prophet and their intention to conform to the divine commandments; in other words, they declared themselves Muslims. In the Second Pledge of ^{c}Aqaba (622, about a month before the *hijra*), they declared their readiness to fight on behalf of the Prophet. Thus even before setting out for Medina, the Prophet assured himself that he would be able to exercise a permanent authority in Medina after his arrival. This would make possible the establishment of a sovereign Muslim community under his headship.

The new Muslim community, or *umma*, as it is called in Arabic, materialized immediately upon the arrival of the Prophet in Medina. In outward form, it was a federation of clans--eight Medinan clans plus the Prophet's followers from Mecca, who were now constituted as a ninth clan under the name of Quraysh. The Prophet was careful to lay down regulations governing the conduct of member clans. These regulations were eventually embodied in a document frequently referred to by Western scholars as the Constitution of Medina. The internal affairs of the clans were left virtually untouched. These continued to fall under the jurisdiction of clan leaders as before. In this respect, it can be said that daily life within the umma proceeded more or less as before; the internal structure of the clans remained basically unchanged.

What the new regulations were concerned with primarily were relationships between clans within the umma and relationships between the umma and parties outside Medina. It was with respect to these relationships that the authority of the Prophet became operative. Whenever disputes arose between clans, he was to be the final arbiter. The three Jewish clans which lived in Medina were allowed to remain in their places as allies of the Muslims on the understanding that they would not give aid to enemies of the umma. No member clan was allowed to enter into any separate alliances with outside parties. The umma was to be regarded as an indivisible union whose external relations were in the hands of the Prophet. It was he who would, after consultation with his advisors, conduct war and conclude treaties. Similarly, if any member clan was attacked by an outside force, the other clans were obliged to assist in its defense.

The umma was, however, more than a federation in the traditional sense. The bond which united the member clans was religion, not sheer practical expediency. Each clan was part of the umma by virtue of the allegiance rendered by its leaders to the Prophet. The "Islamization" of groups, whether clans, tribes, or even whole towns or regions, was to be a common phenomenon in the subsequent history of Islam. It represented the spread of Islam as a polity. Thus in creating the umma at Medina the Prophet had set a pattern of formal incorporation of groups into Islam. As a confederation of clans bound together by allegiance to God and to His Prophet, the umma was the body politic of Islam. Faith as such was, of course, an individual affair. One could be incorporated into the body politic by virtue of an act of allegiance on the part of the leaders of one's clan, but this did not necessarily make one a believer. The Prophet, to be sure, summoned individuals to personal faith; but at the same time, by creating the umma, he brought into being an order of society within which personal faith, together with obedience, could readily emerge. Islam the polity was an important condition for the growth of Islam the faith.

As revelation continued, the umma was increasingly subjected to the norms of the new faith, and new patterns of life began to emerge. For example, care for the weaker members of the community was made an absolute imperative of the faith. New laws of inheritance were introduced to assure a fairer distribution of estates. A more responsible attitude toward marriage was enjoined, as polygamy was curtailed. A new religious identity was forged, as the forms of worship were worked out in greater detail. In short, the umma was, in accordance with the Prophet's plan, becoming the means through which a new order of society could be fashioned.

The Winning of Mecca

The establishment of the umma in Medina soon thrust the Prophet into the politics of Arabia. The creation of a new center of power could not but arouse concern on the part of the leaders of Mecca. It soon became apparent that the new power was in a position to threaten the all-important caravan route to Syria. The Prophet, on his part, was determined to win the Meccans to Islam, even if power tactics were required. The hostility which they had exhibited toward him in Mecca was bound not to cease after his assumption of leadership in Medina. If Islam was to prevail, this hostility had to be overcome. Accordingly, some of the Meccans who had emigrated to Medina with the Prophet began conducting raids on Meccan caravans, possibly justifying their action as recompense for the confiscation of their property in Mecca and for other hostile acts which the Meccan leaders had committed against them. The Meccan leaders, wishing to rid themselves of the menace to their lucrative trade, organized an expedition against the Muslims in 624. The encounter, which took place at Badr, resulted in an overwhelming victory for the Muslims.

A state of war now clearly existed between the two towns. In the conduct of the war the Prophet exhibited a remarkable control over the course of events. A gifted statesman, he was able to manipulate the forces around him in such a way as to bring about a desired goal. That he wished to bring Mecca to submission is abundantly clear. It is also clear that he entertained a further objective, in relation to which the winning of Mecca was but a means to an end: the winning of all Arabia to Islam. Just when this objective first entered his mind is impossible to say. There is good reason to believe that it was in his mind in the earliest days of his preaching in Mecca. A man as gifted with foresight as the Prophet Muhammad proved to be must have realized from quite an early point that if his mission in Mecca had succeeded this would have laid all of Arabia open to Islam. Mecca was, as we have already noted, the leading religious and economic center of Arabia.

A key factor in the conflict between the two towns was the bedouin. The Prophet sought to create a sphere of influence among the tribes around Medina similar to that which the Meccans had always maintained in their own vicinity. Those tribes which submitted to his authority or entered into an alliance with him were exposed to the teachings of Islam through emissaries sent to them. Thus even before Mecca was won, the mission of the Prophet was already being extended to the bedouin population of Arabia. The great bulk of that population was, however, as yet beyond the reach of his mission. Many tribes, aware of the power struggle between Mecca and Medina, adopted a "wait-and-see" policy. It is often said that bedouin respect power. Whichever side in this power struggle emerged victorious would immediately elicit the respect, and to a very large extent the allegiance, of tribes throughout Arabia.

In 625 and 627 the Meccans launched two further expeditions against Medina, each time adding more numbers to their forces. The expedition of 625, which led to the Battle of Uhud, resulted in a heavy loss of lives for the Muslims but failed to inflict a real defeat on them. The expedition of 627 was the most determined ever and involved the largest number of fighters that Mecca was capable of mustering, including some recruits from allied tribes. The Muslims, anticipating the expedition, prepared for their defense by digging a trench at the point at which a cavalry attack was expected. Upon arrival, the Meccan army, unprepared for this innovation, called off its attack and prepared for a siege of the town. However, the restlessness of the bedouin recruits and inclement weather forced the Meccans to abandon their siege, and after two weeks their army withdrew.

The failure of this last expedition unnerved the Meccans and forced them to reexamine their relations with the umma. A party began to form among them which reasoned that it was much more in the interests of their town to join the Muslims than to fight them. In the meantime, although the Prophet's power and influence was rapidly increasing, rather than attempting a counter-expedition against the Meccans (which may very well have succeeded), he opted for a truce. Ostensibly intending to make the pilgrimage to Mecca, the Prophet and a group of his followers proceeded toward the town in 628 and were stopped at a place near Mecca called Hudaybiyya. There a truce was conducted between the two sides, one of the terms of which was that the Muslims would be permitted to enter Mecca on pilgrimage in the following two years. The truce worked in the Prophet's favor, since it gave him time to deal with certain internal matters in Medina and it allowed more time for the Meccans to think over the situation.

By 630 the Prophet felt that the opportune moment had come for the use of force against Mecca. Judging himself free from the terms of the truce because it had been violated by the Meccans themselves, the Prophet appeared at the outskirts of Mecca in the month of Ramadan with an army of 10,000 men. After receiving a promise of amnesty from the Prophet, the town capitulated with little resistance. Mecca now belonged to Islam.

The Winning of Arabia

Once mastery over Mecca was assured, mastery over the greater part of the rest of Arabia was a foregone conclusion. The Prophet was now indisputably the leading power in all Arabia, to be respected and also--in the bedouin way of thinking--to be feared. This commanding position was confirmed by the delegations which streamed into Medina from all parts of Arabia during the year following the fall of Mecca for the purpose of declaring the allegiance of tribes or tribal factions to the Prophet.

The delegations resulted in a vast system of alliances whereby tribes all over the peninsula were brought within the orbit of the Islamic polity. Tribes over which the Prophet's power was greatest were required to embrace Islam and to pay a religious tax, the Zakat, as a token of their submission. These tribes can be said to have been incorporated within the umma, for the umma was, it will be recalled, essentially a confederation. Certain Christian and Jewish communities were accorded the same treatment as the original Jews of Medina. Some tribes, especially in remote areas, were allowed the status of allies while retaining their paganism. This arrangement may be regarded as a strictly temporary expedient.

Although the Prophet hastened to send emissaries to many tribes to teach them the Koran and to indoctrinate them in the principles of Islam, the religious devotion of the tribes was on the whole shallow. The experience in Medina had shown that genuine faith emerged gradually and was, even in the best of circumstances, in effect limited to a devoted nucleus whose precise identity was known, ultimately, only to God. It was unthinkable that within a single year tribes previously been untouched by Islam and living at some distance from the Prophet should have been transformed into devout believers. Nonetheless, the system of alliances served the Prophet's purpose. It created a sphere in which Islam could be freely propagated. It also brought into being an organism whereby the Islamic polity could be further extended.

The question is frequently raised as to whether the Prophet envisioned or planned for the expansion of Islam beyond Arabia. This is closely related to the question of whether he conceived his mission as limited to the Arabs or as universal. There are good reasons to believe that the Prophet did indeed anticipate some degree of expansion beyond Arabia, although it is unlikely that he foresaw the actual extent of the expansion. For one thing, the Prophet understood the bedouin mentality very well and must have been aware that the tenuous system of alliances could not be held together indefinitely unless some sort of common activity were launched which would absorb the energies of the bedouin. Secondly, there is evidence that the Prophet had a special interest in the situation on the northern borders of Arabia. About a year after the fall of Mecca, he led a large expedition consisting of 30,000 men to Tabūk, along the route to Syria, in the course of which he made treaties with certain Jewish and Christian communities. He also established contact with certain tribes on the border of Iraq, where raiding was on the increase. Finally, tradition attributes to the Prophet a letter to the principal rulers of the day, inviting them to embrace Islam. Western scholars tend to question the validity of this tradition. However, considering that the Prophet, as the most powerful figure in all of Arabia, may well have been conscious of having entered the mainstream of world affairs, the possibility of his having sent out such a letter should not be ruled out.

There is no doubt that the Prophet felt a special affinity with and concern for the Arabs, whose unification he had brought about. They were, in his view, a people lost in the darkness of paganism, in contrast to the peoples around them who had preserved at least a measure of the true religion propagated by earlier prophets. The revelation of which the Prophet was bearer was couched in the language of the Arabs and thus presupposed an Arab audience. The Prophet himself was of Arab stock and is referred to in the Koran as "an Arab prophet." Thus it cannot be denied that there existed in the mind of the Prophet a special relationship between his religion and the Arabs. All this, however, does not provide adequate evidence that he regarded his mission as a strictly national one, limited to the Arabs. The call to submit to God and to His will is, by its very nature, universal. Furthermore, the Prophet regarded his religion as the perfection of all previous religions and himself as the last of the prophets. This presupposes that an invitation to consider the claims of Islam is extended to all mankind, pagan or otherwise.

In retrospect, it can be said that the Prophet accomplished two primary things. He launched a universal religion, which was to become the basis of a world-wide community embracing a variety of peoples and even cultures. And he laid the groundwork for the emergence of an Arab nation and empire. The unification of the Arabs under Islam was to make them more conscious of their oneness, particularly when, soon after the Prophet's death, they became masters over peoples different from them.

The umma, as the prophet left it, was accordingly of a dual character. In essence and potentially it was a religious community open to any who would declare their acceptance of Islam. In outward form, however, it was still a confederation of clans and tribes, membership in which was based on affiliation with a member clan or tribe. In this outward aspect, the umma was roughly coterminous with the Arab nation, although not absolutely so owing to the existence of some Christian tribes. Its inner essence required, however, that this purely Arab character eventually be abandoned so as to make possible the full inclusion of persons of different races, thus fulfilling the universal mission which was the umma's original justification. The umma was, after all, not ummat al-^carab but ummat Muhammad. The de-arabization of the umma was not, however, to be an easy task, as subsequent history was to show.

The Emergence of the Arab Empire

Preliminary Problems

Although by the time of the Prophet's death in 632 the primary conditions had been created for an expansion of the Arabs beyond Arabia, such an expansion could not actually take place until two problems were resolved, each of which was a direct consequence of the prophet's death. The first of these was the problem of leadership. According to the prevailing view (to which Shi^ci Muslims take obvious exception), the Prophet made no provision for his succession but left this matter to the judgment of his community. There was, of course, no possibility of another prophet's emerging to continue his prophetic role. Prophethood had reached its culmination in Muhammad and thus by definition could not be passed on to others. Yet there was a pressing need for someone to succeed the prophet in his role as leader of the community. Without a leader to direct the practical affairs of the umma in keeping with the principles laid down by the Prophet and to maintain the political power which the umma had acquired under the Prophet, the umma would not survive.

Thanks to the timely action of three men, close companions of the prophet and respected members of the community, the problem of leadership was speedily and efficiently resolved. The three agreed that one of their number, namely Abū Bakr, who had been particularly close to the Prophet in his last days, should be presented to the community as its new head. Members of the leading clans of Medina were persuaded to forego their own plans to appoint a leader and to swear the oath of allegiance (bay^{c}a) to Abū Bakr. This made Abū Bakr the first caliph (Arabic: khalīfa), a title meaning successor and deputy of the Prophet.

Thus was born the caliphate, an institution which was to have a long and varied history. Although the caliphate was always to remain in theory an elective office, after the precedent of the appointment of Abu Bakr, it soon succumbed in practice to the dynastic principle. As the first four caliphs, namely Abū Bakr, ^{c}Umar, ^{c}Uthman and ^{c}Alī, were all close companions of the Prophet and men renowned for their piety, to whom the dynastic principle was foreign, they are called in Muslim tradition the "Rightly Guided Caliphs" (al-khulafa al-rashidun), whereas the caliphs thereafter bear the names of their dynasties: Umayyad and Abbasid.

The second problem occasioned by the death of the Prophet was that of the secession of many tribes from the umma. These tribes considered the alliances which they had established with the Prophet to be no longer in effect after the Prophet's death and accordingly refused to continue paying the zakāt. They did not consider themselves as under any obligation to a permanent, impersonal political establishment in Medina. The leaders of the umma, on the other hand, considered that the obligations entailed in the treaties of alliance were not principally to the Prophet as such, but to God, and that the umma was a permanent expression of the will of God. The refusal of the tribes to recognize the suzerainty of the new caliph was therefore a challenge which the Muslim establishment in Medina could not afford to ignore. Survival meant maintenance of the dominant position which the umma had achieved under the Prophet. The slightest indication that the new power would relent would cause a loss of faith, not only among the tribes, but possibly among the Muslims of Medina as well. The defection of the tribes therefore called for an immediate show of strength.

For this purpose the able Muslim commander, Khālid ibn al-Walīd, was dispatched with a sizeable force to deal with the dissidents. These seceders are known in the Arabic historical tradition as "apostates" (murtaddūn), and Khālid's campaigns against them are called "wars of apostasy" (ridda). However, it must be borne in mind that many of the seceding tribes had been incorporated into Islam in a purely political sense. Their Islam had amounted to scarcely more than an acceptance of the Prophet as a kind of supra-tribal magnate with a religious basis of authority.

Khalid's goal in the Ridda wars was nothing less than the extension and consolidation of Muslim sovereignty throughout the peninsula. As one modern Arab historian had said, "Before Arabia could conquer the world it had to conquer itself." In pursuing this goal, Khalid relied on sheer coercion. Coercion had never been systematically applied in Arabia at large under the Prophet; those tribes that had entered into alliance with the Prophet were attracted by the sheer "pull" of the power which he had demonstrated in his dealings with Mecca. The Arabic sources emphasize the fact that the delegations following the fall of Mecca were spontaneous.

Coercion in itself is unsatisfactory as a basis of authority. Islamic rule could hardly have long endured in Arabia had it depended solely on the force of arms. Historically the Arabian heartland has known very little lasting rule. Therefore it was important, if the umma was to maintain its dominant position, that . rallying point be found whereby the energies of the tribes could be deflected from rebellion against authority and channelled into some activity that could be rationalized both by the tribes themselves and by the more religiously inclined members of the umma. This rallying point was provided by excursions beyond the northern borders of the peninsula. From a strictly tribal point of view these excursions were simply raids of a sort long familiar to the bedouin. Through the religious ideology of Islam these raids were transformed into holy wars (jihād), the purpose of which was the extension of Islam to territories beyond Arabia. The Ridda wars were in reality brought to a successful conclusion by inviting the bedouin to give up their senseless rebellion and to join a new offensive on behalf of Islam. The northward expansion of the Arabs was the necessary complement and conclusion of the Ridda wars.

The Expansion of the Arabs

The Arab invasions into the territories beyond Arabia were far too eventful to be recounted in detail here. Suffice it to say that by the end of ^{c}Umar's caliphate (644) the Arabs had made themselves masters of an empire extending roughly from the Zagros mountains in the East to Tripoli (in Libya) in the West. The invasions of Syria and Iraq took place more or less simultaneously. The decisive defeat of the Byzantines took place at a site on the Yarmūk river in 636, that of the Persians at Qādisiyya in 637. After these defeats, the campaigns concentrated on "mopping up." The attack on Egypt commenced somewhat later, in 639, and the defeat of the Byzantine forces there occurred the following year. During the caliphate of ^{c}Uthmān the Arabs gained control of Iran and pushed northward as far as the Caucasus Mountains. In the direction of the Byzantine empire, however, they were never to advance permanently beyond the Taurus Mountains.

The great campaigns under ^{c}Umar and ^{c}Uthmān constitute the first great wave of the Arabs' expansion. During the civil war which broke out after ^{c}Uthmān's death, the expansion came to a temporary halt, and although it was resumed to some extent under the caliphates of al Mu^{c}awiya (661-680) and Yazid (680-683), it was not until the empire had recovered from the second civil war (680-692) that the second and last great wave of Arab expansion (695-715) took place.

How is the great rapidity of the initial expansion of the Arabs to be explained? Modern historians commonly attribute this phenomenon to such factors as the pressure of increased population in the Arabian peninsula, the bedouin instinct for raiding and plunder, the employment of techniques of desert warfare with which the opposing forces were unfamiliar, the cooperation of certain segments of the local population in some of the conquered areas, the disaffection of the general populace in Syria, Palestine, and Egypt toward the Byzantine government, and the internal weakness of the Byzantine and Persian states.

That Arabia prior to Islam had undergone an increase of population creating pressures which could conceivably seek an outlet in conquest and expansion is generally conceded. It is also well known that bedouin possess an inborn instinct for raiding for the purpose of acquiring booty. Furthermore, there is no doubt that the Arabs enjoyed definite advantages over their enemies, owing to their skillful use of techniques of desert warfare. The armor of the desert warrior is relatively light, which together with the use of the camel permits a high degree of mobility and the traversing of great distances. The desert provides a sanctuary into which to retreat after a quick strike against the enemy. Thanks to the camel, the desert can also be transformed into a vast communications network in which all forces can have ready contact with each other and with headquarters.

As for the attitudes of the existing populations in the areas overrun by the Arabs, this too, in certain cases, worked in favor of the Arabs. Possibly as a result of the increase of population in Arabia mentioned above, there had been, long before the appearance of Islam, an infiltration of Arabic-speaking populations into Syria, Palestine and Iraq. The bond of language and, to some extent, of culture made these populations well disposed toward the Muslim invaders, and in fact made possible their ready absorption into the newly established Arab empire, adding strength to the Arab forces. The rest of the populace in the Byzantine Empire's eastern provinces (Syria, Palestine, Egypt), if not enthusiastic supporters of the Arabs, were at least not well disposed to their own rulers from whom they differed linguistically, culturally, and even religiously. Whereas the Byzantine rulers were Greek and rigidly orthodox, their eastern subjects were essentially oriental, spoke languages unrelated to Greek, and adhered to non-orthodox Christian creeds. To this we may add that the people of Syria, Palestine, and Iraq spoke a semitic language (Aramaic) akin to Arabic, which engendered a certain degree of affinity with the Arabs.

The internal weakness of the Byzantine and Persian states was due largely to a series of wars which had taken place between them, in the course of which the energies and material resources of both states had been exhausted. At the time of the hijra, the Persians seemed to have the upper hand. They had managed to penetrate deep into Byzantine territory. But during the Prophet's years in Medina, the Byzantines had made a comeback and had inflicted a decisive defeat on the Persians in Persian territory. All this was at great cost to both sides.

All these factors must certainly enter into any explanation for the phenomenon of Arab expansion. However, they do not provide the whole explanation. Religiously inclined Muslims will, of course, lay great stress upon divine action as the primary factor behind the Arab expansion, which was, from the religious perspective, an expansion of Islam itself. But even the secular historian, who does not care to speak in such terms, necessarily must regard Islam as the decisive factor in the expansion of the Arabs. That bedouin tribes, which constantly for centuries had engaged in warfare with each other and were known to prize their independence, should have suddenly placed themselves obediently under the order of Muslim commanders is inconceivable apart from Islam. It was Islam that provided the necessary rallying cry and instilled in the bedouin warriors a sense that they were fighting for a grand and noble cause. Whatever may have been the original material motivations of the bedouin, as the conquest progressed the bedouin felt themselves caught up in a movement much greater than anything they had dreamt of before, a movement not of their own making, which they could explain only in terms of a divine intervention in human affairs.

Political and Social Structure of the New Empire

The territorial gains of the Arabs confronted them with the problem of how to rule both themselves and the new peoples who now lived at their mercy. Some of the rudiments of government had already been created at Medina under the Prophet. The original umma has, in fact, been described as an embryonic state. At Medina a number of common or "public" functions had emerged which were concentrated in a central authority, principally the Prophet. For example, the Prophet (usually in consultation with his close associates) conducted foreign affairs, directed military expeditions, collected taxes, supervised the disposition of "public" wealth, promulgated regulations governing many aspects of communal and individual life, and judged disputes referred to him. To draw upon a distinction postulated by modern theorists, it may be said that the prophet exercised executive, legislative and judicial functions. The army and the central treasury provided the umma with the material bases of statehood; Islam gave it the necessary ideological basis. It has been said that the Prophet, in establishing the Islamic state, had accomplished for the Arabs, and especially for the Meccans, limited as they were by tribal notions of social organization, what they had been unable to accomplish for themselves.

The acquisition by the Arabs of a vast empire required that the existing machinery of state be expanded and further organized. The embryonic state now matured into a fully-formed state. A kind of "state-consciousness" emerged among the Arabs. This may be attributed to a number of factors.

For one thing, the wealth of the state increased spectacularly. The treasury emerged as an all-important public interest; a public domain (fay') came into being. The proper disposition of these interests required a centralized administrative authority. Such an authority was the caliph, who was regarded as the trustee of all communal property. It was he who was responsible for the distribution of wealth to members of the conquering community in the form of pensions. For this purpose, the caliph ᶜUmar took a census, on the basis of which he compiled a register of all persons entitled to pension. This amounted to a register of the entire citizenry, since all citizens were in theory soldiers and therefore pensionaries. The register, called in Arabic dīwān, was probably the first major undertaking of the caliphal government.

Secondly, once the conquests were in full swing, the ranks of the army swelled enormously. Although the caliph was unable to direct all the campaigns of such a vast and widely scattered army, his prestige was nonetheless heightened, as signified by the alternate title which he now assumed, namely amīr al-mu'minīn (Commander of the Faithful).

Thirdly, along with the growth of the army and the rapid progression of the conquest, the administration necessarily expanded with equal rapidity. This expansion tock place by means of a grafting of the Arab military administrative machinery on to the existing administrative machinery of the conquered lands. The provincial organization of these lands was left more or less as it was found. ᶜUmar placed in charge of the various provinces military commanders who thus functioned as governors, combining military and civil responsibilities. These commanders were responsible not only for supervising the affairs of the Muslim soldiers under their command, but also for collecting tribute from the subject peoples. (In some cases this latter responsibility was assigned to an independently appointed official, the ᶜāmil). The actual financial administration of the empire rested heavily upon native officials who had served under the previous governments. These officials were simply reinstated in their offices and carried on the business of taxation and bookkeeping in much the same way as they had done before, except that they handed over the receipts to Arab instead of Byzantine or Persian rulers.

Finally, not the least among the factors contributing to "state-consciousness" was the awareness, following the first wave of conquest, that a great empire had fallen and another had retreated from much of its territory and that the Arabs had filled the vacuum. The Arabs were not slow to regard their commonwealth as a greater emper than those which it had replaced. The Arabs, as Muslims, had entered into the mainstream of world-history, and they knew it. The caliph was the greatest statesman of the world, Medina the capital of its greatest empire.

In the course of the conquests the Arabs became increasingly aware of their distinctiveness vis-à-vis their new subjects, and in time a system of society emerged which served to preserve this distinctiveness. This system may be depicted by means of the diagram on p. 62.

The system embraced two units which were, in theory, symbiotically related to each other: an Arab aristocracy and a non-Arab subject population. A kind of contract existed between the two parties whereby the Arabs provided protection and security for their subjects in return for payment of tribute. This tribute consisted of the taxes formerly paid to the Byzantine and Persian governments

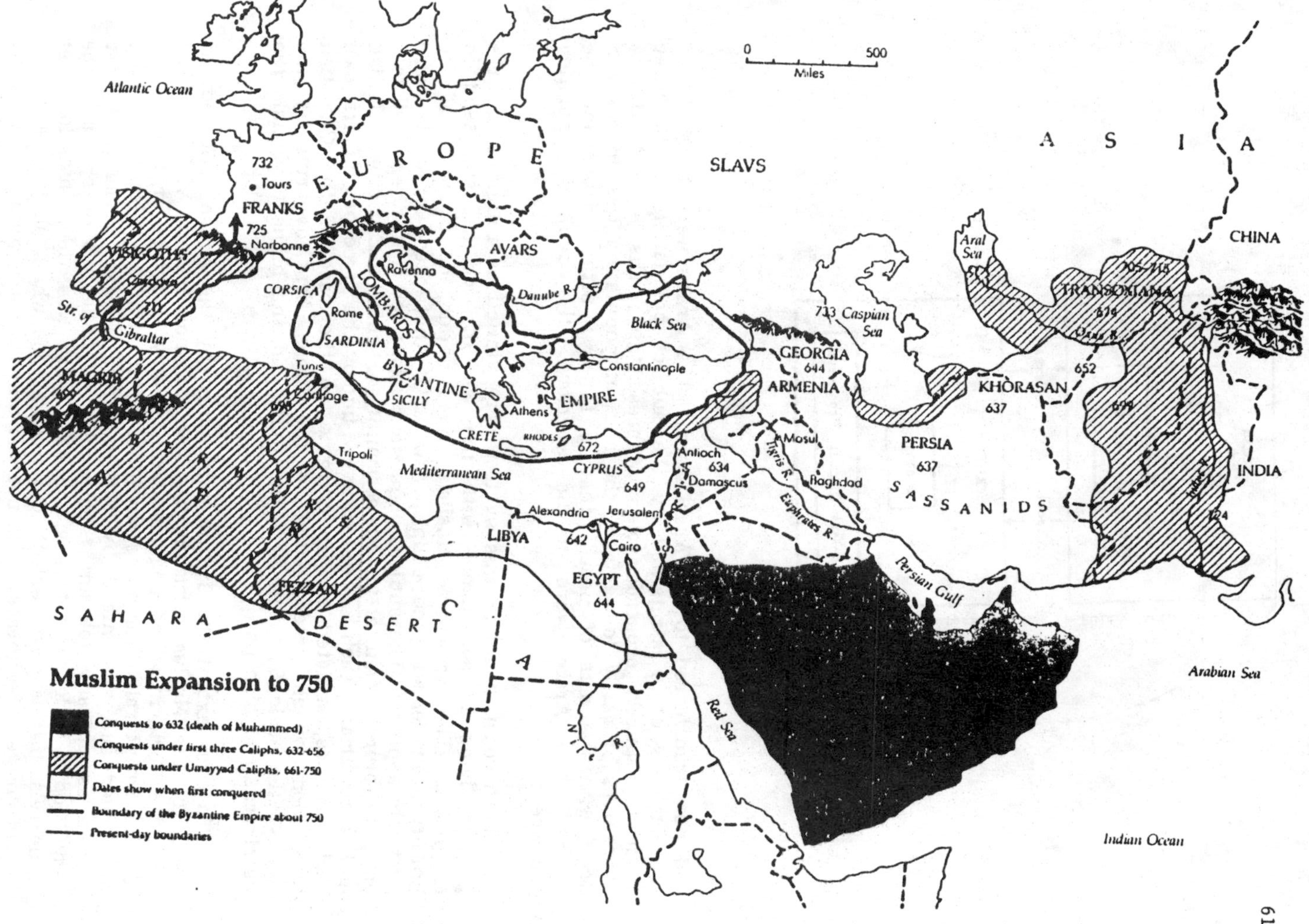

from A. Esler, The Human Venture

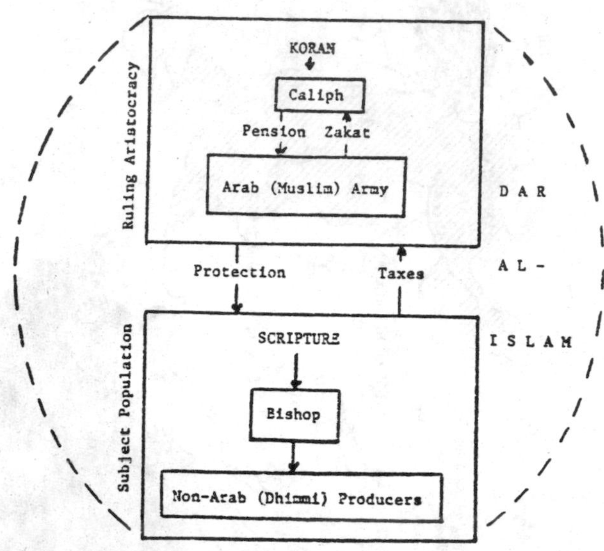

and now transferred to the Arab state. The Arabs were thus viewed as a military caste maintained by the subject population. The latter assumed a purely economic role. Whereas the Arabs were to devote themselves primarily to warfare, the subject population was to concern itself with the arts of peace, that is to say, with farming and the crafts. The Arabs were to be warriors, the subject population producers.

Both constituents in this system were viewed as religious congregations living in accordance with the will of God as expressed in scripture. The Arabs, as Muslims, lived under the precepts of the Koran; their leader, the caliph, saw to it that these precepts were properly applied. The subject population comprised a number of different "scriptural" (ahl al-kitāb) communities, chiefly Christian, Jewish and Zoroastrian, each of which lived under the precepts of its own scriptures as mediated by its clergy. In the case of the Christian population, which predominated in the areas first overrun by the Arabs, the basic Scripture was the Bible and the highest officials the patriarchs and bishops.

To some extent the system established by the Arabs reflected the ideals of the Muslim community. The original Islamic vision looked toward a world in which paganism and idolatry would be eradicated and all the Scriptural communities would co-exist in peace within an order maintained and guaranteed by Muslim arms. These communities were viewed as mutually tolerant theocracies, all believing in one and the same God. Underlying this vision of society was the conviction that while Islam is the most perfect of religions, one which all people should be encouraged to embrace, it is not the only religion worthy of respect. The exercise of power was to be confined to the Muslim community, but power was to be used for the good of all. Within a secure and prosperous order of society maintained by Muslim arms, Islam was to be propagated through persuasion, not by the sword. As the non-Muslim communities were freed of the responsibility for bearing arms, they were expected to pay higher rate of taxation. By virtue of this taxation they were classified as dhimmī ("protected") communities, in contrast to the dominant Muslim community. The caliphal government did not, in the strict sense, rule the dhimmīs. It exacted taxes from them and regulated their relations to the Muslim community, but as far as their internal affairs were concerned it allowed them to rule themselves. It was incumbent upon the dhimmīs simply to pay taxes and not to disturb the public peace.

There were certain differences, however, between the system which came to prevail within the Arab empire and that which was envisioned in the Islamic ideology. For one thing, whereas Islamic ideology regarded the community of Muslims as a racially open community into which Arabs and non-Arabs who embraced Islam could be admitted as full equals, the system which came to prevail treated Islam as the national religion of the Arabs and while it did not prevent non-Arabs from embracing Islam, it incorporated them into the community as inferiors or second-class citizens and not as full equals. Thus the community of Muslims was viewed as being predominantly Arab; as it was tribally organized, it was possible for non-Arabs to be admitted only by being attached to Arab tribes as client members. Non-Arab Muslims, in fact, came to be known by the Arabic term for client: mawlā (plural mawālī). As inferiors of the Arabs, the mawālī who entered the army were barred from the cavalry and obliged to fight as infantrymen, and their names were not inscribed in the dīwān, or pension list. The dīwān, in fact, became a symbol of Arab exclusiveness. Most seriously, the mawālī were for a time obliged to pay a land-tax from which the Arabs as Muslims were exempt.

In the second place, the ideal Islamic pattern of society did not exclude Muslims from the arts of peace, as did the system which was operative in the Arab empire, at least in principle. It did, as we have noted, confine arms-bearing to Muslims, but it did not look upon the Muslim community as a fundamentally military community maintained by a non-Muslim subject community of producers. As we shall see, Muslims were eventually to enter fully into the economic life of the conquered provinces.

During the first wave of conquests Arab separatism was reinforced by the policy of settlement adopted by the caliphal government. Although some of the Arabs who migrated into the conquered territories retained a nomadic life, a great part of them were cut off from nomadism by being made to settle, together with their families, in military camps called in Arabic amsār (singular misr). In either case, the Arabs remained apart from the indigenous population. Very few, if any, settled in the villages and towns of the conquered territories. Originally the camps were conglomerations of make-shift huts or tents, intended merely to be a dwelling place for Arab soldiers in the intervals between campaigns. However, in the course of time they developed into permanent settlements of towns; huts and tents gave way to houses made of brick or stone. At first, these settlements were organized into quarters corresponding to tribal divisions, but later they were reorganized into districts which had no connection with particular tribes. The isolation of the Arabs in these settlements from the surrounding population was not to last very long, for non-Arabs, particularly mawali, began to flock to them in search of employment and a better life. This influx increased the population and contributed to the transformation of the settlements into permanent towns. However, the Arabs maintained their superiority over the mawali and imposed on them their language. The amsar, the most famous of which were Basra and Kufa in Iraq and Fustat in Egypt, stood in sharp contrast to the territory around them.

The great majority of the Arabs did not acquire landed property in the conquered territories. Being of bedouin background, the rank and file of the Arab forces were drawn primarily to the spoils of war and consequently, during the wars of conquest, did not display any great eagerness to become property owners. However, a small number of Arabs did acquire property, and that on a rather large scale. As a result of the death or flight of royalty and much of the Byzantine and Persian nobility in the face of advancing Arab forces, the Arabs encountered large tracts of abandoned land. This land became the responsibility of the caliph, who, wishing to assure that it remained under cultivation, parcelled it out among high-ranking Arab notables in the form of land-grants called in Arabic qatai^c (singular qati^ca). Owners of qata'i^c were exempted, as Muslims, from the normal land-tax (kharaj) and were required to pay a smaller religious tax called ^cushr. As a rule, these landowners lived in the amsar and leased the land to tenant farmers.

The Civil Wars, 656-692

The unity which seemed to characterize the Arabs under the vigorous leadership of ^cUmar did not long outlast his death. Under ^cUthman (644-656) a movement of opposition to the caliphal government developed, resulting finally in ^cUthman's assassination, an event that plunged the Arabs into violent civil war (called in Arabic fitna). The first conflict extended over a period of five years (656-661) and was finally resolved when the fifth caliph, Mu^cawiya (the first of the Umayyad caliphs), was able to establish order. On Mu^cawiya's death in 680, conflict broke out once again, lasting this time twelve years (until 692). Thus within half a century, two great civil wars were fought which threatened the very life of the empire erected by the Arabs.

The central issue in these wars was that of succession to the caliphate. As noted earlier, the first caliph, Abu Bakr, was appointed to office by means of an essentially elective process, based on previous Arab custom in the appointment of tribal shaykhs. That is, the choice of an inner circle of close associates of the Prophet was ratified by the community-at-large through a general bay^ca (oath of allegiance). This procedure was workable so long as the Arabs remained united, making a universal bay^ca possible. But once personal rivalries exacerbated by social tensions set in, the caliphate could--and in fact did--become a bone of contention between conflicting parties, causing serious civil strife.

The rebellion against ^{c}Uthmān which led to the First Civil War was spearheaded by certain malcontents in the Arab army who seem to have been upset over pensions, which they believed to be inadequate, and over the whole system of distributing the spoils of war, which they considered to be unfair. These malcontents seem to have been mostly bedouin. As the conquests had progressed, a great stream of bedouin from Arabia had entered the Arab army. By increasing the number of pensionaries, this influx of new recruits had placed new pressures on the central treasury (<u>bayt al-māl</u>), the source of all pensions, creating something of a financial crisis. To this we may add the fact that the bedouin were by nature unruly and unaccustomed to being under the firm command of a central government. By confining them to the amsar rather than allowing them to roam freely in the rich agricultural lands of the conquered territories, the caliphal state had from the very beginning provoked a degree of resentment among the bedouin.

To make matters worse, ^{c}Uthmān seemed to be practicing unabashed nepotism. Although himself an early convert to Islam, he was nonetheless a member of the Banū Umayya, the Meccan clan which, with few exceptions, had held out to the last possible moment against the Prophet. Seemingly a tool in the hand of his own clan, ^{c}Uthmān began to appoint his fellow clansmen to high offices in the empire. This, not surprisingly, gave rise to suspicion in many quarters that the old anti-Islamic Meccan aristocracy was taking over the Islamic empire. In particular, those who had been ousted from office to make way for ^{c}Uthmān's appointees quite naturally bristled with resentment and joined the opposition.

The assassination of ^{c}Uthmān in 656 by a group of malcontents who had come to Medina to deal directly with the caliph created an enormous stir throughout the empire. In Medina ^{c}Alī, the Prophet's cousin and son-in-law, was proclaimed caliph by Uthman's killers. His appointment was contested, however, by three prominent figures, who refused to give him their allegiance so long as the assassins went unpunished. Alī's reluctance to have the assassins punished seemed to imply support of their cause. Two of ^{c}Alī's opponents, Talha and Zubayr, were companions of the Prophet, who withdrew from Medina to Mecca, where they were joined by ^{c}Ā'isha, the Prophet's wife. From there they proceeded to Iraq in search of supporters in the military camps. ^{c}Alī soon followed them and was able himself to get considerable support from the warriors at Kūfa. A great battle took place in which Talha and Zubayr were defeated and killed. The battle came to be known as the Battle of the Camel, because ^{c}Ā'isha had watched it while seated upon a camel.

The third opponent of ^{c}Alī was Mu^{c}āwiya, a member of the Banū Umayya, who demanded that the assassins of ^{c}Uthmān be handed over to him as kinsman of the slain caliph. Mu^{c}āwiya had been governor of Syria for twenty years, having been appointed to the post by ^{c}Umar. He had under his command a disciplined and loyal army, whereas ^{c}Alī's army was made up largely of bedouin from the military camps of Iraq, the very element from which the opposition to ʿUthmān had drawn its support. In the battle which took place at Siffīn in 657 ʿAlī, by virtue of the superior strength of his forces, gained the upper hand. However, before the battle reached a conclusion, Muʿāwiya instructed certain of his soldiers to hoist copies of the Koran on the tips of their lances as an appeal to the enemy to settle all differences through arbitration, not through armed conflict. ʿAlī was persuaded by a group of his followers to accept this arrangement, and a court of arbitration was set up consisting of two persons, one appointed by ʿAlī and the other by Muʿāwiya. After long deliberations, the arbiters decided that ʿUthman had indeed been unjustly killed and that the customary law of revenge should accordingly be applied. This decision was in effect a vindication of Muʿawiya's demand and a denial of ʿAlī's fitness to be caliph. In the meantime, a segment of ʿAlī's army which had rejected the principle of arbitration from the beginning, preferring rather to pursue the battle to its finish, withdrew from ʿAli's camp and regathered at a place called Nahrawān. Once the decision of the arbiters was announced, ʿAlī rejected it as inconsistent with the requirements of the Koran and began planning another campaign against Muʿāwiya. However, as the defectors who had gathered at Nahrawan proved to be implacable, ʿAlī was required first to deal with them. The defectors were attacked and a great many of them killed. ʿAlī then retired to Kūfa where he hoped to strengthen his position. Before he was able to gather sufficient forces for a renewed campaign against Muʿāwiya, however, he was murdered by one of the survivors of Nahrawan. Muʿawiya was thereupon proclaimed caliph in Damascus.

In seeking to explain the social forces involved in the First Civil War, some historians place great emphasis on the bedouin support of ʿAlī's cause. As a result of the continuing migration of bedouin into Iraq in the wake of the initial conquests, the camp-towns had become overcrowded with warriors who could not immediately be absorbed into the frontier warfare. This congestion gave rise to frustration and restlessness, which was further aggravated by the economic grievances mentioned earlier. In eliciting support from the bedouin soldiery, ʿAlī in effect placed himself at the head of those same forces that had been involved in the opposition to ʿUthmān. Thus ʿAlī's movement was, in the view of historians who take this interpretation, at bottom a reaction of bedouin forces to unfair practices of the caliphal state. Some go so far as to say that it was an expression of bedouin resistance to all centralized control, to government <u>per se</u>.

This is not to say that ʿAlī's movement did not involve other elements within the Arab Muslim community. At the time of his accession to the caliphate, ʿAli had the support of many of the Companions of the Prophet, who were still living in Medina and who now looked to ʿAlī as their leader. These Companions were the spiritual elite of the community, and ʿAlī in many ways epitomized their search for a new order more in line with Islamic ideals. However, in the contest with Muʿāwiya the possession of a strong army was of capital importance, and for this reason ʿAlī had left Medina for Iraq in search of recruits among the soldiers in the camps, the majority of whom were bedouin. His move signified that the real center of power in the empire lay no longer in the Arabian Peninsula but in the conquered territory.

It has been suggested that the contest between ʿAlī and Muʿāwiya entailed some degree of territorial competition between Iraq and Syria. The Arabs of Iraq, it is said, were resentful of the higher pay enjoyed by the soldiers in Muʿāwiya's army and feared that a victory for Muʿāwiya would mean Syrian hegemony over the rest of the empire.

It may be noted in passing that the events of the First Civil War brought about the beginnings (though by no means the full development) of the three most important religious sects in Islam: Shīʿism, Khārijism and Sunnism. Even though in the course of these events ʿAlī lost many of his original supporters, a certain group remained faithful to him to the very end. These came to be known in time as shīʿat ʿAlī, or the Party of ʿAlī, whence the terms Shīʿism and Shīʿi. Upon the death of ʿAlī, his partisans transferred their loyalty to his offspring, and there emerged among them a legitimist conception of the caliphate, according to which this highest office in Islam was transmissible only within the line of ʿAlī. This legitimist outlook is the bedrock of Shīʿism, which was to develop subsequently into several different branches. Khārijism, on the other hand, emerged out of the group which withdrew from ʿAlī's army and regathered at Nahrawān. This group adopted, in contrast to Shīʿism, a radically democratic view of the caliphate, coupled with a puritanical ethic. According to the Khawārij, it was up to members of the community to choose the best man among them to be caliph. Being the best man meant not so much possessing political acumen as adhering to the highest standard of righteousness. A caliph thus chosen was entitled to lead the community only so long as he fulfilled the community's righteous expectations. Once any caliph lapsed into wrongdoing, the community should depose him (as the Khawārij had in effect deposed ʿAlī for his "wrongful" act of accepting arbitration) and choose another. It was not necessary that a caliph be a descendant of ʿAlī, or even that he be an Arab. The only requirement was that he be a righteous Muslim.

Sunnism was, in effect, born in the minds of the great majority of Muslims who accepted neither the legitimist Shīʿi nor the puritanical Khārijī views of the caliphate. For this majority, any ruler who could effectively use power to maintain the unity of the community was worthy to be caliph, so long as he outwardly professed Islam and conformed to its standards of public behavior. It was not necessary that he be a descendant of ʿAlī or that he be flawlessly righteous. This emerging Sunnī position was, like the Khārijī, in principle elective, the difference between the two positions having to do with the standard of conduct expected of the caliph. The more lenient Sunnī position made possible the acceptance of caliphs from the religiously suspect clan of Banu Umayya (such as Muʿawiya and, later ʿAbd al-Malik, both of whom certainly enjoyed the support of the majority of Muslims, even if some Umayyad caliphs, such as Yazīd I and the last Umayyads, did not). Later on, Sunnī theorists added certain formal qualifications to candidacy to the caliphate, which included descent from the Quraysh. They also allowed for the "election" of a caliph by his predecessor.

The Shīʿis and Khawārij were in the final analysis religious minorities within the larger community of Muslims. As minorities, they held fast to what they believed to be right and true without regard to whether or not their views were accepted by the majority of Muslims. The emerging Sunnī attitude, on the other hand, was that nothing could be true or right which was not widely accepted among Muslims. This community as a whole was, in the Sunnī view, divinely guided and could not lapse into serious error. Any doctrine which was not widely accepted therefore failed to pass a crucial test of its truth and should be rejected lest it disrupt the unity of the community. The Shī^cis and Khārijis, as minorities, did not concern themselves with preserving the unity of the larger body of Muslims. For the Sunnī, this unity was sacrosanct.

It must be emphasized that Shī^cism, Khārijism and Sunnism were, in the period just after the First Civil War, very loosely formed movements and did not yet have the precise sectarian character which they were later to assume with the evolution of distinctive bodies of legal doctrine and theology. The most amorphous of these movements was Sunnism, which embraced the main body of Muslims and was therefore the least self-conscious. The term Sunnī begins to have a more concrete significance in the Abassid period. (The term is actually somewhat misleading because it implies that a Sunnī is simply one who adheres to the Sunna, or Tradition, of the Prophet. Since Shī^cis and Khawārij also hold fast to the Sunna, a further characteristic is required to define Sunnī. We have tried to state this in the preceding paragraph. It is implied in the longer Arabic phrase sometimes used of Sunnis: <u>ahl al-sunna wa'l-jamā^ca</u>. The Sunnī is thus the one who, in addition to holding fast to the Koran and Sunna, also holds fast to whatever is accepted within the professing Muslim community at large and promotes the unity of that community. The Sunnī is, in other words, a "main-line" Muslim.)

Mu^cāwiya's caliphate (661-680) brought two decades of relative stability and peace to the Arab empire. Mu^cawiya's power was clearly Syria-based, and the capital of the empire was now Syria's great and ancient city, Damascus. As noted earlier, this Syrian basis of power had been built up by Mu^cāwiya during his years as governor. Mu^cāwiya used it to control the rest of the empire, particularly the turbulent amsār of Iraq, where resentment continued to smolder. Under Mu^cāwiya's successors this Syrian basis of power was retained until finally, in 744, it was destroyed. In order to keep the Arab soldiers in Iraq in check, Mu^cāwiya appointed capable and tough-minded men as governors over them. One of these, the famous Ziyād ibn Abīhi ("Son of His, i.e., Mu^cāwiya's, Father," so named because Mu^cawiya had proclaimed him to be his half brother), is said to have declared in a speech after his arrival in Basra:

> You allow kinship to prevail and put religion second.... Take care not to creep about in the night; I will kill every man found in the streets after dark. Take care not to appeal to your kin; I will cut off the tongue of every man who raises that call.... I see many heads rolling; let each man see that his own head stays upon his shoulders. (Translation from G. E. Grunebaum, <u>Classical Islam</u>, pp. 70-71.)

In Kūfa, Ziyād attempted to offset the influence of tribal divisions by reorganizing the town into districts having no connection with particular tribes. At the same time, he endeavored to cultivate friendly relations with the heads of tribes.

The relative tranquility of Muᶜāwiya's caliphate was due in no small measure to his own personal capabilities as a ruler. Without a doubt the most effective ruler of the empire since ᶜUmar, Muᶜāwiya achieved his purposes more through diplomacy than through the use of force. His style of government was in accordance with Arab tradition, and for this reason he commanded the respect of the majority of dignitaries throughout the empire. His one major departure from tradition related to the succession. He was determined that he should be succeeded at his death by his son Yazīd. However, even in this matter Muᶜāwiya showed deference to Arab sensitivities. Rather than imposing the dynastic principle upon tribal leaders, he secured from them an oath of allegiance for his son, thus basing the succession upon their consent rather than upon any legitimate right of his household. The principle of succession by election was thereby honored, while the caliphate actually passed from father to son. This arrangement constituted an important precedent for the future, for it made possible the perpetuation of a de facto dynasty while keeping within the bounds of the Sunnī concept of the caliphate as de jure an elective office.

Unfortunately for the cause of the Banū Umayya, the succession of Yazīd was not universally accepted. Opposition to his rule arose simultaneously in Iraq and in the Hijāz, giving rise to the Second Civil War. The Shīᶜi faction in Kūfa, which was gaining strength, decided that the opportune moment had come to place a son of ᶜAlī on the throne and accordingly persuaded al-Husayn, who was living in Medina, to come to Kūfa to stage a revolt. However, word of this plot reached the ears of Yazīd's governor in Iraq, who led a force to crush the revolt. Al-Husayn and his party were attacked at Karbalā', twenty-five miles northeast of Kūfa, and killed. This happened in October 680, six months after Yazid's accession. This murder of a grandson of the Prophet (al-Husayn's mother was Fātima, daughter of the Prophet) and son of an eminent Companion of the Prophet caused great consternation, particularly among devout Muslims, and served to intensify the opposition to Yazīd. For the Shīᶜi movement itself the Karbalā' massacre provided a martyr whose violent death was to increase devotion to the line of ᶜAlī to the point of fanaticism and would be commemorated annually thereafter down to the present day.

In the Hijāz, the opposition to Yazīd gathered around another son of a Companion of the Prophet, ᶜAbd Allāh ibn Zubayr, who like al-Husayn had refused to pay homage to the new caliph. In 682 news of Yazīd's profligate life style caused the people of Medina to rise up in open rebellion. Yazīd, who until this moment had attempted to conciliate his critics in Medina, decided that the time had come to crush the Hijāzī opposition. In 683 the caliph's army sacked Medina and laid siege to Mecca, where ᶜAbd Allāh ibn Zubayr was living. Before Mecca could be taken, however, news arrived of Yazīd's death (December, 683), and the caliphal army withdrew. ᶜAbd Allāh was thereupon declared caliph by his partisans in the Hijāz. In Syria Yazīd's son,

Muʿāwiya II, was proclaimed caliph but died of ill health only a few months later. This brought to an end the Sufyānid line, as Muʿāwiya and his descendants are called, after Muʿāwiya's father Abū Sufyān.

The Second Civil War now entered its most dramatic phase. The Banū Umayya rallied behind a cousin of Muʿāwiya named Marwān ibn al-Hakam. At the same time, however, the succession became a matter of dispute between the two principal Arab tribes living in Syria, the Kalb and the Qays. The former remained loyal to the Banū Umayya and proclaimed their acceptance of Marwān ibn al-Hakam, whereas the latter decided in favor of ʿAbd Allāh ibn Zubayr. In 684 the two sides came to battle over the issue at Marj Rāhit, a plain outside Damascus. The long-range effect of this confrontation was enormous, as it exacerbated tribal tensions throughout the empire. Its immediate result was a victory for the Kalb and the House of Umayya. Marwān became the founder of a new line, the Marwānid line, which was to rule the Arab empire until its fall sixty-six years later.

Marwān, who was nearly seventy at the time of his accession, died after a brief reign in 685 and was succeeded by his energetic and capable son ʿAbd al-Malik, who ruled for the next twenty years. To ʿAbd al-Malik fell the task of restoring unity to the divided empire. Thanks to the victory at Marj Rāhit, Umayyad control over Syria was secure, while control over Egypt had been established under Marwān. The principal areas remaining to be restored to Umayyad rule were the Hijaz and Iraq, the eastern provinces being an extension of the Iraq governorate. The former had become the stronghold of ʿAbd Allāh ibn Zubayr. In Iraq the situation was complicated by the success of a Shīʿī revolt in Kufa (685) led by a native of al-Tā'if named Mukhtār who posed as the champion of ʿAlī's last surviving adult son, Muhammad ibn al-Hanafiyya, whose mother (as the name indicates) was a woman of the Hanīfa tribe and not, as in al-Husayn's case, a daughter of the Prophet. Mukhtār ruled Kūfa for about a year and a half. His end was brought about, not by ʿAbd al-Malik, but by Musʿab ibn Zubayr, brother of ʿAbd Allāh, who subdued all of Iraq in the name of the rival caliph. The revolt of Mukhtār was an important event in the history of Shīʿism because it was at that time that certain doctrines that were to become distinctive of radical Shīʿism first appeared. Mukhtār, as agent of an ʿAlid remaining in retirement, represented a new type of leader and propagandist, which was later to become commonplace among radical Shīʿis.

In 691 ʿAbd al-Malik directed his energies against the rival Zubayrid caliphate. First he marched into Iraq and defeated Musʿab, whom ʿAbd Allāh had appointed viceroy. Weary of two decades of strife, the heads of the Arab tribes in Iraq swore allegiance to ʿAbd al-Malik, whom they looked upon as a restorer of peace. In the following year (692), ʿAbd al-Malik sent his able general, Hajjāj ibn Yūsuf, to deal with ʿAbd Allāh in the Hijāz. Mecca fell to Hajjāj's army, and the rival caliph was slain. This event marked the final end of the Second Civil War. Not for another half century was there to be a civil conflict of such major proportions. The next conflict, however, was to bring down the Arab empire.

Problems Under the Later Umayyads, 699-750

Under the capable rule of ᶜAbd al-Malik (692-705), the Arab empire made a spectacular recovery from the turbulence of the Second Civil War. Syria was brought firmly under control and became once again, as under Muᶜāwiya, the basis of power of the empire. ᶜAbd al-Malik and his successors saw to it that another Marj Rāhit would not occur. The use of Syrian power to control the rest of the empire was symbolized by the building of a new fortified provincial capital in Iraq, called al-Wāsit, where Syrian troops were stationed and placed under the command of Hajjāj ibn Yūsuf, the newly appointed governor of Iraq. Hajjāj ruled Iraq in an even more ruthless manner than had Muᶜāwiya's governor, Ziyād.

The building of al-Wāsit was but an aspect of a general policy of increased centralization pursued by ᶜAbd al-Malik. The Arab empire was gradually being transformed into a centralized bureaucratic regime typical of advanced agrarian states. The informal, patriarchal style of rule of the earlier caliphs was giving way to a more absolutist style. (We will see in the next chapter how this tendency reached its culmination under the ᶜAbbāsids.) In order to assure a more direct control over the bureaucracy, ᶜAbd al-Malik ordered that the language of administration, which thus far had been Greek (and, in the former Sasanian provinces, Pahlavi), henceforth be Arabic. This action meant that from this point on only persons who had mastered Arabic could hold positions in the government. Although the bureaucratic personnel continued to be drawn from the non-Arab indigenous population, it was now fully arabized and thus became more integrated with ruling circles, especially the court. ᶜAbd al-Malik also issued new coins bearing Islamic symbols and Arabic inscriptions. These measures helped to accelerate the spread of the Arabic language among the non-Arab subjects of the empire, preparing the way for the later arabization of the wider population.

Under ᶜAbd al-Malik and his successor (and son) al-Walīd (705-715), the Arab armies made their last spectacular advances into new territories. In the East two great river valleys were conquered, that of the lower Indus in northwest India (Sind) and that of the Oxus river in Central Asia. Meanwhile, in the West, a combination of Arab and Berber forces crossed the strait of Gibraltar and established a foothold in Spain. With these events the Arabs reached the peak of their expansion.

Despite the efforts of ᶜAbd al-Malik and his successors to maintain a tightly controlled empire administered by a centralized arabized bureaucracy, the empire nonetheless suffered from a number of internal problems that were in the end to contribute to its collapse. Two of these problems in particular deserve our attention.

Inter-tribal Tension

One of the primary problems that sapped the strength of the Arab empire was posed by the Arabs themselves. As the Arabs settled in the camp-towns of the conquered territories, they retained their tribal identities. Almost inevitably, this resulted in inter-tribal rivalries in the course of which tribes coalesced to form larger tribal groupings. Consequently, in each of the garrison towns major tribal groupings emerged to carry on lively competition. In time, as contact between the garrison towns increased, coalitions were formed between tribal groups in different towns. The end result was a tendency for the entire Arab population of the conquered territories to be polarized into two major blocs. The Arab genealogical tradition, in the form in which we have it, is heavily influenced by the alliances which were thus formed during the age of the conquests. It may be noted in passing that the formation of two rival groupings is a common feature of the social structure of certain parts of the world, especially the Middle East, and is a subject of great interest to anthropologists, who commonly refer to it as "dual organization." It is a particularly prominent feature of bedouin society.

The polarization of the tribes was, to a large extent, an outcome of the Battle of Marj Rāhit. As noted earlier, that battle pitted the Kalb tribe, supporters of the Umayyads, against the Qays tribe, who supported the caliphate of Ibn Zubayr. The Kalb tribe was reckoned to be of South Arabian origin and thus among the descendants of Qahṭān, whereas the Qays were reckoned to be descendants of Adnān. In spite of the order which ᶜAbd al-Malik was able to establish in Syria, the memory of the bloodshed at Marj Rāhit lingered on, especially among Arabs located elsewhere, and the major tribal groupings and coalitions which emerged in the garrison towns aligned themselves along the lines of the Kalb versus Qays dispute. That is, certain tribes identified themselves as South Arabian in origin and therefore as allies of the Kalb, whereas other tribes traced their origins to ancestors located in the central and northern regions of the Arabian peninsula and therefore saw themselves as allies of the Qays.* Frequently, these two major groups are referred to by historians as the southern and northern Arabs, "southern" in this case signifying origins in South Arabia and "northern" indicating origins in the great steppe and desert regions lying to the North of South Arabia (including both Central and Northern Arabia, that is to say the original Arab heartland). Frequently the southern Arabs are called Yemeni Arabs (implying a broad application of the term Yemen to the whole of South Arabia). It should be remembered from Chapter One that the people of South Arabia were not, in most ancient times, strictly speaking Arabs, that term having been originally confined to camel-breeding bedouin. Owing to the arabization of South Arabia in the period just before Islam, the South Arabians were easily absorbed into the Arab movement of expansion under Islam and therefore reckoned as Arabs, albeit of separate ancestry from the rest of the Arabs; hence the appellation "southern (or Yemeni) Arabs." It must be emphasized that the terms

*Although the polarization of Arab tribes was primarily along the "northern" versus "southern" lines, there was at least one exception to this scheme. A group of "northern" tribes known as the Banu Rabīᶜa frequently aligned themselves with the southern tribes.

"southern" and "northern" do not indicate the actual location of tribes in the period just prior to the conquests. What they indicate, rather, is place of ultimate origin. Thus the Kalb tribe, though reckoned to be "southern," was actually located in Syria prior to the conquests. Other tribes living in Syria and North Arabia, for example the Ghassanids and Lakhmids, were also reckoned to be southern.

Some modern scholars have suggested that the southern tribes represented that part of the population of Arabia which, before Islam, had lived in the larger sedentary communities located on the periphery of the Arab heartland, particularly in the north and south but also elsewhere (such as at Yathrib in the Hijāz), whereas the northern tribes (with some exceptions, such as the Quraysh of Mecca) represented that part of the population among whom nomadism predominated. The same historians also suggest that the southern Arabs, because of their sedentary background, adapted more readily than the northern tribes to the urban environment of the garrison towns and assimilated more easily the civilization of the conquered territories.

The bone of contention in the original conflict between the Kalb and the Qays had been the caliphate itself, with the two tribes aligning themselves with the Umayyads and Ibn Zubayr respectively. After Umayyad power had been fully restored by ᶜAbd al-Malik, the continuing tension between southern and northern tribes became focused on the governorships of Iraq and Khorasan, rather than on the caliphate, which was now firmly in Umayyad hands.

Although the greatest of the later Umayyad caliphs (ᶜAbd al-Malik, Walīd, ᶜUmar II, and Hishām) tried to keep above the tribal conflict by appointing neutrals as governors in these provinces, the others were not so careful. Two caliphs favored the southern tribes by appointing favorites of these tribes to office. The general trend among the later Umayyads, however, was to lean toward the northern tribes. In the end, the Umayyad state came to be based, for all practical purposes, on an alliance with the northern tribes. The last Umayyad caliph, Marwān II, depended so heavily on the Qays tribe that he transferred the capital to North Mesopotamia, where the Qays were particularly strong. When rebel leaders appeared among the Arabs of Syria, who were resentful of their loss of predominance, Marwān II destroyed the walls of the major Syrian cities, thereby in effect putting an end to the Syrian basis of Umayyad power.

Thus alienated from the Umayyads, the southern Arabs were quick to join a revolutionary movement launched in 747 in Khorasan in the name of a new line of claimants to power, the ᶜAbbāsids.

Before leaving the subject of inter-Arab tension behind, it should be noted that one modern historian, M. A. Shaᶜban, has argued that the real conflict among the Arabs was between those Arabs who were becoming assimilated into the indigenous society, intermarrying with the local population and engaging along with them in peaceful occupations such as farming and commerce, and those Arabs who preferred the traditional life of the warrior and thus remained aloof from the indigenous society, clinging to those privileges which the conquests had brought to them and retaining strong tribal leanings. Arabs of the first type to a very large extent took the point of view of the subject peoples and looked upon the later Umayyad state, with its strong connections with the Qays, as an imperialist regime designed to benefit a privileged class of military colonists. These Arabs were predominantly Yemeni or southern, whereas the warrior-colonists (muqātila) belonged primarily to the Qays or northern camp. The reaction to "Arab rule" was thus not confined to non-Arabs but had support among the Arabs themselves, especially among the Yemeni Arabs.

The Mawali: Islamic Universalism versus Arab Exclusivism

In the long run the most serious problem of all besetting the Arab Empire was the problem of the mawālī, or non-Arab Muslims. The very term mawālī is suggestive of the nature of the problem. As the conquering Arab Muslim community was tribally organized, it was possible for non-Arabs to be admitted into the community only by being attached to particular tribes. This placed the non-Arabs somewhat on the fringe of the community and gave them the status of second-class citizens. As noted earlier, the mawālī occupied an inferior rank in the army, and their names were not included in the official register of pensionaries. Furthermore, intermarriage with Arabs was often strongly discouraged, and a certain amount of social segregation was practiced in some towns. In Kūfa, for example, the mawalī worshipped in separate mosques.

But the most aggravating of all the discriminatory measures imposed upon the mawali had to do with taxation. As noted earlier, some Arab notables had, during the conquests, acquired estates called qaṭā'i^c, which consisted of abandoned lands which the caliphal state had parcelled out among them as the legitimate fruit of the conquests. Lands which had not been abandoned remained in the hands of their former owners and were subject to taxes corresponding roughly to taxes which had been paid to previous governments. These taxes, which were called in Arabic kharāj, were not required of Arab landowners, who, as Muslims, were subject only to a lower tax called the ^cushr.

In the course of time, as great numbers of people in the conquered territories embraced Islam, many who owned land insisted that, as Muslims, they too were subject to the ^cushr and not to the kharāj. However, this the caliphal state was not prepared to allow, since it would have meant a loss of revenue. Accordingly, many non-Arab Muslim landowners were compelled to continue paying the higher rate. This aroused deep resentment, since the ^cushr had been originally defined as a religious tax applicable to all Muslims. In imposing the kharāj on non-Arab Muslims, the caliphal state seemed to be engaging in an unfair and irreligious policy. Feelings reached the boiling point during the reign of ^cAbd al-Malik. Rather than continue paying the kharāj many non-Arab Muslims had left their lands and migrated to the camp-towns in search of a better life; but the Umayyad

Governor of Iraq, Hajjaj ibn Yusuf, forced them to return to their lands.

The mawālī embraced with enthusiasm the universalism which had been implicit in Islam from the beginning. In their view all Muslims were equals in the sight of God and should be treated so by any state that professed to rule on behalf of Islam. In this they were supported by the majority of the religiously minded Arabs, particularly those who had devoted themselves, along with similarly inclined non-Arabs, to pious studies and had, together with their non-Arab colleagues, become what might be called the spiritual elite of Sunnī Islam. Islamic universalism was also strongly emphasized by the two non-Sunnī sects, Shīᶜism and Khārijism. The mass of Arab warriors, on the other hand, tended to regard Islam as a national religion and the caliphal state as a military machine whose primary function was to keep the conquests in motion and to look after their interests as the dominant aristocracy.

The relationship between Islam and Arabism was not an issue in the time of the Prophet and during the first conquests. The Prophet himself had carried on his mission primarily among Arabs and had utilized Arab resources for the furtherance of his purposes; but in no sense was his mission limited to Arabs. Historical circumstances produced a community of Muslims that was nearly coterminous, though not identical, with the Arab nation; Islam was, in fact, the primary agent in the formation of the Arab nation. The relationship between the two collectivities in the earliest period of Islam may be represented by means of the following diagram.

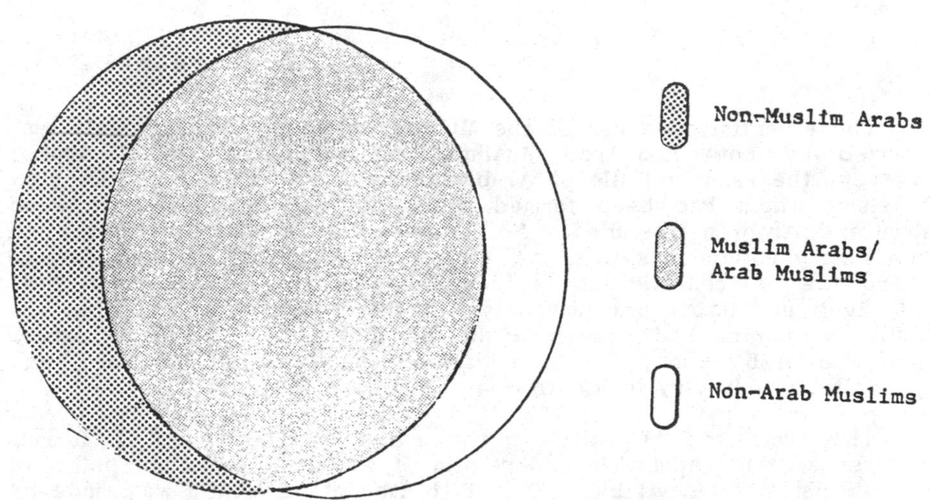

After 700 great masses of non-Arabs embraced Islam and before long outnumbered their Arab coreligionists. When this happened, the Muslim community assumed a more open character and the universalism of Islam, implicit from the beginning, became more evident. A new relationship now obtained between Islam and Arabian which may be represented as follows:

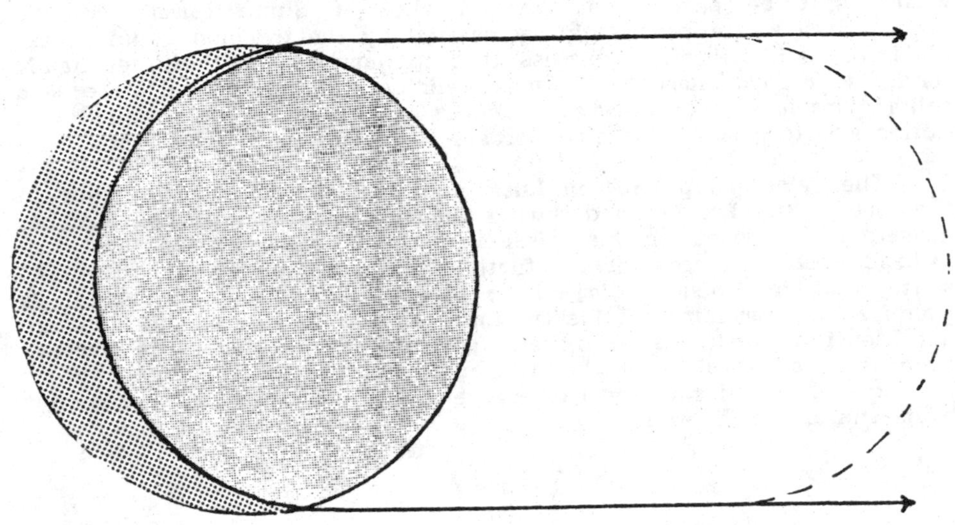

The essential openness of the Muslim community was strongly emphasized by both non-Arab Muslims and religiously-minded Arabs. However, the rank and file of Arab warriors retained a parochial view of Islam, which had been formed when the old relationship between Islam and Arabism prevailed. So long as the Muslim community had been nearly coterminous with the Arab nation, it had been tempting to regard the two collectivities as identical, and the Arab warrior class had given in, almost unconsciously, to this tendency. Now that the Muslim community had proven to be distinct from, and much larger than, the Arab nation, the Arab warriors persisted all the more, and now quite consciously, in identifying the former with the latter.

Time was on the side of the mawālī. The logic of Islamic universalism was undeniable and reform of the inequitable tax policy of the caliphal state inevitable. The first attempt at reform was made by ᶜUmar II, regarded by tradition as the most pious of all the Umayyad caliphs. ᶜUmar's efforts were continued under Hishām. The policy worked out by the latter caliph drew a distinction between poll-tax (jizya) and land tax (kharāj and ᶜushr). The former alone was linked to religion, since it was essentially a tax on persons and religion is clearly an attribute of persons. Non-Muslims (dhimmīs) thus paid this tax; Muslims did not, but were responsible only for the alms-tax (zakāt) required of all Muslims. The land tax, however, was considered to be entirely unrelated to the religious status of the person. According to the theory now adopted, the proper object of the land tax was the land itself, not the landowner. The land tax was, in other words, a tax on land, not a tax on persons. Thus, if a landowner converted to Islam, he continued to pay the kharāj. As a Muslim, he was exempt only from the jizya; conversion changed his status as a person, but did not affect the status of his land. Similarly, if a Muslim acquired land from a non-Muslim, the transfer of ownership did not change the status of the land; the Muslim continued to pay the same tax as the former landowner. Land was divided into two categories: kharāj land and ᶜushr land. The distinction between these categories arose out of the particular circumstances of the age of the conquests. ᶜUshr land was in theory (if not always in fact) land which had been abandoned by its former owners and reassigned as qaṭā'iᶜ to Arab notables, kharāj land was land whose owners had remained and submitted to the rule of the conquerors. Whatever status a given piece of land acquired during the age of the conquests became, so the theory held, its permanent status, unless its owners chose to transfer it into a religious endowment (waqf).

Hishām's reforms satisfied the religiously minded Muslims, since they upheld Islamic universalism by establishing a tax, the jizya, from which all Muslims, Arab and non-Arab, were equally exempt. The issue of taxation, which had aroused strong feelings among the mawālī during the caliphate of ᶜAbd al-Malik and Walīd I was thus, for all practical purposes, resolved. However, the reforms came too late to mollify antagonisms which had been building up among the mawālī for half a century. Furthermore, while they may have defused the issue of taxation, they did not alter, in the eyes of the mawālī, the basic character of the state. As the Umayyad state in its last years became increasingly more dependent on the Qays, it seemed as much as ever to be serving the interests of a privileged class of Arab warriors. The day of the Arab empire was, in fact, over. The cessation of conquests after caliphate of Walīd I (705-715) had made the Arab aristocracy parasitical and the expansionist military machine obsolete. The time had come for a new order to be ushered in.

CHAPTER THREE

THE COSMOPOLITAN EMPIRE OF THE ABBASIDS

750-945 A.D.

Despite the efforts of ᶜUmar II and Hisham to redress the grievances of the mawālī over unfair taxation, the House of Umayya was unable to redeem itself in the eyes of its opponents. The opposition became too widespread and deepseated to be appeased with reforms of the tax system. In the minds of a large part of the growing Muslim populace, the Umayyads had forsaken the principles of Islam and the time had come to replace them with new rulers who would set the community of Islam back on its proper course. This sentiment was espoused not only by the mawālī but by a significant number of Arabs as well, especially Yemeni Arabs who turned increasingly against the Umayyad state as the latter, after the reign of Hisham, came to rely more and more on the northern tribal groupings.

The Umayyads had indeed failed to adjust to changing times. They had played into the hands of an exclusivist Arab military class, now made up primarily of northern tribes, which had no future and which was fast proving to be obsolete and parasitical. In so doing, they had tried to perpetuate an Arab empire inherited from their predecessors in a time when such an empire was no longer a true expression of the Islamic umma. Rather than look upon the Arab empire as a temporary phenomenon which must pass away once it had served its purpose and give way to a cosmopolitan social and political structure more in keeping with the realities of the expanding umma, the Umayyads had come to look at their empire as an end in itself. This way of thinking proved to be suicidal. Once the opposition had spread and found expression in an ideology calling for a restoration of true Islamic rule, revolutionary forces were set in motion which could not be stopped.

The revolution replaced the defunct Arab empire with a new cosmopolitan empire ruled by descendants of an uncle of the Prophet, al-ᶜAbbās. The Abbasids viewed their empire as the proper expression of the ideal Islamic polity and themselves as true caliphs on the order of the "rightly-guided caliphs" of the earliest period. The Umayyads, in the official Abbasid view, had not been caliphs at all but kings who had ruled in their own interests and not in the interests of Islam. The Abbasids had ended the "evil days" of Umayyad rule by restoring the caliphate, which they regarded as the primary symbol of an Islamic order rightly so called. The new empire was cosmopolitan in the sense that it was based on a partnership between Arabs and non-Arabs and no longer served the interests of a dominant Arab elite. Among the non-Arabs who served in the new regime, the Persians played the leading role, and one can therefore speak of the cosmopolitanism of the new empire as based on a partnership of Arabs and Persians.

With the coming of the Abbasids to power in 750, we enter a new chapter of Arab history. As noted in the Introduction, it is at this point that an earlier history dominated by Arabs (in the classical sense) comes to an end. Henceforth, Arabs and non-Arabs join hands in the making of our history. We have not yet, however, reached the point where our attention can be focused primarily on the Arab lands. Although the process of arabization is well under way in 750, it has by no means run its full course. The Fertile Crescent has taken great strides toward full arabization, but in Egypt and North Africa the process is still in its early stages. Furthermore, under Abbasid rule much of the lands which are later to constitute the present-day Arab lands are still inextricably tied to the Muslim lands to the East, particularly the Iranian plateau, both politically and culturally. It is not until the collapse of the Seljuk empire around 1100 that we can begin to disregard these eastern lands and shift our attention to the Arab lands as such.

Between the earlier history dominated by Arabs and the later history of the Arab lands, the period of Abbasid rule (750-945) forms a chapter of its own. The main theme of this chapter is the attempt on the part of the Abbasids to establish once and for all a single universal Islamic empire based on the principle of equality of all Muslims, Arab and non-Arab. As we shall see, the attempt failed. The Abbasid empire soon proved to be as ephemeral as the Arab empire which it had replaced. After less than a century of efflorescence the new caliphate entered upon a course of decline leading to ultimate collapse. The Abbasids were thus in the long run unable to live up to their promise of a truly Islamic empire. Once their empire fell apart, the dream of a politically united Islamic world would never again be so nearly realized, and the unity of the umma would eventually be worked out along other lines. However indispensible a powerful universal caliphate may have seemed to the first Abbasids, such an institution was not to belong to the future. The umma would learn to flourish in time without a caliphal empire, and the notion that the political unification of all Muslims was indispensible to the interests of Islam would eventually be abandoned.

In this chapter we will consider first how the Abbasid revolution succeeded in placing the new dynasty in power and how the dynasty managed to get firmly established. We will then take notice of some of the principal characteristics of the new regime. Next we will consider the general economic conditions within which the early Abbasid caliphate flourished, noting in particular the important role played by the bourgeoisie. We will then give attention to some important religious and cultural developments under the Abbasids and note how these affected the shaping of Islamic thought and of the Arab cultural heritage. The remainder of the chapter will be devoted mainly to factors contributing to the decline of the Abbasids.

The Abbasid Revolution and the Founding of a New Caliphate

The movement which brought the Abbasids to the throne was well organized and had been active for a quarter of a century prior to its final successful bid for power. Ideologically the movement had much in common with Shīʿism. It contended that the right to rule the Islamic community belonged to descendants of the "House of the Prophet" (ahl al-bayt), an expression that could be interpreted broadly to mean the immediate household of the Prophet, with which ᶜAlī was connected by virtue of his marriage to the Prophet's daughter. The Abbasid movement adopted the broad interpretation, the favored line being that descended from al-ᶜAbbās, an uncle of the Prophet.

Shīᶜism as such was, in the Umayyad period, more a mood than an organized movement. The ᶜAlid family grew with time, and periodic revolts were attempted in the names of various members of this family. The most successful of these revolts was staged in the name of Muhammad ibn al-Hanafiyya, ᶜAlī's son by a woman of the Banū Hanīfa. The leader of the revolt, Mukhtār, had managed to rule Kūfa for a year and a half. Subsequent Shīᶜī revolts were more ephemeral and on the whole less dangerous, though always a nuisance to the Umayyad government.

The Shīᶜīs were not the only group which agitated for the downfall of the Umayyads. So also did the Khawārij, another of the three principal sects in Islam, whose origins were discussed in the last chapter. The activities of the Khawarij were often more violent and dangerous than those of the Shīᶜīs. However, like the Shīᶜīs, the Khawārij were unable to organize themselves into a single, coherent movement; in fact, they suffered even more than the Shīᶜīs from division within their own ranks. They did, on the other hand, manage to achieve some degree of political success, especially among the Berbers of North Africa. As for the Sunnīs, their attitude toward the Umayyads was ambivalent. Although most Sunnīs had supported the caliphate of Muᶜāwiya and many remained for a long time faithful to the Umayyads, others, such as the famous religious scholar Hasan al-Basrī, became critical of Umayyad rule. It is said that in the discussions which Sunnī theologians conducted over the issue of free will versus predestination, the upholders of free will (known in Arabic as the Qadariyya) were also opponents of Umayyad rule, whereas the upholders of predestination defended the Umayyads. The doctrine of predestination seems, in fact, to have become something of an official theology of the Umayyad state. In the end, the great majority of the Sunnīs turned against the Umayyads.

The Abbasid movement began in 718, when a great grandson of al-ᶜAbbās named Muhammad ibn ᶜAlī first sent agents into the eastern lands of the empire to rally support for his claim to the caliphate. Special appeal was made to the mawālī. In order to draw support from those mawālī who were inclined toward the Shīᶜī way of thinking, Muhammad proclaimed that the son of Muhammad ibn al-Hanafiyya had bequeathed to him the right to be caliph. Thus the great grandson of al-ᶜAbbās tied his own movement to the movement which had grown out of the mawālī-supported revolt staged by Mukhtār thirty-three years earlier. Even the organization of the earlier movement was adopted. The Imam (the title which the Shīᶜīs preferred over caliph as the designation of the rightful ruler) lived in seclusion (the Abbasids chose Humayma, an oasis in Transjordan, as their hiding place), while the propagandizing activity of the movement, called in Arabic daᶜwa, was carried on by agents. The headquarters of the Abbasid movement was in Kūfa, where Shīcism had flourished since cAlī himself had taken up residence there, although the principal field of operation of the movement was Khorasan. During Muhammad ibn cAli's lifetime, the movement achieved only limited success and at times suffered serious set-backs. However, at his death in 743 the leadership of the movement was taken over by his son Ibrāhīm, and activities were intensified. The headquarters in Kūfa was placed under the charge of an Arab named Abū Salama, who assumed the title of wazīr. In Khorasan, the leading role was played by a mawla of Persian origin named Abū Muslim.

It was in Khorasan that the Abbasid bid for power began in 747. Abū Muslim had managed to gain wide support among both mawālī and disaffected Arabs. (We noted in the last chapter that it was mainly Yemeni Arabs who joined the movement.) An army was assembled from the two groups, and the Abbasid military offensive began. Abū Muslim was assisted by a capable Arab general named Qahtaba, who led the Abbasid army to its first victories. The capture of Merv in 747, which was the principal Arab stronghold in the East, gave the Abbasids almost immediate control over the whole of Khorāsan. In 749 Abbasid forces victoriously entered Kūfa; and, as the Imām Ibrāhīm had in the meantime been seized and killed under orders of the last Umayyad caliph, his brother Abu'l-cAbbās was now proclaimed caliph. In the following year a decisive defeat was inflicted on the Umayyad army at the Battle of the Great Zāb.

The first years of Abbasid rule were taken up with the consolidation of the new regime and the elimination of rivals. Abu'l-cAbbās, determined to eliminate Umayyad influence forever, ordered the seizure and execution of as many members of the Umayyad House as could be found. It was because of this action that his royal title, al-Saffāh, which can mean "the Generous One," was taken in its other meaning of "the Bloodshedder." One of the few who escaped al-Saffāh's purge was cAbd al-Rahmān ibn Mucāwiya, who found his way to distant Spain where he established a remnant Ummayad dynasty. Within the Abbasid movement itself there was felt a need for a purge. The first to fall was the wazīr Abū Salama, whom al-Saffāh had come to regard as untrustworthy. Under the next caliph, Abū Jacfar al-Mansur, the great Abū Muslim himself became a victim of the purge. Owing to his great popularity in Khorasan, Abū Muslim's murder aroused strong feeling among a certain section of the masses, among whom the belief spread that he had gone into hiding and would return soon to deliver them once again from the evils of the day.

In many respects the real founder of the Abbasid empire was the second caliph of the new line, al-Mansūr (754-775), brother of al-Saffāh. Dissatisifed with Kūfa, which was a center of constant turbulence, al-Mansūr undertook to build a new capital for his empire. The site he chose was Baghdad, then a small village on the Tigris at the point where that river flows nearest to the Euphrates. The location was a crossroads where several important routes leading in all directions met. The new capital was designed to be primarily a residence for the caliph and a garrison for his troops, although markets and residential areas were soon to grow up around it.

To al-Mansūr goes also the credit for giving sound organization to the army of the new regime and to the administration. The mainstay of the army was a standing corps made up of soldiers from Khorasan who had fought in the revolution. These constituted a truly professional army, who were maintained on fixed salaries paid from the central treasury and whose services were full-time. The new troops stood in contrast to the old Arab military aristocracy, who considered themselves entitled by right, rather than by service, to fixed pensions and who offered their services only when called up for particular campaigns. Alongside the standing army of the Abbasid regime, lighter corps of volunteers, many of them bedouin Arabs, were maintained on the frontiers. These lived either on raiding or on pious contributions to religious warfare.

The new administration was built up with the aid of a number of seasoned bureaucrats of Persian origin enlisted by the Abbasids, the chief of whom was Khālid ibn Barmak, who together with his sons were to play a leading role in the affairs of state for around three decades. Through careful management and by keeping a personal eye on state finances, al-Mansūr was able to provide the Abbasid government with a strong financial basis. He understood very well that a sizeable treasury was essential to the maintenance of a professional army and bureaucracy. An efficient spy network and postal system (barīd) kept al-Mansūr in touch with developments throughout the empire.

Characteristics of the New Caliphate

The character of the new regime established by the Abbasids may be summed under three primary headings: cosmopolitanism, religious zeal, and absolutism. The cosmopolitanism of the regime was a reflection of the universalist emphasis of the movement which brought the Abbasids to power; it applied, in fact, not only to the regime itself but to the entire social order which emerged as a result of the revolution. The old Arab military aristocracy had been unseated, and in its place there now arose a new aristocracy consisting of both Arabs and non-Arabs, especially Persians. Social discrimination continued to persist, but it was no longer based primarily on considerations of ethnic origins. Wealth, power, and social standing were no longer the monopoly of the Arabs. The old indigenous aristocracies of the conquered lands were now admitted into full partnership with the descendants of the conquerors, and the distinction between conqueror and conquered in fact disappeared. The new cosmopolitan aristocracy was essentially civilian rather than military, being made up of three primary categories: those associated with government, those commanding great amounts of private wealth, and those exercising religious leadership by virtue of their learning. The first category comprised the army, the personnel of the court, and the civilian bureaucracy, with the latter as the dominant element, even though subject in principle to the orders of the caliph. The second category comprised the great landowners and merchants and the bankers. These will be discussed in the next section. The third category consisted of the ᶜulamā', whose prestige and influence rested upon their command of the religious sciences, especially law.

Among the non-Arab peoples who participated in the new cosmopolitan society of the Abbasid era, the dominant role was played by Persians. This is because the Abbasid revolution had been launched in central Iran (Khorasan), with the result that both the standing army and the bureaucracy was made up primarily of Persians. The Persians were also to play a lively role in the development of culture, as we shall see. As for the Arabs, they were to remain a distinct element in Islamic society for some time to come. Although much of the original Arab aristocracy became assimilated into the indigenous population, forming a kind of Islamic melting pot, certain Arab tribes retained their identity, especially in lands adjacent to the Arabian Peninsula (not to mention the Peninsula itself), and many noted individuals continued proudly to trace their descent from Arabian ancestors, not the least of those doing so being the caliph himself.

The partnership of Arabs and Persians is very evident in the Abbasid regime itself. The caliph, being a descendant of the Prophet's family, the Banū Hāshim, retained a strong Arab identity, and the first Abbasid caliphs were careful to see that their sons were thoroughly schooled, not only in Islam, but also in Arabic letters and traditions. (After Hārūn al-Rashīd, most caliphs had non-Arab mothers, but as lineage was reckoned through the father their Arab identity was not considered compromised.) Furthermore, the first caliphs kept in their entourage a number of notables of Arab descent, including other members of their own family, thus giving an Arab flavor to the court and to their social life. Arabs also constituted part of the original Abbasid army, in which they fought mainly as auxiliaries. On the other hand, the main standing army of the Abbasids was made up of Khorasani soldiers, many of whom were Persian. (Those Arabs of Khorasan who had fought for the revolution probably also formed part of this army, although they appeared to have been outnumbered by the Persians and had, owing to their close contact with the indigenous population, adopted Persians ways.) The bureaucracy was made up almost entirely of Persians, and Persian traditions of government were adopted.

The second major characteristic of the Abbasid regime, we have said, was religious zeal. The Abbasids took very seriously their role as restorers of true Islam and delivers from the "aberrations" of their predecessors, a role which they had assumed during the revolution. Once in power, they were quick to identify themselves as champions of orthodox Islamic doctrine and to disassociate themselves from all heresy. Al-Manṣūr put to the sword the leaders of a group of fanatical supporters who had proclaimed him to be an incarnation of deity. He also ordered the execution of a prominent bureaucrat and literateur, Ibn al-Muqaffaᶜ, who was accused of heretical ideas. His successor, al-Mahdī, instituted an inquisition, the primary target of which was a heresy known as <u>zandaqa</u>. (Exponents of this heresy were known as zindiqs.) Although this term later became synonymous with unbelief, in early Abbasid times it applied to persons accused of harboring certain philosophical ideas which were considered inimical to Islam, chiefly dualism (the belief that good and evil, spirit and "matter," are both eternal principles perpetually in conflict with each other). Persons guilty of <u>zandaqa</u> were considered enemies of the state and therefore liable to death. It may be that the anti-zandaqa inquisition was a device used to weed out from the ranks of the bureaucracy persons whose loyalty was suspect.

The position of the Abbasids towards the Shīᶜis was somewhat ambivalent, although the general trend was toward persecution of them as political enemies. A certain segment of the Shīᶜis, later known as the "extremists" (ghulāt), to whom heretical doctrines of Persian and Gnostic origin were attributed, were repudiated altogether. The rest of the Shīᶜis adopted a more moderate posture, the difference between them and the Sunnīs being largely political; consequently the Abbasid position toward them was somewhat more difficult to define. The Abbasids themselves had been brought to power on the crest of an essentially Shīᶜi type of movement and had consequently come to regard themselves as the fulfillment of the Shīᶜi longing for the rule of the House of the Prophet. However, many Shīᶜis had refused to accept their coming to power, and a Shīᶜi rebellion (which was supported by the noted jurist Mālik ibn Anas) broke out during the reign of al-Mansūr and had to be put down by force. Al-Mahdī attempted a reconciliation with the Shīᶜis, but al-Hādī and al-Rashīd resumed the repressive policy of al-Mansūr. Al-Ma'mūn again attempted a reconciliation, even going so far at one point as to name an ᶜAlid as his successor; but the experiment ended in failure. Thereafter the Abbasid state in general regarded the Shīᶜis with disfavor, sometimes persecuting them (as under al-Mutawakkil), sometimes simply letting them alone. Because the Abbasids had in their early days stressed the rights of the House of the Prophet, they had felt a certain bond with the Shīᶜi temperament. However, they could not, as rulers who considered themselves the fulfillment of Shīᶜi expectations, countenance the continuing Shīᶜi devotion to the ᶜAlids. Their conception of the House of the Prophet was a broad one embracing both themselves and their ᶜAlid kinsmen, but among the Shīᶜis the more narrow conception, limiting the House of the Prophet to the ᶜAlids, prevailed. A compromise between the ᶜAbbasids and the Shīᶜis could only have been worked out on the basis of the broad conception; this the Shīᶜis were unwilling to accept.

On the other hand, the Abbasids found wide acceptance among the Sunnīs and cultivated close ties with their ᶜulamā'. As relations with the Shīᶜis deteriorated, the Abbasids leaned all the more toward the Sunnī form of orthodoxy and became in the end its ardent champions. Under their patronage, Sunnī religious scholarship flourished, the sacred law (sharīᶜa) was codified, and the all-important traditions of the Prophet were collected in authoritative volumes. The Abbasids were particularly eager to see the sacred law applied and for this purpose created the post of Chief Judge (qādi'l-qudāh), to which was assigned the responsibility of appointing and dismissing other judges (subject, of course, to the approval of the caliph) and of advising the caliph in matters of law. The most renowned occupant of this office was Abū Yūsuf, author of a famous work on taxation and a leading figure in the development of Sunnī Jurisprudence.

In order to emphasize the religious character of their rule, the Abbasid caliphs adopted throne names indicating special divine favor, such as al-Mansūr ("Rendered Victorious"), al-Mahdī ("Rightly Guided") and al-Rashīd (also "Rightly Guided). They also changed their official title from khalīfat rasūl allāh ("Vicegerent of God's Prophet") to khalīfat allāh ("Vicegerent of God"). To this was added the preposing title "Shadow of God." The early Abbasids also assumed personal command over the principle holy war (jihād), that against the Byzantine empire, considered to be the chief remaining adversary of the world of Islam.

The third major characteristic of the Abbasid regime, its absolutism, was a legacy of the pre-Islamic empires. Both the Byzantine and Persian emperors had enjoyed immense power and had surrounded themselves with pomp and ceremony in the midst of a splendid court, thereby engendering in the minds of their subjects, from whom they maintained a calculated distance, a sense of awe and mystery. The first caliphs of Medina, by contrast, had adhered to a style of rule which was simple and austere, being based on Arab custom. They were, in effect, "super-shaykhs," for whom easy access to their presence was a matter of pride. Following the example of the Prophet, they had carried out major decisions after careful consultation with the leading members of the community. Under the Umayyads this "patriarchal" style of rule, as it has been described, gradually gave way to the more absolutist pattern known in the ancient oriental empires. Muᶜāwiya had retained many features of the "patriarchal" caliphate, including easy accessibility and consultation in decision making, but at the same time had built up for himself a courtly atmosphere unknown to his predecessors. ᶜAbd al-Malik and his successors went further in the direction of absolutism, perhaps following the Byzantine model originally but, from the time of Hishām onward, adapting more and more to the Persian model.

The Abbasid revolution brought the transition of absolutism to completion. The Abbasid regime may be described as a Persian autocracy cloaked in Islamic garb. The symbol of its power was the ever present court executioner, whose sword was ready to fall upon anyone who defied the caliph's orders. The absolutist outlook of the Abbasids was presaged in their extermination of the Umayyads at the very outset of their reign and in their subsequent elimination of other political enemies, including their massacre of a group of ᶜAlids at Fakhkh. Such uses had been given the sword by the Umayyads but never on so great a scale. Like previous emperors, the Abbasids maintained a lustrous court governed by an ancient court etiquette, and they elevated their own personages above their subjects by means of elaborate ceremonial and high-sounding titles. Audiences with them was attained only through the offices of a court chamberlain.

The basis of this autocracy was, of course, the standing army of professional soldiers, housed in the main citadel in Baghdad and rewarded with high salaries. So long as the caliph could rely on the loyalty of his troops, his power was virtually unlimited, even if he delegated many functions of government to others. The early Abbasids in fact delegated immense power to their ministers of the Barmakid family (Khālid ibn Barmak and his sons), who for a time enjoyed a virtual monopoly over the government; but the extermination of this family by Hārūn al-Rashīd in 803 demonstrated that such power could be recalled at a moment's notice if not prudently used.

Such absolute power was not destined to endure for long. Two factors were ultimately to check it: the gradual encroachment of army officers upon the affairs of state and the assertion of legal and spiritual authority by the ᶜulamā'. But while it lasted it represented a version of the Islamic order that was the distinctive contribution of the ᶜAbbasid House: absolute power exercised by the Vicegerent of God in the interests of true religion.

Economic Prosperity and the Growth of the Bourgeoisie

In strict economic terms the Abbasids were more the beneficiaries of the Arabs conquests than were any of their predecessors. The conquests accomplished two things the benefits of which were not to be fully realized until after the Abbasids came to power: (1) through raiding and through confiscation of treasures by the caliphal state they released great amounts of wealth which had hitherto been hoarded by the indigenous aristocracy, making it possible for this wealth to be put into circulation, and (2) they created a vast zone of peace within which trade could flourish on a large scale and grow. It was in the nature of things that the full impact of these accomplishments on economic life could not be felt until a certain period of time had elapsed during which economic techniques and institutions could be developed whereby the new conditions would be properly exploited. This preparatory period turned out to be roughly a century, ending just about the time that the Abbasids came to power. In the first half-century or so of Abbasid rule, the economic benefits of the conquests came to fruition, and the Islamic world entered the period of its greatest economic prosperity, a period lasting roughly two centuries (750-950).

The conquests had enabled many individuals to amass vast fortunes. The rank and file of the Arab soldiers were well paid, receiving pensions which were on the average about double the income of a skilled craftsman, not to mention the additional wealth which they often received as their share in booty. But as compared to the wealth of the average soldier, that acquired by the great Arab notables was sometimes astronomical. Such wealth was concentrated in the amṣār, where native craftsmen, affiliated with the Arabs as mawālī, scurried to produce goods to meet the demands of Arab consumers. The Arabs were *nouveau riches* whose consumer demands exerted a powerful stimulus on industry and trade. An unusually clever and enterprising native craftsman or merchant could himself acquire a considerable fortune and thus join the ranks of the *nouveaux riches*. Through intensive economic activity in the amṣār, wealth was kept in circulation. This mobilization of wealth helped to promote by Abbasid times a high degree of social mobility. Just as in the era of the conquests impoverished bedouin had suddenly become men of means and status, so also in the course of time the native population, no matter how low-brow, could rise to great heights through clever business practices or carefully cultivated connections. Where wealth is in free circulation, less depends on birth, more on talent and resourcefulness. The social mobility of Abbasid times was further strengthened by the Islamic emphasis on the equality of all believers.

One of the most important acquisitions of the Arab conquerors was precious metals, gold and silver, which were obtained in the form of coins, precious vessels, and jewelry. Much of these metals found their way into the treasury, either in the form of revenue from taxation or as confiscated wealth. This made possible an increase in the supply of coins, since the metals provided material for fresh minting. To this must be added the fact that the conquests had given access to the silver mines of Central Asia and the gold mines of Nubia and West Africa. The incorporation of these areas into the caliphal empire made possible the circulation of coins on an unprecedented scale. This was itself an important stimulus to economic activity and assured that the economy of the empire would be thoroughly monetary.

Two basic coins came into use, corresponding to the two precious metals: the gold dīnār and the silver dirhem, the former Byzantine in origin, the latter Persian. M. Lombard has called attention to the great importance of the influx of large amounts of gold from West Africa, making possible a vast increase in the output of dīnārs. This had two main consequences. First, it caused the dīnār to be introduced into areas where only the dirhem had been in use, thus fostering bimetallism in a large part of the empire. Secondly, by creating a great abundance of gold coins, it helped to reduce hoarding and to assure a steady circulation of money.

The extensive use of money stimulated banking. Money could not be carried over great distances except at great risks, and consequently travellers were in need of a checking system whereby money could be deposited in one locality and withdrawn in another. ("Check" is in fact thought to be a derivative of the Arabic word sakk.) This was provided by banks. Furthermore, banks provided loans for business ventures and similar purposes--even, in some cases, to meet state expenses. Finally, banks carried on the all-important service of currency exchange, made necessary by bi-metallism. As the two coins fluctuated in value independently of each other, the rates of exchange varied and had to be determined by financial experts.

The Arab conquests made possible the transformation of vast regions extending from the frontiers of China to the Atlantic Ocean into a single, gigantic economic unit. The advantages which this afforded were enormous. For one thing, raw materials could be transported to regions far from their origin, making possible the spread of certain industries. For example, a textile industry might be stimulated in a given locality by introducing wool produced elsewhere and dye produced still elsewhere. Secondly, industrial techniques could also spread from one region to another. An example of this is provided by studies of Egyptian glass products which show that the Egyptian glass industry was very much influenced by that of Iraq. Thirdly, currency could flow freely throughout the entire area. Finally, a ready exchange of manufactured goods could take place, stimulating both industry and trade.

Of the various industries which flourished in the Abbasid empire, the most successful were the textile (weaving) industries, which included the production of cloths, carpets, tapestries, and upholstery fabrics. The primary materials used in these industries were flax (for the production of linen), cotton, silk, and wool. These were in great abundance in various parts of the empire, Egypt being particularly famed for its production of flax. Other flourishing industries were those producing glass, pottery, paper (introduced from China under the early Abbasids), and perfumes.

Trade was not confined to the empire but embraced areas beyond, particularly Saharan and sub-Saharan Africa in the West and India and the lands beyond it in the East. The importance of African gold has already been mentioned. The imports from the East were primarily luxury goods--perfumes, spices, precious stones, silk, and dyes. Demand for these goods was increased by the development of a lavish style of life at the Abbasid court and among the upper classes generally, who endeavored to simulate the court. Arab navigators had mastered the Eastern seas in the Umayyad period, having become familiar with the behavior of the monsoon winds, and Arab merchants had established enclaves as far away as China. Under the Abbasids, with the increased demand for luxury goods Muslim trading activities in the East increased rapidly. Both sea and land routes were used, although the sea routes predominated. Important coastal towns grew up along the shores of the Persian Gulf. Trade was also carried on with peoples in the North, especially those living in the Volga region. Through these peoples the Muslims obtained furs and skins from places as far away as Sweden.

Wherever Muslim merchants travelled, they carried their religion with them. Consequently, merchants became as important a force in the spread of Islam as warriors. Indeed, in certain areas, such as Turkish Central Asia and the coastal areas of India, Southeast Asia and China they were the sole bearers of the faith.

Trade between the Islamic world and West Europe was limited during the Abbasid apogee. The famous historian, H. Pirenne, put forward the thesis that the Arab conquests disrupted the economic integrity of the Mediterranean world, which had flourished as an economic unit since ancient times and had reached its zenith under the Roman empire. In place of the Mediterranean world, the Arabs created a new land-based ecumene, uniting the southern and eastern shores of the Mediterranean with the lands to the East. After 1000, however, Mediterranean trade was revived, as we shall see in the next chapter.

The economic boom which took place under the Abbasids was accompanied by a growth of population throughout much of the empire. This was due not simply to a higher birth rate but to an increase in longevity as a result of better health and living conditions. During the first two centuries of Abbasid rule public health was unusually good and fatal epidemics rare, as compared to other periods. Furthermore, there was an appreciable influx of populations from areas outside the empire, for example, slaves from Africa and slave-troops (mostly Turkish) from Central Asia. The growth of population was greatest in towns and thus was tantamount to urbanization. The number of new towns which emerged in the period under consideration is remarkable. Although some towns dwindled or disappeared, the emergence of the new towns and the marked growth of existing towns cannot be accounted for solely on the basis of a shift from town to town. Demographic growth was particularly noticeable in Iraq, to which populations from other areas were attracted owing to its being both the political and economic center of the empire. But definite growth was also evident in Syria and Egypt.

The great emphasis on industry and trade brought to prominence a class of persons whose primary interest was in the profitable investment of capital. This class has been described by some economic historians as a Near Eastern bourgeoisie. Although made up primarily of Muslims, it also included men of other faiths; and in keeping with the spirit of the age it was ethnically cosmopolitan as well, comprising both Arabs and non-Arabs. The backbone of the bourgeoisie were the merchants. These may be divided into two categories: local merchants, or shopkeepers, whose wealth was generally speaking very modest and who were often tradesmen selling their own products, and the great merchants, called in Arabic tujjār (sing: tājir), who involved themselves in large-scale long-distance trade. It was the latter, obviously, who formed the upper echelons of the bourgeoisie. But the bourgeoisie was not limited to merchants as such. It comprised all persons with sufficient capital to engage in major investment and thus, in addition to merchants, landowners and government officials as well. In fact, the line between these categories was always somewhat hazy; landowners and government officials invested capital in commercial operations, and merchants acquired land (always regarded as an investment in itself) and bought their way into public office. Nonetheless, the categories still stand, since one can still make distinctions on the basis of primary interests. Thus, one can distinguish, for example, between merchants who owned land on the side and landowners who invested in trade on the side.

Generally speaking, investments took the form of joint enterprises based either on full partnerships or on limited partnerships called in Arabic qirāḍ. (In the qirāḍ the investor entrusted money to a merchant in return for a fixed share in the profit.) By means of such arrangements, investors were able to spread the risk and reserve capital for other investments, thus diversifying their business activities as much as possible. The legitimacy of profit was never seriously questioned by Muslims who participated in such operations, and the Muslim jurists, particularly those of the Hanafī school, were able to develop a commercial law quite adequate for the needs of the age.

Although under the early Abbasids a Persian aristocracy of the traditional type, exemplified by the all-powerful Barmakid family, had exercised a paramount influence in the affairs of state, by the middle of the ninth century their position was beginning to be taken over by the bourgeoisie. For about a century, men whose wealth had been gained largely through capitalistic enterprises held high office and made themselves indispensable to the efficient working of government. Their weight was also felt in religious circles. It has been estimated that about sixty percent of the ᶜulamā' in the ninth century were merchants or from a merchant background.

In view of the prevalence of capital investment in the economy of the Abbasid empire, is it appropriate to describe that economy as capitalistic? As E. Ashtor has suggested, two considerations require us to give a negative answer. First, the Abbasid economy was never dependent upon capitalistic activities in the sense that if these activities had been stopped the economy would have collapsed. Such dependence is usually taken to be an essential mark of a truly capitalistic system. In the Abbasid empire, land remained the principal source of wealth and basis of security; land was preferred to sheer capital, and rather than regarding landownership as a device for acquiring capital for further investment, most landowners preferred to retain their lands on a permanent basis, using its profits as a source of livelihood (and often to support a luxurious life style) rather than as capital for investment. Such investments as were undertaken by the wealthy were thus often marginal to their main interests. Furthermore, a large part of both the industry and the commerce of the Abbasid empire was carried on by the government or by persons associated with government. Certain industries, such as arms production, paper production, and the manufacture of luxury fabrics for the court (called tirāz in Arabic) were monopolized by the government. Other industries, in principle free, were under compulsion to supply the government with certain commodities and were subject to governmental regulations. Furthermore, men of government, often including the caliph himself, engaged extensively in trade and sometimes did not hesitate to use their power to gain unfair advantage, occasionally dipping into public funds or utilizing state facilities, for example, state-built ships, to further their ends. Thus, private enterprise was exposed to fierce competition from rulers and officials. To this may be added the fact that wealthy bourgeois were frequently granted tax-farming concessions by the government. These concessions were highly profitable as they permitted the tax-farmer to turn a fixed share of the tax revenues to the government and keep the rest for himself as a commission. Such practices militates against the existence of an autonomous free enterprise system operating on the principle of laissez-faire.

Secondly, several factors prevented a high concentration of wealth in the hands of individuals on a permanent basis. For one thing, the Islamic law of inheritance, based on the Koran, required that the estates of deceased persons be distributed among certain specified heirs. Thus, whatever the size of a fortune which a man might gain during his lifetime, it was destined to be broken up at his death. Huge fortunes could not be passed intact from generation to generation. Furthermore, confiscations of wealth by the state was common, undermining the security of the bourgeoisie. As towns had no municipal autonomy, the bourgeoisie had little protection against the whims of the state, and the state, often hard pressed to maintain the huge expenses of court and army, was tempted to look to the very wealthy as a convenient source of funds. Confiscations took the form of fines (musādarāt) imposed on the ground of some alleged violation of regulations. In a certain respect, these factors stimulated economic activity by keeping wealth in circulation. However, at the same time they militated against the development of a true capitalistic system in that they prevented the emergence of merchant barons (such as arose in Italy, for example) possessing sufficient capital to control industry and commerce and to restrain government and able to retain this capital within their families for several generations.

The Contest for Spiritual Authority: the ᶜUlamā' against the State

As noted earlier, the Abbasids came to power as restorers of Islam and champions of orthodox doctrine. However, at the beginning of their rule orthodoxy was not yet fully defined, especially with regard to certain theological issues which had not yet been posed. These issues were to arise in due time; as soon as they did, the need to formulate an orthodox position with respect to them became obvious. This gave rise to a crucial question of procedure: who has the authority or right to declare what orthodox doctrine is? In 827 the caliph al-Ma'mūn took a bold step. One of the principal issues that had emerged was whether the Koran belongs to the created order or is, like God himself, beyond creation and thus eternal. Al-Ma'mūn issued a decree proclaiming the Koran to be created and requiring all of the ᶜulamā' to subscribe to this doctrine or face prosecution. Thus, in effect, al-Ma'mūn declared himself to be authorized as caliph to define correct doctrine on behalf of the entire community and to impose doctrine on the community by force. This way of thinking resembled somewhat a theory of rule which had existed in the Byzantine empire under the name of "caesaropapism," according to which the ruler is both "caesar" and "pope," that is to say, both temporal and spiritual head of the community. Al-Ma'mūn's action provoked widespread opposition among the Sunnī ᶜulamā', who adhered to the doctrine of the eternality of the Koran and maintained that the right to define doctrine belonged to them as a body and not to any one individual, caliph, or otherwise. Thus a conflict emerged between the caliph and the ᶜulamā' over spiritual authority.

Theological issues such as the createdness of the Koran arose in part from the exposure of Muslims to Greek rationalism, which took place as a result of contact with non-Muslim theologians and philosophers influenced by Greek thought and as a result also of the translation of Greek philosophical writings into Arabic. A group of Muslim theologians called Muᶜtazilīs, whose origins go back to Umayyad times, began under the early Abbasids to call for a rationalist interpretation of Islam which required that the Koran be regarded as created. These theologians argued that, if the Koran is eternal, then the belief in one God is compromised, since a kind of pluralism arises: the Koran is given a status equal to that of the Divine Being Himself. The great majority of the ᶜulamā' rejected the Muᶜtazilī teaching and adopted a hostile attitude toward rationalistic theology in general, which they regarded as alien to Islam. They believed the affirmation of the eternality of the Koran to be required by revelation, even if it could not be rationalized by the human intellect.

Al-Ma'mūn, who himself had strong leanings toward rationalism, decided that the Muᶜtazilī position was superior to that of the opposing culamā' and adopted the Muctazilī theology as the official theology of the state. As a token of allegiance to the state, all culamā' were required to make public confession of the doctrine of the createdness of the Koran by means of signed statements. Those who refused were put to "test" (mihna), that is to say, dismissed from office (if they were judges), flogged, imprisoned, or persecuted in some other manner. Under al-Wathiq, one of the most respected of the culamā', a traditionalist named Ahmad ibn Nasr al-Khuzācī, was actually put to death. Some culamā', not wishing to undergo such persecution, made public confession of the official doctrine, while repudiating it inwardly. The most popular figure in the movement of opposition to the Muctazilī doctrine was the eminent traditionist, Ahmad ibn Hanbal, founder of the Hanbalī law school, who had wide popular support, especially in Baghdad.

The Muctazilī theology enjoyed official sanction for a period of twenty years (827-847), being retained after al-Ma'mūn's death by the two following caliphs, al-Muctasim and al-Wāthiq. Throughout this period popular antipathy toward it, as well as the antipathy of the majority of culamā', remained undiminished. The strong feeling aroused by Ahmad ibn Hanbal among the populace of Baghdad was one of the factors contributing to the turbulence of that city and inducing the caliph al-Muctasim to transfer his residence to Samarra. Finally, the caliph al-Mutawakkil, soon after his accession in 661, rescinded the unpopular doctrine and announced his adherence to the doctrine of the eternal Koran and to the other tenets generally held by the culamā'.

In the course of these events, orthodoxy achieved greater definition at the theological level, but the agent in the process of definition, in the end, was not the caliph but the culamā'. The experiment in caliphal spiritual supremacy had failed. The caliph would henceforth follow the lead of the culamā' in spiritual matters and restrict his role to guaranteeing insofar as possible that law and theology as defined by them were properly maintained and applied. The culama' emerged from the experiment with a keener sense of their own independence vis-a-vis the state. Twenty years of conflict with the state had produced among them a cautious attitude toward earthly power that was to remain a permanent feature of the culamā' grouping, even when the state was fully committed to their definition of orthodoxy.

The assertion of spiritual authority by the culamā' gave notice to the Abbasid House that its absolutism could not be extended to the domain of faith. The Shīcī conception of rule, which did assign spiritual authority to the caliph-Imām and which had influenced the Abbasid self-conception in the early days of the dynasty, proved unworkable in a society whose population was predominantly Sunnī and whose religious leaders (the culama') were on the whole resolutely opposed to it. The Sunnī view of the social order had triumphed, and the Abbasid caliphs henceforth became the unqualified supporters and patrons of an autonomous Sunnī religious establishment.

Arabization and the Development of Arab Culture

We have already noted that, although the Abbasid revolution had brought an end to the political domination of the Arabs, it by no means removed Arabs from the scene altogether. While many Arabs became absorbed into the indigenous populations of the empire, others retained their Arab identity by preserving credentials of descent from Arab ancestors or by continuing to live an "Arab" way of life as bedouin. Especially in the Arabian Peninsula and in parts of the neighboring countries of Syria, Palestine and Egypt, there continued to exist an authentically Arab population, the majority of which was bedouin; and the Peninsula itself continued to be regarded as an Arab homeland. Moreover, persons of Arab descent lived at the Abbasid court and were active in all fields of endeavor, from commerce to religious studies.

Arab influence in Abbasid life was not limited to bonafide Arabs. The spread of the Arabic language and literature and of Arab traditions among the indigenous populations of the empire resulted in an active participation in the development of Arab culture by persons who were not Arabs in the classical sense. As a result, a cosmopolitan Arab culture blossomed under the Abbasids, with literature as its principal ingredient.

The spread of the Arabic language was almost universal within the lands of Islam. Wherever Islam was established, Arabic accompanied it as the language of the Koran and of administration. As a result, there emerged everywhere a class of natives fully conversant with Arabic. However, in many areas Arabic did not displace the native language; those who acquired Arabic became bilingual, retaining their native language as the primary spoken language. In such areas Arabic was the language of culture, administration, and religion, but not the language of the street. Furthermore, Arabic was restricted to towns and did not penetrate the countryside to any appreciable degree. In other areas, however, Arabic gradually gained ground over the native language, finally replacing it altogether, not only in the towns but eventually in most of the countryside as well. It is this Arabic monolingualism that constitutes the true mark of arabization. Quite understandably, it was those countries nearest to the Arabian Peninsula and subject to the influence of large Arabic-speaking populations, mostly bedouin, within their borders that were the first to succumb to arabization: Syria (including Palestine), Iraq, and Egypt. In all cases arabization began in the major towns, spread to other towns, and thereafter, much more gradually, into the countryside. Syria was probably far along the way to arabization by the end of the Umayyad period, owing to the influence of the Arab tribes and the Umayyad court. In the case of Iraq, the presence of the Arab camp towns and, under the Abbasids, the caliphal court promoted arabization. In Egypt the process of arabization was no doubt somewhat more gradual, although the influence of a centralized administration based in the Arab town of Fustat, together with that of bedouin tribes living on the edges of the Nile Valley, were powerful impetuses to arabization. The progress of arabization in these countries brought into being an Arab culture zone characterized not only by Arab high culture but also by an emerging Arab general culture in which certain dominant Arab traits were fused with native traits. Arabization also proceeded slowly but steadily in the principal towns of North Africa and Spain. In North Africa the process was much accelerated by the bedouin invasions after 1000.

Although Arab high culture, that is to say Arabic literature, was eventually to find its real home in the Arab culture zone, in Abbasid times it flourished in all areas of the empire. The Abbasid court was, of course, the primary center of all literary activity, but various provincial courts also attracted men of letters. So long as Arabic retained its literary primacy, Arabic literature had an assured place wherever men of taste and means were present to patronize it. Only after the emergence of new Persian (Farsi) as the primary literary language of Iran and Central Asia (it later spread to India and Turkey) did Arabic as a literary language have to withdraw from part of its original domain and retreat into the congenial atmosphere of the Arab culture zone. It remained in all these areas, however, as the primary language of religious studies and of science and philosophy.

The involvement of non-Arabs in the development of Arabic literature under the Abbasids brought into sharper focus an issue that was perhaps the most crucial in the entire history of that literature, at least in the pre-modern period: To what extent should Arabic literature incorporate new tendencies in content and style? Otherwise stated: To what extent was Arabic literature bound to the themes and styles of the old poets of pre-Islamic times? This issue had first been raised in Umayyad times when a certain group of poets attached to the Umayyad court had explored new avenues of expression, departing cautiously from the antiquated vocabulary and motifs of the desert but without seriously violating the general norms of the older literature. Chief among these poets were the famous trio, al-Akhtal, Farazdaq and Jarīr. Another group, which departed even further from tradition, were the ᶜUdhrī poets, who set aside the time-honored ode (qaṣīda) as the primary poetic form and developed a new type of love poetry in which love was treated as an independent theme rather than as one ingredient in a more complex thematic structure, as in the ode. Over and against these poets, a more conventional school of poets clung firmly to the subject matter and vocabulary of pre-Islamic times, for which reason its poetry was contemptuously called "camel poetry."

The more innovative of the Umayyad poets, and especially the ᶜUdhrī poets, foreshadowed the "new poetry" of the Abbasid period, which aroused lively controversy among men of letters. The primary representatives of this poetry were Abu'l-ᶜAtāhiya and Abū Nuwās, both of whom lived during the reign of Hārūn al-Rashīd, of whom the latter poet was a boon companion. The new poetry flourished under the patronage of the court and consequently reflected standards of taste created by the influx of Persians into courtly life. The courtly atmosphere also accounts for the strong tendency of the new poetry toward bombastic modes of expression. Abu'l-ᶜAtahiya's poems display a reflective and even didactic attitude which is typical of some of the poetry of the period. His unrequited love for a slave-girl of the royal harem drove him to a morbid preoccupation with death and vanity of life. Abū Nuwās, on the other hand, was the prime representative of the so-called "licentious poets" (*al-shu^{c}arā' al-mujjān*). His hedonistic verse was a clear reflection of the pasttimes enjoyed by the court and by the upper classes who emulated the court. In general the new poets made no pretense of imitating the old Arabian poetry. Though a restricted number of forms were still used, the themes which poetry might explore were no longer limited by convention.

The cultivation of the new poetry was accompanied by an intensive development of the art of literary criticism among men of letters. The reactions of the critics to the new poetry varied widely. Some condemned it, while others praised it. One critic, al-Tha^{c}alibi, went so far as to declare the new poetry superior to the old. The greatest of the earlier critics, Ibn Qutayba, took a more cautious approach, approving the new poetry while at the same time upholding the preeminence of the older poetry. His attitude thus strengthened the more conservative tendency among the critics, while allowing for a degree of creativity within limits. The triumph of conservatism is reflected in the work of later poets who sought to reproduce the pre-Islamic *qasīda* and to incorporate the bedouin spirit in their poems. The greatest of the later poets, al-Mutanabbī, travelled among bedouin to draw inspiration and master correct usage.

An even more serious controversy developed as to what was proper in the field of prose writing. The pre-Islamic Arabs had given rather little attention to prose as an art form, concentrating rather on poetry as the consumate art. Their prose consisted mainly of an oral tradition of stories of great battles, called in Arabic *ayyam al-^{c}arab*. These stories were usually punctuated with poems, which brought to a climax the sentiments aroused by memories of the events recounted. As important as it was to tribal life, at least in the heyday of pre-Islamic paganism, story-telling, always remained subordinate to poetry as a vehicle of artistic expression.

With the coming of Islam, prose composition received an important impetus from the emergence of a religious prose literature. The Koran itself was written in a type of prose which, although rhymed, was carefully distinguished from poetry as such and was in fact given a different name, *saj^{c}* (poetry is called in Arabic *shi^{c}r*). Alongside the Koran there emerged a large body of religious literature in ordinary prose, which included sayings of the Prophet, anecdotes about the Prophet's activities, and commentary on the Koran. Later there was to emerge also a historical literature dealing with the great events of the early days of Islam. This material (with the exception of the Koran) developed orally for several generations and was only subsequently put into writing.

This early prose literature, despite its novelty in certain respects, adhered to the basic standards of the literary language (*al-fusha*) used by the pre-Islamic poets. This language, which had emerged as a common literary medium among the pre-Islamic tribes and was distinct from the tribes' spoken dialects, became the object of special study after the appearance of Islam, giving rise to a class of philologists. Thanks to their efforts, the grammatical, morphological and stylistic norms of the literary language were spelled out and codified and the meanings of words recorded. Out of such efforts standards of correct usage emerged which were considered binding on all those who wished to express themselves in the literary language. The literary language of pre-Islamic times thus became a classical tongue, and the philologists became the classicists of their age, the custodians of a classical tradition.

The preservation of the literary language had a strong religious motivation. Since the Koran and the sayings of the Prophet and reports of his contemporaries were couched in the literary language, it was imperative that that language be preserved so that future generations would not lose touch with the sources of their religion. The Koran itself was regarded as untranslatable, and its recitation was an integral part of worship and piety. Furthermore, the religious conscience of the community required that the literary language used in the Prophet's time be kept alive. As a consequence, religious studies and classical philology became wedded to each other.

Toward the end of the Umayyad period a new type of Arabic prose made its appearance, a development which was rapidly accelerated under the Abbasids. This prose was secular in spirit and had as its main purposes the entertainment of the listener or reader. It may be described as an Arabic belles lettres. The use of prose for secular purpose had received its first great impetus when ᶜAbd al-Malik had adopted Arabic as an official language of government near the end of the seventh century. Arabic was thereafter used not only as the language of records but more importantly as the language of official correspondences. This gave rise to an Arabic epistolography, or art of letter-writing. However, it was not until the last years of Umayyad rule that the first great work written in secretarial Arabic appeared. This was a treatise on the secretary's art written by ᶜAbd al-Hamīd, a mawla of Persian origin, and based on the Persian secretarial tradition. Epistolography was not belles lettres as such. However, it was closely allied to it, since it endeavored to employ elegant phrases which were pleasing to the ear; belles lettres was, furthermore, developed to a large extent among persons of the secretarial class, called in Arabic <u>kuttab</u> (sing. <u>katib</u>). The first major work in belles lettres proper appeared about the same time as ᶜAbd al-Hamīd's treatise. This was a collection of stories of Indian origin entitled <u>Kalīla wa-dimna</u>, which a secretary named Ibn Muqaffaᶜ translated from Pahlavi (pre-Islamic Persian) into elegant Arabic.

Under the Abbasids, the new secular prose became a primary ingredient in the culture of high society, that is to say, of the court and upper classes of society, including high government officials and wealthy merchants and landowners. At the same time, owing to the large role of the secretarial class in the production of this prose literature, it began to develop along new lines at variance with the classical literary tradition preserved by the philologists. The primary influences in the shaping of the new prose were drawn from Persian sources, including the Persian court literature of pre-Islamic times. The secretaries, not being thoroughly schooled in the grammar and stylistics of the classical philologists, wrote in a free and (from the classical point of view) innovative, undisciplined manner, ignoring many of the conventions held dear by the classicists. Furthermore, their writings were imbued with a moral outlook that was not in complete harmony with the principles of Islam, being essentially aristocratic and worldly in spirit.

The combined impact of the new poetry and the belles lettres prose resulted in a disdain among a certain segment of high society, led mainly by secretaries, for the "antiquated" standards upheld by the classicists. The more the classicists insisted upon these standards the greater became the disdain of the secretaries. This disdain found expression in an anti-Arab movement among certain secretaries and literary critics known as the *shu^{c}ūbiyya*. The shu^{c}ūbiya advocated the cultural superiority of the indigenous, non-Arab "natives" (whence the name of the movement) over the Arabs. Supporters of the movement ridiculed the classical Arabic literature as naive, obscurantist, and desert-bound and regarded the Arabs as barbarians who had little to offer the world culturally.

The literary contest which ensued between those secretaries who upheld the tenets of the shu^{c}ūbiyya and the philologists (often called the "Battle of the Books") had serious ramifications. A triumph of the shu^{c}ūbiyya would undoubtedly have resulted in a future development of Arabic in a direction leading away from its classical foundation. Like the major European languages, Arabic might have evolved through stages into a language much different from its original prototype. This would have broken an important tie with the original Arabs and would have made difficult the perpetuation of an Arab cultural identity within the world of Islam. Perhaps ultimately Arabic, without its classical foundation, would have given way universally as a primary literary language to Persian and other languages. Such developments would obviously have had serious consequences for religious life. The language of the Koran and the other primary sources of Islam may have become a "dead" language of liturgy and esoteric religious studies, and not a living language of people.

The fate of the classical tradition within Abbasid high society was thus a matter of grave consequence for the future of Arab culture. The culture of high society, called in Arabic *adab* (the translation of this term as "literature" is too narrow), was a powerful determinant in the cultural life of the empire as a whole. The only thing that could compete with it in influence was the religious culture of the ^{c}ulamā' and the pious, who although sometimes involved marginally in high society, were intrinsically outside it. All members of high society, whether secretaries, high officials, merchants or landowners, aspired to be *udabā'* (sing. *adib*), that is, "men of culture." As high society grew as a result of the economic boom of Abbasid times and the consequent growth of the bourgeoisie and expansion of officialdom and the court, the *adab* culture took on greater and greater importance.

The credit for the ultimate triumph of the classical tradition goes largely to two men: Ibn Qutayba and ^{c}Amr al-Jāhiz. Ibn Qutayba, whose influence on the development of poetry has already been mentioned, was also instrumental in creating a new Arabic belles lettres which was fully grounded in the classical tradition. But his work in the prose field was overshadowed by that al-Jāhiz, the greatest of all the Arabic belles lettres writers. Al-Jāhiz's greatness lay in his ability to incorporate into his writings themes of lively interest to the flourishing high society without violating the standards of proper Arabic writing established by the philologists. In the urban environment of the Abbasid age, the favorite themes of the old Arabian literature commanded little interest. Al-Jāhiz's own urbanity and comprehensive knowledge of the world provided a type of outlook fully in keeping with the times. At the same time al-Jāhiz's writings maintained a true Arab character, as defined by the classicists, not only by adhering faithfully to classical usage, but also by including material drawn from genuine Arab sources, such as bedouin proverbs. Al-Jāhiz was also a deeply religious man and a profound theologian who injected into his writings a truly Muslim spirit. Thus, in effect, al-Jāhiz laid the foundations of an Arab-Muslim humanities that was to become a vital ingredient in the on-going development of Arab culture.

The Decline and Breakup of the Abbasid Empire

The decline of the Abbasid empire was a gradual process, the beginnings of which are faintly perceptible as early as the reign of Hārūn al-Rashīd. Under Hārūn the Abbasid state lost its control of North Africa (the Maghrib), and Abbasid hegemony was confined thereafter to the lands of the Muslim "East" (the Mashriq) including Egypt. However, Abbasid control over North Africa had been slight from the beginning, and Spain had never come under effective Abbasid control at all, so that the Abbasid empire, based in the politically powerful and economically prosperous province of Iraq, can be fairly described as an essentially "eastern" Empire from its earliest days.

A more serious manifestation of decline was the four-year civil war between the two sons of Hārūn al-Rashīd, al-Amīn and al-Ma'mūn, which ended with al-Ma'mūn's defeat of his brother in 813. Although the empire made a reasonable recovery, it was beset thereafter with a series of serious social disturbances and with separatist tendencies in large parts of the empire. The recruitment on a large scale of Turkish slave troops, beginning in the reign of al-Mu^{c}tasim (833-842), also brought trouble to the empire; commanding officers, gradually usurping the powers of the caliph, assumed an ever larger role in political life.

Decline was particularly rapid in the two decades between 861 and 881. During 861-871 the central government became embroiled in rivalries between factions in the army, and the caliph degenerated into a pawn in the hands of powerful officers. This weakening of the central government was an invitation to rebels and opportunists throughout the empire. In 869 a revolt broke out among African slaves known collectively as the Zanj, who were working on a salt extraction project in the marshy areas of lower Iraq. The revolt was led by an Arab who claimed descent from ^{c}Alī. The rebels managed to gain control of a large part of Southern Iraq and Khuzistan, thus cutting off access to Baghdad via the southern routes. The caliphal army had great difficulty in fighting the rebels, who adopted guerilla tactics in the marsh lands, for which the caliphal cavalry was ill-suited. It was only after a struggle of fourteen years (968-883) that caliphal forces were able to mount an attack sufficient to defeat and wipe out the rebels. In the meantime, ambitious rulers in Egypt and southeast Persia took advantage of the central government's preoccupation with the Zanj rebellion by defying caliphal orders and extending the sphere of their rule. One of these was Ahmad ibn Tulūn, who had become governor of Egypt in 868. In 877 the central government, perturbed at the trifling amount of money which Ibn Tulūn had remitted to support the war against the Zanj, sent troops against him. These failed to subdue him, and instead Ibn Tulūn used the opportunity to occupy Syria. As a result, a complete rupture between Ibn Tulūn and the caliph took place. In Sijistan (Southeastern Persia), a popular leader named Ya^{c}qūb al-Saffār had emerged in 867 as the head of a volunteer army formed in order to defend the towns in the area against brigands. Having obtained firm control over Sijistan, Ya^{c}qūb then used his army to subdue surrounding areas. By 873 he had made himself master of Khorasan. In 876 he marched against Baghdad itself, compelling the caliph to divert his energies from the war against the Zanj in order to stop his advance.

After these set-backs, the caliphate was able to make a temporary recovery under the capable rule of al-Muwaffaq, brother of the caliph al-Mu^{c}tamid (870-892), who exercised authority as regent in place of the inept caliph. It was under al-Muwaffaq's command that caliphal forces finally succeeded in subduing the Zanj rebellion in 783. Meanwhile, the deaths of Ya^{c}qūb al-Saffār (879) and Ibn Tulūn (884) and the succession of less aggressive rulers (Ya^{c}qūb's brother and Ibn Tulūn's son) brought relative peace and stability to the empire.

The period between 880 and 925 (nearly half a century) was the calm before the storm for the Abbasid Caliphate. During this period, the central government was blessed with a number of capable rulers and administrators, beginning with the Regent al-Muwaffaq and continuing with a series of outstanding wazīrs. For the most part harmonious relations were maintained between the caliph, the civilian administration (under the wazīr) and the military. Many of the wazirs of the period were exceptionally capable administrators and experienced financiers who were able to keep the government on a reasonably sound financial footing. They were respected by the army officers and, thanks to the cooperation of the latter, the civilian element in government was able to maintain a dominant position. However, despite these improvements the caliphal empire was but a shadow of its former self. The loss of control over the eastern parts of the empire proved to be permanent and, although the caliphate was able to regain nominal control over Egypt in 905 and could claim hegemony over the entire Fertile Crescent, as well as the northern territories (Armenia and Adharbayjan) and southwestern Persia (Khuzistan and Fars), Abbasid rule in parts of this domain was shaky. In Egypt the administration was in shambles, in Syria serious disturbances were created by a radical Shī^{c}ī sect called the Qarmatians, and in southwestern Persia various insurgents continued to be active.

After 925 the military began to assume greater power over the central government, eclipsing the civilian administrators. In 936 the new title of Commander-in-Chief (amīr al-umarā') was conferred upon the leading general, to whom was assigned complete power over affairs of government. Thus the central government was transformed into a military dictatorship. The post of Commander-in-Chief became a bone of contention between rival officers, and in the ensuing chaos various adventurers from outside Baghdad managed to usurp the post and to control the city for short periods of time. In the meantime, the caliph was constrained again to relinquish Egypt again to an autonomous local ruler (935), while Syria and northern Mesopotamia came under the control of chieftains of an Arab family, the Hamdanids. Finally, in 945 Persian Shi'i tribal chieftains called the Buwayhids captured Baghdad, and the caliphate remained under their domination for more than a century thereafter.

The decline of the Abbasid empire calls for an explanation. How do we account for the fact that an empire as mighty and majestic as was that of the Abbasids in 800 should have been in ruins a century and a half later? The general, long-range causes of the Abbasid decline are complex, as with the decline of all great empires, and no answer can do absolute justice to the facts. However, it is possible to single out two main factors in the Abbasid decline: social unrest and separatist tendencies in important parts of the empire. Social unrest was the inevitable outcome of tension which were endemic to Abbasid society from the very beginning. Despite their promise of social justice during their revolutionary days, once in power the Abbasids were quick to align themselves with the dominant elements in society--the rich and influential. Although the Abbasids had eliminated an exclusively Arab aristocracy, they had merely replaced it with a new aristocracy made up of certain high Arab dignitaries together with the native non-Arab aristocracy, to which were added in increasing numbers the rising bourgeoisie.

Abbasid society was thus no less elitist than Umayyad society had been. Now that conflict between the conquerors and conquered had come to an end, the cleavage between the rich minority and the masses of poor became more obvious, causing frustration and unrest. The poor comprised two categories: the poor peasants of the countryside, and the poor of the towns, that is, the urban proletariat or working class. The condition of the peasants varied, but generally speaking was miserable. Some peasants owned their own land, but were subject to a heavy burden of taxation. The official rate of taxation varied from about one-half of the crop to about one-fifth, depending on the degree of fertility, but the greed of tax-farmers often led to more extortionary rates. When the tax burden became unbearable or cultivation of the land too difficult, peasants would abandon or sell their land and either migrate to the towns or become tenant farmers. The majority of the tenant farmers worked on large estates owned by wealthy landowners, who often themselves lived in towns. The tenant farmer paid a rent which, in the cases of fertile land, could consist of as much as four-fifths of the crop. Generally speaking, the peasants lived at a bare subsistence level, and the fruits of their labor went to the government and into the pockets of wealthy landowners or tax farmers. Owing to their desperate conditions, the peasants were receptive to revolutionary ideas, and organized revolts among them were common from the earliest days of the Abbasids. One of the most serious of these was a 21-year revolt led by a religious radical named Bābak, which broke out in Adharbayjan three years after al-Ma'mūn's accession and spread quickly to other parts of the empire. Later in the ninth century, the radical Qarmatian movement got its start among peasants in lower Iraq. As for the urban working class, these too often led desperate lives and were open to subversive propaganda, particularly those who were not highly skilled. Unemployment was not uncommon, and the jobless constituted a particularly troublesome segment of the urban population. The city of Baghdad was especially prone to urban turmoil and violence. However, organized and sustained revolutionary movements like that of Bābak among the peasants never took shape among the urban poor, whose frustrations were released only in sporadic revolts and outbreaks of violence.

Other sources of unrest in Abbasid society were the bedouin and the slaves. The bedouin were an ever present menace to the government and the settled agricultural population. It was among bedouin rather than peasants that the Qarmatians achieved their first spectacular military successes. The impact of bedouin extended throughout much of the Fertile Crescent and Egypt. Slave movements, on the other hand, were a rare phenomenon. The movement of the Zanj is the only thing of its kind in the history of the caliphate, although its impact on the empire was enormous.

The threat of rebellion among these various segments of Abbasid society made the services of the standing army indispensable to public order. The recruitment on a large scale of Turkish slave troops by al-Mu^{c}tasim was occasioned, not only by disorder in the city of Baghdad, but also by the Bābak revolt, which made the need for an effective and dependable army more apparent. The days when the caliph's army fought on frontiers were fast departing. By the end of the ninth century, frontier warfare was turned over to religious volunteers (ghāzīs) and bedouin, while the standing army was concerned exclusively with maintaining the caliph's authority within the empire.

No less disastrous for the empire in the long run than the disturbances caused by the oppressed classes were the separatist tendencies which gave rise to independent regimes and brought about the empire's political fragmentation. Some of these regimes have been alluded to already. The first area is to slip from Abbasid control, we have noted, were North Africa and Spain. In Spain a survivor of the massacre of the Umayyads, ^{c}Abd al-Rahmān, established an independent state just six years after the coming to power of the Abbasids. As the Abbasids had not in any case effectively ruled Spain prior to this event, we may say that for all intents and purposes it was never a part of the Abbasid empire. The same may be said of Morocco where in 788 Idris, a descendant of ^{c}Alī who had survived a massacre of the ^{c}Alids under the caliph al-Hādī, likewise established an independent state. In Ifriqiya (Tunisia) an important new precedent was set in 800 when the caliph Hārūn al-Rashīd granted to the amīr (governor) Ibrāhīm ibn al-Aghlab, who had become all-powerful in this North African province, the right to pass the amirate on to his descendants. By this action a dynasty was in effect created under the auspices of the Abbasid caliph. In return for this favor the Aghlabids, as the new dynasty is called, agreed to recognize the suzerainty of the caliph and to pay a tribute at certain intervals. Thus by 800 two types of independent regimes had emerged in North Africa: a dissident type (the Spanish Umayyads, the Idrisids), which gave no recognition to the Abbasids whatsoever, and a loyalist type (the Aghlabids), which accepted the nominal suzerainty of the Abbasids while in fact ruling independently. Some regimes which were later to emerge vacillated between these two types. The advantage to the Abbasids of regimes of the loyalist type was that, in situations where the Abbasids could no longer exercise effective control over an area, they were able to retain a certain prestige by having due respect paid to them, even if only in a ceremonious manner. This was much to be preferred to outright repudiation of Abbasid authority as it kept the empire nominally intact.

During the ninth century, areas closer to the center of the empire produced independent regimes. The first of these was to emerge in Khorasan. The separatist inclinations of the Khorasanians was first evident during the civil war between al-Amīn and al-Ma'mūn, when the latter established his base in Khorasan and defeated his brother with Khorasanian help, after which he remained as caliph in Khorasan for some time before deciding to transfer himself to Baghdad. When this happened, he left his general Tāhir in charge of Khorasan and in 820 conferred the amīrate of Khorāsan on Tāhir's line, thus creating a loyalist dynasty, the Tahirids, similar to that of the Aghlabids. Later in the same century, Yaᶜqūb al-Saffār (867) and Ahmad ibn Tulūn (868) established themselves as independent rulers of Sijistan and Egypt without the express sanction of the caliph and, while the caliph was preoccupied with the Zanj wars, defied his orders, thus adopting the posture of dissidents. However, their successors (the Saffarids and Tulūnids) improved relations with the caliph, taking up a loyalist stance. An important loyalist dynasty was established in Central Asia in 892, that of the Sāmānids, a Persian aristocratic family. The Sāmānids ruled until the end of the tenth century, extending, after the demise of the Saffārids, their rule throughout Central and Eastern Iran. Meanwhile, during the tenth century a dissident regime, that of the Fātimids, replaced the Aghlabids (909) in Ifriqiya, and a new loyalist regime, the Ikhshīdids, established itself in Egypt (935) but later succumbed to the expanding Fātimids (969), while in Syria and northern Mesopotamia the loyalist (but highly independent with Shīᶜi tendencies) Hamdānid family set up autonomous states in Mosul (905) and Aleppo (944).

The loss of large territories to independent rulers imposed great financial hardship on the caliphal government, because it meant a reduction of revenue for the central treasury. The tributes which the caliph was able to obtain from some rulers was no substitution for regular tax revenues. The local rulers were eager to keep the revenues of their territories under their own control in order to strengthen their own government and improve their economies. Egypt, for example, had previously seen a large part of its resources drained off to the central lands of the empire, and Egypt's governors had administered Egypt primarily for the benefit of the caliphate in

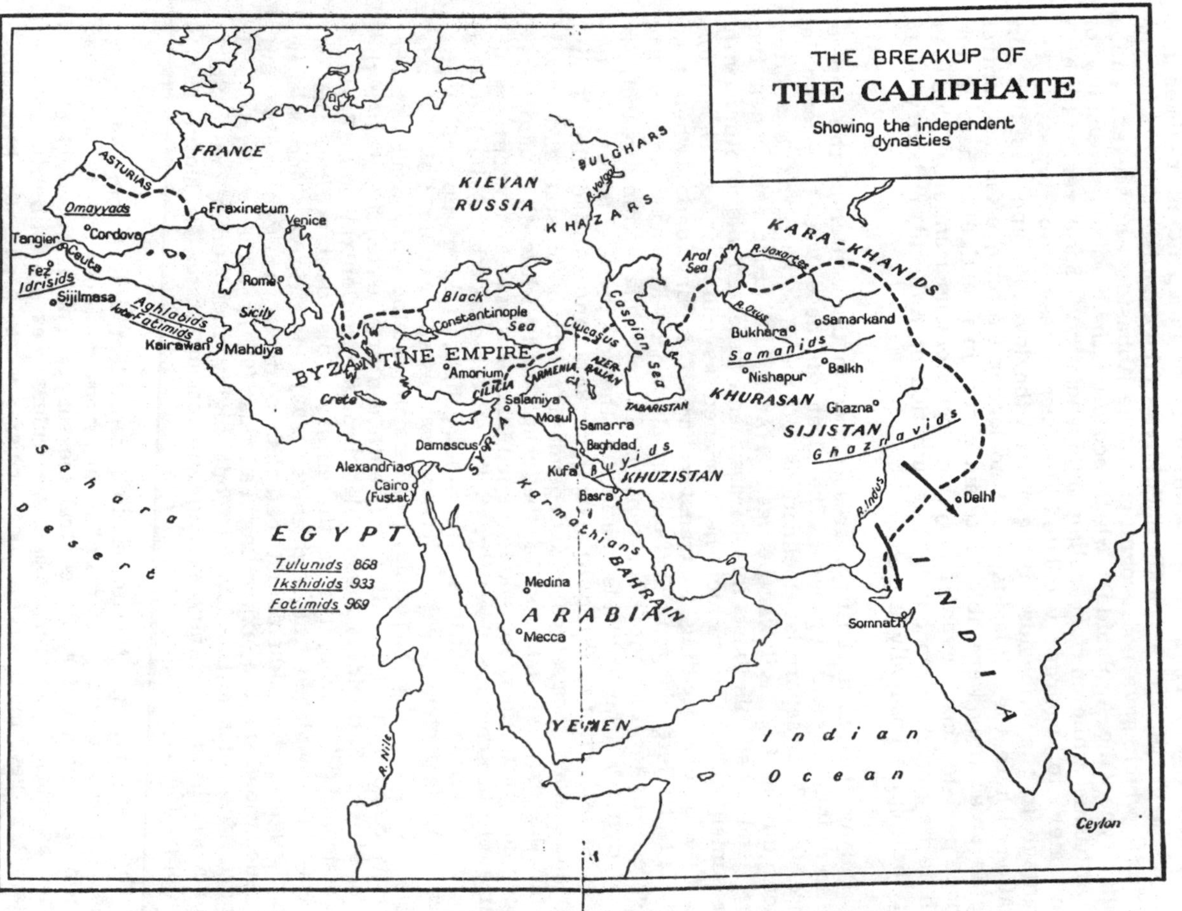

from J. J. Saunders, A History of Medieval Islam

Abbasid Empire's Fragmentation into Local Regimes

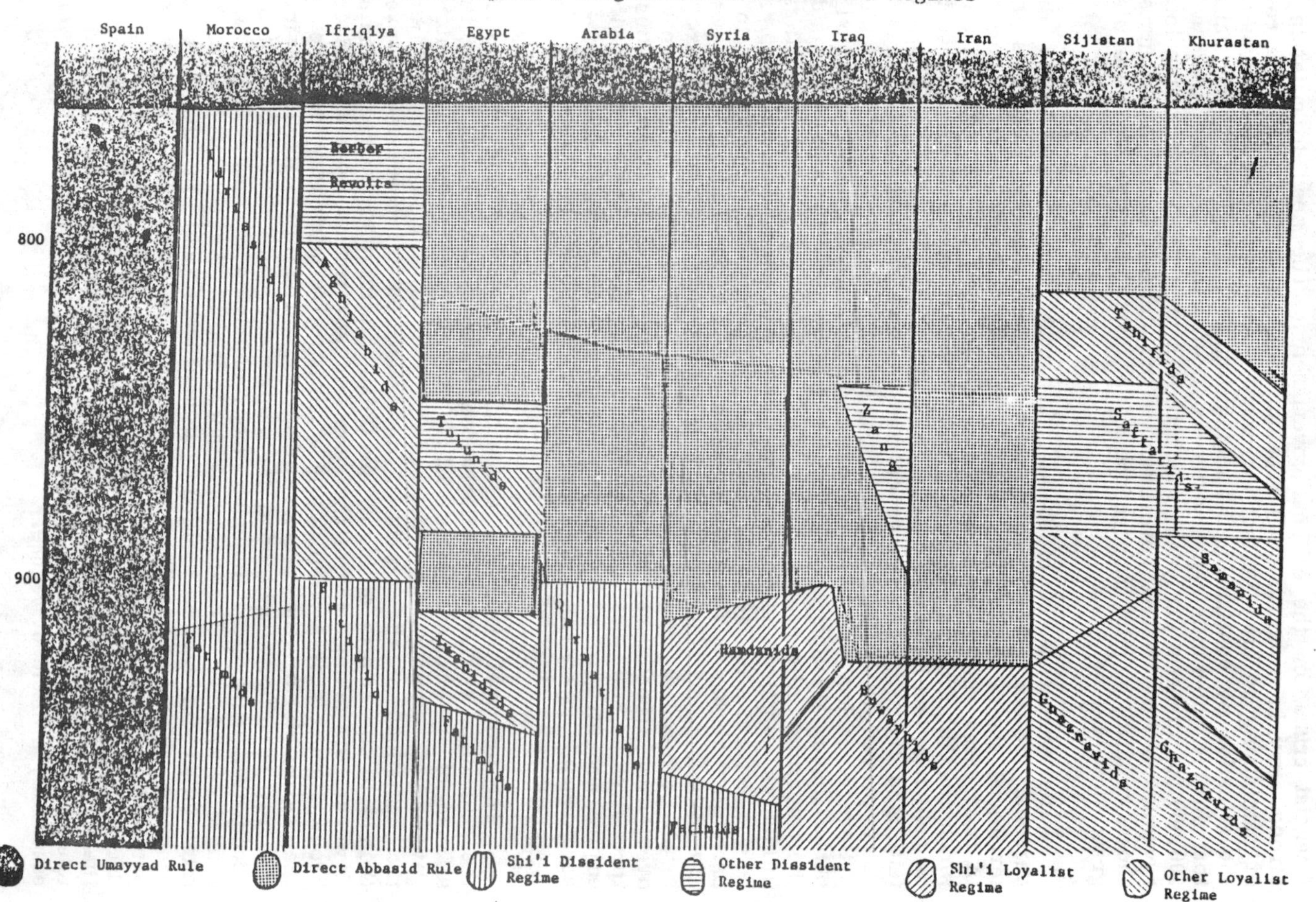

Baghdad. Under Ibn Tulūn, an "Egypt first" policy was adopted for the first time, and the country's economy improved rapidly. Similar developments occurred in other areas. This loss of revenue created a financial crisis for the caliphal government. The need to maintain a strong army in order to quell rebellion did not diminish, and the cost of maintaining an army in fact increased. The army itself exacerbated the situation by continually demanding higher pay. One source claims that in the mid-ninth century the cost of maintaining the army was 200,000,000 dirhems per year, which represented two-thirds of the total revenues of the central government. In addition to these expenses, those entailed by the maintenance of a lavish courtly life were also great.

The emergence of independent regimes sometimes reflected the personal ambitions of the local rulers or their families, sometimes the territorial aspirations of the people who helped bring them to power. In most cases both factors were involved in some degree. The empire which the Abbasids had originally ruled was too vast and too diverse to be held together indefinitely as a single political unit. While the Islamic faith and the Arabic language created a large measure of unity, this unity proved to be essentially non-political. It entailed a particular pattern of society and even of government, but, as things turned out, not a universal empire solidly united under the caliphate. Alongside the unifying influence of Islam and Arabic were many centrifugal influences which undermined the unity of the Abbasid empire: languages, cultures, sectarian commitments, and even sheer loyalty to a particular region. To impose unity on the empire by force was unthinkable, since this would have required firm command over troops in all parts of the empire. It was in fact by virtue of their control over local troops that independent rulers were able to establish themselves in the first place. Failure to control the whole of the empire amounted to a failure to control the empire's armies. It was hard enough to control the standing army stationed in the capital, let alone armies in outlying provinces.

The principal, immediate cause of the collapse of the caliphate in the mid-ninth century was the ascendancy of the military over the affairs of government after 925. Before that time the central government, although hard pressed by the demands of the army and the limitations of the treasury, had managed to meet its expenses thanks to the efforts of highly proficient wazīrs and their assistants. However, the taking over of the reigns of government by army officers brought about a breakdown of the administrative machinery built up by the wazīrs during the previous decades. The army itself fell into disarray as officers contended for supremacy, and the lack of stable administration produced financial chaos, depriving the army of a steady source of income. The resultant confusion in the capital led to the intervention of various military adventurers and to the ultimate conquest of the city by the Buwayhids. The Buwayhid takeover was particularly humiliating because the Buwayhid chieftains were Shī^{c}ī who decided to retain the Abbasid caliphate only as a means of rendering their rule more acceptable to their Sunnī subjects. Despite their toleration of the Abbasid caliphate, the Buwayhids as Shī^{c}is were essentially a dissident regime.

The capture of Baghdad in 945 by the Buwayhids may be regarded as the final event in the downfall of the Abbasid empire. Never again would Abbasid caliphs rule in their own right. The caliphal office would, it is true, continue to exist for another three centuries as a symbol of legitimacy and moral force, and members of the Abbasid line would continue to occupy it. However, it would henceforth be stripped of all real power, and the great caliphal empire would become but a memory.

CHAPTER FOUR

THE ISLAMIC WORLD IN AN AGE OF INTERNATIONALISM

From 945 onward the Abbasid empire was clearly a thing of the past. An Abbasid caliphate continued to exist, but it was a caliphate without an empire. Even the central lands were no longer under its rule. The real masters in these lands were the Buwayhid amīrs, who ruled western Iran as well. As Shīʿis, the Buwayhids felt no genuine loyalty toward the Abbasids, but rather treated the caliphate as a political convenience, a means for pacifying a predominantly Sunnī population who still looked to the caliph as the true Commander of the Faithful. Elsewhere other regimes, whose emergence was discussed in the previous chapter, held sway. For about three centuries (945 to 1258) an Abbasid caliph continued to sit on a throne in Baghdad. Deprived of all real power, the caliph played a purely symbolic role. He was now but a figurehead of the moral and spiritual unity of the emerging international world of Islam. This role was, of course, acknowledged only by the Sunnī population, but as that population was in the majority the caliph's position in this role was secure. Sunnī rulers would obtain investiture from the caliph, who would thus use the prestige of his office to legitimize their rule.

The failure of the Abbasids to create a universal Islamic empire capable of standing the test of time was of great significance. The demise of the Abbasid empire meant in effect the demise of the single Islamic polity which had originated in Medina and had been perpetuated and extended by the earlier caliphs. Henceforth, the Islamic world would not be a single polity under a ruling caliph having great armies and bureaucracies under his command. Rather, it was destined to become a politically diverse, international world community embracing a plurality of independent principalities, some large enough to be termed empires. Islam the religion and the great civilization which it would foster, including the specifically Muslim patterns of life prescribed in the Sharīʿa, would become in time a sufficient basis for the unity of the Islamic world. A caliphal empire would no longer be deemed a prerequisite of that unity. Political pluralism would engender a concept of unity conceived along non-political lines. Islamic rule would continue to exist in order to carry out the task of creating those conditions within which the Sharīʿa could prosper, but it would be a diversified rule exercised by an indeterminate number of rulers, some great and others small.

Although internationalism and political pluralism were the new realities after 945, the time-honored notion of a single centralized Islamic polity would not die easily. The period 945-1258 witnessed several attempts to restore this polity. The disappearance of the Abbasid empire cleared the stage for new ventures in empire-building. One such venture was attempted by a series of rulers claiming ʿAlid descent and adhering to the Shīʿi conception of the Islamic polity, namely the Fāṭimids. The Buwayhid chieftains who puppetized the caliphs and ruled over the central lands were not true empire-builders, owing to their practice of dividing their realm among themselves and thus fragmenting it into smaller principalities. However, in the middle of the eleventh century two nomadic invasions occurred almost simultaneously at opposite ends of the Islamic world which gave fresh impetus to empire-building. These were the invasions of the Seljuk Turks coming from Central Asia and the Lamtūna Berbers coming from the sub-Saharan region of West Africa. Both of these nomadic peoples created empires (the Seljuk and Murābit empires) that were short-lived but had important long-range historical consequences. Both were loyal to Sunnī ideals and to the Abbasid caliphate. However, whereas the Murābit rulers never seriously aspired to extend their sway beyond the Maghrib (North Africa), the Seljuks clearly saw themselves as restorers of the universal Islamic polity. Their loyalty to the Abbasid caliphate went beyond the verbal allegiance of the Murabits and took the form of an active championship of the right of the caliph to universal dominion. The Seljuk empire collapsed around 1100, having failed to achieve its fundamental aspiration. Somewhat later, with the collapse of the Fatimid state in Egypt in 1171 and the mobilization of Muslim forces against the Crusaders, a Kurdish general named Salāh al-Dīn was able to build a Syro-Egyptian empire (the Ayyūbid empire), which was in certain respects modeled on the Seljuk empire but without evident commitment to restore the universal caliphal polity. During the period of Ayyūbid hegemony in Syria and Egypt, a remarkable caliph named al-Nasir (1180-1225) succeeded in establishing in Iraq a basis of real power for the caliphate; for the first time in nearly three centuries a caliph actually ruled over a limited territory. There is no evidence, however, that al-Nāsir seriously contemplated universal dominion within the Islamic world. Rather, it seems that after the collapse of the Seljuk empire the pluralistic conception of the Islamic umma as an international world community prevailed. In the Maghrib, the empire of the Murābits was, around the middle of the twelfth century, supplanted by that of the Muwahhids, who established a caliphate of their own based on revivalist notions and implicitly calling for universal dominion but without seriously contemplating achieving it.

The collapse of the Seljuk empire around 1100 also represents a point in our study of Arab history where we can begin focusing attention to a greater extent upon those areas which eventually became the present-day Arab lands without regard for developments in the lands to the East, particularly Iran. Earlier, the eastern part of the emerging Arab domain had been closely linked politically to the Iranian lands, owing to their inclusion along with these other lands in the universal empire erected by the Arabs and perpetuated by the Abbasids. After the collapse of the Abbasid empire, the Iranian lands continue to occupy our attention for another century and a half. This is because the Seljuks, whose empire is essentially Iranian-based, not only rule over a part of the eastern Arab lands, but more importantly, because the social and religious institutions which are developed under their rule have an enormous impact on the future of the Arab lands. We will see later in this chapter, as well as in Chapter Seven, that the Seljuk legacy eventually finds a pied-a-terre in the eastern Arab lands under Ayyubid and Mamlūk rule, and an aspect of it (the madrasa) even finds its way to the Maghrib. Once the Seljuks disappear from the scene, the relevance of Iran to Arab history diminishes sharply. Although the process of arabization in large parts of the future Arab lands, namely Egypt and North Africa, has not fully run its course by

1100, these lands are patently on their way to becoming--with the culmination a century or two later of developments now set in motion--a relatively self-contained object of history study. Arab history is moving toward its last great chapter, the history of the Arab lands as presently constituted.

Since we will focus in this chapter on those areas which are to become the Arab lands of our study in subsequent chapters, we will not deal with developments which take place, after the collapse of the Great Seljuk empire, in the eastern lands of Islam. We should note, however, that those lands are also very much a part of the emerging international world of Islam and that out of those lands a new momentum of expansion is launched in the direction of India, resulting in an even larger and more diverse world of Islam. Furthermore, in these more eastern lands literary culture becomes the domain of the Persian language, as Arabic is confined mainly to the Islamic religious sciences and philosophy (along with natural science). The result is a bifurcation of the Islamic world into two literary cultures, Persian and Arabic.

Through the period under consideration in this chapter (945-1258) a number of important changes and new developments took place within the area which were to become the present-day Arab lands. One of these was the further arabization of the Eastern and Central Maghrib as a result of a large-scale migration of bedouins into these areas. Despite the predominance of the Arab language in the towns along the North African coast, the general population of North Africa had remained until the end of the tenth century more Berber than Arab. As a result of the new bedouin invasions, North Africa assumed the predominantly Arab character which it has retained to the present day (notwithstanding the survival of the Berber language and way of life in certain regions). Thus, during the period under consideration, North Africa was incorporated more fully into the Arab culture zone, and by the end of the period the Arab world had assumed the general geographical shape which it has today. The Fertile Crescent lands had been more or less arabized before 945. The extent of arabization in Egypt prior to that date is, as has been noted, uncertain. In all probability the greater part of Egypt was still undergoing substantial arabization in the period under consideration.

Other important developments were the consolidation and spread of the feudal (iqṭāᶜ) system throughout the eastern Arab lands (Egypt and the Fertile Crescent) as well as Iran; the gradual over-all decline of urban life and of economic activity; the triumph of Sunnī orthodoxy, standardization of intellectual life and the rise and spread of the Ṣūfī orders.

The beginnings of feudalism occurred under Buwayhid rule. One of the most severe problems which Abbasid government of the early tenth century faced was that of how to pay the army. Inheriting this same problem, the Buwayhids hit upon a new scheme. Instead of paying their officers salaries drawn from the central treasury they granted them fiscal rights over districts assigned to them. This arrangement permitted each officer to collect taxes in the district assigned to him on his own and to keep the revenue thus acquired as personal income in lieu of a paid salary. The only financial obligation of the officer to the government was the payment of ᶜushr, although later on this obligation was dropped. The assignment of fiscal rights in this manner was called iqtāᶜ, a term which suggested a connection with the older qatīᶜa (see Chapter Two) but must be distinguished from it, since the qatīᶜa was a grant of the land itself and not of the fiscal rights over land. The iqtāᶜ was to become, under the Seljuks, the basis of a new "feudal" or decentralized order, one which would take root in the eastern Arab lands under Ayyūbid rule and would later be perpetuated by the Mamlūks (see Chapter Seven) and Ottomans (see Chapter Eight). The spread of this feudalism, based on the primacy of the military, would bring an end to the years of mercantilism and bourgeois ascendancy which had been inaugurated by the coming of the Arabs.

The Fātimid Empire in Egypt (969-1171)

The circumstances which led to the establishment of the Fātimid empire bear certain similarities to those which produced the Abbasid empire. Both empires were the product of revolutionary movements which were able to seize power in outlying areas and then commence a drive toward the central lands of the Islamic world. In the case of the Fātimid empire, the revolutionary movement which prepared the way was that of the Ismāᶜīlīs, and the place of initial success was Ifrīqiya (Tunisia). But, unlike the Abbasids, who having established themselves in Khorasan proceeded immediately toward the central lands, the Fātimids remained in Ifrīqiya for sixty years (909-969) before undertaking their final drive eastward. During those sixty years, however, they did spread their rule westward to Morocco, creating a North African empire.

The Ismāᶜīlī movement represented the most radical branch of Shīᶜism. Its beginnings go back to the death of the ᶜAlī Jaᶜfar al-Sādiq in 765 (during the reign of the second Abbasid caliph, al-Mansūr). Jaᶜfar had been a religious teacher with a large following among the Shīᶜis; at the time of his death his followers split into two groups over the issue of the succession. The majority supported his son Mūsā. A small group, however, remained faithful to an older son named Ismāᶜīl, whom Jaᶜfar had appointed as his successor but who had predeceased him. These partisans of Ismāᶜīl, who came to be known as Ismāᶜīlīs, rallied to Ismāᶜīl's son. From this split came the distinction between Ismāᶜīlī Shīᶜis and Twelver (ithnā ᶜasharī) Shīᶜis. The latter, who grew out of the followers of Mūsā, are so named because they believed that the true line of Imāms (or caliphs) ended with the twelfth Imām, who disappeared in 873 and will return at an unknown time in the future to establish the reign of God upon the earth. The Ismāᶜīlīs, on the other hand, adhered to a continuing line of Imams.

The Imams of the Twelver Shīᶜis:

1. ᶜAlī ibn Abī Tālib, d. 661.
2. Al-Hasan, d. 669.
3. Al-Husayn, d. 680.

4. Zayn al-cĀbidīn, d. 712.
5. Muḥammad al-Bāqir, d. approx. 731.
6. Jacfar al-Ṣādiq, d. 765.
7. Mūsā al-Kāẓim, d. 799. (versus Ismācīl)
8. cAlī al-Riḍā, d. 818.
9. Muḥammad al-Taqī, d. 835.
10. cAlī al-Naqī, d. 868.
11. Hasan al-cAskarī, d. 873.
12. Muhammad al-Mahdī, disappeared in 873.

During the course of the ninth century, the Ismācīlīs found adherants primarily among the more radical type of Shīcīs (known in Arabic as ghulāt, "extremists"); by the end of that century their movement had assumed a revolutionary character and had already achieved minor success in southern Iraq, where the Ismācīlīs Qarmatians had fomented revolt among the peasants. The Twelver Shīcīs developed, in the meantime, into a more moderate movement. Particularly after the disappearance of the twelfth Imām in 873, the Twelvers were in a better position than the Ismācīlīs to come to terms with the existing authorities, since they no longer advocated the claims of an earthly Imām but now simply awaited the return of the the "Expected One."

In the first decades of the tenth century, violent outbreaks were instigated by the Ismācīlīs in Syria, where the Qarmatians created havoc among the bedouin, and in Ifrīqiya, where the Fāṭimids came to power in 909 with Berber support, overthrowing the Aghlabid government. It was the latter success which was by far the more important in the long run, since the new Fāṭimid state developed rapidly into an empire, engulfing first the areas west of Ifrīqiya and then, from 969, Egypt and a large part of Syria as well as Western Arabia and Yemen. After their conquest of Egypt, the Fāṭimids transferred their seat of power from Ifrīqiya to Egypt, where they constructed a new capital, the city of Cairo. From 969 until its final dissolution in 1171, the Fāṭimid empire was Egyptian-based.

Under the Fāṭimids Egypt entered one of the most brilliant periods in its history. Egypt was now not simply an independent amirate but the center of a great empire comprising North Africa, most of Syria (including Palestine), and the shores of the Red Sea. Hegemony over the Hijāz made the Fāṭimids protectors of the two holy cities, Mecca and Medina, a role which brought enormous prestige within the Islamic world at large. The new city of Cairo became a religious center in its own right. The great mosque of al-Azhar, which was constructed in 971, was developed into a center of learning of major importance.

Even though the great majority of the population living within the Fāṭimid empire were Sunnī Muslims, the Fatimids themselves remained faithful to the principles of Ismācīlī Shīcism and to the objectives of the revolutionary movement which had brought them to power. The ultimate objective was to overthrow the Abbasid caliphate and to establish the supremacy of the cAlid line throughout the world of Islam. The Fāṭimids sought to accomplish this objective through three closely related means: military expansion, commercial expansion, and subversive propaganda in lands not under their rule.

The main thrust of the Fātimid military expansion was eastward through Syria in the direction of Baghdad and the central and eastern lands. The Fātimids attributed great importance to their army, which at the time of their conquest of Egypt had numbered, according to one source, 1,000,000 men, mostly Berbers. The Berber forces remained the most important element in the Fātimid army for half a century (until 1021), after which soldiers of other nationalities began to assume a larger role. The Fātimid advance into Syria began immediately after the conquest of Egypt; although the Fātimids never won Syria as a whole, they managed to acquire a substantial part of it. The further advance of the Fātimids eastward was prevented by the Buwayhids, who although Shī^cis were Twelvers and thus in conflict religiously with the Fātimids. The Abbasid caliphate was thus, ironically, saved from disaster at the hands of Shī^cī conquerors by Shī^cī protectors.

The expansion of Fātimid commerce was more successful than the military offensive eastward. The Fātimids succeeded in building up the Red Sea trade route as the primary artery of international (east-west) trade, thereby luring this trade away from the Persian Gulf. In this way they were helped to some extent by the political decentralization of the central lands under the Buwayhids, owing partly to the Buwayhid policy of dividing the realm up among members of the ruling family and partly to the spread of the iqtā^c system. As the power of the military increased in the central lands, both amīrs and high-ranking officers began to interfere in the international trade in order to obtain profits for themselves. This subjected the merchant class to constant perils and insecurity. The Fātimids, on the other hand, offered strong, highly centralized government and protection and maximum freedom to merchants. Of all periods in Arab history, merchants probably enjoyed greatest freedom of operation and the least interference from government in the early Fātimid period (up to around 1050). A greatly expanded Egyptian navy assured protection on the waters of the eastern Mediterranean, and merchants from the Italian commercial republics of Amalfi, Venice and Genoa were encouraged to trade in Fatimid-controlled ports. By opening eastern markets to Italian merchants, the Fātimids broke down the wall that had long separated Western Europe commercially from the Islamic world and inaugurated a new area of Mediterranean trade. The prosperity of Fātimid Egypt became famous all over Europe, and European travellers of the eleventh century described the splendour of the mosques and palaces of Cairo and the magnificence of the great bazaars of both Cairo and Alexandria.

Thanks to the favorable conditions for trade provided by the Fātimids, the bourgeoisie prospered under their rule; the transition from a mercantile economy to a feudal one dominated by the military, which was already far advanced in the central and eastern lands, was delayed for about a century in the case of Egypt. Something of the old glitter of early Abbasid times now shown forth from Cairo. The heyday of the bourgeoisie, though destined in time to come to an end, was not yet entirely over. The freedom afforded to merchants extended not only to the great international merchants but to local merchants as well. Industry flourished. In particular, Egyptian textiles became more famous--and more on demand--than ever. Economic activity was further stimulated by a steady supply of gold, made possible by the Fātimid ascendancy in North Africa until the mid-eleventh century.

Fātimid commercial expansion eastward was accompanied by a spread of Ismaʿīlī propaganda. Ismaʿīlī communities were established in far away North India, where they were to develop into permanent sects. The seeds of Ismaʿilism were also sown in Yemen. It was in these areas, rather than in Egypt and North Africa, that the far future of Ismaʿīlī Shīʿism was to lie. In keeping with their objective of promoting subversion in the lands not under their rule, the Fātimids built up a vast propaganda machine, called the daʿwa, the headquarters of which were in Cairo. (The term daʿwa refers to the propagation of Islam. As the Fātimids considered Ismaʿīlī doctrine to be the true form of Islam, they applied this term to their propaganda effort.) The daʿwa had two purposes: to rally all Ismaʿilis solidly behind the Fātimid caliphate, and to win non-Ismaʿīlīs over to the Fātimid cause. The agents of the daʿwa were known as dāʿīs. They were organized in pyramidal fashion under a Dāʿī-in-Chief. Dāʿīs were thoroughly trained in Ismaʿīlī doctrine and in techniques of subversion and sent out to all parts of the Islamic world. Thus, the revolutionary techniques and methods of organization which had been developed by radical Shīʿis since Umayyad days were incorporated into the Fatimid state; the daʿwa in fact became a department of the Fatimid government, with the Dāʿī-in-Chief as its head.

Although the period of prosperity of the Fātimid empire can be said to have lasted until the mid-eleventh century (around 1050), the forces of disruption were already at work even before that time. The eccentric behavior of the third Fātimid caliph in Egypt, al-Hākim (996-1021), may be interpreted as a symptom of an internal crisis. Al-Hākim has often been described as deranged, owing to strange measures such as his prohibition of business activities during the daytime and his slaughter of dogs. Religiously, al-Hākim was a fanatic. He prohibited women from appearing in the streets and imposed heavy penalties on non-Muslims, requiring them to wear a special dress and ordering the destruction of many of their churches and synagogues. His crowning deed was his laying claim to be an incarnation of deity. For Sunnīs especially this was the ultimate sacrilege. The crisis which occasioned these actions arose from the fact that the Fātimid political objective and the Ismaʿīlī ideology was not being realized. The Fātimid political objective was the destruction of the Abbasid caliphate and the conquest of Baghdad and, ultimately, all of Muslim Asia, whereas the Ismaʿīlī ideology called for the rule of the Islamic world by an infallible, rightly-guided Imām-Caliph, who would embody all the expectations which Shīʿis had for centuries pinned on the figure of the Mahdī. Al-Hākim's predecessor, al-ʿAzīz, with his close fraternization with non-Muslims and his mundane preoccupation with trade and material prosperity, had not conformed fully to the Ismaʿīlī image of the divinely favored ruler. These failures of the Fātimids to live up to the expectations of their adherents had created unrest and dissatisfaction, threatening the stability of the state. This accounts for al-Hākim's efforts at suppressing dissident groups and his intolerance toward non-Muslims. His claim to incarnation was in keeping with certain Ismaʿīlī tendencies and was probably designed to enhance his authority.

However, despite the method that may be detected in al-Hākim's madness, his measures did not halt the disruptive tendencies at work in the Fātimid empire. Under his successors these tendencies were accelerated; not the least of them was the ascendancy of the military over the government. Al-Hākim himself disappeared in 1021 under strange circumstances; out of the body of followers who had adhered steadfastly to his claim to divinity there emerged in the course of time a religious sect, that of the Druzes.

The great turning point in the history of the Fātimid empire is the so-called Great Calamity (*al-shidda al-ᶜuzmā*), a period of extreme upheaval lasting some fifteen years (1057-72) from which the empire never fully recovered. During this period, struggles between rival factions within the military came to a head, and open warfare broke out in the streets of Cairo working great havoc on the urban scene. The primary contestants in this struggle were the Turkish and Sudanese corps (called in Arabic *mushāriqa* and *sudaniyya*), who had risen to prominence with the gradual fading out of the original Berber troops (*maghāriba*). Along with this turmoil within the military went the collapse of the civilian administration, which had been responsible for the efficient functioning of government during the heyday of the empire. It is said that no less than forty wazīrs held office during this period. Finally, in 1066, a terrible famine broke out, caused by low Nile waters, and lasted for six years, during which time the population was considerably reduced and agricultural production diminished.

These developments were accompanied by losses of territory. Already before the Great Calamity, the Fātimids lost the North African part of their empire to local Berber rulers who declared their allegiance to the Abbasid caliph (1047 or 1049). The coming of new Turkish invaders from the East, namely the Seljuks, resulted in the loss of important footholds in Syria: Aleppo slipped from Fātimid control in 1060, Jerusalem in 1071 and Damascus in 1076.

The period of the Great Calamity was followed by a partial recovery under the dictatorship of Badr al-Jamālī and his son al-Afdal (1073-1121). Badr had been governor of Acre when the despairing Fātimid caliph had invited him to accept the office of wazīr. Himself an Armenian, Badr had in his service an Armenian bodyguard and a loyal and reliable army. These assets he, as wazīr, now used to full advantage by establishing a military autocracy. Rival officers were rounded up and executed, and the Fātimid army regained something of its former stability and effectiveness under the firm command of Badr, who assumed the title of Commander of the Armies (amīr al-juyūsh).

After the death of al-Afdal, new disorders broke out, and the Fatimid caliphate spiraled rapidly to its downfall. Despite its brilliant beginnings, the Fatimid caliphate finally went the way of the Abbasid caliphate before it. An original asset--a strong and seemingly invincible army--became a heavy burden and, in the end, a detriment to efficient government and a prospering economy. With this triumph of the military over the domestic scene, the way was prepared for the onset of feudalism. Just as in Baghdad the domination of the military had produced anarchy, laying the Abbasid caliphate open to invasion from outside, so now, two centuries later, history repeated itself; in the midst of the chaos which prevailed in the last days of the Fātimid caliphate appeared a remarkable figure from outside, the Kurdish general Salah al-Dīn, who not only made himself master over the Fātimid caliphate but in the end abolished it altogether, thereby opening a new chapter in Egypt's history.

The Seljuk Empire (c. 1040-1100)

Around the middle of the eleventh century, as the Fātimid empire was entering its decline, two new empires appeared in the eastern and western parts of the Islamic world. One of these empires, that of the Seljuks, embraced at its peak most of the Fertile Crescent together with the Iranian lands, while the other, that of the Murābits, embraced Morocco, southern Spain, and a large part of Saharan West Africa. Both of these empires were the creations of nomads. Both arose quite rapidly, existed for a relatively short period and then collapsed as rapidly as they had arisen. Both were to have a great impact on the social and cultural life of the lands which they embraced, and the long-range impact of one of them, the Seljuk empire, was to extend even beyond its own proper domain.

The Seljuk empire was the product of a mass movement of Turkish nomads from the Central Asian Steppe into the eastern lands of Islam. Although Turks had begun to filter into the Islamic lands long before their entrance en masse, they had done so in limited numbers and as slaves rather than as conquerors. The mass movement of Turkish nomads began in the second quarter of the eleventh century, when a group of Turkish tribes belonging to a larger Turkish grouping known as the Oghuz Turks crossed the Oxus river into Iran. These nomads were led by chieftains belonging to an aristocratic family called the Seljuks, which name has come to refer to the entire group, chieftains and followers alike. In 1040 the Seljuks became the undisputed masters of Khorasan and then moved steadily westward across Iran into the Tigris-Euphrates valley where they soon put an end to the remaining branches of the Buwayhid ruling family. The city of Baghdad, seat of the Abbasid caliphate, was seized temporarily in 1055 and permanently in 1060.

The caliph and his entourage were initially joyful over this development and received the conquering Seljuk prince, Tughril Bey, with open arms. There was cause for this rejoicing. The Seljuks had been converted to Islam before their wanderings into Iran, the agents of their conversion having been Muslim merchants who had carried Islam into the Steppe. The caliph was thus confronted with Sunnī co-religionists, not Shīʿi pagans. But more than this: the Seljuk leader had declared himself a champion of Sunnī Islam and foe of all heresy. In the caliph's eyes there was only one "heresy" that mattered, namely Shīʿism. The caliph had been obliged to live for some time as best he could under the domination of Shīʿi rulers, namely the Buwayhids, who had reduced his status to that of a puppet monarch. The appearance of a Sunnī conqueror at the gates of Baghdad, with thousands of tough nomadic warriors under his command, therefore signaled liberation of the caliphate from the tutelage of heretics and its restoration to former glory. Indeed, Tughril Bey himself at first gave every appearance of being the caliph's loyal servant and of making the caliph's cause his own; there were strong indications that the Seljuk leader would unleash his forces against the caliphate's remaining enemy-number-one, the Fatimid state, thus winning Egypt and its dependencies back to Abbasid rule and to orthodoxy. Nothing short of the re-integration of the old Abbasid empire seemed to be in Tughril Bey's mind.

But the Seljuk ascendancy soon proved to be a mixed blessing for the caliph. For one thing, it speedily became clear that the role which the caliph would play under the new dispensation, as conceived by Tughril Bey, would be a modest one. Far from becoming true sovereign in the image of the caliphs of old, the caliph was to be a kind of puppet senior partner of the ruling Seljuk prince. The latter, with the title of Sultan, would be in full command, the former would conveniently acquiesce, declaring the prince to be his vicegerent and spokesman in the realm of political affairs and retaining for himself, in addition to the religious duties which he had exercised under the Buwayhids, jurisdiction over the city of Baghdad, which would be constituted as a kind of caliphal "Vatican State." Furthermore, Tughril Bey's attention came to be so taken up with the internal affairs of his newly acquired dominions and with the maintenance of order among his unruly nomads that any major offensive against the Fatimids proved out of the question for the time being.

The main body of westward-moving Turkish nomads, or Turkomans, as they are usually called (just as Arab nomads are called bedouin), migrated into the mountainous regions north of the cultivated plains of the Fertile Crescent. Although they were, to some extent, attracted to these regions by their suitability for grazing, they were also encouraged by the Sultan to move into the north country. The Seljuk leaders were quick to understand the threat which nomads posed for their new empire. The tax structure of the empire, being based on the traditional Islamic pattern, was geared primarily to an agrarian type of economy. A large-scale substitution of a pastoral for an agrarian economy would mean the virtual dismantlement of the state. While in certain areas, especially in eastern Iran, but also in peripheral agricultural areas to the West, the nomadic encroachment upon cultivated land could not be prevented, the Seljuk leaders were determined that their Turkomans would not get the lion's share of the more fertile lands; hence their deliberate encouragement of the northwestward migrations. However, once the Turkomans were ensconced in the northern highlands, independent-minded tribes and ambitious chieftains were more readily tempted to throw off the yoke of the central authority. Dissident tribesmen might also give asylum to rebel princes. The affairs of the north country thus became a major concern to the Sultan.

As the Turkomans migrated into the northern fringes of the empire, the Sultan was in the meantime making every effort to build up the empire from within, following traditional Islamic models. In this he was assisted by the Khorasani notables with whom he had formed an alliance shortly after his initial incursions across the Oxus river. This partnership between the Seljuk ruling family and the Khorasani nobility was advantageous to both parties. The Seljuks themselves had no experience in the art of government and therefore saw the administrative expertise of the Khorasanis as a valuable asset. The Khorasanis on their part welcomed the opportunity to acquire administrative control over the new conquests. Furthermore, being primarily Sunnī, they delighted at the prospect of a Sunnī political triumph. These Khorasanis were, in fact, the perpetuators of a tradition of statecraft going back to Abbasid times and earlier. It was no doubt they who inspired the Seljuks with the dream of a reconstituted Abbasid caliphate under Seljuk auspices.

The preponderance of Khorasanis within the ranks of government gave Khorasan a leading role within the Seljuk empire that is reminiscent of earlier times. The Abbasids had originally been brought to power in the eighth century on the crest of a Khorasani offensive led by Abū Muslim, the men of East Iranian origins (among them the famous Barmakids) had risen to positions of great prominence in the Abbasid government. Similarly, al-Ma'mūn had wrested the caliphate from his brother in 813 with Khorasani support. Now under the Seljuks the "enter Khorasan" theme seemed to be repeating itself.

In addition to incorporating the Khorasani elite into the political structure of their empire, the Seljuks also took over much of the existing armies of the conquered territories, which enabled them to add to their Turkoman soldiery a standing army of the traditional type--i.e., a professional army composed mainly of Turkish slaves. This army, by virtue of its great discipline, proved to be a more effective instrument of the Sultan's will and more reliable as a support for the state. However, a professional army required pay, whereas the Turkoman warriors demanded nothing more than pasturage for their flocks. The latter were thus virtually self-sustaining and continued, despite their unruly tendencies, to be the mainstay of Seljuk strength.

During the reign of Tughril Bey's successor, Alp Arslan (1063-1072), the activities of the Turkomans in the North brought the Seljuks into conflict with the Byzantine army. Some of the Turkomans settled within Byzantine territory, an action which amounted to annexation of the lands involved since Turkoman settlement made it virtually impossible for Byzantine officials to collect taxes there. Alp Arslan did not wish to start trouble with the Byzantines, but preferred rather to neutralize the Byzantine frontier in order to concentrate on what he considered to be the primary business of the Seljuk army, namely overthrowing the Fāṭimids, which he saw as a prelude to uniting the Islamic world for the Abbasid caliph. But the Turkomans forced his hand. In 1071 the inevitable confrontation between Seljuk and Byzantine forces took place, resulting in an overwhelming victory for the Seljuks and the complete destruction of the Byzantine army. This event laid Byzantine territory wide open to the Turkomans, who quickly moved in. In a few years' time Byzantine administration was rooted out of large areas of western Anatolia. Anatolia was on its way to becoming Turkish.

The movement of the Turkomans across the northern territories into Anatolia had important implications for the Arab lands of the Fertile Crescent. The new Anatolian pasturelands and frontiers absorbed a steady flow of Turkomans, as new waves of them poured out of the Asian Steppe. These migrations resulted within a few generations in the Turkification of vast areas that had previously been Greek-speaking and Christian. Had the doors of Anatolia remained closed and had the tidal wave of Turkomans moved southward instead, the effects upon the cultural and linguistic make-up of present-day Syria and Northern Iraq would have been enormous. The feasibility of large-scale Turkoman settlement in the Fertile Crescent lands is purely speculative. However, the fact that such settlements did not occur, that the Fertile Crescent lands were hardly touched by the Turkoman migrations despite their proximity, must surely be regarded as a fact of great importance for the history of these lands. The Arabness of present-day Syria and Iraq should not be taken for granted.

Alp Arslan and his successor (and son) Malik Shāh (1072-1092) were served by a remarkable wazīr named Nizām al-Mulk, to whom some of the most important developments of the Seljuk period are due. Nizām al-Mulk was a Persian who had been trained in the civil service in Khorasan under a previous regime. It was in Khorasan that the bureaucratic legacy of Abbasid times had remained most nearly intact, and Nizām al-Mulk proved to be a zealous advocate of that legacy. Endowed with a keen sense of propriety and social order, Nizām al-Mulk set himself to the task of rebuilding the Islamic state. In pursuing this objective, he was quite clearly inspired by the memory of the early Abbasid empire; his program of reform reflects an underlying wish to bring back the "good old days." However, Nizām al-Mulk was not one to ape an earlier generation. Times had changed, and Nizām al-Mulk was fully aware of the new conditions that had arisen since the early ninth century. He also seems to have been eager to benefit from the lessons of the past and, where possible, to improve upon the system of the early Abbasids.

Two principal measures characterize the reforms of Nizām al-Mulk. One of these was the expansion of *madrasa* education. The madrasa, or religious college, was primarily a means of inculcating Sunnī orthodoxy. It was not in itself an innovation of Nizām al-Mulk, as the first madrasas had been established before his time in the eastern Iranian lands which had escaped the domination of the Buwayhids; however, it is to Nizām al-Mulk that the credit must be given for extending the madrasa system into western Iran and the Fertile Crescent and for making the madrasa the primary teaching institution for a new Sunnī political and social order. During the Buwayhid period, government had become increasingly detached from society. It lacked what one modern authority has called an organic relationship to society as a whole. This was due largely to the heterodox (Shīʿi) leanings of the Buwayhid regime. Even before the Buwayhids, however, earlier regimes had shown themselves to be out of touch on occasion with the sentiments of the main body of Muslims. In the ninth century the Abbasids themselves had sponsored a theology branded as heretical by the majority of ʿulamā'. Nizām al-Mulk had a great appreciation for the role of religion as a social force; it could make and unmake societies.

His reforms were predicated upon the principle that the cause of social cohesion is best served when the government espouses those religious sentiments which are dominant in the society as a whole. Accordingly, it was important to foster orthodoxy within the ranks of government. For this reason the primary purpose of the madrasa, in Nizam al-Mulk's eyes, was to train government personnel. The madrasa graduate would represent a new type of bureaucrat. Unlike the bureaucrats of earlier generations who, more often than not, looked askance at strict orthodoxy, preferring the intellectually more stimulating alternatives offered by the various heretical movements, the new madrasa-trained bureaucrat would be thoroughly grounded in the orthodox religious sciences--i.e., Koran and Hadith studies, Sharīʿa studies, and the like. As bureaucrats of the new type infiltrated the government service, government would assume a more orthodox tone and a link would be forged between government and the orthodox religious establishments.

The other important measure carried out by Nizām al-Mulk was the regularization of the iqtāʿ system. Under the Buwayhids the practice of assigning fiscal rights over given districts to officers in lieu of pay had become so entrenched that, with the coming of the Seljuks, all hope of abolishing the practice was virtually gone. Nizām al-Mulk seems to have realized this and to have adopted the view that the next best measure, the only practicable one under the circumstances, was to bring the granting of iqtāʿs under the firm control of the central government. The iqtāʿ system was a powerful decentralizing force. It militated against one of the most important bases of centralized power: the treasury. Possession of a rich treasury not only gives government great control over the military, rendering the military dependent upon it for its upkeep; it also enables government to expand its bureaucracy and the ruler to maintain a more impressive court. Once the central treasury was reduced to meager proportions, the only remaining way of bolstering the central government was to give it a larger role in the assignment (and re-assignment), registration and supervision of iqtāʿs. The granting of an iqtāʿ gave the grantee complete rights to the tax revenues in the area involved and the authority to collect taxes. However, the central government might see to it that the taxes collected were fairly assessed and that no illegal taxes were levied. It might also make certain that officers received iqtāʿs commensurate with their rank, that proper concern was shown for the maintenance of the productivity of the area involved, that the term of each iqtāʿ was duly observed, and that upon expiration of the term specified the iqtāʿ was reassigned to a qualified person. Under the Buwayhids iqtāʿs had been granted in a somewhat haphazard way such that the conditions pertaining to iqtāʿ grants varied from case to case. Nizām al-Mulk tried to put an end to this confusion by consolidating the various types of iqtāʿ into a single well-defined institution subject to fixed rules and procedures. Thus, the central government would, if Nizām al-Mulk's reforms were successful, have a measure of fiscal control over the empire, although on a different basis than before.

Nizām al-Mulk's reforms did not produce the permanent results which he had envisioned. His measures helped to reenforce the iqtāʿ system and even to extend it, without achieving the hoped for bureaucratic control over it. Thus, feudalism became more entrenched than ever; the iqtāᶜ system, rather than being integrated into a more centralized administrative structure, continued as before to undermine the strength of the central government. As for the madrasas, owing to the rapid disintegration of the Seljuk empire in the early twelfth century, they did not have sufficient time or opportunity to have their intended effect as the training centers of a new corps of bureaucrats. The strong central government which they were to imbue with orthodoxy never materialized.

As feudalism spread and became more consolidated under the Seljuks, it continued to sap the economy of the Fertile Crescent lands and Iran. One of the principal features of the iqtaᶜ system was the temporary nature of the iqtaᶜ grants. The system was based on a belief that the military should not become permanently attached to the land. Thus, an iqtaᶜ grant might be revoked after a certain period of time, and at the death of an iqtaᶜ-holder the grant could not be passed on to heirs in the manner of an ordinary estate. This feature of the iqtāᶜ system made for a very short-sighted and exploitative attitude on the part of iqtāᶜ-holders, who neglected the long-term development of the lands appointed to them and concentrated rather on immediate gains. As a result, irrigation was not properly maintained in many areas, the amount of cultivated land further decreased, and the condition of the peasantry became even more oppressed. Trade also suffered, as the Seljuk state, eager to replace revenues lost through the granting of iqtāᶜs with new sources of income, imposed on merchants a type of taxation known as maks (plural: mukūs), which included duties and sales taxes. Although all merchants suffered from these taxes, the hardest hit were the local merchants, who constituted the middle and lower ranks of the bourgeoisie. Moreover, the military continued to encroach upon the activities of the merchants by undertaking commercial ventures of their own. Along with this economic decline went a breakdown of public health, and there were numerous fresh outbreaks of the bubonic plague.

The frustration of the lower and middle classes gave rise to movements of revolt, the most effective and best organized of which was a branch of the Ismāᶜīlī movement organized by a fiery dāᶜī named Hasan al-Sabbah. Hasan's base of operations was a fortress in Daylam called Alamūt which his armed bands were able to capture in 1090. From Alamūt Hasan directed an underground revolutionary movement which included among its principal activities, missions of assassination. Nizām al-Mulk was himself one of the early victims of the movement (1092). In 1094 Hasan repudiated the accession of al-Mustaᶜli to the throne in Cairo and withdrew his allegiance from the Fatimid state, instituting a "new daᶜwa" in favor of Mustaᶜlī's brother Nizār and his descendants. Meanwhile, the movement spread to other areas, as Hasan's followers managed to seize other fortresses, creating a network of bases. Although the new movement was unable to bring about a real revolution, it did manage to spread terror throughout the eastern Arab lands and Iran.

The Great Seljuk Empire collapsed rapidly after the death of Malik Shāh in 1092, which was also the year of Nizām al-Mulk's death. Its real strength from the beginning had lain in the Turkoman tribes which had placed themselves under the direction of the Seljuk chieftains. As time passed, the Seljuk rulers found themselves more and more embroiled in the affairs of the tribes as well as the affairs of the Seljuk household itself. Once the initial wave of Turkoman migration across the eastern and northern lands had subsided, the centrifugal tendencies of the tribes became pronounced. The allegiance of the tribes to the central power was, as among all nomadic peoples, in principle voluntary; if a tribe found it expedient to strike out on some independent venture, it did not hesitate to do so. Much of the energy of the Seljuk Sultāns was therefore spent on trying to maintain their leadership over the tribes and to suppress revolts. Their success in this effort lessened with the passing of time. To make matters worse, the Seljuk family itself was beset with internal divisions. The Seljuks inherited from their Steppe homeland a conception of empire as the patrimony of the extended family. The Great Sultans ruled as first among equals within the family. So long as a member of the family was strong enough to maintain this primacy, a semblance of unity was maintained. But upon the death of Malik Shāh the impulse to divide up the inheritance prevailed. This fissiparous tendency was accelerated by the fact that various Seljuk princes had acquired large iqtāᶜs, especially those iqtāᶜs which had been taken over from the Buwayhids.

Malik Shāh's death was followed by a struggle for power between various factions of the Seljuk army, headed mostly by members of the Seljuk family. In the course of this struggle the Great Seljuk empire was dismembered; there arose in its place a network of lesser states, some larger than others, but none of them vast in their extent. These states had one important feature in common: they were all purely military. In each of them there ruled a military commander or amīr supported by his own army. This was a heyday for military adventurers. Any man strong or charismatic enough to place himself at the head of a band of warriors might enter into the fray. Most of the commanders who emerged initially from the struggle with territories under their command were of the Seljuk line, but many were not; in subsequent years non-Seljuk rulers became more and more common. Since an aura of legitimacy had been associated with the Seljuk name, many of these adventurers posed as regents--or, to use the Turkish title, atabegs--ruling on behalf of a Seljuk minor. The title stuck and came to be used even after regency ceased to be a fact; it became a title denoting prestige and legitimate power. The great majority of these adventurers, if not of the Seljuk line, were at least Turkish. Only in the eastern Iranian lands was a semblance of the Great Seljuk empire created under the Seljuk prince Sanjar (1118-1157). Elsewhere opportunism and instability prevailed. In the Fertile Crescent lands, this situation continued until, under the stimulus of the Crusades and with the effective leadership of the Zangids, a new unity was to emerge.

The Arab-Islamic World in ca1100: Seljuks, Fatimids, Murabits

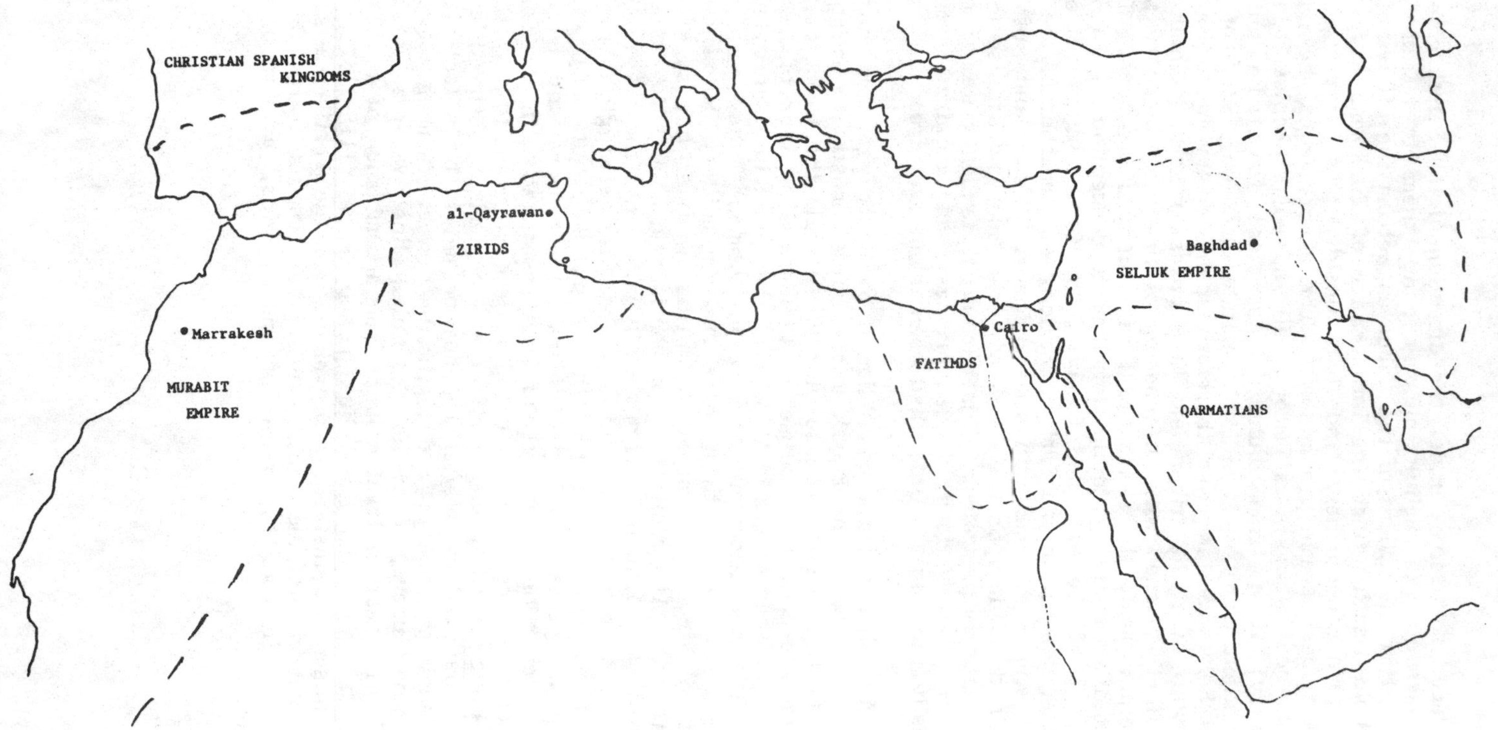

The Murābit Empire (c. 1070-1150)

At about the same time that the Seljuk armies were victoriously entering the gates of Baghdad, an important movement was taking shape in the far-away Saharan regions of West Africa. There a religious reformer named Abd Allāh ibn Yāsīn established a fraternity of religious warriors, whose stronghold was a fortress located, it is believed, on an island in the lower Senegal river. From the Arabic term for this fortress, ribāt, is derived the name by which these warriors are commonly known, murābit (plural: murābitūn). These Murābits were Berbers belonging to the Lamtūna tribe, which had roamed for some time between Morocco and the Negro kingdoms south of the Sahara. Ibn Yāsīn imposed on his warriors the strictest discipline. As a condition of admission into the fraternity, each new member had to undergo a hundred lashes as absolution for all former sins. Thereafter a strict observance of Mālikī law, as administered by Ibn Yāsīn, was required, and harsh penalties were applied against offenders.

The Murābits soon became a powerful instrument. Ibn Yāsīn was careful to delegate military leadership to one of the Berber chieftains and retain only the spiritual leadership of the movement for himself. Under their Berber generals, the Murābits began to attack first the black people to the South, who were as yet pagans, and then their own fellow Berbers, whom they regarded as apostates. Soon the Murābits succeeded in subduing all of their fellow Berbers, making themselves masters of the entire Western Sahara. As more and more Berber men were absorbed into the movement, the number of warriors increased rapidly; the Murābit army soon found itself poised for expansion into the Islamic territory to the North. The expansion northward was justified on the basis of the moral laxity of those in power. The Murābits had become an instrument of religious reform beyond their own homeland.

Ibn Yāsīn did not himself live to see the full establishment of the Murābit empire, although he may have sensed in his last days that it was in the making. At the time of his death in 1059 Murābit power had encompassed southern Morocco up to the High Atlas. Ibn Yāsīn's spiritual leadership was within a few years taken over by the Mālikī scholars, or fuqahā', as a group. Military command was assumed by the Berber general, Abu Bakr ibn ᶜUmar. The Murābits were now ruled by men of Lamtuna nobility.

Under Abū Bakr, Murābit forces moved north of the Atlas Mountains and gained mastery over Central Morocco. There, on the plain below the High Atlas, they founded a new capital city, Marrakesh, which was to become a leading center of activity until the present day. Shortly after the building of the new city had started, the command of the Murābit army was taken over by Abū Bakr's cousin, Yūsuf ibn Tāshfīn. Fez was conquered in 1075, and soon thereafter all of Morocco as well as the Western part of what is now Algeria fell under Murābit control. Finally, in 1086 Ibn Tāshfīn crossed the Strait of Gibraltar into Spain in response to an appeal for help from several Muslim rulers of Spain following the capture of Toledo by the Christian ruler of Castile. The Christian rulers of northern Spain were making startling advances in their campaign of reconquest. Ibn Tāshfīn brought their advance to a temporary halt by inflicting a decisive defeat on the Christian forces at the Battle of Zallāqa in 1086. In 1091 Ibn Tāshfīn assumed direct rule over the whole of Muslim Spain. The Murābit empire now stretched all the way from the Senegal in the South to the middle of Spain in the north.

Having become ruler of such a vast empire, Ibn Tāshfīn was obliged to define more carefully his relationship to the Abbasid Caliph in the East, who was enjoying new prestige under Seljuk auspices. Political rivalry with the Fātimids coupled with deep-set devotion to the Sunnī Mālikī school of law ruled out any dealings with the Shīʿī state. In the face of the Sunnī revival in the Seljuk lands, Ibn Tāshfīn seems not to have seriously entertained the idea of forming a separate Sunnī polity. Instead, he chose to incorporate his empire within the universal Sunnī state system by having the Abbasid caliph's name mentioned in mosque services and by regarding his own office as having been conferred on him by the caliph. Accordingly, the title which Ibn Tāshfīn assumed for himself was amīr al-muslimīn, not amīr al-mu'minīn, the latter being a title reserved for the caliph alone.

Ibn Tāshfīn died in 1106, leaving his empire to his son ʿAlī ibn Yūsuf (1106-1143). The son, unlike his father, was "born in the purple," that is to say, born and raised amid the luxuries of courtly life and far-removed from the harsh nomadic existence which had shaped the character of his father. Given to religious studies and pious exercises, ʿAlī cared little about matters of government; the historian al-Marrākushī goes so far as to say that "his neglect of the interest of his subjects was utter and entire." In keeping with his strong religious inclinations, ʿAlī allowed the Mālikī fuqahā' to exercise almost complete control over him.

The immense pre-eminence accorded to the Mālikī fuqahā' is a characteristic feature of the Murābit period as a whole. To an extent the Maghrib experienced under Murābit rule the same sort of development toward greater religious--and consequently cultural--uniformity as was taking place in the eastern lands under the Seljuks. The fuqahā', like their counterparts in the East (the ʿulamā'), were, as the custodians of the Sharīʿa, representatives of the divine order of society. As Mālikīs they belonged to the larger Sunnī community, and as they gained greater power Sunnī orthodoxy became more entrenched. Like the Islamic lands to the East, the Maghrib had been subjected to a variety of religious tendencies since the days of the Arab conquests, and in the tenth century the Fātimids had sown the seeds of Ismāʿīlism, that ever present "heresy." It required a powerful state such as that of the Murābits to give Sunnī orthodoxy the boost which it needed in order to attain a true political triumph.

However, the orthodoxy propagated by the fuqahā' was in one major respect very different from the orthodoxy of the East: it was strongly anti-intellectual. Whereas theology, and with it a certain intellectualism, had triumphed among the ʿulamā' of the East, it was roundly condemned by the fuqahā' of the Maghrib. The latter allowed law alone as the proper preoccupation of pious minds, all else was strictly off limits. This legalistic bent is suggested by the very term by which Maghribī religious scholars were generally known, fuqahā' ("lawyers"). (The term ᶜulamā' means "men of learning"; strictly speaking, the terms are somewhat interchangeable.) The most dramatic expression of the anti-intellectualism of the Maghribi fuqahā' was their demand during the reign of ᶜAlī ibn Yūsuf that all the writings of al-Ghazzālī, a great eastern theologian, be burned.

The Maghribī orthodox movement was not as yet tied to the madrasa. Religious learning was still developed within the setting of the mosque (especially the central mosques of Fez, Marrakesh and Toledo), along informal lines reminiscent of pre-madrasa learning in the East. The madrasa with its broad curriculum of religious studies was not to appear in the Maghrib until the fourteenth century.

The Murābit army, which originally had consisted of warriors from the Lamtūna tribe, was in the course of the conquests in Morocco and Spain enlarged through the addition of mercenaries. The use of mercenaries was required by the tribal character of the original army. The Murābit rulers dared not include large numbers of warriors from tribes other than the Lamtūna lest inter-tribal competition cause the army to disintegrate. Thus, non-Lamtūna Berbers could be recruited only to a limited extent, and these had to be placed under the firm command of Lamtūna chiefs. The Lamtūna warriors themselves were not sufficiently numerous to bear the entire burden of warfare as the conquests proceeded. Hence the need for mercenaries. "The logic of the tribal state requires that when the rulers sense the military insufficiency of their own group they should seek reinforcement from elements with no tribal ties in their territory" (Abun-Nasr, A History of the Maghrib, p. 101). Not only were mercenaries more reliable than tribal warriors, they were prized for their orderly line tactics in battle and were useful for their collection of taxes among hostile tribes. Mercenary soldiers were by no means a new phenomenon. They had been utilized for generations by the Muslim rulers of Spain. Those who served the Murābit state as a rule were mostly Christians. They were stationed in garrisons in the vicinity of Marrakesh and were allowed to build churches and to exercise their religion freely.

The government of the Murābits was of the militarized type common also in the East. No distinction was made between military and administrative functions; most administrative posts were filled by military officers. There was not in the West that highly developed bureaucratic tradition which Nizām al-Mulk had sought to revive under the Seljuks. The two primary functions of the Murabit state were the administration of the army and the collection of taxes. The army appears to have been maintained primarily from the government treasury, not, as was becoming increasingly common in the East, through iqtāᶜs. The commanding positions in the army were assigned to Lamtūna chieftains, who constituted the Murābit aristocracy. Over them stood the amīr al-muslimīn as the supreme head of the community.

The political unification of Muslim Spain and the Maghrib under Murābit rule made possible an unprecedented intermingling of peoples of the two areas. The result for the Maghrib, and particularly Morocco, was a rapid diffusion of Andalusian civilization in the cities. Many Spanish architects, craftsmen and men of culture made their way into Morocco; Fez saw its famous Qarawiyyīn mosque enlarged in the Andalusian style, and Tlemcen witnessed the construction of its Great Mosque on the model of the Great Mosque of Cordova.

Urban life, benefitting from lively trade and industry, flourished. Marrakesh mushroomed into a bustling center of activity. Fez, Morocco's most ancient major city, experienced the most remarkable growth of its history thus far. The Maghribī cities were not adversely affected by the advance of the nomadic Lamtūna. The movements of the Lamtūna did not represent a massive nomadic tidal wave comparable to the Turkish movements under the Seljuks. Furthermore, much of the population of the Maghrib was, in any case, already nomadic, or at least semi-nomadic, and the people of the cities had long since learned to deal with surrounding tribes. The economy into which the Maghribī cities were integrated was not as solidly agrarian as was the case with most of the great eastern cities.

The continuing development of urban culture meant a further strengthening of the Arabic language. Although the process of arabization in the Maghrib was to be greatly spurred by the coming of bedouin tribes from the East, it was also furthered by the primacy of the Arabic language in urban cultural life. The infusion of Andalusian literary influences reinforced this primacy all the more.

The civilization of Spain, which the Murābit rulers absorbed rapidly after their conquest of Spain and which they helped to disseminate in the Maghrib, had in the end a seductive effect upon the Murābit aristocracy and ruling elite. Originally austere and hardy, they were soon softened by the niceties of the refined civilization which now surrounded them. The end result was a greater disposition to the pleasures of cultured life than to the call of battle. The Murābits were losing their original esprit de corps. This rendered them vulnerable to charges of corruption levelled against them by an opposition movement, the Muwaḥḥids, whose military challenge they were unable to meet. Upon the death of ᶜAlī ibn Yūsuf, the Murābit empire collapsed within the space of a few years. Hemmed in by the forces of the Spanish Christian reconquest from the North and by the Muwaḥḥids in the South, the Murābits found themselves hopelessly outdone. The final undoing of the Murābit state owes much to the dynamism of the Muwaḥḥid leader, Ibn Tūmart. The rise of the Muwaḥḥids will be described in a later section.

Despite the rapidity of the Murābit collapse, the achievements of the Murābits are considerable. They ushered in Morocco's first period of greatness by unifying the country, which they had found split into petty tribal chieftaincies, and by making it the basis of a large empire. Thus, they left to posterity the concept of Morocco (the Western Maghrib) as a political unity in its own right. By unifying Morocco, they paved the way for their successors, the Muwaḥḥids; although Maghribī civilization entered its most illustrious age under the latter dynasty, it may be said that the Muwaḥḥids stood upon the shoulders of the Murābits.

The Hilalian Migrations and the Arabization of the Maghrib

The Murābits, as we have seen, never succeeded in dominating the entire Maghrib. Only that part of the Maghrib which comprises what is now Morocco and western Algeria came under their rule. The rest of the Maghrib underwent a very different fate. Shortly before the western Maghrib was overrun by the Murābits coming out of the Sahara, the eastern Maghrib fell victim to another invading people, Arab bedouin coming from regions surrounding the Nile Valley. Since the leading tribe among these bedouin were the Banu Hilal, the movement as a whole is frequently referred to by historians as the Hilalian invasion, or migration, and the people themselves are described as Hilalian Arabs. Another tribe which achieved prominence somewhat later were the Banu Sulaym, although even they are usually subsumed under the epithet "Hilalian." The ultimate origin of these tribes appears to have been in the Najd (in Central Arabia). However, for several decades prior to their arrival in the Maghrib around 1050, they had been living on the fringes of the Nile Valley, where they had been disturbing the local cultivators. The Fātimid ruler of Egypt, it is said, lured them westward with the prospect of more readily obtainable pasturage, his purpose being not only to rid Egypt of the bedouin menace but also to inflict that menace on the ruler of Ifriqiya, a former vassal of the Fātimids who had declared his allegiance to the Abbasid caliphate, as a punishment for his perfidy.

The strategem met with spectacular success. The Hilalian bedouin arrived in Ifriqiya in full force in 1052, defeating the army of the local ruler and causing the region to be fragmented into a number of minor principalities. Thus, while the western Maghrib was being integrated along with Spain under Murābit rule, the eastern Maghrib was disintegrating politically under the Hilalian impact. Unlike the nomadic Berbers, who were able to form powerful solidarities and thus erect empires, these Arab bedouin spread out in various directions in search of pasturage, thus remaining divided into smaller units. In this respect, they stand in sharp contrast to the original Arabs who marked across North Africa under the banner of the newly arisen Islam. The contrast also extends to the very nature and scope of the two Arab invasions. The Hilalian invasion was a bedouin phenomenon pure and simple, undirected by an urbanized Arab leadership comparable to that which had been supplied, earlier, by Mecca and Medina; and it entailed a much vaster transference of bedouin population into the Maghrib, one which was, in fact, to take place over three centuries (1050 to 1350), in contrast to the earlier Arab movement which, in comparison seems like a blitzkrieg. The Hilalian invasion in 1050 was thus the beginning of a long-term demographic phenomenon. The fame of the pasturelands of the Maghrib spread all over the Nile Valley and Arabia, bringing tribe after tribe in search of a better life in this new world. The Hilalian tide did not stop in Ifriqiya but continued westward, probably after the fall of the Murābits, into Morocco, where the bedouin found pasturage in certain parts of the countryside, undermining but not replacing the political order created by the successors of the Murābits, the Muwahhids.

This long-term demographic phenomenon was to contribute enormously to the process of arabization of the Maghrib. It is important to bear in mind that the arabization of the Maghrib was, as was suggested in the previous section, the result of two complementary developments connected with the two invasions into the Maghrib during the eleventh century, the Murābit in the West and the Hilalian in the East. In the aftermath of these invasions, the Maghrib was divided into two halves which were subject to two different processes of arabization. The Murabits, although Berbers, fostered the development of Arabic literary culture, which was inspired mainly by influenced from Spain; the Islamic religious sciences cultivated by the influential Maliki fuqaha' found expression exclusively in Arabic. Against this pre-eminence of the Arabic language, the Berber language had no chance of maintaining a position of importance within urban culture. Consequently, the Berbers were subject to the same forces of arabization that had been at work among the non-Arab populace of Egypt and the Fertile Crescent. In the eastern Maghrib, a new kind of arabization occurred, one which influenced the larger countryside outside the cities and complemented the high-cultural arabization going on within urban society. The Hilalian Arabs were the agents of this arabization, partly by virtue of their representing a sizeable new element within the population, partly by virtue of their mingling and intermarrying with the nomadic Berber population. This intermingling was fostered by two factors: (1) a common nomadic way of life and (2) a common religious allegiance, namely Islam. When this intermingling occurred, the result was generally a predominance of the Arabic language over the Berber.

As in Egypt, arabization in the Maghrib is difficult to trace with precision. We are unable--and will probably always be unable--to put our finger on a point in time when the Maghrib as a whole assumed a predominantly Arab character. The periodization adopted in this book (and explained in the Introduction) assumes that that point had been reached--if not fully, then nearly--by 1250, so that one may regard the present-day Arab lands as in place from that date onwards and ready to be treated as the primary object of our study. 1250 thus becomes the terminus a quo for a history of the Arab lands as presently constituted for two reasons: (1) the assumption by the Maghrib of a predominantly Arab character qualifying it for inclusion within the Arab lands and (2) the Mongol invasions, which furthered the separation of the eastern Arab lands, with the exception of Iraq, from Iran (a subject which will be discussed in Chapter Seven).

The two types of arabization, though initially prominent in different parts of the Maghrib, in the long term made an impact, complementing each other, throughout the entire region. High-cultural arabization had been operative in the eastern Maghrib since the coming of Islam to this area. The achievement of the Murābits consisted in their acceleration of this process in the western Maghrib under Hispano-Arab influence. The more ethnological type of arabization, which began in the eastern Maghrib, was, on the other hand, to spread into the western part as Arab bedouin began to pour into that area during the period of Muwaḥḥid rule and after.

It is important to emphasize that the assumption that the Maghrib had assumed a predominantly Arab character by 1250 or thereabouts is to be distinguished from the claim that it assumed a wholly Arab character. It has not assumed a wholly Arab character even to this day, as there still remain Berber-speaking enclaves here and there, especially in mountainous areas (as the Atlas mountains of Morocco and the Aures mountains of Algeria). These Berber enclaves have a position in Maghribi society something like that of the Kurds in Iraqi society or the Nubians in Egyptian society in that their specifically Berber culture is marginal to that of the larger society of which they are a part. When a Berber wishes to enter the mainstream of life in a country of the Maghrib, for example by receiving a formal education, he must acquire a native facility with the Arabic language, that is to say, to become arabized.

Another point to be noted is that the arabization of the Maghrib did not mean the immediate demise of the Berbers as a source of politically dominant factions within the Maghribi population. It is a fact that even after 1250 the ruling dynasties of the Maghrib continued for three centuries to be of Berber origin. This ascendency of Berber aristocracies, which had deep roots in North African history, should not mislead us into thinking that Maghribi society retained a predominantly Berber rather than Arab character. Insofar as language is a criterion, the Arab influence reigned supreme even under Berber dynasties. If we wish to probe more deeply the characteristics of Maghribi culture, we will find a complex of Berber and Arab elements with the latter decisively outweighing the former. That Maghribi Arab culture has features which distinguish it from the culture of the eastern Arab lands is undeniable, a fact which is no doubt explainable, at least in part, in terms of Berber influences. Furthermore, it should be noted that the Berber dynasties which ruled the Maghrib after 1250 had to rely heavily on the support of the bedouin tribes. Since these tribes often behaved unpredictably, this contributed to the instability and fragility of the Berber regimes.

One final word is in order concerning the effects of the Hilalian migrations. Historians tend to regard these migrations as having had a long-term adverse effect on the economy of the Maghrib, owing mainly to the large-scale transformation of cultivated land into pastureland and the consequent reduction of agricultural productivity. This, in turn, may account for the failure of Maghribi society after 1250 to produce relatively complex, geographically extended polities on the order of the Murābit and Muwahhid empires. The Maghrib, it seems, was compelled by ecological reversals to settle for more localized, simple political structures. We shall return in Chapter five to the subject of decline of agricultural productivity as it affected the larger world of Islam and its implications for political and social life.

The Ayyūbid Empire (1171-1250)

The collapse of the Fātimid empire in the second half of the twelfth century paved the way for the emergence of a new Syro-Egyptian empire, that founded by Salāh al-Dīn (Saladin) al-Ayyūbī. Whereas the Fatimid empire had been established by an army of North African origin, the Ayyubid empire was the creation of Syrian forces, and the rise of Salah al-Dīn to power must be understood in the context of Syrian developments from the beginning of the twelfth century.

There were two primary determinants in the political history of Syria in the early part of the twelfth century: (1) rivalries between petty Muslim principalities, and (2) the establishment of new states by Crusaders from Western Europe. The Muslim states were centered on the principal cities of Syria and Mesopotamia and were ruled mainly by Turks, either atabegs or Seljuk princes. Some, however, especially the smaller ones, were under the control of Arab chieftains. These states had emerged out of the disintegration of the Great Seljuk empire. They were all essentially military regimes, and there developed among them a very complex system of political relationships. Each ruler ambitiously aspired to add further territory to his domain in order to increase his power and prestige, but this could be done only at the expense of others, and such a military adventure might incur the hostility not only of one but of several adversaries. Because of their divisiveness the Muslim rulers were unable to offer a united resistance to the armies of the Crusaders which marched down the coast of Syria at the end of the eleventh century and established a series of Crusader states: the Principality of Antioch, the County of Edessa, the County of Tripoli, and the Kingdom of Jerusalem. In fact, instead of encountering stiff resistance from the Muslim rulers, the crusading princes soon found some of these rulers ready to form alliances with them in order to gain advantage over Muslim rivals. Thus, the Crusaders themselves became embroiled in the complex politics of the area.

This state of affairs changed in the second quarter of the twelfth century, when the amir of Mosul, a Turkish atabeg named Zangi, commenced a successful campaign of expansion and created a powerful new state which embraced northern Mesopotamia and northern Syria. This proved to be the beginning of a movement of Muslim unification, which in time profoundly altered the relationship between Muslims and Christians. Zangi's crowning achievement was his capture of Edessa from the Crusaders in 1144. The expansion of the new Zangid state reached its peak under Zangi's son, Nūr al-Dīn (1146-1174). After Nūr al-Dīn's capture of Damascus in 1154, the Crusaders were for the first time confronted with a single, powerful adversary. This new situation engendered a mood of holy war, as the confrontation came to be viewed more and more in religious terms. The era of petty politics had ended, and a new era of Muslim-Christian warfare had begun.

In Syria, the Muslim and Christian forces faced each other more or less as equals, neither side being strong enough to prevail over the other. The decisive factor in the ensuing struggle would be the control of Egypt. There internal disorder and the decrepit condition of the Fatimid caliphate invited intervention. Nūr al-Dīn was the first to respond, but the Crusaders followed in short order. In 1163 Nūr al-Dīn sent a Syrian army under the command of a Kurdish general named Shīrkūh to Egypt on the pretext of restoring order on behalf of the Fatimid caliph. A few years later (1168), in Shīrkūh's absence, a

Crusader army marched on Egypt, captured Bilbays and began a siege of Cairo. Shīrkūh returned promptly and the Crusaders withdrew. Shīrkūh was then appointed wazīr by the Fātimid caliph, thereby acquiring full power over Egypt's internal affairs. At his death in 1169, he was succeeded in this role by his nephew Salāh al-Dīn.

The position which Salāh al-Dīn inherited from his uncle was ambiguous: nominally wazīr of the Fātimid caliph, he was in fact really the representative of a Syrian power. In 1171 Salāh al-Dīn decided to terminate the first role by doing away with the Fātimid caliphate itself. By officially abolishing this institution, he ended a two-century long chapter in Egypt's history. Egypt was now ruled in the name of the Abbasid caliph. Salāh al-Dīn's responsibility toward Nūr al-Dīn was not so easily brushed off. However, the death of the latter in 1174 gave Salāh al-Dīn a free hand. He was now not only master of Egypt but a sovereign ruler in his own right.

With the passing away of Nūr al-Dīn, the unity which had been built up under his rule and that of his father quickly collapsed. A new unity was now to emerge under the aegis of Salāh al-Dīn, with Egypt as its primary base. For a full dozen years after Nūr al-Dīn's death, Salāh al-Dīn's attention was taken up almost entirely with the consolidation of his power in Syria. Egypt was firmly under his control, but in Syria various contenders rushed in to fill the vacuum left by Nūr al-Dīn. In dealing with these would-be rulers, Salāh al-Dīn combined diplomacy and warfare, using the latter only as a last resort. His success in gradually winning the allegiance of most of the leading men of Syria has been attributed by the noted British scholar H. A. R. Gibb to his remarkable personal qualities, particularly his sense of honor, his faithfulness to his word and his strong religious commitment, all of which commanded admiration and respect.

With Muslim Syria firmly in hand, Salāh al-Dīn was ready in 1187 to concentrate on the war against the Crusaders. In that year he achieved a smashing victory over the Crusaders at the Battle of Hittīn, which resulted in the capture of Jerusalem and the restoration of that city to Islamic rule. This event provoked the famous Third Crusade, in which some of the royalty of Europe participated, including the famous Richard the Lion-hearted of England. But although the Crusaders were able to recapture the important fortress of Acre, they were unable to achieve their main objective--the winning back of Jerusalem. Instead, after hard fighting, they settled in 1192 for a truce with Salāh al-Dīn, by virtue of which they retained only the coastal region of Palestine. Salāh al-Dīn died the following year.

From the perspective of Islamic history, Salāh al-Dīn's most important achievement was not his victory over the Crusaders, who were more a nuisance than a serious threat to the Islamic world as a whole, but rather his restoration of Egypt as the center of a Muslim empire in the eastern Mediterranean and his revivification and strengthening of Sunnī Islam as the dominant faith in the lands formerly ruled by the Fātimids. Under Salāh al-Dīn, the madrasa system, a legacy from Seljuk times which had already implanted in Syria by Nūr al-Dīn, was further expanded and carried into Egypt. It became a principal means whereby orthodox Sunnī doctrine supplanted Ismāᶜīlism, and even the Azhar, which had previously been a center of Ismāᶜīlī education, was now transformed into a bastion of orthodoxy.

Another legacy from Seljuk times came to prevail in Egypt under Salāh al-Dīn and his successors: the iqtāᶜ system. The iqtāᶜ was not altogether new to Egypt, as the later Fātimids had granted some iqtāᶜs to their officers. However, the rise of Salāh al-Dīn to power gave the further development of the system a strong impetus. The army which Salāh al-Dīn brought to Egypt was alien to the country, and its officers were accustomed to the iqtāᶜ system as practiced in Syria since Seljuk times. This army was made up of a core of Kurdish cavalrymen, who functioned as a kind of bodyguard, together with a larger body of Turkish cavalrymen. As for the Fātimid army, part of it was absorbed into Salāh al-Dīn's army, while the remainder was driven out of Egypt. The iqtāᶜ system which Salāh al-Dīn implemented in Egypt more or less approximated that which Nizām al-Mulk had envisaged for the Seljuk domains. Not all the land was transformed into iqtāᶜs under Salāh al-Dīn and his successors; moreover, some land remained in private hands. Feudalism thus did not engulf the entire country. The period was still one of transition. Furthermore, the iqtāᶜ-holders in Egypt and Syria seem to have had a more responsible attitude toward their land than elsewhere, being required, for example, to keep irrigation systems in working condition so as to keep up the level of production. As a result, agriculture fared rather well.

After Salāh al-Dīn's death, the Syrian part of his empire broke up into a network of small principalities ruled by his Ayyūbid relatives--sons, nephews and cousins. Egypt, however, remained unified under a single ruler. Furthermore, the ruler of Egypt, by virtue of his superior power, enjoyed a certain preeminence over his relatives in Syria, thanks to which a measure of unity was maintained within the Ayyūbid household under Egyptian auspices. Consequently, the Ayyūbid empire did not suffer the complete dismemberment which befell the Seljuk empire after the death of Malik Shāh.

Economically, Egypt and Syria flourished under the Ayyūbids. Precious metals were on the increase and coins plentiful. Trade flourished, and the population of some cities increased. Peace with the Crusaders allowed a resumption of commercial relations with Europe, in particular with the Italian republics. Trade with Europe was, in fact, on the increase, as a result of the increased demand for eastern goods stimulated by the Crusades. The Italian merchants were allowed to live in Ayyūbid territories with certain privileges, such as freedom of commerce and the right to have their own commercial warehouses and quarters. Among the commercial operations in the East, the spice trade became all-important, owing partly to new markets in Europe. During the Ayyūbid period, an association of rich merchants known as the Kārimīs, whose origins went back to Fātimid times, achieved a virtual monopoly on the spice trade, which was to make them a leading force in economic affairs for some time to come.

The Ayyūbid period also saw some important cultural developments. It was under the Ayyūbids that Egypt and Syria assumed that cultural primacy within the Arab culture zone which they were to enjoy thereafter. In both countries Arabic literature and scholarship flourished under the stimulus of urban expansion, court patronage, and the Sunnī religious revival. The Ayyūbid period, in fact, inaugurated what has been called the Silver Age of Arabic letters.

The end of Ayyūbid rule in Egypt in 1250 came about as a result of an increased recruitment of Turkish slave troops, or mamlūks. Although the presence of mamlūks was a long-established phenomenon in Egypt, the last Ayyūbid ruler, al-Malik al-Sālih, was the first of his household in Egypt to acquire mamlūks in large numbers and to make them the principal basis of his personal power, owing to the increasing unreliability and factitiousness of the regular troops. These mamlūks were quartered in special barracks located on an island in the Nile river (called by Egyptian al-bahr), from which they drew their name, the Bahrīs. In the confusing circumstances which followed the death of al-Malik al-Sālih, the Bahrīs emerged as the most important single force in Egypt, and power was ultimately transferred to their leading general, opening a new chapter in Egyptian and Syrian history, which will be dealt with later.

The Caliph al-Nāsir (1180-1225)

Within a few years after the death of Nūr al-Dīn and just as the Zangid realm was being absorbed into the new Syro-Egyptian empire of Salah al-Dīn there emerged in Iraq a remarkable political figure. This was none other than the Abbasid caliph himself, al-Nāsir. Al-Nāsir must be regarded as one of the most outstanding members of the Abbasid line; among the Abbasids of the tenth century onwards he is perhaps the sole example of true greatness. His greatness lay in his ability to take advantage of the political conditions of his time to build for himself a basis of real power. The caliphate had for centuries been virtually powerless. Even in Seljuk times when the prestige of the caliphate was increased the institution was still deprived of real political power, being eclipsed by the sultanate. Al-Nāsir saw a way to bolster not only the prestige but also the actual power of the caliphate. His attempt to realize this plan is one of the most unusual episodes in Abbasid history.

At the time Zangi and his son Nūr al-Dīn were extending their power in North Mesopotamia and Syria, thus ending in that area the political fragmentation that had resulted from the break-up of the Seljuk empire, Iraq and Western Iran remained fragmented among various petty military principalities. Political relations in such a setting were complex; stability among rival amirs could be maintained only through a delicate system of alliances. The alternative to such alliances was a political free-for-all. For the caliph this situation had a certain advantage: he was not faced with a single powerful ruler capable of keeping him firmly under his thumb. The spirit of opportunism was in the air, and the caliph as one of many potentates might try his hand in the political game. If a man should emerge in the caliphate as capable as his peers, or more so, he might well bring new power and glory to the age-old office.

Such a man was al-Nāsir. In the political game which he undertook to play he had an important advantage not given to others which he exploited to the fullest, namely the venerable status of the caliphal office itself. Al-Nāsir placed special emphasis on the religious character of the office and sought to strengthen his relationship with the ᶜulamā' by having himself recognized as a religious scholar capable of expounding the Sharīᶜa according to the doctrine of all four of the recognized Sunnī schools. By taking this step al-Nāsir hoped to acquire greater prestige as virtual head of the ᶜulamā' establishment.

But this was only one aspect of al-Nāsir's bid for greater power. Where possible, he extended his rule over neighboring territory through military means. At the same time he was enough of a realist to recognize that, in the fragmented political order of his time, he could not create a large empire through coercion. He was not enough of a military man, or did not have a sufficient army at his disposal to overpower rival amirs in the manner of the Zangids. He preferred rather to extend his influence through peaceful means. This he did by making himself head of an organization of a type known in Arabic as futuwwa and persuading many of the amirs of his day to join it.

Futuwwa organizations had become common in the Eastern Muslim cities in the preceding centuries. In spite of many differences, they all had certain features in common. They were voluntary associations dedicated to the promotion of "manliness" (this is in fact what the term futuwwa means), with all the virtues which that had entailed, especially that of hospitality. In the urban environment where the individual might otherwise feel isolated and insecure they provided a sense of belonging. Their group activities entailed a great deal of ceremonial, especially the initiation of new members. Generally, these organizations fostered sports activities and thus helped to fill up leisure hours. Most of the futuwwa organizations drew their membership from the lower working classes, and often the members bore arms for the purpose of self-defense. For this reason, the upper classes tended to view the organizations with misgiving and even fear. As Sūfī teachings spread throughout the Eastern cities, the futuwwa ideology became increasingly tinged with Sūfī ideas. Indeed, one cannot draw a hard and fast line between the futuwwa and the Sūfī order (tarīqa); the two blended into each other to a remarkable degree.

Al-Nāsir saw the futuwwa as a powerful social force which could be rallied to the side of the caliphate. Just two years after his accession as caliph he had himself initiated into one of the futuwwa organizations, and then began encouraging others, including his own courtiers and various amirs, to join. In this way he not only gained the favor of futuwwa men generally but also incorporated part of the ruling class into the structure of the futuwwa. Al-Nāsir was using the futuwwa as a means of intergrating society under his own headship. In 1207 he felt his popularity with the futuwwa organizations to be strong enough to permit him to take the final step: he declared himself to be the head of all the futuwwa organizations, banning any organizations that did not acknowledge his headship. Al-Nāsir now had both the ᶜulamā' and the futuwwa organizations working in the service of his revived caliphate.

The futuwwa organization into which courtiers and amīrs were admitted took on a distinctly courtly character. As head of this organization--and as head of the ᶜulamā'--al-Nāsir was in a position to exercise a large measure of moral and spiritual direction over the rulers and to act as mediator in their quarrels. The Sūfī-oriented ideology of the futuwwa inculcated a strong feeling of reverence for the futuwwa leader, whose role was not unlike that of the Sūfī Shayreh. Thus while al-Nāsir was unable to match the combined might of the amīrs of his day, he succeeded in acquiring a moral mastery over them which he believed to be consonant with the dignity of his office. Even the powerful Salāh al-Dīn (who died before al-Nāsir reached the height of his power) respected him.

There was even a further aspect to al-Nāsir's program. Wishing to overcome insofar as possible the Sunnī-Shīᶜī schism, al-Nāsir took pains to come to terms with both the Ismāᶜīlī and Twelver Shīᶜī communities. With respect to the Ismāᶜīlī community, he scored a spectacular victory when the Ismāᶜīlī Imām at Alamūt announced his conversion to Sunnī Islam. The good will of the Twelvers was cultivated by a show of special reverence for the descendants of ᶜAlī. For example, a shrine was built at Samarra over the place where the twelfth Imām was believed to have disappeared. Sūfī ideology had already incorporated a certain degree of ᶜAlid loyalty by emphasizing the special place of ᶜAlī in its spiritual hierarchy.

Al-Nāsir's program remained in effect for a generation after his death. The futuwwa-based caliphate was not, however, without its enemies. A powerful line of rulers, the Khwārizm-Shāhs, emerged in Eastern Iran and seemed bent on building up a polity of the old Persian type, much as the Seljuks had done, in which the caliph would again be reduced to little more than a figurehead. These rulers had challenged al-Nāsir and continued to challenge his successor, al-Mustansir (1226-1242). However, the real undoing of the caliphate was to take place at the hands, not of the Khwārism-Shāhs but of the pagan Mongols. The tragedy of the destruction of the Abbasid caliphate in 1258 is heightened by the fact that on the eve of the Mongol disaster the caliphate had, thanks to the ingenious efforts of al-Nāsir, made a remarkable return to life.

The Muwahhids (1130-1269)

While the Zangids and after them the caliph al-Nāsir endeavored to create new political units out of the hodge podge of the post-Seljuk period, the Arab West was re-integrated politically under the rule of a new Berber dynasty, that of the Muwahhids, which followed close upon its predecessor, the Murābit dynasty. In contrast to the Murābit movement, whose origins were among the nomadic Lamtūna, the movement which brought the Muwahhids to power originated among the sedentary Masmūda Berbers of the High Atlas mountains.

Like the Murābit movement, the Muwahhid was inspired by a program of religious reform. Its founder, Ibn Tumart, himself a Masmūda Berber, had journeyed to the East to study religious subjects and had come into contact with a number of noted teachers. As a result of these studies, he had been exposed to the two great influences which had permeated the religious thinking of the East, the theology of the Ash^c arite school and the mysticism of the Sūfī movement, particularly as represented by al-Ghazzālī. In the course of his studies he had also become familiar with the classical system of Muslim jurisprudence (usūl al-fiqh), which laid down methods of deriving rules of conduct directly from the Koran and Hadīth. These studies had intensified his deep dissatisfaction with the moral and intellectual climate which prevailed in his homeland under the Murābits.

Upon returning to the Maghrib, Ibn Tūmart began going from place to place preaching reform and condemning the evils of the day. This preaching was directed against two targets: the Murābit rulers, who had, in Ibn Tūmart's view, surrounded themselves with luxury and departed form the true faith, and the Mālikī fuqahā', who had succumbed to a legalistic frame of mind and had neglected the life of the spirit. Ibn Tūmart was particularly incensed with the anthropomorphic understanding of God encouraged by the fuqahā'. He had learned from the theologians of the East that God is entirely beyond the physical world and that verses in the Koran which seem to attribute physical characteristics to God must be interpreted figuratively (through ta'wīl), not literally. He insisted (with the theologians of the East) that if God is truly One, then He cannot be a conglomeration of separate parts or characteristics. A literalistic interpretation of Koranic descriptions of God was, in his view, tantamount to polytheism and alien to the true spirit of the Koran itself. Because of Ibn Tūmart's strong emphasis on the Unity of God, his doctrine came to be described as tawhīd ("affirmation of Unity") and those who accepted it became known as muwahhids ("affirmers of God's Unity"). But Ibn Tūmart was also incensed with the dry legalism of the fuqaha, who observed meticulously the code of law built up by generations of legal experts but were unwilling to use the Koran and Hadīth directly as a basis of law. Ibn Tūmart called for a return to these "original sources" (usūl) of law.

Quite understandably a clash soon occurred between Ibn Tūmart and the Murābit authorities, and Ibn Tūmart was obliged to retreat with his followers into the security of his native country in the High Atlas. Choosing the mountain village of Tinmal as a place in which to settle, he proceeded to organize his followers into a militant community. Proclaiming himself to be the Mahdī (the one chosen by God to usher in the Final Age), Ibn Tūmart made himself supreme head of the new community. In some respects, Ibn Tūmart's community resembled that which Ibn Yāsīn had established a century before among the Lamtūna nomads. As with the nomads so among the strong-willed mountaineers of Tinmal an iron-tight, relentless discipline was required. The whip was used freely to shape character and assure conformity. Lukewarmness, not to mention dissidence, was not tolerated. The basis of the discipline was not, however, as in the case of the Murābit community Mālikī law but rather the teaching of the Mahdī as the final expositor of the Koran and Hadīth.

It has been said that Ibn Tūmart sought to model his activity on that of the Prophet Muhammad; it was indeed the function of the Mahdī to restore the conditions of earliest Islam. Tinmal seems to have been a kind of Medina; those who came from outside--i.e., the earliest followers of Ibn Tūmart plus newcomers--were called "Emigrants" (muhājirūn), and the people of Tinmal itself were called "Helpers" (ansār). The oligarchy that surrounded Ibn Tūmart was not unlike that of the Companions (sahāba) who surrounded the Prophet.

This oligarchy was made up of two councils. The highest in authority of these was made up of the ten men who were closest to the Mahdī. This council was called simply "the Ten." Directly under it was the council of "the Fifty." The rest of the community was organized into a hierarchy consisting, it is said, of twenty ranks. Thus, the community was highly structured, and the rule of the Mahdī, though in principle absolute, was carried on in consultation with the community's notables.

The first Muwahhid offensive was attempted in 1130 when Ibn Tūmart decided to attack Marrakesh. The result of this encounter was defeat for the Muwahhid troops; for the next fifteen years the Muwahhids confined themselves to the mountains and the Saharan regions of Morocco. Ibn Tūmart himself died soon after the attack on Marrakesh. He was succeeded by ᶜAbd al-Mu'min, one of the "Ten," who had distinguished himself in the service of Ibn Tūmart. In the first years of ᶜAbd al-Mu'min's reign, the Muwahhids extended and strengthened their control over the mountain regions.

In 1145 the time came to strike out again against the Murābits. This time the Muwahhids had no difficulty overpowering Murābit forces and within a short time swept over all of Morocco, taking both of the key cities of Marrakesh and Fez. The conquest of Morocco paved the way for further penetration into Spain and the Central and Eastern Maghrib. In Spain the Muwahhid penetration was facilitated by the fact that a number of governors had joined the rebellion against the Murābits. These encouraged the Muwahhids to cross the strait, and with their co-operation the Muwahhids had by 1148 become masters of south-western Spain. The rest of Muslim Spain came temporarily under the rule of an opponent of the Muwahhids named Ibn Mardanish. Since ᶜAbd al-Mu'min's main concern lay with the further expeditions in North Africa, he contented himself for the time being with a partial mastery of Spain.

The advance of the Muwahhids eastward across North Africa brought them into conflict with two major forces: the Arab (Hilālian) bedouins, who had recently seized a number of coastal cities. In 1152 the Muwahhid forces dealt a crushing defeat to a group of bedouin tribes in an important battle near Sitif. The Muwahhids then proceeded to occupy Ifrīqiya (the Eastern Maghrib), driving the Normans out of their main stronghold, Mahdiyya, in 1160. Thus, by the time of ᶜAbd al-Mu'min's death in 1163, the Muwahhids were masters of the largest empire ever to be ruled from Morocco. In the course of these conquests, the Murābit dynasty was wiped out completely.

ᶜAbd al-Mu'min was not only a brilliant conqueror but also a capable administrator. He devoted a great part of his time during his last ten years of rule to organizing his state internally. Within the new state, the Masmūda tribes, to whom alone the term Muwahhid properly applied, constituted the dominant element. The council of "the Fifty," which included the heads of the tribes, was retained as the principal advisory body. In this way the heads of the tribes were able to continue functioning as a ruling elite. Within this elite, the family of ᶜAbd al-Mu'min himself occupied a position of special pre-eminence. ᶜAbd al-Mu'min saw to it that the succession was secured in favor of his son, thus causing recognition to be given to the dynastic principle. This was a departure from pure Berber custom, to which dynastic rule was unfamiliar. ᶜAbd al-Mu'min himself as ruler assumed the titles of caliph and amīr al-mu'minīn, no doubt with the precedent of Abū Bakr in mind. Members of the caliph's family came to be called "sayyids." With this honorific designation they were distinguished from the Masmūda tribal aristocracy, who were called "shaykhs."

ᶜAbd al-Mu'min displayed special interest in fiscal administration. Muwahhid legal doctrine made it possible to regard all non-Muwahhid Muslims as subject to the Kharāj tax and the Muwahhids themselves as exempt from this tax. Accordingly in 1159, ᶜAbd al-Mu'min conducted an immense geographical survey of the area from Cyrenaica to the Atlantic for the purpose of designating lands subject to the Kharāj. Certain nomadic tribes, including some Arab bedouin, which were on good terms with the Muwahhid state, were charged with the responsibility of collecting taxes from settled tribes, their reward being exemption from the Kharāj. These tribes were known as "makhzan tribes." In addition to being responsible for the collection of taxes, they were also required, when called upon, to provide military service and thus formed part of the army.

The original mainstay of the Muwahhid army were, of course, the Masmūda warriors who had been disciplined and endoctrinated at Tinmal. (One may recall the similar position of the Lamtūna in the Murabit army.) Later, recruits from other tribes--including even some Arab bedouin--were included. Cavalrymen from ᶜAbd al-Mu'min's own tribe, the Kumia (not a Masmūda tribe), came to form a special body guard. Finally, as the empire reached the peak of its power, the caliph began to recruit mercenaries, as the Murabits had done earlier. Under ᶜAbd al-Mu'min's successors, the number of these "foreign" troops increased as the number of Masmūda warriors grew smaller.

One of the most sensitive issues which ᶜAbd al-Mu'min had to deal with was that of the relations between the Muwahhid state and the Mālikī fuqahā', whom Ibn Tūmart had clearly repudiated. Because of the great influence which the fuqahā' exercised among the people and because of the practical needs of justice, ᶜAbd al-Mu'min was constrained to tolerate, at least tacitly, the Mālikī system of law. However, at the same time he endeavored to remain faithful to the original Muwahhid goal of unifying the Muslim community of the Maghrib on the basis of Ibn Tūmart's teaching. Accordingly, he allowed only young men from the Masmūda tribes to take posts in the administration. These were subjected to special training supervised personally by ᶜAbd al-Mu'min himself. Because they were required to memorize the writings of Ibn Tumart, this new breed of administrators were called huffaz ("memorizers"). In addition to this heavy indoctrination, their training also included horsemanship, archery, swimming and other skills.

Under ᶜAbd al-Mu'min's two successors, Abu Ya'ᶜqub (1163-1184) and Abu Yusuf Ya'ᶜqub (1184-1199), the Muwahhid power was further extended in Spain. The Spanish rebel Ibn Mardanish was killed in 1172 as a result of intrigues within his own family, and his sons declared their loyalty to the Muwahhids. This enabled the Muwahhid state to extend its rule over all of Muslim Spain. A new offensive was subsequently organized against the Christian powers in the North culminating in a notable Muslim victory at Alarcos in 1196.

The Eastern Maghrib proved to be a trouble spot. Here, amid the increasing turmoil caused by the bedouin migrations, a family of former governors of the Murabits in Spain and the Balearic Isles, the Banu Ghaniya, was able to establish itself in Bougie on the coast in 1184 and began to extend its rule to other areas. It was not until 1206 that the Muwahhid caliph al-Nasir (1199-1214) was finally able to defeat the Banu Ghaniya. Wishing to establish a stronger government in the area, al-Nasir appointed Muhammad ibn Abu Hafs, son of one of Ibn Tumart's closest companions, as viceroy of Ifriqiya. This marked the beginning of a new governatorial dynasty which was later to survive the Muwahhid state itself.

Under the Muwahhids there was a considerable efflorescence of economic life. Spain was the most active center of agriculture, industry and trade, but its economic prosperity had an impact on the Maghrib as well. The merchants of the coastal cities of the Maghrib traded not only with Spain but also with Pisa, Genoa, Venice, and Marseilles.

Cultural life also flourished, particularly art, music, and most of all, philosophy. Both Abu Yaᶜqub and Abu Yusuf were cultured men who encouraged intellectual activity privately, even though publicly they had to cater to a strong distrust of philosophy. The period of their rule produced two philosophers of major importance, Ibn Tufayl and Ibn Rushd (Latin: Averros).

Abu Yusuf went further than his predecessors in attempting to enforce the official Muwahhid doctrine at the expense of Maliki orthodoxy. Embued with the conviction (derived from Ibn Tumart) that the Koran and Hadith alone should be consulted in legal matters, he ordered the burning of the Maliki law books and directed his own scholars to compile fresh compilations of hadith. This extremist position was abandoned by his successors, however, and the Maliki school retained its dominant position throughout the Maghrib.

After the death of Abu Yusuf, Muwahhid power began to decline. In Spain a great Christian offensive was mounted in revenge of the loss sustained at Alarcos. All the Christian rulers of Spain and Portugal

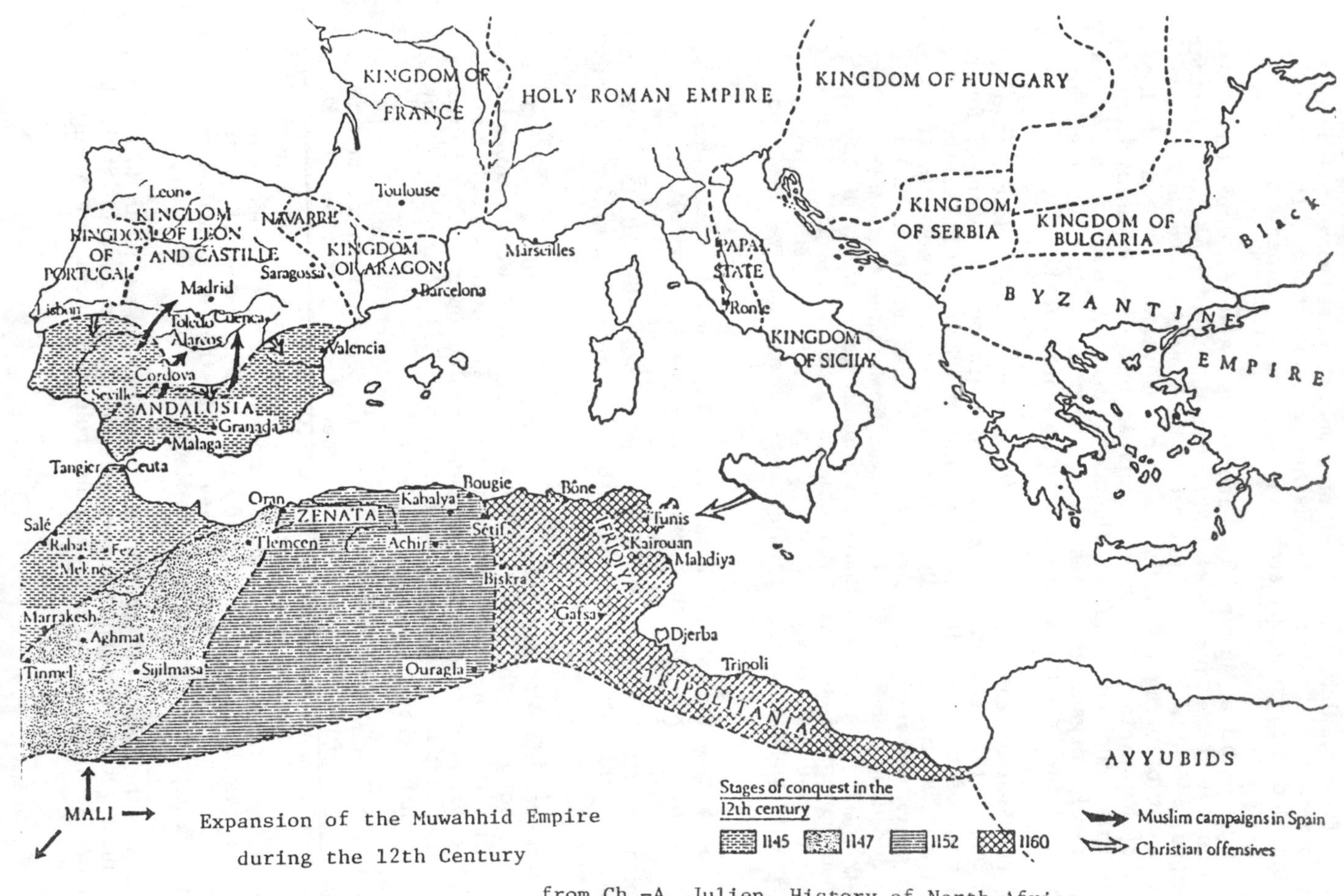

Expansion of the Muwahhid Empire during the 12th Century

from Ch.-A. Julien, <u>History of North Africa</u>

co-operated in the venture. The Pope himself declared a crusade against the Muwahhids, which brought knights and adventurers from all quarters. The decisive battle took place in 1212 at Las Navas de Tolosa, in which the Muwahhids suffered an overwhelming defeat. It is said that with this battle all hope of a Muslim recovery in Spain disappeared. Thereafter, Muslim forces in Spain maintained a steady retreat until eventually all traces of the Muslim presence were erased.

Several factors may be cited as accounting for the decline of the Muwahhid empire. For one thing, the aristocratic Masmūda Berbers became obsessed with its privileges, keeping the rest of the population in an inferior status. Consequently, the masses of people had great difficulty identifying their own interests with those of the state. Thus, as soon as the state showed signs of weakness, many were eager to throw off the yoke. Furthermore, a conflict developed within the Muwahhid aristocracy itself between the Masmūda notables or shaykhs, who remembered the egalitarianism of the early days of the Muwahhid movement, and the ruling family or the sayyids, who were seeking continually to strengthen the position of the dynasty and to make all others the subjects of a hereditary monarch. Thirdly, the character of the rulers themselves weakened. After Abū Yūsuf, the rulers had little control over their own empire but were rather themselves controlled by various factions. Some were more interested in the pleasures of courtly life than in the affairs of state. Fourthly, the Muwahhid doctrine lost its original vitality and ceased to fire the enthusiasm of those who ran the empire, much less the masses. Last but not least, the incursions into Morocco of Arab bedouin, those which had earlier entered the Eastern Maghrib as part of the Hilālian migrations, caused economic regression and political instability in the very heart of the empire. This was an unfortunate consequence of a step taken by ʿAbd al-Mu'min. Wishing to relieve Ifrīqiya of the pressure of nomadism, he had transported several bedouin tribes to Morocco.

The sign of the end came in 1235, when the governor of Ifrīqiya and the chief of a tribe which controlled Tlemcen both ceased to obey the orders of the caliph. In thus asserting their independence, the former founded the separate Hafsid state and the latter the independent Zayānid state. By 1250 the Muwahhids were left with Southern Morocco as their only domain. The final blow came in 1269 when a nomadic tribe from Central Morocco, the Banū Marīn, conquered Marrakesh, driving the Muwahhids into the High Atlas from which they had originally come. The last Muwahhids were annihilated in 1275.

Among the important developments of the Muwahhid period, the following deserve special notice. (1) The process of arabization continued apace under the Muwahhids. Even though in its early days the Muwahhid movement had leaned toward a kind of Berber nationalism, it ended up by giving further impetus to the cultivation of the Arabic humanities. The permeation of the Muwahhid court with Arabic culture was, in fact, one of the factors contributing to the alienation of the less cultured Berber-speaking Masmūda tribes. The rulers lost their Berber ways. The arabization process was also accelerated by the incursions of bedouin into Morocco. (2) In spite of the antipathy of the original Muwahhids toward Mālikism, the Muwahhid movement was never able to unseat the Mālikī fuqahā'. Its attempt to do so only increased the intransigence of the fuqahā', and as a result Māliki orthodoxy was at the close of the Muwahhid period stronger than ever. It had lost, for a time, the official status which it had acquired under the Murābits but it soon regained this status under the dynasties that replaced the Muwahhids. (3) Certain features of Muwahhid doctrine were to make a permanent imprint on North African life, however, especially the puritanical strain reflected in the segregation of the sexes and the veiling of women. (4) The great reverence which a large section of the masses felt toward Ibn Tūmart as the impeccable Mahdi, an attitude which the caliph Abū Yūsuf had opposed, strengthened the tendency in North African popular piety to focus upon saintly figures. At the same time, Sūfism, with its own galaxy of saints, made rapid inroads into North Africa. The French historian H. Terrasse wrote, "It is very striking that the great mystical leaders of the Maghrib--those who were to remain the most popular of its saints--nearly all lived under the Almohads [Muwahhids] and died at the end of the twelfth century."

CHAPTER FIVE

SOCIETY AND INSTITUTIONS: THE MEDIEVAL ORDER

The centuries which we have considered in the previous chapters witnessed the gradual formation of a social and political order which was to persist until the dawn of the modern era. This order extended throughout the world of Islam and may, because of the integrative role which Islam played in it, be described as an Islamic order. It was therefore not distinctively Arab--that is, it was neither distinctive of Arabs alone, since both Arabs and non-Arabs were part of it, nor was it distinctive of the Arab lands exclusively, since it prevailed in other lands as well. One could, of course, look for features of social life that were distinctive of the Arabs or of the Arab lands. But one would soon discover that, once one goes beyond those overriding features that characterize Islamic society in general, one encounters a marked variation of features from one area to another, even within the lands inhabited by Arabs or Arabic-speaking peoples. These specifically regional features are, in any case, for our purposes secondary and need not occupy our attention.

In speaking of an Islamic social order, we are speaking of a social order which existed throughout a period in the history of the world--or at least of Europe and the Middle East--which is frequently called "the Middle Ages" or "the medieval period." We are thus distinguishing the social order in question from the highly fluid and somewhat erratic social conditions that prevail in most parts of the modern Islamic world, including the Arab lands. Since modern Islamic countries are subject to such a wide range of novel influences and developments, owing largely to the penetration of new technology and secular ideas into these countries, it is premature to describe any particular pattern of society visible in these countries as Islamic. Attempts to create a new Islamic order in certain countries have not yet led to results that may be judged long-lasting; these attempts are still too recent to allow any such judgment. The modern situation remains for Islamic countries, as for the rest of the world, generally speaking one of great flux. In contrast, the Islamic order of society to be considered in this chapter exhibited over a period of at least a millenium a high degree of integrity, stability, and equilibrium. Such changes as occurred within the social order during this period occurred gradually and perceptibly, (by modern standards) and did not significantly alter certain fundamental patterns, on the basis of which a sense of the underlying stability of the social order may be predicated.

The phrase "Islamic social order" is not meant to suggest that the social order to be examined in this chapter was identical with the <u>ideal</u> Islamic order. The latter was considered to be manifest in the Umma under the Prophet and the first caliphs and in the Sharīʿa as worked out by the ʿulamāʾ. The actual social and political order within which Muslims lived during the Middle Ages was viewed by the more devout Muslims as somewhat removed from Islamic ideals, even though it was shaped to a large extent by those ideals.

The most formative period in the emergence of the medieval Islamic order was unquestionably the seventh through the tenth centuries, although certain important developments took place in the two following centuries. Certainly by the mid-thirteenth century the medieval order of society was well established and more or less fully formed. It would persist with minor modifications up to the modern period.

The concept of society as the total aggregate of people living together in a certain territory and conforming to certain common patterns of social behavior admittedly did not have a prominent place in the thinking of Muslims (or, for that matter, of any human beings) prior to the modern age. There is in classical Arabic (as distinct from modern Arabic) no precise equivalent of the English word "society." There were within Islamic society solidarities which were stronger than that of society as a whole and which had the effect of overshadowing the concept of society as such. Chief among these solidarities was that of the religious community, the most comprehensive religious community being the Islamic umma. Religion was thus the primary basis of social cohesion. Secular conceptions of community (such as that embodied in the modern concept of the nation) were virtually unknown. The only solidarity which compared in strength with that of the religious community was that of the extended family; whereas the individual belonged to the former by virtue of religious affiliation, he was bound to the latter by the natural tie of kinship. To some degree other solidarities existed, for example, that of towns or quarters, that of regions, that of particular trades or professions, but these were always overshadowed by the religious community. Among Muslims the most serious threat to the overriding solidarity of the umma was posed by sectarian differences, which were in principle religious in nature (even if there were concealed social or economic factors behind them in given instances). However, this threat must not be unduly exaggerated. Ultimately the sects were able to establish a modus vivendi, in spite of occasional outbreaks of violence. (The most serious sectarian division was that between Sunnīs and Shīᶜis, but even between these a large measure of peaceful coexistence was achieved.) In any case, the vast majority of Muslims were Sunnīs, and it is among them that the solidarity of the umma was achieved on the largest scale, despite certain variations in law and theology. Among Sunnis the view came to prevail that certain differences in regard to law and theology were inevitable and that the unity of the umma was not compromised by these differences. A saying attributed to the Prophet in fact stated that the umma would be divided into seventy-three sects.

The Muslim umma was, of course, vast. This vastness, which might have militated against its solidarity, was partially offset by two things: the mosque and the pilgrimage. The mosque provided a setting in which the solidarity of the umma could be expressed locally. One of the two Arabic terms for mosque, namely jāmiᶜ (the other is masjid), means "gathering place." The mosque is the place where Muslims in a particular locality gather together for worship and social intercourse. It thus engenders a local congregation which epitomizes the Islamic umma. Muslims who worship together in a given mosque acquire a feeling of congregational unity while retaining a sense of belonging to the universal umma. The travelling Muslim is always welcomed in their midst. The universal umma is epitomized in an even more dramatic way in the Great Pilgrimage to Mecca. Here local ties disappear as pilgrims from all parts of the Islamic world gather for common religious observances. Though they constitute only a segment of the umma, their varied origins make them a living embodiment of the universality of the umma, and each pilgrim returns to his home with tales of the great event that foster the universalist spirit in others.

Despite the vastness of the Moslim umma, it cannot be equated with society as such. It was rather a part of society, as were also the other religious communities which were accorded legitimacy under the Sharī^{c}a. While the larger concept of society as a whole may play a somewhat secondary role in medieval thinking, this is not to say that the concept did not exist at all. While there is no precise equivalent in classical Arabic to the English term "society" (taken in the broad sense which the term has in modern social science usage), there is a term in whose meaning the concept of society was very strongly implied. This is the term dār al-Islām (literally, "abode of Islam"). Strictly speaking, this term has more a territorial than a social connotation. It refers to that part of the physical world in which Islam is secure by virtue of the presence of an Islamic state and where the Sharī^{c}a is honored. But the people who inhabit the dār al-Islām clearly constitute an Islamic society, whether all be Muslims or not. Non-Muslims who adhere to legitimate revealed religions are as much a part of Islamic society as the Muslims. Although they are not subject to all parts of the Sharī^{c}a, they are subject to those parts that govern intercommunal relations, and as dhimmīs (or ahl al-kitāb) they have a distinctly Islamic status. They are incorporated into Islamic society as affiliated religious congregations. In this respect, the system of mutually tolerant theocracies established by the Prophet and the first caliphs persisted. Non-Muslims enjoyed religious freedom provided they observed those intercommunal regulations laid down in the Sharī^{c}a and fulfilled their obligations to the Islamic state, the primary one being that of payment of the poll tax.

The Agrarian Setting

Any system of society is better understood when viewed from the perspective of the long-term ecological setting within which it emerged and then persisted. Ecology is concerned with the interrelationship between a society and its physical environment. Before the emergence of modern technology-based civilization, the fundamental relationship between the more complex human societies--those which we commonly described as "civilized" (in contrast to "primitive")--and the physical environment was an agricultural one. Marshall Hodgson has, accordingly, described the premodern civilized societies, including the Islamic, as "agrarian-based." In an agrarian society the economy centers upon agricultural production as the primary productive activity. This agricultural base is reflected in the social structure, and upon it all cultural activity and institutional development, in the end, depend. The great mass of people are peasants who employ relatively simple methods of cultivation. The civilized arts and sciences are made possible by the existence of a privileged wealthy class who live off a surplus of agricultural products and who dwell in cities, which arise by virtue of this surplus. Thus cultural life is dependent on the vicissitudes of agriculture. Insofar as the surplus is reduced in difficult times, cultural life is restricted, and the level of complexity and sophistication of the society's institutions lowered; insofar as the surplus increases and is well managed, city life and culture are able to flourish. Change is uncommon, and when it does occur it is slow. The pace and extent of change are limited by the limits of animal power and the natural elements. As a result, the prevailing mentality is, by modern standards, on the whole conservative, including social attitudes. The structure of society tends to be hierarchical.

The lands in which the Islamic social order arose and developed--that is to say, the Middle East and North Africa--appear to have undergone a general decline of agricultural productivity in the centuries following the break-up of the Abbasid empire. In order to understand why this was so we must appreciate the vicissitudes to which agriculture in this region has always been subject. The region is, to begin with, among the more arid regions of the earth, and from the time of the earliest civilizations cultivation of the soil has always depended to a large extent on irrigation in the alluvial plains of great river valleys or around underground water sources, although in certain areas rainfall has been a significant source of water. Irrigation has always depended on a complex hydraulic technology. Both large-scale cultivation and the proper maintenance of the hydraulic technology which supports it require a high degree of cooperation made possible only by centralized bureaucracies. But such bureaucracies have often proven to be fragile, succumbing periodically to external conquest, internecine strife, political fragmentation, or decentralization and irresponsibility in the systems of land tenure. When cultivation has, as a result of any of these factors, been interrupted over a period of years, agricultural land has been transformed into grassland, suitable only for grazing. Once the land had been incorporated into a pastoral economy, its reclamation became all the more difficult. Overuse of grassland for grazing purposes within a pastoral economy could then reduce the land to desert. On the other hand, continuous cultivation of land was not always a good thing. Land could be overworked and thus ruined. Agrarian society did not possess an agricultural science or technology (or political system) capable of assuring adequate soil conservation. So, whether cultivated or not, land suffered. Long-term deterioration of agriculture was therefore extremely difficult to ward off.

Beginning with the aggressive and well-planned administration of the Umayyad governor of Iraq, Hajjāj ibn Yūsuf, or even earlier, the most productive alluvial (silt-nourished) land of the Tigris-Euphrates valley--the area which the Arabs called the "Sawād"--began to sustain a very lively agriculture, thanks to improvement and effective maintenance of the irrigation systems. This agriculture of the Sawād was the mainstay of the prosperity which reached a peak under the early Abbasids. Despite the blossoming of commerce and growth of the bourgeoisie under the Abbasids, the fundamental source of wealth was still land as was noted in chapter three. Islamic society, under

Abbasids, remained essentially agrarian. The prosperity of the period therefore owed much to the agricultural productivity of the Sawad.

With the breakdown of the Abbasid state, the deterioration of agriculture in Iraq suddenly accelerated and, according to Hodgson, "came to a head." The spread of the iqta system, mentioned in Chapter four, contributed to this acceleration by preventing the fostering of long-term interests on the land. But the deterioration of agriculture in Iraq was only symptomatic of a general trend throughout the Middle East and North Africa. Its effects were especially dramatic in that it eliminated the agricultural foundation upon which the grandiose scheme of building and maintaining a single Islamic polity under Abbasid auspices had been based. The emergence of a politically diverse world of Islam after the collapse of the Abbasid empire was very much a function of the backward slide of the agrarian economy of the areas inhabited by Muslims. With a much slimmer and more precarious agricultural base, Islamic society would have to settle for less complex and sophisticated institutions than had previously existed, especially in the political sphere. While attempts would continue to be made to set up empires with complex bureaucratic structures and would in some areas such as the Nile valley be relatively successful, many parts of the world of Islam would become subjected to much simpler political and administrative institutions: those associated with the rule of amirs (to be discussed shortly). Cultural life, too, would exhibit the effects of lowered general prosperity.

The State

One of the principal earmarks of the Islamic social order was the presence of an Islamic state, of Islamic rule. The Arab conquests had given rise to a highly elaborate state structure, one having a vast territorial domain extending from eastern Iran to Ifriqiya (modern Tunis) and beyond. This state structure was, as we have noted, built upon Persian and, to some extent, Byzantine models. It reached its apogee under the early Abbasids, after which it succumbed to the process of disintegration described in the last section of chapter three. What emerged thereafter was a network of smaller state formations most of which came to form a Sunni international political order. Each ruler within this network looked to the caliph, who continued to reside in Baghdad, as the theoretical bearer of ultimate political authority and was careful to secure official recognition from him. Thus the caliph, who could now no longer be considered a head of state, had become a legitimizing agent within a network of states whose unity under the aegis of Sunni Islam he symbolized. Some of the states within this network were able to achieve sway over considerable territory--for example, that established by Salah al-Din. However, many of them were limited to a small territory sometimes consisting of no more than a city and its immediate environment. In the case of these latter states, the level of bureaucratic complexity and sophistication was sometimes very low, particularly if the state consisted merely of a local military adventurer and his troops. Furthermore, while nominal allegiance was always paid to the caliph and nominal recognition given to the unity of all states within the network, violent rivalries often existed between competing rulers, each anxious to enlarge his domain.

It is common for historians to refer to the states that made up this pluralistic political order as amīrates and the rulers themselvs as amīrs. The term amīr had from the time of the Arab conquests been used for those who governed the provinces of the far-flung caliphal empire. Theoretically, the rulers who belonged to the new pluralistic system were still governors ruling their domains on behalf of the caliph. However, since the caliph had no effective power over them and generally granted legitimacy to any military commander who could effectively assume control over a given area, the rulers were in reality heads of state in their own right; their rule was clearly independent of any outside power. The term amīr in any case has the literal meaning of "commander" and need not connote a subordinate status.

After the destruction of the caliphate in Baghdad in 1258, a remnant caliphate was maintained for a time in Egypt. It did not, however, enjoy universal recognition among Sunnis, and the need arose for a new conception of legitimacy which did not entail the official sanction of a caliph. This need was met with a doctrine known in Arabic as al-siyāsa al-sharᶜyya, according to which the Islamic state existed wherever the ruler was a professing Muslim and used his power to preserve the public peace and, in collaboration with the ᶜulamā', to uphold the sacred law, the Sharīᶜa. Under this new conception, the Islamic state, although able to exist without a caliphate, still continued to carry on the essential functions of the caliphate. Islamic rule per se remained a reality.

As was noted in chapter four, the Seljuk rulers adopted the title of Sultān, and in the centuries following the breakup of the Seljuk empire this title came to be widely used among Muslim rulers. It did not signify a status essentially different from that of amīr, however, and the two titles (sultān and amīr) may be regarded as more or less interchangeable, at least in theory. The title of sultān may have implied a higher degree of grandeur, especially in consideration of its historic association with Great Seljuk rule, and it is perhaps not inaccurate to speak of the sultān as a sort of super-amīr. The coexistence under the Seljuks of caliph and sultān has seemed to some modern scholars suggestive of a separation between spiritual and temporal powers. In reality, the powers of the caliph had been, during the Abbasid apogee, much more temporal than spiritual, so that the later relationship between caliph and sultān (or amīr) is more correctly understood in terms of a de jure delegation of temporal power.

The Islamic state reached the high point of its development under the early Abbasids, and the various state-formations which emerged in subsequent centuries reflected in varying degrees--in some cases only remotely--the structure of the Abbasid state. Where a local amīrate consisted of merely an amīr and his leading officers, the resemblence to the Abbasid prototype would indeed be slight. However, even in such cases certain parameters of Islamic statehood, harking back to Abbasid times or before, were always discernible. Two primary functions defined almost universally the role of the Islamic state: (1) the maintenance of the internal peace, security, and decency of the Islamic social order and (2) the maintenance--and, where possible, the advancement--of the frontiers separating the Islamic domain from the realms beyond. In the case of relatively small amīrates located far from the Islamic frontiers, the second function would of course recede into the background, but where they were located in proximity to frontiers this function could become paramount. With larger state-formations, such as the Great Seljuk empire, it always played a role; to it was related the all-important task of corresponding or concluding treaties with non-Muslim powers.

The carrying out of these functions naturally required an army together with a corps of administrative personnel capable of carrying on the important business of taxation and financial accounting, which were needed in order to meet the expenses of equipping and maintaining an army. This bureaucracy could itself be a major expense, not to mention the lavish courts sometimes maintained by the rulers themselves and other high officials. Thus the activities of the state were costly, and the relationship of the state to the people tended to be essentially fiscal. It was difficult for the masses to view the state as consisting of anything but a revenue-consuming army and bureaucracy. The bureaucracies and courts maintained in the smaller amīrates were of course far less extensive than those of the highly centralized imperial regimes; but, on the other hand, the population base was much thinner. Generally speaking, the financial burden imposed by states, great or small, upon the masses was heavy. As was typical in pre-modern agrarian societies, the burden was heaviest for the peasants who worked the soil.

Public welfare was, on the whole, a marginal concern of the state. Occasionally the state took an interest in public works which were clearly crucial to the economy, such as the maintenance of irrigation systems. Generally speaking, however, public welfare was left more to the initiative of wealthy individuals than to that of the state. Hospitals, schools, institutions for the poor, and the like were classified as charitable establishments and were funded from private sources and organized legally under the name of awqāf (religious endowments). Amīrs themselves or bureaucrats might establish awqāf out of their private assets.

The maintenance of the internal peace, security, and decency of the Islamic social order entailed prerogatives which are frequently described, using modern jargon, as executive and judicial. An oft-repeated dictum has it that the Islamic state cannot exercise legislative powers since in Islam God is the sole legislator; the state merely applies and enforces God's law, the Sharīʿa. This dictum is correct if we restrict the term "law" to the Sharīʿa. To do so, however, is to disavow the positivist conception of law common among modern historians. In positivist thinking, law tends to be viewed as a body of norms which people are in some sense compelled to adhere to by virtue of threats of punishment (frequently called coercive sanctions). Without these threats, the norms in question do not constitute genuine law. Since the state is normally the initiator of threats and the possessor of instruments that can be used to carry out the threats, it is in some degree involved in the process of making law. We may thus distinguish between the law of God, in the making of which the Islamic state theoretically plays no role, from Islamic positive law, for which the state is largely responsible. Islamic positive law would consist of all those norms which members of Islamic society feel compelled to adhere to by virtue of the presence of a state capable of punishing in the event of nonadherence. Ideally those norms should, from a Muslim point of view, be on conformity with God's law, although in fact this may not always be the case. The Sharīᶜa spells out the prerogatives of the ruler as well as the sanctions he should apply; to the extent that a ruler follows steadfastly the Sharīᶜa, he proves himself to be a good Muslim ruler.

The primary means whereby the Islamic state transforms the Sharīᶜa into positive law is a judicial system called in Arabic qadā'. This system centered upon a court over which a judge bearing the title of qādī presided. Theoretically, the ruler himself could act as qādī; it was in fact a prerogative of the ruler--whether the caliph or the 'amīr standing in his place--to do so as he saw fit. In actuality, however, it had been the practice of rulers since early Islamic times to delegate the judicial function to others, upon whom the title of qādī was thereupon conferred. In the court of the qādī, claimant and defendent stated their cases, witnesses were heard, and a decision was rendered. In applying the Sharīᶜa to particular cases and in relying upon sanctions provided by the state to undergird his decisions, as an agent of the state the qādī helped to bring about the realization of an Islamic positive law.

But the qādī did not have a complete monopoly over judicial procedure. The 'Abbasids had established a court of appeals known generally to historians by its Arabic name, the mazālim ("wrongs") court. This court came to be widely regarded thereafter as an essential part of the Islamic state apparatus. None other than the ruler himself, caliph or amīr, presided over this court. To it were addressed complaints concerning unfair decisions of qādīs or wrongs committed by other state officials or powerful persons. The mazālim court did not have an appellate jurisdiction in the sense understood in Western legal systems. In principle, the decision made by a qādī was final and not subject to review by a higher court. If an individual felt that a qādī's decision was unfair, he could bring his complaint to the mazālim court, but that court, instead of reviewing the qādī's decision to determine its legal soundness, would investigate the qādī's character and qualifications and, where these were in doubt, call for a rehearing by another qādī.

Criminal jurisdiction theoretically belong to the qādī, although in fact it was largly exercised by a special agency of the state known as the shurta (often translated as "police department"). Since the rules of evidence to which the qādī was subject were very stringent, making prosecution difficult, and since the penal code contained in the Sharīᶜa did not take into account certain types of crime, criminal justice became in effect much more the business of the shurta than of the qādī.

Also important to the state's function of maintaining public decency was the muhtasib, an official appointed by the shurta and supervised by the qadi. We will consider his role later in this chapter.

Local government as such was nonexistent. The city, for example, was not a self-governing entity but was ruled directly by representatives of the state. In the case of small amirates which encompassed a single city together with the villages of its surrounding countryside a semblance of municipal autonomy may seem to have existed. However, the local amir in such a situation, if he were not a subordinate of a strong amir would invariably be eager to carve out a larger domain for himself, one inclusive of other cities, thus showing a lack of commitment to the city as such. Furthermore, the amir and his troops remained largely aloof from the rest of the population of the city, seldom seeing their interests as identical with those of the civilian population.

The ᶜUlamā'

The Sharīᶜa, which the qādī was to apply to cases brought before him, was a vast body of regulations the knowledge of which was cultivated by a special class of scholars known as ᶜulamā' (literally, "possessors of knowledge"). In principle, therefore, the qādī should himself be an ᶜalim (singular of ᶜulamā'), since only one who is well-versed in the Sharīᶜa should be in a position to apply it to specific cases. But a knowledge of the Sharīᶜa had a value that extended far beyond the sphere of judicial application. Since the Sharīᶜa defined not only what was obligatory and forbidden but also what was merely advisable or inadvisable, much of it lay beyond the scope of positive (that is, judicially applicable and enforceable) law. This is true even for much that fell under the categories of obligatory and forbidden, since these categories did not always entail enforceability through agencies of the state. The ritual prayer, for example, is obligatory but not enforceable in the ordinary sense. The devout Muslim was much more concerned with sanctions which God would surely apply in the present life.

Since the devout Muslim aspired to conform to the Sharīᶜa, not only when he was in the court of qādī, but throughout the whole of his daily life, he stood in need of ongoing guidance from the ᶜulamā'. It is a platitude in Islam that the Sharīᶜa has not been given to mankind in the form of a detailed code. What has been given is a divine revelation contained within two repositories: the Koran and the Sunna (Custom of the Prophet Muhammad). From this body of revelation, scholars, working in the service of the entire Muslim community, are to derive through careful study and interpretation (entailing a methodology which we will explore in chapter five) the details of the Sharīᶜa, which they may then systematize into a code. The results of this scholarly activity are so vast that only the scholars themselves may claim a mastery of them. Since ordinary Muslims depend heavily on these scholars in their effort to live according to the Sharīᶜa, the scholars--that is to say, the ᶜulamā'--play an extremely important role within Islamic society.

Some modern scholars have referred to the ᶜulamā' as the clergy of Islam or even as the Muslim church. This terminology is valid to some extent, although it can be very misleading. In Islam there are not sacraments which must be administered exclusively by an ordained clergy, and there are no formally constituted conciliar bodies which make authoritative pronouncements on doctrinal matters or issue official confessional statements. However, if the terms "clergy" and "church" are used in a very broad sense to refer to a body of persons possessing superior understanding in matters of vital importance to the religious life of people and representing collectively what may be regarded as a religious establishment, then the ᶜulamā' may be considered to be a kind of clergy or church. They are, after all, the bearers of the ideal law of God. Without them God's law would be very imperfectly known, if known at all, and the salvation of mankind would therefore be in jeopardy. It is their superior knowledge of God's law and that alone which gives the ᶜulamā' the degree of authority which they enjoy within Islamic society. They dispense this knowledge to others and thus keep the community as a whole on the right path. They are, as it were, the keepers of the community's conscience, the guardians of its basic values.

The training which the ᶜulamā' received embraced all of the "religious sciences" (to which reference will be made in the following chapter). The paramount sciences were, as might be expected, those related to the Koran and Hadīth, the two fundamental sources of law. Mastery of the law books, in which the legal doctrine of earlier ᶜulamā' was found, was also required. These studies of course required a thorough knowledge of the Arabic language, its vocabulary and grammar, and for this reason the linguistic sciences became an important adjunct to the religious sciences in the curriculum of study of the ᶜulamā'.

The training of the ᶜulamā' was highly personal. The worth of one's training depended, not upon what institution one studied at, but what teacher one studied under. Until the eleventh century all instruction took place in the mosque. Beginning in the eleventh century, schools of higher religious studies, called madrasas, were founded on a wide scale, and it was in these madrasas that most of the ᶜulamā' received their training. Despite this institutionalization of learning, however, religious instruction continued to revolve around the personal connection between teacher and student. One did not, upon completion of his studies, receive a degree from an institution but rather a certificate of approval, called *ijaza*, from a teacher or teachers. This certificate amounted to a permit to teach to others the material learned from the teacher. Learning was thus, to a very large extent, transmitted orally from generation to generation. Not the library but the lecture hall was the primary center of learning (notwithstanding the many splendid libraries which the Islamic world produced).

In principle, higher religious education was open to all. In no other field was equality of opportunity so nearly achieved as in the religious field. A religious education was inexpensive, and anyone could seek it. As a consequence, the ᶜulamā' constituted an open class which anyone might enter regardless of background. The sole requirement was an aptitude for learning. Needless to say, those who were exposed to learning early in life (which was more often the case among upper than among lower classes) had a better chance of success than others.

Although the ᶜulamāʾ were in full agreement on most major points of law, they allowed some variation of opinion in matters of detail. Consequently, "schools" (madhāhib) of law, or jurisprudence, emerged among them, based in theory on the teaching of prominent masters of the formative period of Islamic legal development (eighth and ninth centuries). Two such schools failed to survive. Four, however, remained: the Hanafī, Mālikī, Shāfiᶜī, and Hanbalī schools. The Hanafī and Mālakī schools, although they claimed the famous jurists Abū Hanīfa and Mālik ibn Anas as their founders, were in reality an outgrowth of two regional schools of earlier times, the Iraqi and the Hijāzī (based in Medina). The former, being more exposed to the legal traditions of the conquered territories, was the more flexible in its doctrine, allowing a rather liberal application of Islamic norms, whereas the latter, based as it was in the original homeland of Islam, was more bound to the traditions and practices familiar to the first Muslims.

The origins of the Shāfiᶜī and Hanbalī schools are much more closely linked up with the jurists from whom their names derive. Muhammad ibn Idrīs al-Shāfiᶜī has been called the master architect of classical Islamic jurisprudence. It was he who worked out a theory of sources and a system of interpretation that was to become the foundation for all future generations of legal theorists, even those belonging to the other three schools. Although he did not intend to form a separate school, he gathered around himself a number of devoted students who, after his death, soon constituted a school. The last to appear of the four schools was that of the Hanbalīs. Ahmad ibn Hanbal was more an authority on traditions (hadīth) of the Prophet than on law as such. The school which emerged out of his circle of followers is generally regarded as the strictest and most conservative of all the schools.

The Hanafī and Mālikī schools, in addition to being the first to develop, also became the most geographically widespread of the four schools. The Hanafī school, having originated in Iraq, enjoyed the important advantage of official Abbasid support. This connection with the ruling authorities was to remain a feature of the Hanafī school down to the time of the Ottoman empire. As a consequence, the Hanafī school predominated throughout Muslim Asia. North Africa, on the other hand, became a Mālikī stronghold. As for the Shāfiᶜī and Hanbalī schools, they claimed the allegiance of many important individuals--especially scholars--and of communities here and there (there were, for example, Hanbalī and Shāfiᶜī quarters in some cities), but on the whole their followers were in the minority as compared to other schools.

The City

One of the most striking features of medieval Islamic society is the predominance of cities. It was in the cities that the influence of the ᶜulamā' and of the state was greatest. It is paradoxical that a society which did not accord to the city any autonomy or individuality as a legal entity in its own right should have been so thoroughly city-centered. One modern scholar has gone as far as to say that in the Muslim world "the whole of civilization was found in the town; it was only there that administration, law, religions and culture existed." Islam, from the time of its inception, had a very strong urban underpinning, and as it spread it fostered a development of urban life. Its spread was, in fact, largely from city to city. Islamic law was developed within the context of the city, and many of the regulations pertaining to worship presuppose an urban setting. The mosque itself, although possible in the smallest villages, is not its true self except in the city. It was indeed in many respects a pillar of urban life.

Even though the typical medieval Muslim city has appeared to some Western observers to be lacking in organization, it was not without an overall plan. The basic elements in its layout were: the main mosque, the commercial area or bazaar, the official quarter (where public buildings were located), and the residential areas. (To these we might add the burial area; but since this area was marginal to the city itself, we will ignore it.) The arrangement of these elements was essentially concentric (allowing, of course, for some variation from city to city). The hub of the city was the main mosque. Its central position was indicative of the primary importance of religion in urban life. In the immediate vicinity of the main mosque was the bazaar, which had an internal organization of its own based on the segregation of the various trades and crafts. Gold merchants, jewelers, perfume merchants, booksellers, clothsellers, carpet merchants, leatherworkers, workers in wood and metal--all these occupied certain sections of the bazaar. Proximity to the mosque was reserved for the more noble trades, such as that of perfume and incense, while the less noble trades, for example pottery and tanning, were situated further from the mosque. The main mosque, together with the bazaar, formed the kernel of the city. At the edge of this kernel was the official quarter, in which not only officialdom was located, but also the soldiery, whose function it was to maintain order and to defend the center of the city against popular disturbances. The mosque area, the bazaar, and the official quarter together constituted what might be called the public section of the city. Surrounding this public section were the residential areas comprising the private dwellings. Beyond them, the city gradually merged with the countryside, as sophisticated urban dwellings gave way to simpler, more village-type dwellings inhabited mainly by cultivators who worked the land adjacent to the city.

The residential or private section of the city was organized into quarters, which were often separated from each other by empty spaces. Each quarter was almost a city in itself; in fact, the medieval Muslim city has been described as a conglomeration of separate towns. Running through the middle of many quarters was a main street, from which smaller dead-end streets or alleys extended outward on either side. The main street was enclosed at both ends by great gates, which served to isolate the quarter physically from the rest of the city. The basis of solidarity of a quarter might be any one of a number of things, such as religion (Christians and Jews lived in separate quarters), ethnic identity (some Syrian towns, for example, had Turkish and Kurdish quarters), sectarian differences (Shi^c^is and Hanbalis, for example, had their own quarters in some towns), common village origins (migrants from Harran, for example, lived together in Damascus and Aleppo), or even common occupational interests (as in Aleppo, where millers and tanners lived together). On the other hand, social class was not, generally speaking, a basis of solidarity or urban quarters. They were no "upper class" neighborhoods in the modern Western sense, no Beverly Hills, where only the rich lived in isolation from the less affluent or poor classes. Rather, the quarters had a mixed social character. Those nearer to the central part of the city tended to be wealthier and more sophisticated than the outlying quarters, but always the social classes could be found living together. Every quarter had its religious leaders (the ^c^ulama', in the case of Muslim quarters), its merchants, great and small, its craftsmen and laborers, and its poor.

The residential quarters showed few, if any, signs of municipal organization. The streets were very narrow and winding, being designed only for human and animal traffic, not for wheeled vehicles. Priority was given, in the use of space, to the private dwelling; consequently, very little space was available for public traffic. Public areas, such as parks and squares, were virtually non-existent. Daily life was concentrated almost entirely in the home. The private dwelling, although drab on the outside, might contain spacious and attractive courtyards or patios, where relatives and friends could gather for refreshment and social intercourse. The order and unity of the interior stood in sharp contrast to the chaotic labyrinth of streets outside. The residential quarter seemed designed to provide retreat from the public life of the central districts of the city. This dichotomy of public and private is a major feature of the medieval Muslim city.

Since the residential quarters fostered a spirit of separatism among the city's inhabitants, the unity of the city depended entirely on activities in the public section of the city. The main mosque gathered people from all quarters (except non-Muslim ones) for worship; it also gathered them for public purposes, such as to listen to an address by the ruler. The bazaar also brought people together (non-Muslims included) in very active exchange, both commercial and social.

The one public official who exercised what might be described as a municipal, or at least quasi-municipal, function was the muhtasib, the "inspector of the market." Appointed by the police and supervised by the qadi, this official's duty was to see that public morality was properly maintained in the bazaar. This included not only the maintenance of fair business practices but also the observance of general standards of decency and propriety on the part of the public. Thus, the muhtasib kept a watchful eye against dishonesty in manufacturing and selling, fraud, unfair competition, as well as against rowdiness, drunkenness, theft, and indecent dress. Empowered to bring violators

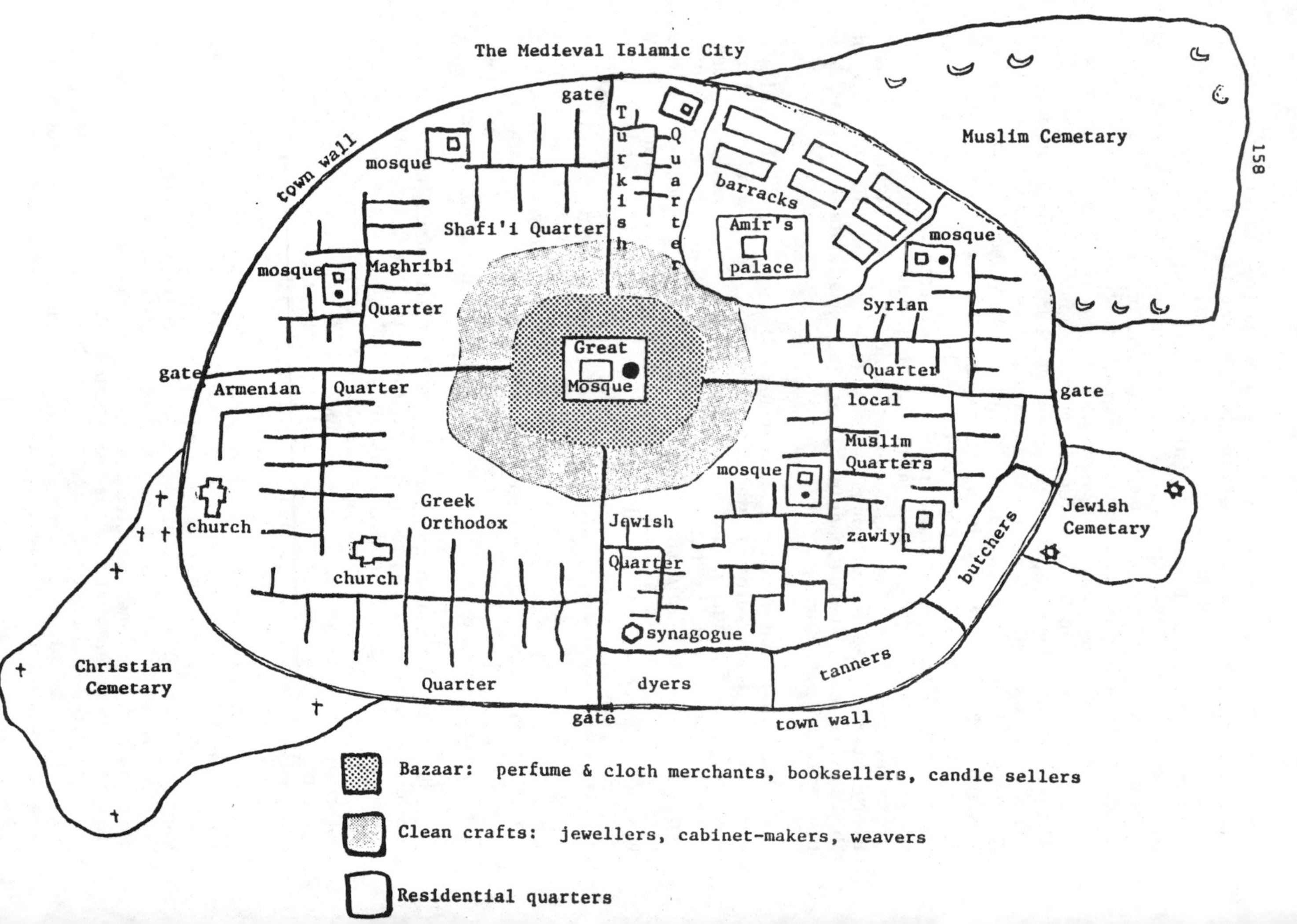
The Medieval Islamic City
Muslim Cemetary
town wall
gate
mosque
Turkish Quarter
barracks
Amir's palace
mosque
Shafi'i Quarter
mosque
Maghribi Quarter
Syrian Quarter
Great Mosque
gate
Armenian Quarter
local Muslim Quarters
gate
mosque
church
Greek Orthodox
church
Jewish Quarter
zawiyh
butchers
Jewish Cemetary
synagogue
Christian Cemetary
Quarter
dyers
tanners
gate
town wall
Bazaar: perfume & cloth merchants, booksellers, candle sellers
Clean crafts: jewellers, cabinet-makers, weavers
Residential quarters

to immediate justice, the muhtasib could impose penalties on his own authority, such as the flogging of drunk persons and sexual offenders and the amputation of the hand of the thief caught in the act. His jurisdiction, called in Arabic hisba, was conceived in religious terms. Through him the communal duty of promoting good and preventing evil (al-amr bi'l-ma^{c}ruf wa'l-nahi ^{c}an al-munkar) was discharged. Beginning in the eleventh century, some ^{c}ulama' began to write treatises devoted specifically to the duties of the muhtasib and the regulations he was supposed to enforce.

As inspector of the market, the muhtasib exercised authority over the various trades and crafts. There has been a great deal of debate among scholars over whether or not these trades and crafts were organized into guilds such as were found in Byzantine or medieval European cities. One scholar who has made a careful study of this question has concluded that, if the term "guild" be taken to mean an association restricted to a particular trade or craft and designed to serve not merely the social but also the economic interests of its members, then there were no guilds in the medieval Muslim city. It did happen that occasionally members of a particular trade or craft formed a Sufi brotherhood or lived together in a particular quarter, in which case they maintained an active social life among themselves; but in these cases economic interests seem to have been secondary. Probably all the trades and crafts had some degree of organized social life. This would seem to follow from their being grouped together physically in different sections of the bazaar. Also, there must have been some organized system of apprenticeship whereby skills could be transmitted from generation to generation. However, incorporation of entire trades and crafts for the purpose of insuring fair prices, controlling quality, and eliminating ruthless competition was unknown. These matters were tended to by the government as represented by the muhtasib and his assistants. Often the government appointed a particular merchant or craftsman ra'is (or shaykh) over his fellows; but such appointments did not entail incorporation of the trade or craft concerned. The ra'is was simply an intermediary between the muhtasib and the artisans.

The Countryside

Owing to the dominant position of the city in medieval Islamic society, the countryside had very little life of its own. The chief figure in the rural scene was of course the peasant, who lived close to the land which he cultivated. As has been the case everywhere in pre-modern times, a rather high concentration (by modern standards) of human labor on the land was necessary for proper cultivation, resulting in an accumulation of peasants in villages, the size of a village being determined largely by the density of peasant population. Some peasants owned the small tracts of lands which they cultivated. Many others, however, worked as tenant farmers on large estates owned by wealthy individuals who lived, generally speaking, in the cities. The commonness of the latter arrangement has led one modern scholar to remark: "The cultivator does not own and the owner does not cultivate." This absenteeism of landowners militated against the proper development of many lands. Nothing comparable to the medieval

European manor, which was a self-contained, self-sufficient agricultural unit supervised directly by a resident landlord and relatively cut off from city life, ever developed in the medieval Islamic world.

Absentee landownership and the urban domination of the countryside was the outcome of two factors: (1) the cultural, political, and social primacy of the city, which made residence in the country undesirable or unnecessary in the eyes of the wealthy, and (2) the economic importance of land as the chief basis of wealth. Despite the great interest in trade that is so characteristic of medieval Islamic society, land remained the primary (and most secure) source of income. Hence, wealthy city-dwellers, including merchants, continually sought to buy rural property. Since industry was never developed on a scale sufficiently large to absorb a significant part of the available capital and since, in any case, the prohibition against usury discouraged financial speculation, free capital tended to be put into land.

Written medieval sources tell us practically nothing about rural life, since this subject had little or no interest for most writers, all of whom were city-dwellers. We would like to know more than we do about the customs, folklore, and religious beliefs of peasants, but unfortunately our information about them is extremely sparse, and such information as exists is usually provided by writers who themselves were alien to the rural scene and took a dim view of peasants. To a large extent we must infer information about peasants in medieval times from the research of modern ethnographers.

The predominance of peasants was an essential feature of the village distinguishing it from the city. This is not to say, however, that all its inhabitants were peasants. Even peasants required certain services; therefore, tool-makers, carpenters, millers, barbers (who also did some surgery), religious teachers, and the like were found in most villages. Furthermore, the peasants' lives were not confined entirely to their own villages. The markets of the nearest city were a constant attraction to peasants, and many of them occasionally left their normal routine to get a glimpse of urban life and to obtain goods not available locally, such as clothing, medicine, metal implements, and exotic items from distant lands.

Social Stratification and the A^{c}yān-Amīr System

In virtually all societies there is some degree of ranking of individuals into strata or classes. Medieval Islamic society was no exception. Sociologists commonly single out three criteria for this ranking: power, wealth (socioeconomic status), and prestige. These three categories represent resources which are obviously limited in quantity and will therefore inevitably be distributed unequally among members of a society. Since they are limited, they will (like many scarce commodities) be coveted and therefore valued by most people. Those who possess them in large degree will be regarded as particularly eminent or as superior to others. Those who possess them in a very limited degree or not at all will be regarded as inconsequential and inferior. The presence of strata or classes indicates that the ranking of individuals is not based on a continuous scale but involves a grouping of individuals on the basis of these categories. Very often this grouping is by occupation or status. A high official of the state, for example, has access by virtue of his status to a large degree of power, and probably of wealth and prestige as well, and is therefore grouped in the upper stratum or class of his society.

Within Islamic society, social stratification was most evident in the cities, because that is where power, wealth, and prestige were located in the largest degree. The village, being much smaller than the city and made up primarily of peasants, was more egalitarian. This is not to say that there were no social distinctions in the villages. In many villages some families were distinctly more prosperous than others, and these might exercise a kind of political leadership. If the village population was not dominated entirely by absentee large landlords, these more prosperous elements might actually be landlords in their own right (although their landholdings would be very small compared to those of the absentee landlords). In many villages, the more influential families might choose a village chief who would be responsible for supervising the internal affairs of the community. Such projects as repairing irrigation canals or reaping a large harvest often required the managerial functions of such a chief.

It was in the cities that the greater disparities in power, wealth, and prestige were to be found, giving rise to fairly conspicuous class distinctions. These distinctions are evident in certain Arabic terms that appear frequently in the writings of medieval Muslim authors. Two of these--<u>khāṣṣa</u> ("elite") and <u>ᶜāmma</u> ("commoners")--form a pair, implying a two-level stratification of society. This two-level stratification is common in pre-modern societies: one was a member either of the aristocracy or of the unwashed masses. In some cases, the term <u>khāṣṣa</u> referred only to the ruling elite, that is to the ruler, high military officers and high officials of the state, in which case the accent obviously was upon power as the basis of stratification and the term <u>ᶜāmma</u> would include all the subject people, even those wealthy and prestigious ones who were not a part of the ruling elite. However, in many other instances, the term <u>khāṣṣa</u> has a broader sense, including not only the ruling elite but also a category of persons called <u>aᶜyān</u> ("notables"), which embraced the most influential members of the civilian population. When <u>khāṣṣa</u> has this broader sense, a more widely-based stratification of society results, one which entails wealth and prestige as much as power, and the opposite term <u>ᶜāmma</u> definitely takes on the sense of commoners.

The aᶜyān and the amīrs played complementary roles within the urban scene. Included among the aᶜyān were all persons who were in a position to influence in significant ways the activities of a sizeable body of fellow civilians and thus to determine in large measure the affairs of the city. Since the amīr concerned himself only with certain fairly well-defined aspects of city life, considerable room was left free for the creation of spheres of influence by elements within the civilian population. Thus military and civilian elements worked together to direct the life of the city. Hodgson has called this system of social control in the Islamic city "the aᶜyān-amīr system."

Civilians could exercise influence over their fellows in a variety of ways. Some did so through their association with the ruling circles of public officials. This was the case, for example, with qādīs, muhtasibs, high-ranking civilian bureaucrats, and officially appointed representatives (ra'īses) of trades. Others--the leading merchants and large landowners--owed their ability to influence others entirely to their wealth, while still others--the ^{c}ulamā', Sūfī masters (see next section) and non-Muslim religious leaders--owed this ability to prestige of a religious nature, although this latter category could also sometimes be quite wealthy. Thus the ranks of the a^{c}yān included various sorts of persons, the principle common criterion of membership being the ability to exercise sway over a significantly large segment of the urban population. To be counted among the a^{c}yān meant to have a following upon whose loyalty one could consistently rely and which was large enough to have an appreciable impact on city life.

Hodgson has placed strong emphasis on two closely interrelated features of the a^{c}yān-amīr system: (1) the contractual nature of the relationship between the a^{c}yān and their followings, and (2) the high degree of fluidity of social life within the system as compared to other agrarian societies. To say that a relationship is contractual is to say that it is a relationship *voluntarily* entered into by both parties, even if the relationship entails a social superiority of one part over the other. Hodgson further describes the relationship between the a^{c}yān and their following as a *patron-client* relationship, both of which terms are suggestive of the voluntary nature of the relationship. A person could exercise sway over others only to the degree that he could offer benefits such as protection, employment, or religious counsel. In return for these benefits, one received, by virtue of the loyalty of the clientele thus acquired, the benefit of enhanced social standing. The patron-client relationship was thus freely entered into because it was seen by each party as serving his particular interests. The a^{c}yān could not, in other words, lay claim to pre-eminence in Islamic society simply on the ground of status conferred by long-standing custom.

The Islamic social outlook was not status-oriented. One earned the position one had in society through the prudent use of one's resources and wits. This is not to say that one could not be born with important advantages; but birth itself never assured one, or one's posterity, of an ongoing position of advantage. The only sphere in which relationships were determined by long-standing custom was that of family life. Outside the family one negotiated one's way through life. Even the amīr's position depended more on his ability to elicit the loyalty of his troops than upon status as such. This contractualism of social life made for a high degree of social mobility relative to other agrarian societies. One could climb up or slide down the social ladder. Social stratification there was, but it was not a stratification which held people in absolute captivity within a given stratum, as was the case with the more caste-oriented agrarian societies. Family would of course attempt to keep wealth and other socially important resources within their possession from generation to generation, sometimes with considerable success. But prevailing social attitudes did little to guarantee that this would happen. Hodgson has suggested that this fluidity of social life and relative disregard of status was, partly at least, a function of the ecological setting of Islamic society. The gradual and persistant decline of agricultural productivity, while by no means eliminating the agrarian base of the social order which was the hallmark of all agrarian societies, had undermined that base to a considerable degree. This gave the commercial marketplace, with its penchant for contractual relationships, greater relative weight than it had in most other agrarian societies. It also gave greater relative weight within the larger social context to the pastoral economies which existed on the peripheries of Islamic agrarianate society, thus strengthening the position of merchants in the cities, with whom the pastoralists, being by nature traders, formed common cause.

Thus far the categories we have been considering have suggested a two-part stratification of society, the two strata being an elite consisting of the ruling circles (the amīr and his entourage) and the aᶜyān on the one hand, and a mass of commoners on the other. Other categories which appear in classical Arabic texts suggest a class division of sorts among the commoners. These categories are represented by terms such as ayyārūn, ghawghā', and zu'ar, which taken together seem to denote a class best described as the disreputable poor, or the rabble. They constituted the lowest stratum of society, the scum of the earth. Membership in this class entailed a lack of those resources that gave others higher standing in society, but it entailed something more: the adoption of a disreputable style of life and means of livelihood. The disreputable poor were generally semi-skilled or unskilled workers who were forced by unemployment or the harshness of circumstances to resort to devious sources of income, such as thieving or begging or wheeling and dealing. A poor person who struggled to make an honest living, no matter how meagre, did not belong to this disreputable class, although he might at any time be tempted to join it.

Thus, we have what amounts to a tripartite stratification of society. Clearly the ruling elite and the notables represent the top stratum of medieval Islamic urban society, and clearly the disreputable poor represent the bottom stratum. What remains is a middle stratum: the respectable commoners, the good solid citizens who made an honest living and kept within the bounds of law and propriety. This stratum included the petty bureaucrats, the small-scale merchants (especially shopkeepers), the lesser ᶜulamā', the honest working population (especially skilled craftsmen)--in other words, those who did not have sufficient power, wealth, or prestige to be regarded as khāssa or aᶜyān, but yet did not belong to the despised segments of society.

It is to be noted that not all those associated with government, commerce, or religion were entitled to be considered as upper class. In fact, among those associated with these things the greater majority were classified as commoners; only the very few stood in the upper echelons of society. The great majority of ᶜulamā', for example, were petty teachers, Koran-readers, mosque officials, and judges would never have been considered among the very great. Most merchants likewise operated small-scale businesses, which placed them among the general throng. Workers, no matter how skilled, almost by definition were excluded from the upper classes, since the most consummate craftsman was unable to amass wealth to be counted among the truly wealthy.

Obviously, there were great economic differences within the middle stratum. Presumably most merchants made an adequate living, as did the skilled craftsmen. Semi-skilled or unskilled workers, however, were often very poor and faced the threat of unemployment. These were subject to the temptation to join the rabble. Even religious functionaries sometimes received small pay and were obliged to live at near-poverty level. The middle stratum thus cannot be defined in purely economic terms. Certainly the line of demarcation between middle and lower classes was not a purely economic one but had to do with the life style and means of livelihood adopted.

The lower or disreputable stratum is of great interest to social and economic historians because it was always a key factor in the urban scene. In every city there were a sizeable number of young and early middle-aged men who possessed no particular skills and who earned a living from whatever work they could find. Usually poor and living from hand to mouth, these men hovered between the respectable and disreputable segments of society. When times were good, they managed to keep employed and would have respect for the public peace. In hard times, they were readily drawn into disruptive activities, such as rioting and pillaging. Unemployment brought leisure time in which to plan such activities. On the whole, the working population in medieval Muslim cities had no organized channels through which to communicate their complaints or demands to the authorities. Consequently, rioting was their only outlet in times of distress, with pillaging as the inevitable complement. Such activities fostered an anti-social and ultimately criminal attitude in many. Those who wished to avoid criminal acts could, and often did, take to begging. To the upper classes, these lower segments of society were coarse, lazy, and mischievous--hence the perjorative appellations which were applied to them. Sometimes they had experience with arms, in which case they were all the more dangerous. In fact, in some towns armed units called ahdath were formed among young men of the lower classes.

It was primarily among the lower classes that a type of spontaneous organization known generally as the futuwwa arose in many towns, especially in Iran and the eastern Arab lands. The futuwwa was essentially a young men's club designed to provide organized leisure-time activities, including sports, and to inculcate certain ideals, especially those associated with manliness. In contrast to the upper classes, which remained highly conscious of their privileged status, the futuwwa organizations laid great stress on the equality of all human beings. Futuwwa members tended to be hostile to the rich and powerful and often, when authority was poorly enforced, provoked disorders. On the other hand, the government sometimes sought to win their favor by recruiting some of their number into the police force, and powerful individuals occasionally used them as henchmen. The code of behavior of the futuwwa members was to always be in line with Islamic norms as defined by the ʿulamāʾ. Critical of the established order, they sometimes set aside conventional morality by engaging in such practices as the public drinking of wine. They tended to look upon the ᶜulamā' notables as hypocritical and the ruling elite as guilty of injustice, praising rather the virtues of those who championed the cause of the poor and oppressed. From time to time there emerged among them Robin Hood-like heroes noted for their chivalry, respect for women, and noble deeds on behalf of the poor.

The Ṣūfī Orders

One of the most pervasive forms of organized social life in the medieval Islamic world was that represented by the Ṣūfī orders. These orders, which arose in the eleventh and twelfth centuries and rapidly spread throughout the Islamic world, were the result of the popularization of mysticism. Although Ṣūfī mysticism per se will be discussed in the following chapter, a brief consideration of its rise and character will be necessary here for introductory purposes.

Mysticism, which is a universal phenomenon found in all civilizations, is a type of religious experience in which the focus is on a heightened sense of the reality of God. Ṣūfī mysticism takes its clue from the monotheistic affirmation, which it interprets as meaning that God is the sole ultimate reality and everything other than He is but an appearance. The Ṣūfī (as the Muslim practitioner of mysticism is called) seeks through various spiritual exercises to become so wholly preoccupied with God that he becomes heedless even of his own selfhood. This state is known in Arabic as fanā' (disappearance of self), and it is accompanied normally by strong feelings of ecstasy.

Ṣūfī mysticism had roots in earliest Islam. The Koran itself places great emphasis upon the reality of God and of the world beyond. Among the first generations of Muslims there were some who adopted an ascetic manner of life, choosing to renounce all worldly concerns in order to meditate more fully on God. This early asceticism (zuhd) developed gradually into a more explicit mysticism, as formal techniques of meditation and a repertoire of mystical concepts were introduced. Beginning in the ninth century, there emerged a number of prominent Ṣūfī shaykhs, or masters of the art of meditation, who attracted large followings. Through them Ṣūfī mysticism achieved great popularity among the masses. In contrast to the somewhat rigid legalism of the ᶜulamā', Ṣūfī mysticism appealed to the deeper religious needs of people; it offered them the possibility of a direct personal relationship with God, and it was thoroughly grounded in the vocabulary of the Koran.

It is characteristic of Ṣūfī mysticism, in contrast to many other types of mysticism, that it emphasized group experience. Whereas mysticism often leads to withdrawal from society and solitary isolation, the mysticism of the Ṣūfīs, generally speaking, drew people together. Two factors account for this: (1) the influence of the Ṣūfī shaykhs, who worked with adepts in groups, and (2) the Ṣūfī liturgy, or dhikr, which was designed to be performed by groups. The physical basis of Ṣūfī mysticism was the convent (zāwiya or ribāṭ in Arabic, khāniqāh in Persian), at which a Ṣūfī shaykh or group of shaykhs lived together with their disciples. Convents were funded in the same way as mosques and madrasas: through charitable endowments (awqāf). In the convent the shaykh guided his disciples through the various stages of the mystical life. The relationship between shaykh and disciple, or murīd, was very close and intense, and the murīd bound himself in unquesting obedience to the shaykh, abandoning completely all personal desires and opinions. Once a murīd had completed, under the shaykh's direction, his mystical training, he entered the ranks of the fully-fledged Sūfīs and was entitled to gather disciples of his own and to become a shaykh in his own right.

But the convent was not only a place of training; it was also a center of mystical worship. The basis of this worship was the dhikr, which was a liturgy consisting of set formulae describing or addressing deity. The term dhikr means literally "remembrance." By means of the dhikr formulae, the individual worshipper "remembered" God, that is to say focused his attention on God in such a way as to induce mystical ecstasy. Sometimes the dhikr liturgy was accompanied by non-verbal exercises, such as dancing, whirling, and deepbreathing. Among some Sūfīs music was used, in spite of the general disapproval of music by the ᶜulamā' and the absence of music from the regular mosque services.

The dhikr services were usually attended, not only by the shaykhs and their murīds, but also by other persons who were unable or disinclined to engage in spiritual exercises on a full-time basis but derived emotional satisfaction from the service. They did not aspire, as did the murīds, to become fully-fledged Sūfīs, but they did cultivate a facility for the ecstatic mystical experiences of the Sūfīs. It was the involvement of these lay persons in the dhikr services that gave Sūfī mysticism such a wide popular outreach. At the dhikr services shaykh, murīd, and lay-member all gained, in addition to mystical fulfillment, a sense of fraternity that--especially for the lay-members who otherwise were preoccupied with the toils of earning a living--added a great deal of human warmth to their lives.

The Sūfī communities centered on the convents cut across class lines, as well as across the often impenetrable line between town and countryside. No segment of society was untouched by Sūfism. It became indeed one of the most integrative forces within the Muslim community, minimizing social and economic differences and emphasizing brotherhood.

The Sūfī order was essentially an affiliation of convents based on acceptance of a common doctrine and method of meditation, which was that taught by the grand shaykh or founder of the order. Each of the many orders that came to exist arose out of the following of an eminent shaykh. From this original nucleus former disciples of the shaykh, now shaykhs in their own right, journeyed far and wide carrying their master's teachings with them and founding convents in which the methods of the master were practiced. The order thus formed was generally named after the original master, who throughout his lifetime remained the highest spiritual authority in the order. It is a significant feature of the Sūfī movement that the strong allegiance of the murīd to his shaykh remained even after the murīd had completed his formal training and had become a shaykh in his own right--it remained, in fact, to the end of his life. This permanent character of the shaykh-murīd relationship gave the Sūfī movement its hierarchical structure and made possible the formation of great orders. Prior to his death the grand shaykh of an order appointed a khalīfa (i.e., caliph) to succeed him, and thus a spiritual caliphate was established in order to insure direction of the order from generation to generation. The orders varied in the degree of rigidity with which this hierarchical, or pyramidal, structure was enforced; some orders were freer and more congregational than others. However, all orders had this structure in principle. Sūfī doctrine maintained that the earthly structure of the order had its counterpart in the invisible spiritual universe, which was believed to revolve around a central axis, an unidentifiable cosmic shaykh called the Qutb, whom the grand shaykh and succeeding khalīfas typified.

During the early stages of the development of Sūfī mysticism (especially the ninth and tenth centuries), the ᶜulamā' were wary of certain tendencies which were observable in the movement. Some of the more radical Sūfīs adopted slogans which seemed out of harmony with Islamic doctrine. In the early tenth century, for example, a popular Sūfī preacher in Baghdad, named al-Hallaj, exclaimed, "I am the Reality" (by which he meant that he had no reality of his own, that his reality was identical to that of God). This seemed the ultimate sacrilege to the authorities; al-Hallāj was apprehended and later executed for heresy. Another disconcerting tendency in the Sūfī movement was the disregard of some Sūfīs for the religious law. Furthermore, the movement seemed to be developing rival centers of worship which might detract from the mosque and an independent leadership whose relationship to the ᶜulamā' was far from clear. However, despite the apprehensions of the ᶜulamā', the Sūfī movement grew rapidly within the general population, and it soon became clear to the ᶜulamā' that it was a powerful force which could not be set aside. In the eleventh century, many ᶜulamā' began to see that there was much good in Sūfī mysticism and themselves began to cultivate the mystical experience. To these ᶜulamā' Sūfī mysticism represented the real heart of religion, since it dealt with the inner life, with attitudes and dispositions of the mind, whereas the law as such could deal only with outward behavior. Thus, a wedding of sorts took place between the Sūfī movement and the official religious establishment, and thereafter legal studies and mystical exercises were carried on side by side by the same persons; many ᶜulamā' were also Sufi shaykhs and vice versa. Radical forms of Sūfism continued to exist, especially in rural areas where the influence of the ᶜulamā' was minimal. These the ᶜulamā' continued to condemn. But a large segment of the Sūfī movement preferred to operate in conformity with the religious law.

One of the most widespread of the Sūfī orders was that of the Qādiriyya. Its founder was ᶜAbd al-Qādir al-Jīlānī (d. 1166), who achieved great popularity as a teacher in Baghdad and for whom a convent was constructed outside the gates of the city. ᶜAbd al-Qādir was educated in the tradition of the ᶜulamā' and belonged to the most conservative of the law schools, that of the Hanbalīs. He thus was a typical representative of the conformist or orthodox brand of Sūfī mysticism. The Qādirī order, which was more the product of the organizing activities of ᶜAbd al-Qādir's disciples than of ᶜAbd al-Qādir himself, retained this orthodox character; its dhikr services were conducted in a manner that gave no offense to the law-minded ᶜulamā'. The following formulas are typical of the Qādirī dhikr: "I ask pardon of the mighty God; Glorified be God; May God bless our Master Muhammad and his household and Companions; There is no God but Allāh." Each of these was repeated a hundred times.

Like several of the larger orders, the Qādirī order gave rise to derivative orders. One of these was the Rifaᶜi order, which was inclined to the radical type of Sūfī mysticism and adopted such practices as glass-eating, snake-handling, and walking on fire. Another order which generated many suborders was that of the Shādhiliyya, which arose in North Africa in the thirteenth century. It was more ritualistic and more given to emotionalism than the Qādirī order. No doubt one of the most sensational orders was that of the so-called "whirling dervishes," or Mawlawiyya, which flourished mainly among Turks. In Egypt an order of great popularity was that of the Ahmadiyya (or Badawiyya), based in Tanta. It claimed as its founder Ahmad al-Badawī (d. 1276), who had played a leading role in the resistance against the army of St. Louis, the leader of the Seventh Crusade.

Because of its high regard for men of outstanding spiritual achievement, the Sūfī movement gave strong impetus to a feature of popular religion found in many Muslim countries: the cult of saints (awliyā': more correctly translated as "friends of God"). It is true that a tendency to revere persons of unusual piety existed among medieval Muslims apart from the Sūfī movement. The Prophet Muhammad was revered universally from earliest Islamic times. The Shīᶜis, particularly after the martyrdom of Husayn ibn ᶜAlī, elevated to a position of special sanctity the descendants of ᶜAlī, and in particular, the Imāms, who were believed to be infallible. Sunnī Islam also displayed great deference for persons of superior accomplishments in the field of religion, such as the founders of the four law schools. One may witness, as an example of this, the great respect accorded to the tomb of "al-Imam" al-Shāfiᶜi in Cairo. To this body of spiritual giants the Sūfī movement added a galaxy of others; in many instances it transformed reverence into outright veneration. (Veneration invests its object with a sacred character; reverence does not necessarily do this.) The awe which Sūfīs felt for their grand shaykhs, linked as they were to the cosmic Qûtb, was a new ingredient in popular religion unknown in earliest Islam; it was matched only by the attitudes of the more extreme Shīᶜis toward their Imāms. This awe stemmed in part from the shaykh-murīd relationship described earlier. Many Sūfīs of great renown were endowed by later generations of followers with baraka, or supernatural power (often evidenced in the working of miracles). Their tombs became virtual centers of worship, to which people came to seek answers to prayers, sometimes traveling great distances to reach them. The belief in baraka and in the intercessory offices of saintly persons was particularly strong in Northwest Africa (Morocco and Algeria), where the Sūfī movement absorbed the indigenous Berber belief in holy men to produce the phenomenon of maraboutism. Ibn Tūmart, the founder of the Muwahhid movement, stood within this tradition.

CHAPTER SIX

THE ISLAMIC CULTURAL SYNTHESIS

In chapter three attention was given to the development, under the Abbasids, of an Arab cultural tradition, expressed mainly in literature, especially poetry and belles lettres. Although in the period of Abbasid rule Arabic literature was cultivated throughout the world of Islam, it eventually found its true home in the lands where Arabic became the spoken language of the population. The rise and development of Persian literature in the eastern lands after the ninth century helped to bring about this anchorage of Arabic literature in the Arabic-speaking milieu. While Arabic continued to prevail throughout the medieval Islamic world as a language of religion, philosophy, science and history, its role as a language of poetry and belles lettres within that larger world was considerably diminished after 900.

Literature presents but one facet of the larger cultural whole called civilization. While one may speak of an Arab cultural tradition with reference to literature, it is not quite appropriate to apply this designation to the other components of the civilization of which classical Arabic literature was a part. That civilization is best described as Islamic civilization. True, the Arabic language was used universally in fields other than literature proper. But the religion of Islam, in the final analysis, has had a much greater integrating influence on cultural life than the Arabic language, notwithstanding the pervasiveness of the latter. This is because religion, unlike language, is a set of ideas or beliefs which can determine in large measure the ways in which people structure, beautify, and give meaning to their lives.

The civilization that forms part of the subject matter of Arab history is thus not, at least as far as the medieval period is concerned, a distinctively Arab civilization in the sense of having roots primarily among Arabs or within the Arab lands. Rather, it is the common heritage of all Muslims and of all Islamic lands. Because the Arabs and the Arab lands belong to the world of Islam, Islamic civilization is an essential component of Arab history. Only in the field of literature is it proper to isolate an Arab cultural tradition from other traditions, although even in so doing one must keep in mind that Arabic literature has much in common with the other literature of the Islamic world, that it is, notwithstanding its special anchorage within the Arabic-speaking milieu, an Islamic literature.

It may be noted here that in modern times, as a result of the impact of nationalism, it has become more common to speak of national cultural traditions within the world of Islam--Arab, Persian, Turkish, and so on. These traditions include much more than literature of the tradition sort; they are a good deal more comprehensive than the Arab cultural tradition mentioned above. At the same time, it is seldom that reference is made to Islamic civilization as an ongoing living tradition. It is of Islam the religion (and to some extent of Islamic culture) that one generally speaks in the modern context. Islamic civilization is typically seen to be a heritage of the past, more a medieval reality than a modern one, notwithstanding its lingering effects. In the modern world, Islam the religion lives on within the context of national cultures (producing a certain degree of specifically Islamic cultural activity) and of a world-wide technological civilization.

Medieval Islamic civilization did not arise in a day. Rather, it grew up gradually during the first few centuries after the expansion of the Arabs, and it was the result of close intermingling and collaboration between many different peoples, both Arab and non-Arab. Many elements in this civilization were adopted from older civilizations, but everything was influenced to a greater or lesser degree by the religion of Islam. Islamic civilization was thus a synthesis of many different cultural elements under the aegis of the Islamic faith. This synthesis was a novel one in at least three respects. First of all, it bore the stamp of a new religion, that of Islam. Secondly, owing to the wide extent of the Arab conquests, it brought together cultural ingredients that had never before been assembled on such a large scale. Thirdly, thanks to the creative efforts of its participants, it brought about fresh cultural achievements. This last point bears special emphasis. A synthesis is not merely a juxtaposing of pre-existing elements; it is a creative event whereby the old is woven together to produce something new. Islamic civilization involved much more than a custodianship of ancient achievements; it included a great many achievements of its own that it was able, in its turn, to pass on to other civilizations.

In this chapter we will concentrate on certain elements in Islamic civilization which come under the category of what is often called high culture. High culture, like culture in general, is difficult to define by means of abstract concepts. We may perhaps get an idea of what it is by considering the sort of things it includes. This chapter will deal with ten components of high culture: religious scholarship (excluding theology), jurisprudence, language studies, literature and criticism, theology, philosophy, mysticism, science and mathematics, historiography and geography, art and architecture. These do not represent an exhaustive list of all activities which may be subsumed under the concept of high culture. They are, however, typical of high culture activities; one can scarcely conceive of a high culture which does not embrace these or similar activities.

High culture is generally contrasted to folk, or popular, culture. Unlike the latter, high culture has a very strong literary basis, is found almost exclusively in towns, and is cultivated primarily by persons who belong to the upper strata of society. Most historians, when dealing with cultural life, tend to focus their attention on high culture and leave other categories of culture to the anthropologists. This does not necessarily mean that the historian is disinterested in the other categories; folk culture in particular falls very much within his subject field. However, for most periods of history the historian has relatively little information about folk culture, as compared to the great abundance of material on high culture. It is the latter that most literary sources (which, as we noted in the first chapter, are what the historian relies on primarily) are mainly interested in. Literary sources are the product of persons who, by virtue of their literary inclinations if for no other reasons, are partisans of high culture. The concept of high culture is not as comprehensive as that of civilization. The latter includes, in addition to activities like those named above (as typical of high culture), social institutions and patterns of behavior as well. Indeed, much of the subject matter of the previous chapter belongs under the heading of civilization. The high culture activities considered in this chapter thus represent a part, and not the whole, of Islamic civilization.

Religious Scholarship

Since religion was the primary integrative factor in Islamic civilization, religious scholarship occupied a central place within that civilization. By "religious scholarship" we mean those disciplines and skills that were directly related to the sources of the Islamic faith, especially the Koran and the Hadīth literature. The term therefore does not, in this usage, include religious thought as represented by theology, philosophy, and mystical speculation. The primary aims of religious scholarship were the preservation and correct understanding of the sources of the faith.

The greater part of Islamic religious scholarship was, understandably, devoted to the Koran. Within Koranic scholarship the most important subjects were the recitation of the Koran (qirā'a) and the explication of the Koran (tafsīr: sometimes, but not as appropriately, translated as "interpretation"). The correct recitation of the Koran was a matter of utmost importance to Muslim religious scholars. In order to appreciate why this was (and still is) so, we must realize what the Koran represents to the believing Muslim: the very Speech of God (kalām Allāh). Many writers on Islam describe the Koran as the Word of God. This appellation, though certainly appropriate, is somewhat vague, since it is essentially metaphorical and may be used for any divine revelation, whether verbal or not. In the Bible, for example, the phrase is sometimes applied to moral principles or imperatives which prophets or apostolic writers convey to their contemporaries in their own words. In such cases the Word of God is contained in the words of men. The Islamic tradition, on the other hand, affirms that the Koran consists of words which are themselves from God. The Prophet Muhammad is in no sense the author of the Koran. Both the ideas fouhd in the Koran and the words through which these ideas are expressed have a divine origin. The Word of God is, we may say, contained in the words of God, not of men.

Since the very words of the Koran are from God, they have in the minds of Muslims a sacred character. One modern Muslim writer has described the Koran's character as sacramental, meaning that a transcendent or divine reality is present in its very words. It is through these words that God establishes contact with man and communicates His will to man. This being the case, it is imperative that the words of the Koran be transmitted with the utmost care from generation to generation.

Oral recitation was, for medieval Muslims, the proper mode of the Koran's transmission. A specialist in Koranic recitation taught correct recitation to a group of disciples, who in their turn became specialists and taught recitation to others. In this manner Koranic recitation was passed on from generation to generation. Not only were the words of the Koran thus transmitted; so also was a particular style of recitation, called in Arabic tajwīd. Tajwīd is a type of chanting which is somewhat melodious, although the Islamic tradition carefully distinguishes it from singing as such. It is believed to have originated with the Prophet himself. Through tajwīd the listener is made more aware of the sacredness of the Koran, and strong religious feelings are aroused.

Alongside the oral tradition of Koranic recitation, a written text of the Koran was also preserved from generation to generation, the agents of transmission in this case being scribes who produced a continuing supply of copies of the text. The written text inspired an exquisite calligraphy, which became a vital element in the visual art of Islam. Koranic inscriptions in mosques and other places helped to keep the Koran ever present in the minds of people. Copies of the text were treated with great reverence. The sight of the text evoked much of the same feeling as the sound of the recitation; it fostered an awareness of the scriptural character of the Koran, its character as a Holy Book. Furthermore, for those who did not know the Koran by heart, it was useful for reading purposes. However, important as the written text was in the religious life of Muslims, its position was always subordinate to that of live recitation. It was not copyists but reciters who were the real bearers and transmitters of the Speech of God. This preference for oral recitation as a vehicle of transmission was due partly to the fact that the Arabic script, in the early days of Islam, did not include diacritical marks, and vowel signs were not in use. Without these devices, the text was highly ambiguous and could often be read in several different ways. Consequently, human transmitters seemed far more reliable than the defective written page. Later on, when diacritical marks and vowel signs were developed, the text could be made more precise. However, oral recitation still continued to be preferred as a vehicle of transmission; scribes were viewed as more susceptible to error than reciters, a slip of the pen more feasible than a slip of the memory. Nothing could be more secure than words embedded in the well cultivated and time-honored skills of the reciter. Furthermore, the tajwīd style of recitation, which was itself an integral element in the Koranic corpus, could not in any case be transmitted through written texts. It may finally be noted that, although the Koran is regarded as a book, the term itself (Arabic: al-Qur'ān) is a cognate of the Arabic verb meaning "to recite."

Next to the recitation and transmission of the Koran, the most important Koranic discipline was that of tafsīr, or explication of the Koran. Within this discipline a large literature of commentary on the Koranic text arose. The earliest of the great comprehensive commentaries was that of Ibn Jarīr al-Tabarī (d. 923), a famous scholar of Persian origin who also produced a well-known work of history. Al-Tabarī's method of explicating the Koran was to cite authorities who lived in the earliest period of Islam, especially Companions of the Prophet. Among the Companions, the most renowned as an explicator of the Koran was Ibn ᶜAbbās, a cousin of the Prophet whose father was the eponym of the Abbasid line of Caliphs. Al-Tabarī quotes Ibn ᶜAbbās frequently. The style of writing adopted by al-Tabarī was very much like that of the Hadīth literature, to be discussed presently. Rather than rely on his own ideas in explicating the Koran, al-Tabarī relies primarily on early authorities and restricts his own role to quoting these authorities and demonstrating the authenticity of his quotations. Occasionally, when his authorities hold diverging views, al-Tabarī gives his own view. Generally speaking, however, he was more a compiler of earlier commentary material than a commentator in his own right; his method of explication may therefore be described as the traditional method.

After al-Tabarī's time, a new type of commentary literature arose which employed a method of explication which relied primarily on linguistic principles and lexicographical data rather than on statements of earlier authorities. This method may be called the philological method. Foremost among its exponents were al-Zamakhsharī (d. 1143) and al-Baydāwī (d. 1286). Occasionally, commentators based their explication of the Koran on theological or other philosophical principles. One who is particularly known for having followed this approach is Fakhr al-Dīn al-Rāzī (d. 1210), a famous theologian whose commentary on the Koran is one of the most voluminous in existence.

With respect to the second great source of the Islamic faith, the Hadīth literature, the energies of religious scholars were devoted primarily to authentication and compilation. The Hadīth literature consisted of narratives in which the Prophet's deeds and sayings were recorded. Since these were considered to be inspired, the Hadīth literature came to be regarded as a channel of divine revelation, second only to the Koran. Even though the Hadīth literature did not represent the actual Speech of God, as did the Koran, it was nonetheless a means whereby the will of God could be known. (Occasionally the Prophet did report words of God which were not included in the Koran; these came to form a special class of Hadīth known as Hadīth Qudsī.) The inspired character of the Prophet's sayings and deeds made the task of collecting Hadīth narratives a matter of highest importance. Since there were no set limits to these narratives (as there were in the case of the Koranic corpus), a great abundance of material arose in the course of the first two or so centuries of Islam, and religious scholars were obliged to establish procedures whereby authentic Hadīth narratives could be sorted out from spurious material. Whereas all Hadīth material was originally handed down orally from generation to generation, scholars from the late eighth century began to write down authentic narratives, giving rise to the Hadīth literature per se. The founders of two of the Sunnī law schools, Malik ibn Anas and Ahmad ibn Hanbal, both produced a famous compilation of hadith material. These, however, did not attain the popularity of the so-called "Six Books," compilations which were produced in the ninth and tenth centuries.

The principles and procedures which religious scholars followed in determining the authenticity of Hadīth narratives became an object of special interest, and whole books were devoted to the subject. The focus of this critical endeavor was upon the "chains of authorities" (asānīd, sing: isnād) which were attached to the Hadīth narratives.

No narrative could hope to receive serious attention unless accompanied by a list of persons who had transmitted it from the time of the Prophet. This "chain of authorities" took the following form: "A told me that B told him that C told him that D told him that E told him that the Prophet said (or did) such and such." In this manner, the transmission of the narrative was traced back through several generations to the time of the Prophet. The number of transmitters varied from narrative to narrative, depending on the time span involved or the longevity of the transmitters. Since chains of authorities could be easily fabricated, the scholar who was conducting the evaluation had to be certain that the person from whom he received a narrative was trustworthy and that all the persons cited in the chain of authorities were equally trustworthy. Thus, the evaluation of the authenticity of Hadīth narratives boiled down to an evaluation of the character of the transmitters. Needless to say, men of great piety figured prominently as Hadīth-transmitters. This focus of attention on persons gave rise to a highly developed biographical literature, which was an adjunct to Hadīth-criticism. Indeed, in no other civilization was biographical writing so abundant and so highly regarded.

Although commentaries on the Hadīth books did not have quite the same degree of importance as commentaries on the Koran (owing, perhaps, to the fact that explication of the Speech of God was a much more serious undertaking than explication of humanly composed narratives), such commentaries were written and widely used, especially commentaries on the "Six Books." These commentaries were not, however, categorized as tafsīr (a term that applies exclusively in classical usage to Koranic explication), but as sharh (a general term that can be applied to commentaries on any text, religious or otherwise).

Jurisprudence

Since the ideal law to which the community of Muslims was subject--that is to say, the Sharīᶜa--was considered to be from God, the study of this law (jurisprudence) was closely allied to religious studies and may, in fact, be considered in certain respects as part of religious studies. The Sharīᶜa was an expression of God's will and the basis of man's relationship to God. Only by obeying God's commands could man discover the good life. To disobey was to invite ruin, both in this life and in the life to come. The Sharīᶜa spelled out all of man's duties. These duties embraced not only man's social behavior but also the details of worship. It prescribed both a right way to live and a right way to pray. God's relationship to man was that of a lord (rabb) to his servant: the Lord commanded, the servant obeyed. Since the commands of the Divine Lord were designed to promote man's happiness, they betokened compassion and mercy, not severity or oppression.

Needless to say, the norms laid down in the Sharīᶜa were indistinguishable from moral or ethical norms. The medieval Muslim did not attempt to separate law from morality. As the expression of God's will, the Sharīᶜa necessarily had a moral character; what it declared right or wrong was *really* right or wrong. Furthermore, the norms contained in the Sharīᶜa constituted absolute norms. Right and wrong were such in all times and places. Neither legal nor moral (or ethical) relativism had any place in the Muslim view of things.

Muslim jurisprudence embraced two primary components: the science of fiqh and the science of usūl al-fiqh. The former sought to work out the actual details of the Sharīᶜa; the latter sought to determine the methodological principles which were to guide this effort. These two undertakings presupposed that the Sharīᶜa had not been given to man in the form of a ready-made system of law, one which covered all situations of life; such a system had, therefore, to be constructed by human scholars, the ᶜulamā', on the basis of careful meditation upon the revelation which had come through the Prophet. The chief repository of revelation was the Koran, which the faithful accepted as the very speech of God. But the sayings and recorded deeds of the Prophet, which were enshrined in the Hadīth literature, were also vehicles of revealed truth and therefore constituted, alongside the Koran, a second valid source for the understanding of the Sharīᶜa. These sayings and deeds were regarded as a sacred tradition, or Sunna, which every Muslim must follow to the best of his ability. The Koran and the Sunna were thus the primary foundations upon which the system of law worked out by the ᶜulamā' was to be based. But many cases which called for consideration in this working out of the Sharīᶜa were not explicitly covered in the Koran and Sunna, and therefore some further principle or principles had to be developed whereby the Sharīᶜa could be correctly elaborated. One such principle was the principle of consensus (ijmāᶜ). According to this principle, whatever regulation the Muslim community unanimously agreed upon was a true representation of the Sharīᶜa and was therefore binding upon all Muslims. The consensus of the community was, like the Sunna of the Prophet, thus a vehicle of divine truth; whatever the community agreed upon was considered to be a valid expression of the Divine Will. Another principle adopted by the ᶜulamā' was that of the validity of analogical reasoning (qiyās). According to this principle, whenever a scholar could find no guidance in the Koran, Sunna, or consensus on a particular matter, he was under obligation to draw analogies, or parallels, between cases dealt with in these sources and the case at hand. Thus, if he were asked to render a judgment concerning the drinking of an intoxicating beverage not specifically mentioned in the sources, he might build an argument against the beverage in question by drawing an analogy between it and wine (khamr), which the Koran specifically condemned.

Scholars who specialized in fiqh were the legal experts (fuqahā') of the Muslim community, professionals who were acquainted with the vast details of the Sharīᶜa and from whom one would seek counsel with respect to specific problems; those who specialized in usūl al-fiqh, on the other hand, were called "theorists" (usūliyyūn). Fiqh came eventually to be embodied in enormous books in which the regulations pertaining to the various aspects of life were spelled out and topically arranged. Each of the several law schools, Sunnī and Shīᶜī, had its own fiqh books, which were written by great authorities of different periods. The fiqh books in no sense represented officials codes of positive law; the state had no role in compiling or publishing them. Rather, they contained the legal doctrine of the great jurists, the ᶜulamā'. The jurists were the authoritative exponents of a law believed to be of divine origin. Since they alone were capable of deriving God's law from its proper sources, their doctrine was normative for the Muslim community. Accordingly, certain modern writers have described law in Islam as a "jurists' law," the jurists begin the ᶜulamā'. This is not to say that the ᶜulamā' consciously created law. They as much as any others believed that all law rightly so called was of divine origin, that it stemmed from divine revelation. What the phrase "jurists' law" is meant to convey is that the ᶜulamā' alone, by virtue of their special training, were in a position to declare what the law of God was in particular cases. The Koran and the books of Hadīth, while containing source material for the construction of law, were not in themselves compendia of law. Only in fiqh books compiled by early generations of ᶜulamā' and in declarations made by subsequent generations could formal statements of the law be found.

The fiqh books covered a great variety of topics. This variety is evident from the following list of topics, which are dealt with in a famous Hanāfi law book, the Hidāya of al-Marghīnānī: Alms (Zakāt), marriage; divorce, adoption, manumission of slaves, vows, penalties, trove or booty, missing persons, partnerships (shirka), religious endowments, sales, bail, transfer of debts, duties of the Qādī, rules of evidence, agency, claims, deposits, loans, gifts, hire (ijāra), inheritance, sacrifices, cultivation of wastelands, hunting, pawns, crimes, and fines. It can be seen from these topics that the law books presupposed a highly comprehensive view of law. The law touched upon all major aspects of life, even those relating to worship.

The fiqh books evaluated individual human acts on the basis of five categories. A particular act might be (1) obligatory, (2) commendable, (3) permitted, (4) reprehensible, or (5) forbidden. The second and fourth of these categories have no parallel in modern positive law. Most modern legal systems are content to state what is obligatory and what is forbidden and to lay down penalties or punishments for omitting the former and committing the latter; by implication, acts which are not strictly defined as obligatory or forbidden are permitted. (Sometimes modern law actually states that certain acts are permissible, or "lawful." Some permissible acts are defined by law as "rights.") One must pay taxes, or serve in the armed forces; one must not rob stores, or assault people on the street. On the other hand, one may marry and have children and choose a particular profession and belong to various community organizations. In contrast to the categories of obligatory and forbidden, which are enforced by means of penalties, those of commendable and reprehensible entail the notion of reward; one is not punished for omitting a commendable act but rather is rewarded for performing it. Similarly, one is not punished for performing a reprehensible act but is rewarded for omitting it (that is to say, for refraining from it). Furthermore, the rewards envisioned in Islamic thinking are granted primarily in the life to come, just as punishments are to a large extent meted out in the life to come (notwithstanding the stipulation of a limited number of temporal punishments). This too tends to place the divine law beyond the sphere of positive law.

The medieval Muslim jurists operated on the assumption that all human acts could be evaluated in terms of the five basic categories. However, the evaluation of a particular act was not a human decision but a deduction from the recognized sources of law, especially the Koran and the Hadīth. It was not man but God who evaluated or judged human acts. Deduction from the sources required that the sources be interpreted correctly. The sources did not as a rule say, "This is forbidden," or "This is reprehensible." Generally, the sources contained commands or prohibitions, or statements implying commands or prohibitions, from which the precise evaluation of an act had to be derived. By itself a command (or prohibition) did not necessarily indicate this evaluation. The imperative form of verbs (which is the means whereby commands are expressed) could be used either to require an act or merely to recommend it. Thus, one could not know from the command itself whether the act in question was obligatory or commendable. For this, contextual clues were necessary. Furthermore, one could never know from a general command whether a particular act was meant to be included under it, since there might always be legitimate exceptions to any general command. Consequently, a general command could never stand by itself. It had to be placed in the context of all the source materials, so that the exact scope of application could be determined. Still, further problems of interpretation were created by the language of the sources. For example, a word might have two or more meanings. The interpreter would have to determine which meaning was intended in a given case.

The work of deriving precise evaluations of acts from the sources (an endeavor which is called ijtihād in Arabic) required that basic methodological principles be clearly set forth. These principles constituted the second primary concern of Islamic jurisprudence, and a distinct category of scholarly literature was devoted to it. Thus, alongside the books of fiqh there emerged books of legal theory (usūl al-fiqh). The study of the methodological principles of legal inquiry became one of the most important of all scholarly disciplines within medieval Islam. In theological terms, it represented nothing less than a process of discovering the will of God.

Language Studies

Since the Koran and Hadīth literature occupied a central position in religious studies and in jurisprudence, the study of the language in which they were written, that is to say the Arabic language, took on great importance. The prestige which Arabic enjoyed was also due to the fact that it was for several centuries the language of a ruling elite. This social pre-eminence of Arabic worked together with its religious pre-eminence to make Arabic a universal language of culture throughout the world of Islam, a position which it was to retain until modern times. For nearly as long a time it was to remain also the primary language of government.

As noted earlier, the Arabic language was one of two primary integrative factors in the cultural life of the Islamic world, the other being Islam itself. The integrative effect of Arabic was due to its position as the lingua franca of culture. Everywhere within the Islamic world Arabic was the principal language, not only of worship (had it been only that it could not have had an integrative role separate from that of religion), but also of religious scholarship, jurisprudence, philosophy, theology, science, historiography, and calligraphy. In other words, Arabic left its imprint on virtually all areas of cultural life. Only in the field of literature did other languages make headway against Arabic. But to some extent Arabic compensated for this loss by making inroads into the competing languages themselves. The main competitor, Persian, is heavily influenced by Arabic; indeed, it has been estimated that eighty percent of the vocabulary of Persian is made up of words of Arabic origin. The impact of Arabic upon Persian resembles that of French upon English, except that it was much greater.

The focus of Arabic language study was upon the Arabic spoken in the time of the Prophet. As the language of the Koran and of the Prophet and his contemporaries, the Arabic assumed a normative character. All subsequent generations of speakers of Arabic would be judged on the basis of linguistic patterns current in West Arabia in the early seventh century. The primary task of the specialists in language study was therefore to collect and perceive as much data as possible relating to the Arabic of the Prophet's age. The Prophet's language thus became the classical tongue of all Muslims, the supreme language of the world they knew.

Linguistic data was obtained from two primary categories of sources: literary remains from the Prophet's age and the living speech of contemporary bedouin. The first category was deemed the more important, and within it the Koran was considered to be the foremost model of correct and eloquent usage. Other sources belonging to this category were the Hadīth literature (an obvious choice since it contained the speech of the Prophet himself) and the so-called pre-Islamic poetry, which was still flourishing at the time of the advent of Islam, even though during the first half-century or so of the Islamic era poetic composition was rare. From these various categories of courses linguistic scholars drew supportive evidence (shawāhid) for principles they wished to enunciate or usages they wished to record. Further evidence was drawn from recorded specimens of the speech of bedouin tribes whose genealogies attested to pure Arab descent. Linguistic scholars were aware of the highly conservative character of bedouin speech. Bedouin were considered immune from the corrupting influences of settled life, especially those of the cities where people of various backgrounds constantly mingled.

Language study embraced three primary fields: lexicography, phonetics, and grammar. In all these fields, the requirement of supportive evidence was strictly observed, and the linguistic scholars gathered an immense amount of data. Lexicography is that branch of language study which records the meanings of words. The data compiled by the Muslim lexicographers was contained in huge lexicons, or dictionaries. If we look into any of the great dictionaries of classical Arabic, we find not only that the meanings of words are given but also that examples of the use of words, drawn from the classical sources, are also frequently provided. The study of phonetics had some affinity with the study of Koranic recitation. The latter discipline fostered a preoccupation with correct pronunciation and diction which was to become characteristic of Arabic literary culture in general. The phoneticians made it their task to analyze and to classify all the basic sounds of Arabic and even to explore the physical basis of these sounds. Their work anticipated many of the discoveries of modern phonetics.

Both of the major components of Arabic grammar, namely morphology (sarf) and syntax (nahw), were highly developed by Muslim linguistic scholars. Like other Semitic languages, Arabic is morphologically rich. From a simple "root" consisting of three letters, a host of different words can be formed. From the root K-T-B, for example, we have the words kataba, kitāb, kitāba, kātib, maktūb, maktab, maktaba, to name only some of the derivatives. Even though these are all separate words, they share a common derivation from the root K-T-B. The formation of words on the basis of roots is made possible by the system of forms contained within the Arabic language. Morphology is the study of this system of forms. The morphologist describes and attempts to analyze the system.

Syntax, on the other hand, is concerned with the interrelationship between words in speech. Since words are the bearers of ideas, syntax has a certain affinity with logic, which is concerned with the interrelationship between ideas. To some extent, the Muslim grammarians were influenced by logic, which was useful in rationalizing syntactic structures. However, the main thrust of their work was descriptive. No less than the lexicographers and phoneticians, they too were bound to the evidence they could muster from their sources. This adherence to observed data (whether "observed" in written sources or in the speech of bedouin) in fact gives a strong descriptive bent to the whole of Arabic language studies, a feature which some modern linguists consider to be the most remarkable feature of these studies. While employing logical (ᶜaqli) methods of analysis they found this helpful, the grammarians most often preferred an inductive (istiqrā'ī) approach to their data, drawing from particulars general principles governing the interrelationships between words, while at the same time carefully recording all exceptions.

Theology

That the impact of Islam should have been particularly evident within the field of speculative thought is not surprising. Religion influences not only the way people act but also--and especially--the way they think. The religion of Islam in particular contained many ideas which speculative minds were able to adopt as themes around which to construct integrated systems of thought. Speculative thought is that concerned with ultimate things: God, spirit, the nature of things, the purpose of life. It was unthinkable that any Muslim living in the medieval period should have attempted to construct a system of thought dealing with such subjects without reference to basic Islamic tenets. Furthermore, virtually all speculative thinkers wrote in the Arabic language. This resulted not only in a great intergration of thought through the use of a common tongue; it also resulted in an enrichment of the Arabic language through the introduction of many new terms.

Islamic speculative thought may be divided into three primary fields: theology, philosophy, and mystical thought. Although these fields were closely interrelated, they were nonetheless essentially distinct from one another.

Theology is the systemization of religious beliefs; it transforms a set of beliefs into a system of thought which is rationally coherent. In doing so, it provides a justification for religious beliefs whereby those beliefs can be defended against critics or urged upon nonbelievers. This latter function of theology is usually called apologetics (not to be confused with apologizing!). In Islamic theology, this apological function is very prominent. This is suggested by the Arabic term by which Islamic theology is generally known, namely kalām. Although kalām normally means simply "speech," it can, as a designation for theology, be best translated as "dialectic." (This translation is not intended to explain the origin of the term kalam as a designation for theology, since this has not yet been determined with full certainty. Some scholars think that theology was called kalam because the kalam Allāh was one of its main subjects.) Dialectic is a type of discussion in which the proponent of a given doctrine or set of doctrines builds up a "case" or rationale for his doctrine by responding to particular questions or criticisms raised by his fellow discussants. The dialectical, or discursive, method of building up a system of thought is contrasted to the deductive method. In the latter, one works out a system of thought in isolation from others by deducing from certain basic tenets, taken to be unassailable, further tenets that are implied in the basic tenets. The deductive method does not depend on questioners or critics to elicit a "case" or rationale. It operates, so to speak, in an ivory tower and employs "cold logic"; it is essentially indifferent to whether or not its results will be generally accepted. It is thus clearly the dialectical method which is the more suitable instrument of apologetical theology.

The expansion of the Arabs in the seventh and eight centuries was a great stimulus to dialectical theology. It brought Muslims into close contact with a variety of non-Muslim religious and intellectual traditions, such as Greek and Indian philosophy and Christian, Jewish, and Zoroastrian theology, all of which contained within themselves considerable variation. As a result of these contacts, Muslims were faced with many challenges to their own religious faith. They had to decide whether to respond to these challenges and thus engage in dialectic with disputants who did not share their religious faith or simply to ignore the challenges.

But the challenge did not originate entirely among non-Muslims. Many of them arose from within the Muslim community itself. The civil wars which had occurred during the period of expansion had given rise to a number of important issues. The most pressing of these was the issue of the blameworthy caliph. If a caliph was guilty of a serious offense against the Sharīʿa, should he be allowed to continue as caliph, or should he be deposed? This was linked to the question of whether a serious offender can even be regarded as a true Muslim and member of the umma. If the answer to this question is no, then the offending caliph is not even a Muslim and his deposition should therefore be immediate. Those who adopted this position made membership in the umma conditional upon righteous conduct, whereas those who adopted the opposite position maintained that being a Muslim is a matter of professing publicly the Islamic faith and that all who make such a profession should be accepted as full members of the umma. The quality of a man's conduct, they insisted, must be judged by God, and not by man.

When such issues arose within the community of Muslims, the various contending groups could, if they chose, employ dialectic in advancing their position. Thus, dialectic became an instrument not only for apologetics vis-à-vis non-Muslims but also for sectarian developments within Islam. It was, in fact, by means of dialectic that an orthodox Sunnī theology was ultimately constructed, which would remain basically unaltered until modern times. Among the issues dealt with in dialectic were the following: the existence of God, the nature of God's attributes (power, will, life, speech, sight), the bearing which this plurality of attributes has upon God's unity, the status of the Koran (eternal or created?), the relationship of God's power to human activity (can humans act freely, or are their actions pre-determined?), the ultimate basis of ethical norms, the grounds of Muhammad's claim to prophethood, the nature of miracles, the status of the serious offender, and the nature and basis of the caliphate.

Despite its vigor, dialectical theology was not universally accepted among medieval Muslims. The more conservative Muslims looked upon it as an intrusion of human reason into the domain of religion. In their view, revelation, as contained in the Koran and Hadīth literature, was completely sufficient as a source of religious truth and there was no need to add to it the findings of the dialecticians. If the revelation was silent on certain matters, it was best to leave these matters to God and concentrate on those things concerning which the revelation was absolutely clear. In the final analysis, what mattered most was obedience to the commands laid down in the revelation, not the satisfaction of human curiosity concerning things not touched on in the revelation. The exponents of this point of view frequently called themselves the <u>ahl al-hadīth</u>, or "People of Hadīth," meaning that beyond the Koran itself they accepted only the Hadīth literature as a source of religious truth, thus repudiating human reason as a means for discovering religious truth. A number of books were written condemning dialectic. One of the most famous of these was a book by Ibn Qudāma entitled <u>The Censure of Speculative Theology</u>, which maintained that dialectic in matters of religious faith was contrary to the Sharīᶜa and therefore illegal (<u>harām</u>).

Because of the hostility of most ahl al-hadīth to dialectic, the theologians (mutakallimun) had to take special pains to defend the use of dialectic in the realm of religion and to show that it was fully compatible with the Sharīᶜa. One of the first to do this was Abu'l-Hasan al-Ashᶜarī (d. 935), who wrote a book entitled <u>Highlights</u>

of the Polemic Against Deviators and Innovators, in which he claimed that revelation not only permitted the use of reason but actually enjoined it. As an instrument of apologetics whereby the faith of the community could be safeguarded and strengthened, dialectic was thus, for al-Ash^{c}arī and his followers, a duty which the faithful could not evade. This same conviction inspired a later theologian, al-Fadālī, to write a pamphlet on the question of how much theology the common people (i.e., non-theologians) must know in order to fulfill their duty as Muslims. The prophet maintained that every Muslim must be able to provide a rationale for his faith and provided some arguments, starting with arguments for God's existence, which would enable him to do this.

One of the most significant features of the kalām theology was its cosmology, or theory of the physical world. In order to preserve the exclusive power of God, the theologians denied that the physical world can exist from one moment to the next by virtue of any power or momentum of its own. The notion of a universe endowed by its creator with an independent continuing existence and made to operate in accordance with certain mechanical laws was alien to the thinking of the medieval Muslim theologians. Such a universe, in their way of thinking, would have imposed a limitation on the absolute power of God. Accordingly, they postulated that the physical world is continuously created by God from moment to moment. Each "moment" was viewed as an atomic unit of time having no duration. The rapid succession of divine creations gave an impression of duration, but this duration in no sense pertained to the physical world itself. Continuity and movement, as we perceive them in the physical world, were illusions resembling the illusion of continuity and movement created by the cinematic projector. This cosmology, needless to say, ruled out the possibility of real causality. The relationship between a cause and its apparent effect is imaginary; there is no intrinsic connection between them. (The British philosopher David Hume incidentally argued along similar lines.)

As a kind of compensation for this lack of real continuity and movement in the physical world and for the consequent absence of causal relationships, the theologians postulated the doctrine of the "Divine Orderliness" (*^{c}ādat Allah*). They did not deny continuity altogether; what they denied was simply that continuity is inherent in the physical world. God's creative activity, they emphasized, was continuous and lent continuity, so to speak, to the physical world. But it was not only continuous; it was also orderly, and thanks to this orderliness, certain fixed patterns could be discerned in the behavior of things. Thus, when an object is released by a human hand, it always falls to the ground. There is no reason why it could not on some future occasion fly upward. However, we do not expect it to do so, since the patterns exhibited in the divine creativity thus far in our experience rule this out. The Divine Orderliness made possible a systematic and inductive investigation into the behavior of physical things.

Philosophy

Although Islamic philosophy has many affinities with theology, it differs from it in certain key respects and must therefore be regarded as a separate movement. Broadly speaking, Islamic philosophy is closely akin to theology, since it deals with religious themes such as God, creation, salvation, and prophecy. However, among historians of Islam it has become customary to restrict the term theology to the dialectical or kalām movement and to apply the term philosophy to the movement under consideration in this section. This accords with medieval Muslim practice, which distinguished kalām from falsafa, the latter term being of the same Greek origin as the English term philosophy.

Kalām theology acquired some of its elements from Greek and Hellenistic philosophy; the dialectical method itself was well-known to the Greeks, not to mention certain substantive ideas, such as that of the atomic composition of the physical world. But Islamic philosophy was to a much greater extent a carry-over of Hellenism into the Islamic world, even allowing for the many original contributions of the Islamic philosophers. Kalam theology arose at a time when Greek and Hellenistic ideas were just beginning to percolate into the Islamic world, whereas falsafa was the direct outcome of the massive translation of Greek philosophical books into Arabic which took place in the ninth century. Kalam theology was in large part a product of developments in early Islam; falsafa was more a continuation on Islamic soil of an ancient tradition going back to Socrates, Plato and Aristotle.

It is somewhat more difficult to speak in general terms about falsafa than about kalām theology, since the latter, despite certain variations, was on the whole a more integrated movement. The philosophers did not operate within the framework of an orthodoxy and were able therefore to develop their thinking much more freely along individual lines than were the theologians. Nevertheless, they all adhered to certain common themes and methods of inquiry and shared a common allegiance to the Greek philosophical heritage.

The foremost of the philosophers, by any reckoning, were the famous triad: al-Farābī (d. 950); Ibn Sīna, or Avicenna (d. 1036); and Ibn Rushd, or Averroes (d. 1198). Al-Farābī is famed both for his extensive commentaries on the works of Aristotle and for original philosophical works of his own. His commentaries helped to make the ideas of Aristotle more understandable to Muslim readers, who found Aristotle's own works (in Arabic translation) obscure and difficult to grasp. Thanks to al-Farābī, Greek philosophy became firmly rooted among Muslim intellectuals. For this reason, al-Farābī was to become known as "the Second Master" (Aristotle being the First). Among his original works, the famous is *The Virtuous City*, which presents a view of an ideal political community which resembles in many ways that found in Plato's *Republic*.

Ibn Sīna carried on the tradition of original composition and became the most influential of all the Muslim philosophers. He wrote prolifically and at the same time involved himself actively in political life, even serving on several occasions as prime minister to ruling princes. It is said that his busy life often required that he compose treatises while riding his horse. His major compendium of philosophy is entitled The Book of Healing. Ibn Sīna's expertise extended beyond the bounds of philosophy to include medicine, in which field he conducted many important experiments and produced a definitive book, the famous Canon of Medicine, which was to become a classic of medicine for many generations to come. Ibn Rushd, on the other hand, carried on the tradition of commentary on the works of Aristotle, in which endeavor he far surprised the achievements of al-Farābī. Ibn Rushd, who lived in Spain, was to play a large role in the development of Aristotelianism in Europe.

Among the features of falsafa which distinguish it from kalām theology, the following may be mentioned:

1. The philosophers favored, in keeping with their Aristotelian roots, the deductive method of inquiry and relegated the dialectic of the kalām theology to an inferior position.

2. The philosophers viewed God more as an abstract principle to be contemplated by the intellect than as a living being whose will man should seek to fulfill. The philosophers regarded God as an explanation for the processes of movement and change which are visible in the universe. They believed that all such processes were due to the influence of mind over material forces and looked upon God as the "First Intellect" and "Prime Mover." Ibn Sīna described God as "Necessary Being," as the One Who cannot not exist, since existence belongs to his very nature. He believed that the existence of the world could be explained only in terms of a Necessary Being; since the world does not exist by its own nature (this is proven by the fact that things in the world around us continually perish), its existence must be explained with reference to something else, namely God.

3. The philosophers taught that the world is eternal, in contrast to the kalām theologians, who believed that the world came into existence at a particular point in time and did not exist prior to that time. For the philosophers, creation was a process whereby the world eternally "emanates" from God. The kalām theologians, on the other hand, insisted that God created the world in the manner of an artisan, that he made it out of nothing, and that he sustains it moment by moment by a process of continuous creation.

4. The philosophers tended to regard the human intellect as superior to revelation in the sense that the intellect was able to discover on its own all that is found in revelation--and more. Revelation was designed for the masses whose intellects were not well developed. It contained images or symbols designed to influence the emotions and behavior of the masses, and was thus essential to the social order. Prophets were on a par with philosophers; except that, in addition to possessing superior intellects, they were also endowed with the gift of clothing truth in symbols. These doctrines were contrary to the tenets of kalām theology.

Notwithstanding these unorthodox teachings, philosophy was not without influence on the kalām movement. From the late eleventh century onwards, kalām theologians began to use the deductive method of investigation along with the traditional dialectic, and somewhat later they began to employ certain philosophical themes, the chief one being that of "Necessary Being." If we turn to the great theological compendium of al-Iji, The Stations, we find that a large part of it is devoted to philosophical matters. However, the kalām theologians never adopted falsafa in full but rather continued to adhere to fundamental orthodox tenets.

Mystical Speculation

The kalām theologians and the philosophers were not the only ones in medieval Islam to construct system of thought. So also did a third category of speculative thinkers, the theosophists, or mystical philosophers. Theosophy is a system of thought based on the principle that the knowledge of God and of ultimate things is derived from intuition or mystical insight. Such intuition or insight is called in Arabic maᶜrifa, which is also the closest Arabic approximation of the term theosophy itself. Islamic theosophy represents the speculative as opposed to the practical side of Sūfī mysticism (see previous chapter).

It proceeds from the mystical sense of the oneness of all reality. When in ecstasy, the Sūfī looked upon the plurality of things in the world around him, including his own individual selfhood, as mere illusion. If reality were one, the many objects perceived in a state of ordinary consciousness could not constitute realities in and of themselves. The phenomenal world with its immense diversity must therefore be a mere guise through which the One Ultimate Reality manifests itself to ordinary consciousness. In the mystical state, one came to the realization that the multifarious manifestations of the One have no reality apart from the One. The mystic even saw himself as real only to the extent that he was identical and inseparable from the One. He sought to do away with the sense that he existed as an individual in his own right. As an individual he wished to die so that he might be reborn as his authentic self, a mere drop in an ocean of undifferentiated reality, a self indistinguishable from the Divine Self. Out of these insights Islamic theosophy built up an elaborate edifice of speculative thought and incorporated many ideas of Islamic theology and philosophy while interpreting them in a distinctly mystical way.

Sūfī mystical writing may be said to have begun with a ninth century Sūfī of Baghdad named al-Muhāsibī (d. 837). Al-Muhāsibī exerted great influence on a series of Sūfī writers who appeared during the next two centuries. During this period the Sūfī movement developed a well-defined theory of mystical experience. This theory maintained that mysticism is a progression through various stages of spiritual growth, the last stage being the full attainment of maᶜrifa. Each stage has a two-fold character: it consists of a disposition (maqām) brought about by the Sūfī himself through the observance of certain spiritual exercises and an inner state (hāl), which is solely a product of divine grace. The attainment of the former does not guarantee that the latter will actually occur, although it helps to prepare the way for it.

The greatest and by far the most influential of all the Sūfī theosophists was Muhyi'l-Dīn ibn ᶜArabī (d. 1240). Born and educated in Spain, Ibn ᶜArabī set out at the age of 37 for the East and after visiting Mecca and various places in Iraq, Syria, and Anatolia, settled finally in Damascus where he lived until his death. His two chief works are entitled Meccan Revelations and Bezels of Wisdom. The first was written under intense inspiration during his visit to Mecca, and the second emerged out of his Damascus years. Ibn ᶜArabī's influence can be seen in much of the theosophical writing of later generations, especially in Iran. He also had a considerable impact on the famous Persian Sūfī poet, Jalāl al-Dīn al-Rūmī. Al-Rūmī's voluminous work on Sūfī doctrine, the Mathnawī, which was composed entirely in verse, repeats many of the themes developed by Ibn ᶜArabī.

Science and Mathematics

When we turn from speculative thought to science, we may expect to see the impact of religion suddenly diminish. Is not science a "secular" endeavor, we may ask, which seeks nothing more than to gain an understanding of the physical world and to apply the knowledge thus gained to the problems of daily life? What part can religion possibly play in the study of physical processes? And is not the same true of mathematics, the handmaiden of science? What is religious about the study of numbers?

It is because we moderns have secularized science that we must, in dealing with Islamic science, first realize that that science was inseparable from a religious view of the world. We are conditioned by modern science to think of the physical world as a self-contained entity which is to be studied and understood without reference to anything else. By contrast, the Muslim scientist could only see the physical world as the manifestation of a Divine Presence; he was incapable of seeing it in any other way. This perspective is rooted in the Qur'an, which views common physical events such as the falling of rain and the growth of vegetation as divinely wrought miracles (āyāt). Most Muslim scientists were in fact also mystics or philosophers and brought to their scientific work the strong sensitivity to the presence of God in nature characteristic of Muslim mystics and philosophers. This enabled them to affirm the unity and harmony of the universe to a degree rare among modern scientists. The physical world was for them an organic whole, consisting of closely interrelated parts held together in perfect symmetry; as such it reflected the orderliness and wisdom of the Divine Being Himself. Thus in the field of science, no less than in that of speculative thought, Islam proved to be a powerful integrative force, while the Arabic language, which most scientists used, added to it a second important dimension of unity.

It is perhaps in science that the synthetic character of Islamic civilization is most pronounced, since Islamic science represents the fusion of a particularly wide variety of earlier traditions. A modern Muslim writer has given eloquent expression to this point:

> Islamic science came into being from a wedding between the spirit that issued from the Quranic (Koranic) revelation and the existing sciences of various civilizations which Islam inherited and which it transmuted through its spiritual power into a new substance, at once different from and continuous with what had existed before it. The international and cosmopolitan nature of Islamic civilization derived from the universal character of the Islamic revelation and reflected in the geographical spread of the Islamic world, enabled it to create the first science of a truly international nature in human history.
>
> Islam became heir to the intellectual heritage of all the major civilizations before it save that of the Far East, and it became a haven within which various intellectual traditions found a new lease upon life, albeit transformed within a new spiritual universe. (Seyyed Hossein Nasr, Islamic Science: An Illustrated Study, p. 9.)

The same writer has offered the following scheme showing the transmission of science from the ancient civilizations to the Islamic world.

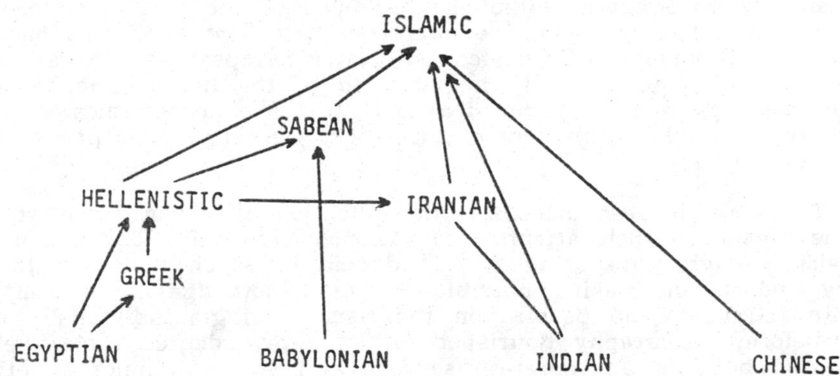

Modern historians of science, when dealing with Islamic science, are often more interested in the quantitative, empirical achievements of medieval Muslim scientists than in the place which science occupied within Islamic civilization and the nature of Islamic science as a kind of contemplation of the universe unrestricted to mere empirical investigation (although including it). Nonetheless, the quantitative achievements of Islamic science are considerable.

To begin with the field of mathematics, we may note that Muslim mathematicians invented both algebra (which term is itself derived from Arabic) and trigonometry, both plane and solid. Islamic numerology (the study of the spiritual significance of numbers), which absorbed many ideas from the ancient Pythagoreans, engendered a great deal of interest in numbers. (The Pythagoreans were a group of Greek philosophers who regarded numbers as higher realities removed from the flux of the phenomenal world.) Islamic art, too, with its emphasis on geometric patterns, helped to promote a lively interest in geometrical theory. Certain theorems of Euclid were re-examined in a new light, and solutions were found to problems which had been posed but not solved by ancient geometricians.

Mathematics was closely related to astronomy, which of all the Islamic sciences produced the most prolific literature. Both the Koran, with its frequent reference to the heavens, and the requirements of Islamic ritual induced Muslims to study the stars. For example, both the times (muwāqīt) and the direction (qibla) of the daily prayers, which vary according to latitude and longitude, had to be determined through careful astronomical calculations. Astronomy also facilitated navigation. Muslim astronomers made new advances, not only in the knowledge of the movements of heavenly bodies, but also in techniques of observation and calculation. Observatories of unprecedented excellence were constructed in a number of places, and the astrolabe, that all important instrument of medieval astronomical calculation (comparable to the slide-rule in modern mathematics), was greatly improved. The use of such facilities, together with the application of the newly developed trigonometry enabled Muslim astronomers to discover data that raised serious questions about the Ptolemaic theory of planetary movements. Although the Muslims continued to adhere to the geocentric conception of the universe, their criticisms of Ptolemaic theory became known to Copernicus and later European astronomers and helped to pave the way for the adoption of the heliocentric theory. Muslim astronomers also produced a vast number of astronomical tables, which represented a refinement of those inherited from their pre-Islamic predecessors.

The same interest that drew the attention of Muslim scientists to the heavens drew their attention to the earth as well. The expansion of Islam brought into being a vast domain in which travel could be freely undertaken, making possible a wider knowledge of the earth's terrain, climates, and peoples on the part of single individuals than ever before. Geography flourished on an unprecedented scale, being cultivated both as a separate discipline and as an adjunct to other disciplines, especially history. Geology, too, made headway, as well as the related discipline of minerology. Muslim scientists were aware of the gradual changes that have taken place in the earth's surface and of the evidence of these changes found in rocks and other formations.

The biological sciences (botany, zoology) and their applied counterparts, medicine and pharmacology, were also avidly cultivated by the medieval Muslims. The great works on botany and zoology contained a wealth of descriptive information about plants and animals, to which was sometimes added a great deal of folkloric and other types of material relating to these subjects. We may take as an example of works which combined descriptive and folkloric material the famous zoological compendium of al-Jāḥiẓ entitled The Book of Animals. This work tells us as much about the medieval Muslim's attitude toward animals as about animals as such. To al-Jāhiz, the animal kingdom was a repository of wisdom, and man could gain personal profit from the observation of animal behavior and from fables told about animals. However, along with the moralistic and even entertaining passages of his book one finds pure description and classification. Al-Jāhiz described and classified about 350 animals and showed an interest in animal psychology.

The principal contributions of the medieval Muslims in the field of medicine related to the identification of diseases of the basis of observable symptoms and the discovery of new remedies (an endeavor belonging properly to the domain of pharmacology). In both of these respects the Muslim physicians surpassed their predecessors and attained a level of excellence that was famed beyond the borders of the Islamic world, and especially in Europe. Research on eye disease and on the nature of vision made possible the founding of the science of optics. In the field of anatomy, Muslim physicians were hampered by the prohibition by the ᶜulama' of the dissection of human corpses. However, in spite of this handicap they achieved a remarkable knowledge of the internal structure and workings of the body, and at least one highly significant advance was made: the discovery of the minor circulation of the blood (i.e., circulation through the heart and lungs), an accomplishment once attributed to William Harvey.

Historiography (History Writing)

A strong historical consciousness, expressed in a great abundance of historical writings, is among the most prominent features of medieval Islamic civilization. The Koran itself, with its accounts of earlier peoples and prophets, fostered a lively interest in the past. After the passing away of the first generation of Muslims, the events of the earliest period became an object of special scholarly interest. The rapid proliferation of Hadīth material demonstrated a kind of fixation on the period of the Prophet in particular, and the critical examination of this material together with its compilation in writing marked the beginning of a distinct historical discipline. Some scholars specialized in Hadīth narratives describing the great expeditions (maghāzī) of the Prophet and attempted to arrange these narratives in chronological order. This led to the emergence of a distinct class of Hadīth compilation known in Arabic as sīra and referred to generally in English as biography of the Prophet. While the Hadīth scholars carried on their work, the philologists undertook the similar task of gathering and sifting the traditions of the Arab tribes, which included tales of ancient battles (ayyām al-ᶜarab) and genealogical legends. Thus, there emerged by the ninth century a considerable body of historical knowledge.

But the interest of Muslim scholars was not restricted to tribal traditions and events of early Islam. Significant history did not, in their view, end with the passing away of the first Muslims but continued on through successive generations. As a modern British scholar has put it, "the remarkable feature [of early Islamic history writing is] that, apart from the philologists, the collectors of the historical tradition were almost exclusively theologians (that is to say, religious scholars) and muhaddiths (hadith compilers). . . . In the theological view history was the manifestation of a divine plan for the government of mankind; and while the historical outlook of the earlier generations might be limited to tracing it through the succession of prophets which culminated in Muhammad, all Islamic schools agreed that it did not end there. In the Sunni doctrine, it was the community, the umma, with which the continuation of the divine plan on earth was bound up; consequently the study of its history was a necessary supplement to the study of the divine revelation in Koran and Hadith." (Gibb, Studies on the Civilization of Islam, p. 115.)

The Muslim historical consciousness reached full maturity with the emergence of a genre of historical writing known generally as universal history. The universal history provided a connected account of the history of the world from the creation to the time of the author. Its treatment of pre-Islamic history contained a great deal of legend, since the sources available to the Muslim historians on this earlier history were largely legendary, and pre-Islamic history was on the whole regarded as introductory to Islamic history proper, which was the primary object of interest. However, the universalistic format showed an awareness of history as a total process having a meaning which could not be fully grasped with reference to any one of its parts.

The most renowned of the great universal histories is the History of Prophets and Kings by Muhammad ibn Jarir al-Tabari (d. 928), who was also the author of a famous commentary on the Koran (see earlier section of this chapter). One can see by reading only a few pages from this work that it is thoroughly embued with the methodology of the Hadith literature ("A told me that B told him, etc."). By assembling and investigating afresh all the material known to him on the history of Islam up to this time, al-Tabari accomplished what no historian of later times would attempt again and in so doing bequeathed to his successors (and to us) an invaluable legacy. Later historians continued to record events of their own time, but none was able to improve on what al-Tabari had done for the first three centuries of Islam. Consequently, in dealing with the earlier centuries later historians either repeated or summarized al-Tabari's material.

In the middle of the tenth century there emerged a new type of history writing, the contemporary chronicle, which was to linger to the end of the medieval period. Unlike al-Tabari and other earlier historians, these historians recorded events as they happened on a year-to-year basis. Also unlike their predecessors, they were not, as a rule, religious scholars, but rather officials attached to the court. This connection enabled them to make use of archives which have since been lost. (In general, archives are not available to a significant degree for Islamic history prior to the Ottoman period.) It also gave to their work an excessive preoccupation with purely political history.

Alongside the universal history and contemporary chronicle, there emerged an important adjunct to historical writing: biography. Although biographical literature was, to some extent, inspired by the sira collections, which combined biographical material on the Prophet with general history, its real beginning as a distinct literary genre should be traced to the Book of Classes by Muhammad ibn Sa^{c}d (d. 844). This book records information about individuals belonging to the first two generations of Muslims and may be described as a biographical dictionary of early Islam. It became an important tool for Hadith compilers, who evaluated Hadīth material primarily on the basis of information about the narrators. In the centuries following the time of Ibn Sa^{c}d, biographical dictionaries multiplied rapidly to produce a literature ultimately more copious even than that of ordinary history. Many of these were specialized, dealing with famous persons of a particular city, scholarly discipline, or law school.

Literature

Since the two major components of Arabic literature, poetry and belles lettres, have been discussed in a previous chapter, we will confine our attention here to some observations about the place of literature within Islamic civilization.

It is common practice among historians to subsume classical Arabic literature under the more general heading of Islamic literature and to include under this heading the other literatures of the Islamic world as well, Persian and Turkish in particular. When we consider certain specimens of classical Arabic literature, however, we may get the impression that the impact of Islam, which we have thus far taken to be a primary integrative factor in cultural life, was very slight in the case of literature. Unlike speculative thought, which originated ideas into closed systems based on commonly accepted Islamic themes, literature is somewhat open-ended, being essentially an art and therefore more oriented to form, style and esthetic function than to any fixed content. We need only consider certain wine-poems of Abu Nuwas to realize how far Islamic norms could be from the mental outlook of a poet. The more licentious poetry preserved to some extent the spirit of pre-Islamic paganism.

On the other hand, a large part of the classical literature is thoroughly saturated with Islamic themes and attitudes. Scholarly and philosophical literature does not fall under the sense of the term literature intended here. Literary works on religious themes (including poetry) abounded, not to mention works in which religious themes, if not the main subject, were incorporated into a larger network of ideas. Even the sīra books were interspersed with occasional poems. More significantly, the Koran itself stood as a primary model of literary art. Because of it, if for no other reason, literary art was firmly linked to the religious outlook.

In view of this variation in the degree of Islam's penetration of literary life, it may seem fitting to think of Arabic literature as a spectrum, with the explicitly religious literature on one end, the licentious or "worldly" literature on the other and all variants in between. With this model, we could speak of works of Arabic literature as more or less Islamic or as not Islamic at all, depending on their position within the spectrum. On the other hand, there is good reason to speak of the whole of Arabic literature in the medieval Islamic world as Islamic in the sense of being conditioned by Islamic norms and ways of thinking. To take this approach is to look at classical Arabic literature as a totality and to regard it as Islamic in terms of the main influences shaping its over-all development and determining the direction of that development. It is also to look at particular works, even the most "worldly," as belonging to this whole and as being to some degree conditioned by the main influences. After all, licentiousness is itself culturally defined. What was shocking in Islamic Baghdad in the ninth century may be commonplace in many modern capitals.

It is important here to bear in mind the main point of the section of chapter 4 on Arabic literary development in the Abbasid period: even though literary life was subject to many influences stemming from pre-Islamic times, the main direction of literary development was determined by religious considerations. While poets praised the indecent pasttimes of courtiers and officials attempted to forge a belles lettres conforming to pre-Islamic tastes and motifs, men of letters with strong religious convictions, such as the great al-Jāhiz, laid the groundwork for an Arabic humanities consistent with the requirements of the Islamic faith.

The eventual emergence of non-Arabic literatures within the Islamic world may seem to militate against the unity of Islamic civilization, the Arabic language being one of the bases of that unity. On this two points may be made. First of all, in the development of these literatures, the Arabic language exercised an influence nearly as great as that of non-Arabic languages themselves. The vocabulary of classical Persian is, as noted earlier, largely of Arabic origin. Furthermore, the terminology and concepts of Persian grammar and stylistics are drawn from the Arabic philological tradition. Persian literature in turn became the principal influence in the shaping of Turkish and Urdu literature, carrying with it the Arabic influences to which it was subject. Although the native genius of the non-Arabic literatures is not to be denied, the pervasiveness of the Arabic influences within these literatures helped to absorb them into that larger entity called Islamic literature. Secondly, where the influence of Arabic ended that of the Islamic religious tradition continued. To support this point we need only refer to the fact that the greater part of the poetry of Sufi mysticism was composed in Persian.

Art and Architecture

As in literature, so also in art and architecture we find great variation in the degree of Islam's influence. However, notwithstanding this variation, the imprint of Islam can be seen everywhere. Although Islamic art and architecture--even that part that was most explicitly religious--was constructed out of pre-Islamic traditions, Islam played a decisive role in producing patently Islamic features and, in fact, a general Islamic type.

The most obvious influence of Islam on art is to be found in the general disapproval of figural art, tendering Islamic art primarily nonrepresentational and decorative. This feature is especially noticeable if we compare the art of the mosque with that of the church. In churches one frequently encounters a rich pictorial art that draws the attention to human forms which play a role in the sacred drama upon which Christian worship is centered. In the mosque, however, there are no figures of any kind upon which the attention may be fixed. The art of the mosque appears to be designed to create an atmosphere but not to focus the attention on anything visual. Rather the attention is to be drawn away from the visual created world to that which is infinite and eternal.

This nonrepresentational character of Islamic art has given prominence to two features: geometric design and calligraphy. Geometric design does not draw the attention to any object. It is uniform and infinitely extendable; it may cover any amount of space. Sometimes the patterns are floral, but the repetitiveness and rigid stylization of a floral pattern guarantees that the pattern will have no representational effect.

Although these features are dictated largely by the requirements of Islamic worship, they are found throughout the art of the Islamic world--even in the art of the private dwelling. Even today when tourists shopping in Middle Eastern bazaars speak glibly of Islamic art, it is these features which they have primarily in mind.

The influence of Islam on architecture can be seen in the great penchant for religious buildings, pre-eminently mosques, but also madrasas, tombs, and convents. In the medieval Muslim city such buildings occupied a conspicuous position. The "Islamic skyline," which even the Western imagination associates with the Islamic city, is no fiction. Whereas in private dwellings little attention was given to the exterior, in the case of religious buildings the exterior counted for much, especially that part of the exterior which arose above the maze of adjacent buildings. Hence the prominence of splendid domes and minarets.

CHAPTER SEVEN

THE ARAB LANDS IN THE AGE OF THE MAMLUKS 1250-1517

During the middle part of the thirteenth century, three developments of major importance for the future of the Arab lands took place: (1) the conquest of Iran and Iraq by a new nomadic people, the Mongols, (2) the emergence in Egypt of a new military regime, that of the Mamlūks, which was soon to extend its rule over Syria as well, and (3) the break-up of the former Muwahhid empire into three separate Maghrabī states, the Marīnid, Zayyānid, and Hafsid states.

The emergence of the Mamlūk regime was to make Egypt the primary political and cultural center of the eastern Arab lands. The Mongol conquest of Iraq placed that land for the time being within the orbit of Iranian civilization. The sack of Baghdad and the devastation of the countryside reduced Iraq to a place of secondary importance within the Islamic world. No longer a center of power in its own right, Iraq now lay on the periphery of an essentially Iranian world. This eclipse of Iraq enhanced the importance of Egypt. Egypt was now clearly the leading power within the Arab lands.

Hostility between the Mamlūk and Mongol states created a barrier between the Arabic-speaking lands under Mamlūk rule and the predominantly Persian-speaking Mongol dominions. As a result of this hostility, the greater part of the eastern Arab lands (Syria and Egypt) became even more separated from Iran than before. This separation, together with the virtual completion around the same time of the arabization of the Maghib as a result of the westward migrations of bedouin over the previous two centuries (leaving Berber-speaking enclaves only in certain areas), enables us from this point onward to make the Arab lands as presently constituted the object of our study. Arab history has become the history of the Arab lands. One important qualification must be made, however. Iraq remained for some time within the orbit of Iranian affairs owing to its proximity to Mongol-dominated Iran and to the inability of the Mamlūks to incorporate it into their empire. In any case, the decrease of Iraq's population together with economic stagnation under the Mongols undermined Iraq's importance as compared with other lands. Later, under Ottoman rule, Iraq again became involved in a common political destiny with the other Arab lands.

The focusing of attention on the Arab lands as a unit of study should not be taken to mean that these lands have an undivided history. We must continue to keep in mind the rather great cleavage separating, as before, the Maghrib from the Arab East. Whereas the Arab East (excluding Iraq) achieves an unprecedented degree of solidarity under the Mamlūks, the Maghrib lapses into division with the emergence of rival regional states and acquires that tripartite character which it has retained to the present day. After the fall of the Muwahhids, a unified Maghrib never again became a reality. Even today the Maghrib continues to be divided into separate political units: Morocco, Algeria, and Tunisia.

The Coming of the Mongols

The most dramatic event in the political history of the Islamic East in the thirteenth century was the Mongol conquest of large parts of the Islamic lands east of Syria. Some historians treat this event as a great watershed in Islamic history dividing the "classical" (or early medieval) from the "medieval" (or late medieval) period. With the coming of the Mongols, nomadism was once again in the ascendancy. Also, as was the case with earlier nomadic movements (Arab, Berber, Turkish), the Mongol movement produced a great empire.

The Mongols resembled the Turks in many respects. They came from the same type of homeland, the Steppe, and possessed similar traditions, values, and qualities of mind. However, they were ethnically distinct from the Turks and spoke a language basically unrelated to Turkish. Moreover, whereas the Seljuk Turks had been Islamized prior to their great conquests the Mongols entered the Islamic world for the most part as pagans, although some of their tribes had been converted to Christianity.

The expansion of the Mongols began around the beginning of the thirteenth century, after an energetic leader known as Genghis (more correctly Chingiz) Khan succeeded in placing himself at the head of a confederation of Mongol tribes. Proceeding from their Mongolian homeland, the Mongol armies first advanced southward subduing North China and then westward toward the Islamic lands. In 1220 the Mongols overran Transoxiana and then crossed the Oxus River in Khorasan, where they had no difficulty overcoming the Muslim resistance. From there they proceeded across northern Iran and up through the Caucasus into southern Russia, where they conducted numerous raids before turning back eastward. By the time of Genghis Khan's death in 1227, the Mongols were masters of a vast empire encompassing virtually the whole of the Central Asian Steppe as well as parts of China and Iran.

As the Mongol forces advanced, they absorbed many Turkish peoples whom they encountered in the way. As a result of this fusion of Turks and Mongols, the army led by Genghis Khan eventually took on a mixed Turkish-Mongol character (Mongolized Turks were known as "Tatars"). The leadership, however, remained firmly in the hands of the Mongol nobility headed by Genghis Khan. This predominance of the Mongol element explains why historians customarily describe the movement as a whole as Mongol.

The death of Genghis Khan created a momentary lull, during which the Mongol empire was divided between the sons of the deceased leader in accordance with the latter's plan. In 1236 Mongol armies were in motion again, the main direction of their movement being toward eastern Europe. Although the Mongols did not create a permanent foothold in Europe, they did establish a state in the area of the Volga River north of the Caspian Sea. The principal leader in these activities was Batu, a grandson of Genghis Khan who had acquired the inheritance originally assigned to his father after the latter's premature death. The armies which fought under Batu's command were called collectively the Golden

Horde, and the state which arose out of their conquests north of the Caspian became known by this name. The capital of the Golden Horde was Serai, a new city erected on the banks of the lower Volga. When Batu died in 1256, he was succeeded after a brief interval by his brother Berke (1257-1267), who converted to Islam. This conversion, which set an example for the Mongol chieftains to follow, made the Golden Horde the first Muslim Mongol state.

The year of Batu's death also marked the beginning of a new offensive against the central lands of Islam. The leader of this campaign was another grandson of Genghis Khan named Hulagu. After crossing the Oxus River, Hulagu's forces occupied northern Iran almost without resistance. By 1258 the Mongols (with many Turks in their ranks) had crossed the Zagros mountains into Iraq and had reached the gates of Baghdad. The city fell immediately into their hands and was given over to plunder for several days, in the course of which the Abbasid caliph was killed and the caliphate itself abolished.

The fall of Baghdad created a shock wave that was felt throughout the Islamic East. The very name Mongol had spelled terror in the minds of the masses for more than a quarter of a century, ever since Genghis Khan's first incursions into Transoxiana and northern Iran. The atrocities committed on occasion by the Mongols against vanquished populations had evoked widespread fear. The great Muslim cities of Transoxiana, for example, had been ruthlessly sacked and a large part of the population slaughtered. A similar fate had now befallen Baghdad, a city rich in past glories.

But the scandal of Baghdad's fall was due not only to the ruthlessness of the Mongols but also to their paganism. Unlike Berke of the Golden Horde, Hulagu and his followers made no pretense of being Muslims. Instead, they deliberately favored the non-Muslim population and themselves clung fast to their ancestral traditions. The Christians enjoyed an especially favored status owing partly to the fact that Hulagu's principal wife professed Christianity. The Sunnī population, by contrast, found themselves out of favor. The Shīʿis, on the other hand, were given a freer hand. In short, the central and eastern lands of Islam and seat of the time-honored caliphate had been ravaged and subdued by a professed enemy of Islam.

After capturing Baghdad, the Mongols proceeded westward toward the Mediterranean, taking by storm the great cities of Syria, Damascus and Aleppo. The Mongol advance seemed unstoppable, and the remaining lands of Islam seemed open to attack. However, at this juncture Hulagu was required to return to Mongolia to deal with an internal political crisis which had erupted among the Mongols. In his absence, the Mongol army, under the command of a deputy of Hulagu, reached the limit of its expansion. In a battle fought near the Palestinian village of ʿAyn Jalūt in 1260, the Mongol army suffered defeat at the hands of a new power which had recently emerged in Egypt, the Mamlūks. Thus, the unstoppable Mongol tide was finally stopped, and Egypt and the Islamic lands to the West were saved from the Mongol onslaught.

The victorious Mamlūks followed up their success at ᶜAyn Jālūt by expelling the Mongols from the captured cities of Syria, in which endeavor they enjoyed the cooperation of these cities' inhabitants who were emboldened by the ᶜAyn Jālūt victory to rise up against their Mongol occupiers. In due time most of Syria became Mamlūk territory, and the Mongols were obliged to settle for their gains in Iraq and the eastern lands.

The new Mongol state maintained its principal capital at Tabrīz, a city located near the northern border of modern Iran within a territory known as Azarbayjan (now divided between Iran and the U.S.S.R.). In the east, a Khorasan (which the Mongols had controlled since the time of Genghis Khan) became a second important center of Mongol power and influence. After Hulagu's death in 1263, the rule over this predominantly Iranian empire passed on to his son Abaqa and remained within the line of his descendants for three-quarters of a century. These descendants bore the title of Il-Khan.

Under the sixth Il-Khanid ruler, Ghazan, a fundamental change in the religious policy of the state took place. Ghazan, a convert to Islam, restored Sunni Islam to its former pre-eminence and encouraged the mass conversion of the Mongols to Islam. In this way, the stigma of paganism was removed from the Il-Khanid state, and a more harmonious relationship between ruler and ruled was achieved. However, the Il-Khanid state continued to suffer from internal disorders. On the whole, the Il-Khanids ruled badly, and their lands, including Iraq, underwent serious economic decline.

The Establishment of the Mamlūk Regime

The rise to power of the Mamluk regime in Egypt was the result of a chain of events set in motion by the death of the Ayyūbid sultan al-Malik al-Sālih in 1249. Al-Malik al-Sālih had created a corps of Turkish mamlūk soldiers, the largest ever in Egypt's history up to his time, and had made this corps the mainstay of his army. These mamlūks were stationed in barracks on an island in the Nile near Cairo and accordingly became known collectively as the Bahrīs (from Bahr, the common Arabic term in Egypt for the Nile). The Bahrīs had demonstrated their military prowess by inflicting a defeat on the Crusader army of Louis IX, which had invaded Egypt just before al-Malik al-Sālih's death. When the son of al-Malik al-Sālih, who had been engaged in duties in Mesopotamia, appeared in Cairo after his father's death to claim the throne, he brought with him mamlūks of his own, whom he proceeded to appoint to high offices. This precipitated an immediate crisis. The Bahrīs interpreted the would-be sultān's action as an attempt to reduce their power. In 1250 a group of them murdered the new aspirant to the throne and rallied behind al-Malik al-Sālih's widow, Shajar al-Durr. The latter in turn appointed as co-ruler a Turkish general named Aybeg, whom she soon married and allowed to assume the title of sultān. This arrangement lasted only until 1257, when both Aybeg and Shajar al-Durr met their deaths as a result of palace intrigues. After a two-year inter-regnum, during which Aybeg's son was accepted as nominal ruler in order to allow time for the real struggle for power to take place, a former general under Aybeg named Qutuz ascended the throne. However, a year later Qutuz was assassinated by his own officers in order to clear the way for one of them to take his place. This new sultan was Baybars, a prominent officer of the Bahri corps. He was to rule as the undisputed master for the following seventeen years (1260-1277). Although later Egyptian historians were to count him as the fourth Mamlūk sultān, Baybars may be considered as the real founder of the new Mamlūk order. His reign, much more than the brief reigns of his ineffective predecessors, marks the real beginning of the Mamlūk era, a period which was to cover two and a half centuries of Egypt's and Syria's history.

A story was told concerning Baybar's rise to power which reveals the conception of rule that was to characterize the Mamlūk system of politics. It was said that after Baybars and his party had killed Qutuz they promptly reported this deed to a Mamlūk officer named Aqtay. "Which of you killed him?" asked Aqtay. "I did," replied Baybars. "Then sit on the throne in his place," said Aqtay. Whereupon all the Mamlūks promptly offered their allegiance to Baybars as the new sultān. The principle underlying this story, namely that the rule belongs to the most powerful, the one powerful enough to seize the throne and eliminate all rivals, was to become a cornerstone of the Mamlūk system. It reflected the circumstances that had given rise to the Mamlūk take-over and the cancellation of Ayyūbid legitimacy. In particular, it determined Baybar's own rise to power. It also was to determine the sequence of events after Baybar's death.

The dynastic principle, which was the exact opposite of this new principle of succession, was by no means completely dead. During the first century and a quarter of Mamlūk rule, the two principles can be seen in competition with each other. Qalāwūn, who came to power in 1279, reversed the tendency which had been at work since the establishment of the Mamlūk regime by securing the succession for his son. The sultanate remained within the household of Qalāwūn until 1382, although it sometimes passed from master to slave rather than from father to son. After 1382 the dynastic principle was abandoned, as a new corps of mamlūks called Burjīs came to power, replacing the Bahris. The Burjīs adhered steadfastly to the original "survival of the fittest" principle of rule.

Although the method of succession was a variable of Mamlūk politics, certain basic features of the Mamlūk system remained constant throughout the two and a half centuries of Mamlūk rule. The most striking of these features was the essentially alien character of the military class. The Mamlūk system seems to have been deliberately designed to keep the military aloof from the indigenous population. Persons born within Mamlūk territories, including sons of Mamlūk soldiers and officers, were barred from serving in the regular armed forces. Only an auxiliary and inferior force called the halqa was open to natives, and service in the halqa offered little opportunity for personal advancement.

The ranks of the regular forces were supplied exclusively from slave markets. The Mamlūk state kept up a lively slave trade, one of the principal suppliers being the Golden Horde Mongols, who obtained Turkish slaves directly from the Steppe. The first Mamlūks are thought to have purchased as many as 800 slaves a year, although the later Mamlūks bought much fewer. By means of these purchases, the mamlūk or slave character of the military was perpetuated from generation to generation. To be part of the Mamluk military class was, by definition, to have a slave origin. The slaves were obtained as youth, immediately Islamized, and then put through a long and arduous training program. Once the training was completed, they were formally manumitted and admitted to the ranks of the adult soldiery. However, even as adults they continued to maintain steadfast loyalty to their original masters.

The rationale of this system appears obvious. Only youths fresh from the Steppe, so it was believed, possessed the toughness and spiritedness required for excellence in the military arts. Only they, by virtue of their slave origins, could be counted upon to be absolutely loyal to their superiors and unreservedly devoted to the military way of life. The native population, softened by the sedentary way of life, was believed to be incapable of cultivating the qualities and physical skills required of the true warrior.

The sons of the Mamlūks, being excluded from the nonhereditary ruling caste to which their fathers belonged, were obliged to enter civilian careers, unless they chose to serve in the socially inferior *halqa* corps. The principal civilian careers open to them were in religion and in the civil administration. In these fields, they worked together with, and soon became absorbed into, the indigenous population.

Of the slaves imported into the country, the most promising were trained to enter the ranks of the royal mamlūks, that is, mamlūks attached to the sultān himself, who were stationed in Cairo and constituted the core of the army. From their number the high officers of the Mamlūk army were recruited. The other slaves found their way into the Mamlūk armies maintained by the officers who held posts as provincial governors in various parts of the empire. Each major city of Egypt and Syria had its own garrison of Mamlūks.

Within the Mamlūk system merit was the primary criterion for personal advancement. Because of this, the Mamlūk military class was highly fluid. A young slave recruit possessing talent and determination could aspire to enter the royal corps and, having succeeded in this, could aspire to rise to the highest ranks of the military, even to the sultānate itself. This upward mobility is evidenced in the personal lives of many of the great Mamlūk sultāns.

The Mamlūk military class was maintained in the traditional manner, that is to say, by means of iqtāʿs. The iqtāʿ system, although dating from Fatimid times, had been much extended by the Ayyūbids, who had inherited the practice of the Seljuks. The system followed by the Mamlūks was essentially the same as that designed by Nizām al-Mulk almost two centuries before Baybar's rise to power. Each officer was assigned the revenue of a particular district or districts on condition that he maintain a certain number of soldiers varying from five to five hundred according to his rank. The districts thus earmarked constituted his iqta^c. The revenue acquired from the iqta^c took the place of regular pay. As Nizam al-Mulk had planned, the assignment of iqta^{c}s was carefully regulated by the state. Although at the beginning of the Mamluk period some iqta^{c}s were heritable, this practice was soon abandoned in favor of the non-hereditary system envisioned by Nizam al-Mulk. Iqta^{c}s might be assigned for a limited term or for an entire lifetime, but they were never passed from father to son. Moreover, under the Mamluks the iqta^c holdings of an individual officer were often scattered over a large area to prevent the emergence of large consolidated iqta^c estates. This scattering helped to assure that the Mamluk class would not evolve into an entrenched landed aristocracy. The extent of an officer's iqta^c holdings depended on his rank. Higher-ranking officers with larger numbers of mamluk soldiers under their command held more extensive iqta^{c}s embracing a number of villages and sometimes a city as well, whereas lower-ranking offices might have only single villages with the surrounding countryside as their iqta^{c}s.

Political Developments under the Bahris

The dominant factor in the political history of the early Mamluk State was the Mongol menace. As noted above, the Mamluks defeated the Mongols at the Battle of ^{c}Ayn Jalut and forced them to withdraw from Syria. However, this by no means brought an end to hostility between the two powers. The Mamluks lived in constant apprehension of a renewed attack by the Mongol state. For this reason the fortification of the Syrian frontiers and defense of the Syrian cities was a matter of utmost urgency. The conversion of the Il-Khanids to Islam in 1295 did not alter this fundamental balance of power, which remained a feature of Middle Eastern politics for a long time, even after the collapse of the Il-Khanid state.

The defense of Syria against the Mongols called for tighter control over the entire region and the elimination of inconvenient rivals. Accordingly, the Mamluks renewed the war against the Crusaders, which they relentlessly pursued until the last vestage of Crusader power in Palestine was eliminated. The major offensives against the Crusaders were undertaken by Baybars, who succeeded in reducing the territory controlled by the Crusaders to a narrow strip along the coast. The final steps were taken by Qalawun and his son and successor al-Malik al-Ashraf Khalil. The former drove the Crusaders into their last stronghold at Acre and was preparing for the siege of this coastal city at the time of his death in 1291. This event marked the end of a two-century long Crusader presence in the Levant.

The Mamluks were careful to make friends as well as enemies within the international scene. Rivalry between the Il-Khanids and the Golden Horde enabled the Mamluks to form an alliance with the latter against the former. Amicable relations were also established with Byzantium, and contacts were maintained, as before, with the Italian city-states.

Within the world of Islam, the Mamlūk Sultans deliberately cultivated the image of pious defenders of Sunnī Islam, making Cairo a bulwark of orthodoxy against the pagan and heretical influences which flourished to the East. In 1261 Baybars installed an Abbasid survivor of the Mongol atrocities as caliph in Cairo. Although the caliphate had exercised little effective power since the time of al-Nāsir, it still remained in Sunnī eyes a powerful symbol of Muslim unity and legitimacy. Now the time-honored institution was restored under Mamlūk patronage. The religious prestige which this action brought to the sultanate was further enhanced by a more active policy with respect to the Hijāz. Baybars used diplomacy to win the allegiance of the sharīf of Mecca, who had been embarking on an independent policy, and in a short time the Hijāz became a dependency of the Mamlūk state. The Mongol conquests had helped to place the Hijāz within the Mamlūk orbit by cutting off momentarily the Pilgrimage from Iraq and the eastern countries, leaving Egypt and the Maghrib as the main source of pilgrims and supplies. To emphasize his patronage over the two holy cities, Baybars adopted the title "Servant of the Holy Places" (Khādim al-haramayn), which was subsequently borne by his successors.

Economic Conditions Under the Bahris

The dominant position of the military, which was a prime feature of political life under the Mamlūks, extended to economic life as well. The military class disposed of great amounts of wealth. Land was, as everywhere, the primary source of wealth, and the iqtā^{c} system made the military the primary landowners. The revenue which the Mamlūks drew from the iqtā^{c} holdings was, on the whole, considerably greater than that of the military in previous periods of Egypt's history. Because of this wealth, the military became a principal participant in economic life. In addition to being the leading consumers, the Mamlūks also invested in economic ventures and were able to use their power to discourage competition from the civilian population.

The ever increasing involvement of the Mamlūk military class and of the state in economic activity was accompanied by a further decline of the bourgeoisie. Whereas the Ayyūbids had allowed the bourgeoisie some measure of self-government, especially in Syria where leading merchants had sometimes been appointed mayors of towns with the title of ra'īs, the Mamlūks did away with such practices altogether. Urban life and administration was taken over almost completely by the Mamlūks themselves. Every town had its Mamlūk governor and garrison, which exercised absolute authority. As for the bourgeoisie, it dwindled in importance and became economically dependent upon the military. Tax-farming, which hitherto had been a major source of income for wealthy civilians, was gradually abandoned, as the iqtā^{c} system became more entrenched. Agricultural production passed almost entirely into the hands of the Mamlūks, and they or their agents became the primary sellers of food. The Mamlūks also invested large amounts of money in the construction of market places (sūqs) and in the leasing of shops.

The exploitative attitude which the Mamlūk officers took toward their iqtā^{c} holdings militated against agricultural productivity. As was always the case with the non-hereditary military iqtā^{c}, the recipient had no interest at heart but to maximize his own profits. Long-term considerations were entirely foreign to his thinking.

These developments notwithstanding, the first century of Mamlūk rule (1250-1350), during which the Bahrīs were in power, proved to be a surprisingly prosperous period economically speaking. The following five factors may be mentioned to account for this prosperity: (1) the effectiveness of the Mamlūk government under the Bahrīs, (2) the improvement of public health, (3) the influx of economically productive populations from the eastern lands, (4) the stability of the monetary system, and (5) continuing trade with Europe.

The government of the Bahrī Mamlūks afforded peace and security within the Mamlūk territories at a time when turmoil prevailed in many other areas. This peace and security were naturally conducive to economic activity. Furthermore, the Mamlūk state itself, continuing in the tradition of its predecessors, encouraged and to a large extent sponsored international trade, granting residential privileges to foreign merchants and maintaining careful control over vital sea routes, especially the all-important Red Sea route.

Judging from the absence of evidence to the contrary in our sources, public health during the first century of Bahrī rule seems to have been good. The chronicles of the period mention very few epidemics or severe famines. The infrequency of such misfortunes increased longevity and reduced infant mortality, resulting in a growth of population and, consequently, of the labor force. Growth of population was also stimulated by the influx of large numbers of people from the land to the East, especially Iraq, as a result of the Mongol atrocities. Among these immigrants were many ^{c}ulamā', merchants, artisans, bureaucrats and soldiers, including even some Mongols, all of whom were capable of being absorbed in a productive manner into the economy of the Mamlūk empire.

The stability of the mamlūk monetary system under the Bahris was due to the existence of a continuing supply of precious metals (gold and silver), making it possible to mint both dīnārs and dirhems of high quality. Gold was particularly abundant, being imported, as before, from West Africa. Close relations with West Africa were maintained. The geographer Ibn Battūta, who travelled to West Africa, mentions in one of his writings that Egyptians lived there, and both he and the historian Ibn Khaldūn testify to extensive commercial contacts between the two areas. Silver came to Egypt, as before, from Europe and Central Asia; while the supply of silver was not as steady as that of gold, it was sufficient to meet the needs of the Egyptian mints.

The trade with Europe provided a vital market for the products of Egyptian agriculture and industry as well as an important source of precious metals in the form of gold and silver coins. The transit trade, too, which entailed the transport to Europe of luxury goods from India and the Far East, brought enormous profits to the Mamlūk empire. European merchants continued to maintain hostels and consultates in Alexandria and to carry on business in Egyptian markets. Syria, on the other hand, attracted rather few European merchants in the Mamlūk period. This was partly due to the growth of rival trading centers in Cyprus and Little Armenia, both of which were Christian lands, and to the increased use of trade routes connecting these centers with the eastern lands.

The fall of Acre to the Mamlūks in 1291 had an adverse effect on trade with Europe. The Pope, hoping to weaken the Mamlūk economy as well as the Mamlūk army, attempted to place an embargo on trade between Europe and the Mamlūk empire. This effort succeeded to some extent in restricting the flow of war materials to Egypt, but it did not put an end to the trade with the Mamlūks, as the Pope had hoped. In fact, so strong was the demand for eastern goods and the desire for profit that the Pope himself was constrained to issue permits for this lucrative trade. Thus, in spite of the papal campaign against the Mamlūks, trade between Europe and Egypt continued after 1291, even if on a restricted basis.

Religious and Cultural Life Under the Mamlūks

The Mamlūk empire has been described as a kind of Islamic Byzantium. As was the case in the later Byzantine empire, the great emphasis in religious and cultural life under the Mamlūks was upon conservation. Very few new discoveries were made or new departures attempted. Religious scholars and men of letters sought rather to hold on to the achievements of their predecessors. Insofar as they had anything of their own to contribute, it was by way of elaborating upon what the predecessors had done or continuing (and perhaps completing) what the predecessors had begun. This conservativism of the Mamluk period may be explained in terms of at least three factors: (1) the desire to preserve Islamic civilization in the face of the Mongol threat, (2) the relative isolation of the Mamlūk territories from other centers of civilization, and (3) the legacy of the Seljuk orthodox revival.

The Mongol atrocities of the mid-thirteenth century caused many Muslims to look to the Mamlūk state as the last remaining bulwark of Islam against paganism. This was especially true after the Mamlūks had proven their superiority over the Mongol armies at the Battle of ᶜAyn Jālūt in 1261. The belief that the Mongols were determined to destroy Islam created in the Mamlūk territories an atmosphere of retrenchment and a preoccupation with the task of preserving the Islamic heritage in the face of implacable enemies. A kind of siege mentality seems to have prevailed, especially under the early Mamlūks.

As a result of enmity between the Mamlūks and the Mongol state erected by the Il-Khanid dynasty, Egypt and Syria became relatively cut off from the eastern centers of Islamic civilization, where a distinctly Iranian-Central Asian tradition was in the making. In the Islamic lands to the North (Turkish Anatolia) and West (the Maghrib) there existed no centers of civilization capable of influencing to a significant degree developments within the Mamlūk territories. The Turkish communities of Anatolia were still in the process of building up a civilization of their own, and Maghribi civilization was more influenced by the lands ruled by the Mamlūks than vice versa and was, in any case, located behind an ever-increasing barrier of nomadism. As for cultural contacts with the Byzantine empire and with Western Europe, these were, despite diplomatic and commercial connections, minimal. This cultural isolation of Syria and Egypt produced an attitude of self-sufficiency. In the absence of challenges or cross-currents emanating from rival centers of civilization, the cultural and religious climate under the Mamlūks became static and somewhat ingrown. Consequently, old ideas and traditions seemed unassailable, and the primary task of learned and cultured men seemed to be that of transmitting faithfully what had been received.

To these factors must be added the third and perhaps most important factor: the coming to fruition under the Mamlūks of the Seljuk legacy. It will be recalled that the Seljuks had inaugurated a revived Sunnī sociopolitical order--that is, a sociopolitical order based on conformity to Sunnī religious teachings, which had taken on the character of an orthodoxy. The primary instrument for the inculcation of this orthodoxy was the madrasa, intended to produce not only ᶜulamā' but civil servants as well. The revived Sunnī order was to be upheld by a military class maintained through iqtāᶜs. The head of the military was the sultān, who commanded on behalf of his spiritual superior, the caliph.

This Seljuk legacy had been zealously embraced by Nūr al-Dīn, who had seen in it a means of strengthening his Syrian realm and of mobilizing resistance against the Crusaders. His subordinate and ultimate successor, Salāh al-Dīn, had carried it into Egypt, where it became an instrument for revivifying Egyptian society and for cleansing it from the effects of Fātimid rule. By the time the Mamlūks came to power, the Seljuk legacy had been operative in Egypt for three-quarters of a century. The Mamlūks further strengthened it by giving it a solid and stable military basis surpassing that of any of their predecessors. It is one of the remarkable facts of Islamic history that the order of society instituted by the Seljuks was ultimately to endure, not in the eastern lands where it had originally been inaugurated, but in Egypt and Syria (as well as, we should note, in the Turkish lands to the North and particularly in the Ottoman empire, which will be considered in the next chapter). Whereas in the eastern lands the Seljuk legacy had scarcely outlived the Seljuk empire, in Syria and Egypt it was to come to its true fruition in an order of society which, thanks to the Mamlūks, was to endure for more than two and a half centuries.

Sunnī orthodoxy, as promulgated under the Seljuks and later under the Mamlūks, was by its very nature conservative. (Indeed, orthodoxy and conservatism, though not synonymous terms, represent closely related ideas.) Not only did it regard the Koran and the Tradition (Sunna) of the Prophet as embodying the final revelation of God to man, more significantly it regarded the law which had been built up by the jurists and the system of beliefs worked out by the kalām thologians as the best possible formulation of received religion and as sufficient for all time. Furthermore, Sunnī orthodoxy had come to regard Sūfī mysticism in its more moderate form and the Sūfī orders as an essential part of Islamic piety. Finally, what is most important from the point of view of social history, it had come to view the sociopolitical order, characterized by a working relationship between the iqtā^{c}-based military and the ^{c}ulamā', as the norm, even if not quite the ideal. The conservatism which prevailed under the Mamlūks was at once cultural, religious, and political.

So enmeshed was Sunnī orthodoxy in the sociopolitical order that the ^{c}ulamā' went to great lengths to justify the status quo and to discourage rebellion. This political conservatism is especially evident in the writings of a prominent jurist who lived in the period of the Bahrī Mamlūks, Badr al-Dīn ibn Jamā^{c}a (d. 1333). Ibn Jamā^{c}a held that usurpation (the seizure of power by force) was legitimate and that when a military commander succeeded in seizing power, the populace was under obligation to submit to his rule. This acceptance of usurpation was necessary, according to ibn Jamā^{c}a, "for the sake of the welfare of the Muslims and of their unity." Like many other ^{c}ulamā', Ibn Jamā^{c}a loathed any political upheaval that might undermine the unity and peace of the umma. The highest premium was placed upon public order. So long as the Law of God, or Sharī^{c}a, was upheld by the ruler, it did not much matter by what means he had gained power. This outlook obviously represented an adjustment on the part of the ^{c}ulamā' to the realities of Mamlūk politics.

To prop up their image as legitimate rulers, the Mamlūks maintained under their patronage a remnant line of Abbasid Caliphs. This line, as noted earlier, was inaugurated by Baybars in 1261, when a refugee of the Abbasid House was proclaimed caliph in Cairo. The Mamlūk-sponsored caliphate was a puppet institution pure and simple. The role of the caliph was to invest each new sultān, for the sultān was, in theory, a delegate of the caliph. In fact, however, the caliph had no real power to appoint sultāns. In the political theory of Ibn Jamā^{c}a and like-minded persons, whenever a military commander seized power by defeating or slaying his rivals (who might include the previous sultān), he had a legitimate claim to rule and the caliph was obliged to invest him with the office of sultān.

The conservative spirit of the Mamlūk period is reflected in its religious literature. In general, religious writers attempted one of two things; either they wrote commentaries on authoritative works of an earlier period or they produced compendia on particular subjects or fields of study in which they endeavored to sum up all previous knowledge. Commentary and summarization were thus the two primary concerns of religious scholars. Only very rarely did a scholar venture new ideas of his own. Perhaps the most typical representative of the class of religious scholars of the Mamlūk period was Jalāl al-Dīn al-Suyūtī, who lived toward the end of the period (d. 1505). Al-Suyūtī has been described as "the greatest polygraph [writer on many subjects] of Islam." He is said to have produced 561 distinct works, of which 450 have survived. Many of these are short treatises, but some are large volumes. Al-Suyūtī's writings covered the whole field of contemporary literary and scientific studies. "By their inclusiveness and easy style, al-Suyūtī's works soon gained an audience from one end of the Islamic world to the other, and have for nearly four centuries held an authoritative position as the interpreter and epitomizer of the Muslim classical tradition" (H. A. R. Gibb, Arabic Literature, p. 147).

Despite the prevailing conservatism, the Mamlūk period produced at least one thinker with a mind of his own. This was the dynamic religious reformer Taqī al-Dīn ibn Taymiyya (d. 1328). Ibn Taymiyya took a dim view of his times. Even though he lived at a time when the Mamlūk state was at the peak of its power and prosperity, he saw the social and religious life around him as defective and in decline. In particular, he singled out the Sūfī orders as a target of criticism, attacking especially the cult of saints and practices related to it, which he considered to be an intrusion into the religion of Islam. He called for a purification of Islam from everything which was incompatible with the Koran and Sunna and for a return to the pristine simplicity of original Islam. He also took to task the legal conservatism of the ᶜulamāʾ, counseling them to seek fresh insight from the Koran and Sunna rather than relying on the statements of later authorities. He even spoke out against certain practices of the Mamlūk state. These criticisms of practices and attitudes that were firmly entrenched among his contemporaries brought Ibn Taymiyya into conflict with the state and the ᶜulamāʾ, resulting in his frequent imprisonment. Although Ibn Taymiyya's ideas had little impact on his times, they came to constitute an important reformist legacy that was to be preserved in his writings and to bear fruit in later (modern) times.

The Mamlūk period is particularly rich in biographical and historical writing, traditions carried forward from earlier times. The greatest biographer of the period was Ibn Khallikān (d. 1282) and the great historian al-Maqrīzī (d. 1441). Ibn Khallikān's Obituaries of Eminent Men contains biographical notes on 865 of the most distinguished Muslims in history and has become an essential tool of Islamic studies. A British scholar, H. A. Nicholson, called it "the best general biography ever written" (Literary History of the Arabs, p. 452). To al-Maqrīzī we owe important works on the topography of Egypt, the history of the Fātimids, the history of the Ayyūbids and Mamluks (to 1440), and a biography of famous Egyptians.

In literature proper, the Mamlūk period is famous not so much for its "higher literature" as for developments which took place in the domain of popular literature. It was in the Mamlūk period that the popular romantic legends centering around the figures of ᶜAntar and Baybars took their present form. It was also in the same period that the famous collection of stories called The Thousand and One Nights entered the final stage of compilation. The earlier history of this collection is poorly known. The Shāhrazād story, which serves as the framework of the collection, has been traced to India, but the stories themselves are of diverse origin. Before these stories were assembled as written literature, they were transmitted by storytellers throughout the world of Islam. Egypt had an especially large share of storytellers, and old stories were often cast in the familiar setting of Egypt itself. For example, the fāris who appears often in the Nights portrays the Mamlūk warrior, rather than the soldier of the Abbāsid period within which the stories are often nominally set. Also, the customs and manners displayed in the Nights often reflect Mamlūk Egypt. Being designed for popular consumption, these stories were of course originally told in the vernacular language and had to be, in assuming a literary character, adjusted at least superfically to the standards of classical Arabic.

In poetry the only figure of the Mamlūk period worth mentioning is al-Busīrī (d. 1296), a poet of Berber extraction who composed what is perhaps the most popular of all Arabic poems, an Ode to the Prophet entitled The Mantle. In some areas where this poem became known it was invested with miraculous powers and its verses were recited as charms. Numerous commentaries were written on it.

Before leaving aside the subject of cultural life under the Mamlūks, one final point should be noted. Whereas in the other Islamic lands (except the Maghrib) the Persian language flourished as a medium of artistic expression and was coming to exercise a great influence on the development of other Islamic literatures, in Mamlūk Syria and Egypt Arabic remained the sole literary language. Thus, while Islamic civilization was developing along new lines elsewhere, in the Mamlūk lands it continued to develop in its original Arabic form. The Mamlūk empire was a haven not only for Sunnī orthodoxy but also for Arab culture.

Decline under the Burji Mamlūks

In 1382 the last of Qalāwūn's descendants to rule as sultān was overthrown by an able Mamlūk commander named Barqūq, who belonged to a corps of mamlūks known as the Burjīs (so named because they were stationed in the main citadel, or "tower," i.e., burj, of Cairo). The Burjī corps had originally been founded by Qalāwūn himself nearly a century earlier. Barqūq's coming to power marked the end of the Bahrī sultānate. The series of sultāns who ruled the Mamlūk empire thereafter are called sometimes Burjīs, after the corps which brought them to power, sometimes Circassians, since all but two of them were of that ethnic origin.

The transition from Bahrī to Burjī rule corresponded to a number of important political and economic changes. Under the Burjīs, the dynastic principle was abandoned altogether and the "survival of the fittest" system of succession became normative. Although this system had the advantage of producing many strong and capable rulers, it made for general instability in political life. When a sultān died he was succeeded pro forma by his son while the real battle for the succession was fought out among the leading Mamlūk officers. The victor emerged as the new sultān, while the previous sultān's son conveniently retired from the scene, his reign having constituted nothing more than an interregnum.

Economically speaking, the Burjī period was one of steady decline. Whereas under the Bahrīs Egypt and Syria had enjoyed economic prosperity under the new line of rulers the economy of these countries went downhill. This retrogression may be traced to several different factors.

1. To begin with, the generally good public health which prevailed under the earlier Mamlūks underwent a sharp decline. This decline had begun even before the Burjīs came to power. Around the middle of the fourteenth century (1347-1350) Egypt and Syria had suffered the ravages of a terrible epidemic known generally as the Black Death or Bubonic Plague, which had also afflicted other Islamic lands and parts of Europe. Thereafter public health under the Mamlūks remained generally poor. Epidemics, although not as severe as the Black Death, occurred with such frequency that foreigners visiting Egypt were told that the plague broke out every seven years. The result was depopulation and a reduction of productivity.

2. After the Burjīs came to power, the Mamlūk economy was further weakened by a concurrence of several different factors. One of these was famine. Low inundations of the Nile in the years 1403 and 1404 produced severe food shortage and malnutrition. This further contributed to the breakdown of public health (malnutrition weakens resistance to disease) and to depopulation.

3. Another factor was the shortage of precious metals available for coinage. The first precious metal to become scarce was silver. Shortly after 1400 (that is, roughly at the same time as the famines mentioned above) the silver dirhem disappeared and was replaced by a copper dirhem. This development was due largely to the drain of silver coins to Europe as a result of trade. Meanwhile, the supply of gold continued for a time, but in the mid-fifteenth century it too began to diminish, owing to the penetration of Europeans into the gold-producing areas of West Africa. Eventually, even copper coins became hard to find at times, and people were obliged in certain instances to resort to the use of wheat in place of coins.

4. Still another factor was the decline of Syrian and Egyptian industry after 1400. A fifteenth-century Mamlūk historian, Ibn Taghribirdī, noted that, whereas in 1388 there had been 14,000 looms in Alexandria, which was a great textile center, by 1433 the number had dropped to 800. Considering the great role which the textile industry had played in Egypt in previous centuries, this rather sudden shrinkage must be viewed as a serious economic setback. Other industries, such as those of sugar, soap and paper, also dwindled. Although this decline can be traced, in part, to reduction of the labor force as a result of depopulation and to the shortage of coins (which reduced consumption), we must turn for a full explanation to an outside factor: the competition of European industry. Early in the fifteenth-century, the superiority of European textiles became apparent, and Egyptian and Syrian textiles were edged slowly out of the market. European textile manufacturers possessed a number of important advantages: better raw materials (especially wool), superior technology thanks to new inventions (e.g., the automatic mill, the treadle-loom and the spinning wheel), and greater scope for free enterprise, creating a more competitive spirit with greater incentives for innovation. Not only were European markets closed to Egyptian and Syrian textiles; more significantly, European textiles found their way into Egypt and Syria. This was true of other products as well. European glassware, paper

and soap, for example, appeared in Mamlūk markets. Even silver inlay, once identified as a truly "eastern" craft, was obtained from Europe.

Particular mention should be made of the economically debilitating effect which the invasion of Timur had upon Syria. In the late fourteenth century, Timur had appeared in the eastern lands of Islam as a re-embodiment of the Mongol horde. Heading an army made up of Turkish and Mongol warriors, he had, like the Mongol conquerors of the thirteenth century, swept like lightning across the central lands of Islam, advancing as far westward as Central Anatolia. In 1400 he entered Mamlūk Syria and within a few months had captured and laid waste the cities of Aleppo, Hamah, Homs, and Damascus, inflicting irreparable damage on the areas, made worse by the raiding of bedouin who got out of control. Syria was ruined economically. Many of her best craftsmen were deported to far-away Samarqand, which Timur had made his capital.

As a result of the economic decline of the Mamlūk territories and the impoverishment of the population, the Mamlūk state itself faced continual financial hardship under the Burjīs. The appetite of the military class for luxury did not diminish, and the cost of conducting wars placed a heavy burden on the state. The wars against Timur in particular were very costly. Owing to the impoverishment of the population, taxation could no longer provide the solution to fiscal strains. Consequently, the state began to explore other sources of income. One of these was the sale of iqtā^{c} lands. This practice, which became fairly common in the fifteenth century, represented an important change in the pattern of land tenure. Whereas independently owned land (amlāk) had previously been rather rare, it now became more common. Even members of the military class themselves, including sultāns, purchased land. This helped, at least temporarily, to strengthen the treasury. Furthermore, public offices went up for sale. Mamlūks were even, for a price, permitted to purchase exemption from military duties. Such practices, fraught as they were with corruption, indicate the desperate nature of the situation which the Mamlūk state found itself in.

One of the most economically ruinous methods of raising money adopted by the Mamlūk state was the establishment of state monopolies over various commercial enterprises. The sultān Barsbay inaugurated this practice in 1423 by making sugar a state monopoly. "All private sugar refineries were closed, and all confectioners, pastry-cooks, and other consumers of sugar were ordered to buy from the state at a fixed price greatly in excess of current commercial prices. A special government department was set up to deal with the sugar monopoly, which, after a brief relaxation, was extended and strengthened during the following years. All traffic and manufacture except by the sultān's agents was forbidden, and existing stocks compulsorily acquired. Even the cultivation of sugar-cane was banned except on the sultān's domain estates. The application of these rules in both Syria and Egypt brought soaring prices and general distress." (The Cambridge History of Islam, Vol. I, pp. 225-226.) Barsbay applied similar measures to other enterprises as well, such as cereal and meat production. In 1429 he stepped into international trade by taking over the spice trade.

The sale of pepper to Europeans by private individuals was forbidden; only the sultan's agents were allowed to make such sales. By eliminating competition, the sultān was able to buy pepper cheaply, since no Egyptian merchants dared to outbid him, and to sell it at an exorbitant price.

These efforts, ultimately, were of no avail. The economic collapse of the Mamlūk empire could be averted by such remedies. The financial predicament of the state only worsened, as its stability was undermined by continual infighting within the military.

The final blows came from two sources--the Portuguese and the Ottomans. By opening up a sea route around Africa connecting Europe with India and the Far East, the Portuguese brought ruin upon Mamluk commerce and particularly on the all-important spice trade, over which Egyptian merchants had for a long time enjoyed complete control. Although the long-term effects of this development upon Levantine commerce should not be exaggerated, the immediate effects were extremely serious.

The decisive blow came from the Ottomans, whose armies entered Syria in 1516 and within a year utterly defeated the Mamlūks, incorporating their empire into their own. In the war between the Mamlūks and the Ottomans, the crucial factor was firearms. Too proud to accept this "modern" innovation, the Mamlūks blindly adhered to their traditional methods of warfare. But history was on the side of the new "dishonorable" weapon, and because the Ottomans were willing to use it they succeeded in overpowering the Mamlūks and in ending their two-and-a-half-century long hegemony over Egypt and Syria.

North Africa Under the Marīnids, Zayyānids, and Ḥafṣids

At the time of the rise of the Mamlūks to power in Egypt in the mid-thirteenth century, the Muwahhid caliphate of Morocco was entering its last days. Already in 1235 the Muwahhid state had relinquished control of the central and eastern Maghrib to local aspirants, the Zayyānids and the Hafsids, and by 1250 could claim only southern Morocco as its proper domain. The final blow came in 1269 when a nomadic people, the Banu Marīn or Marīnids, who had established themselves in central Morocco in 1246, conquered Marrakesh and forced the few Muwahhid survivors to retreat to Tinmal in the High Atlas (the original Muwahhid stronghold), where they lived for six more years until their final annihilation in 1275.

Thus there emerged out of the ruins of the Muwahhid empire three separate successor states, those of the Marīnids, Zayyānids and Hafsids, all of them founded by Berbers despite the predominantly Arab character of the general populace. This tripartite geographical division was thereafter to remain characteristic of North Africa until modern times, although political boundaries would vary considerably from one period to another.

The Marīnid state ruled Morocco until 1465, when power was transferred to another dynasty related to the Marīnids, namely the Wattāsids, who remained in power until 1549. The Zayyānids and Hafsids dominated the central and eastern Maghrib, respectively, until these areas were taken over by the Ottomans in the mid-sixteenth century. The rule of these three states was at best always precarious. All three had to deal constantly with unruly bedouin elements, and their control of their own territories was often restricted to the major cities and surrounding countryside, the remaining territory often being controlled by bedouin. Furthermore, the three states lived in continual competition with each other, each seeking to revive the unity of the Maghrib under its own auspices and at the others' expense.

The Hafsid state in Ifrīqiya (Tunisia) was the first to reach the height of its power. The Hafsids were descendants of a close companion of Ibn Tūmart named Abū Hafs ᶜUmar and for that reason looked upon themselves as the natural heirs of the Muwahhid empire. Even before the Marīnid conquest of Marrakesh and destruction of the Muwahhid state in Morocco, the Hafsids had refused to obey orders of the Muwahhid caliph in 1235 and had proceeded to build up an independent seat of power. By 1260 they had become powerful enough to force the Marīnids and Zayyānids to recognize their suzerainty, and their fame had so spread that ambassadors were flocking to their court from places as far away as Norway. After the destruction of the Abbasid Caliphate in 1258, the Sharīf of Mecca for a time recognized the Hafsid ruler as caliph, until a remnant Abbasid caliphate was set up in Cairo in 1261 by the Mamlūk sultān.

This period of initial greatness ended abruptly in 1277, when rivalries within the Hafsid family plunged the state into upheaval and civil strife, made worse by the involvement of bedouin tribes and of the Marīnids and Zayyānids, who took sides in the conflict in order to further their own interests. Twice in the mid-fourteenth century the Marīnids managed to make themselves masters over the Hafsid territories. This state of turmoil ended in 1357, when an energetic ruler named Abu'l-ᶜAbbās came to power who was able to restore the unity and prestige of the Hafsid state. This new blossoming of Hafsid power lasted for more than a century (1357-1448), after which the state once again lapsed into civil turmoil. By the mid-sixteenth century, the Hafsids were in such decline that the Ottomans were able to intrude into their territory with little difficulty.

Of the many important achievements of the Hafsids, the most noteworthy was their building up of Tunis into the major city of the eastern Maghrib, a position which it has retained to the present day. Not only did the Hafsids make Tunis their principal capital, they transformed it into the primary economic and cultural center of their realm. The Zaytūna mosque became the leading center of learning and attracted scholars from all over the area.

The rise of the Marīnids to power was much more gradual than that of the Hafsids. Unlike the Hafsids, who belonged to the aristocracy of the Muwahhid empire, the Marīnids were originally chieftains of a relatively obscure nomadic Berber tribe, the Banu Marīn, which had roamed in the area southeast of the High Atlas. Under the leadership of an ambitious chieftain named Abū Yaḥyā, they captured Meknes and Fez in 1244 and 1248 and formed a state in Central Morocco, forcing the Muwahhid southward. After twenty-five years of subsequent fighting, they succeeded finally in taking Marrakesh in 1269 and in gaining control over the whole of Morocco. However, their hold over Morocco was tenuous. Not only were they troubled by bedouin, they also expended much of their resources in an unsuccessful attempt to prevent the Christian forces from advancing in Spain. They also encountered opposition from the Zayyānids, who were anxious to enlarge their realm.

It was not until the mid-fourteenth century (1331-1358) that the Marīnids finally reached the peak of their power and greatness, thanks

The Arab-Islamic World in A.D. 1300

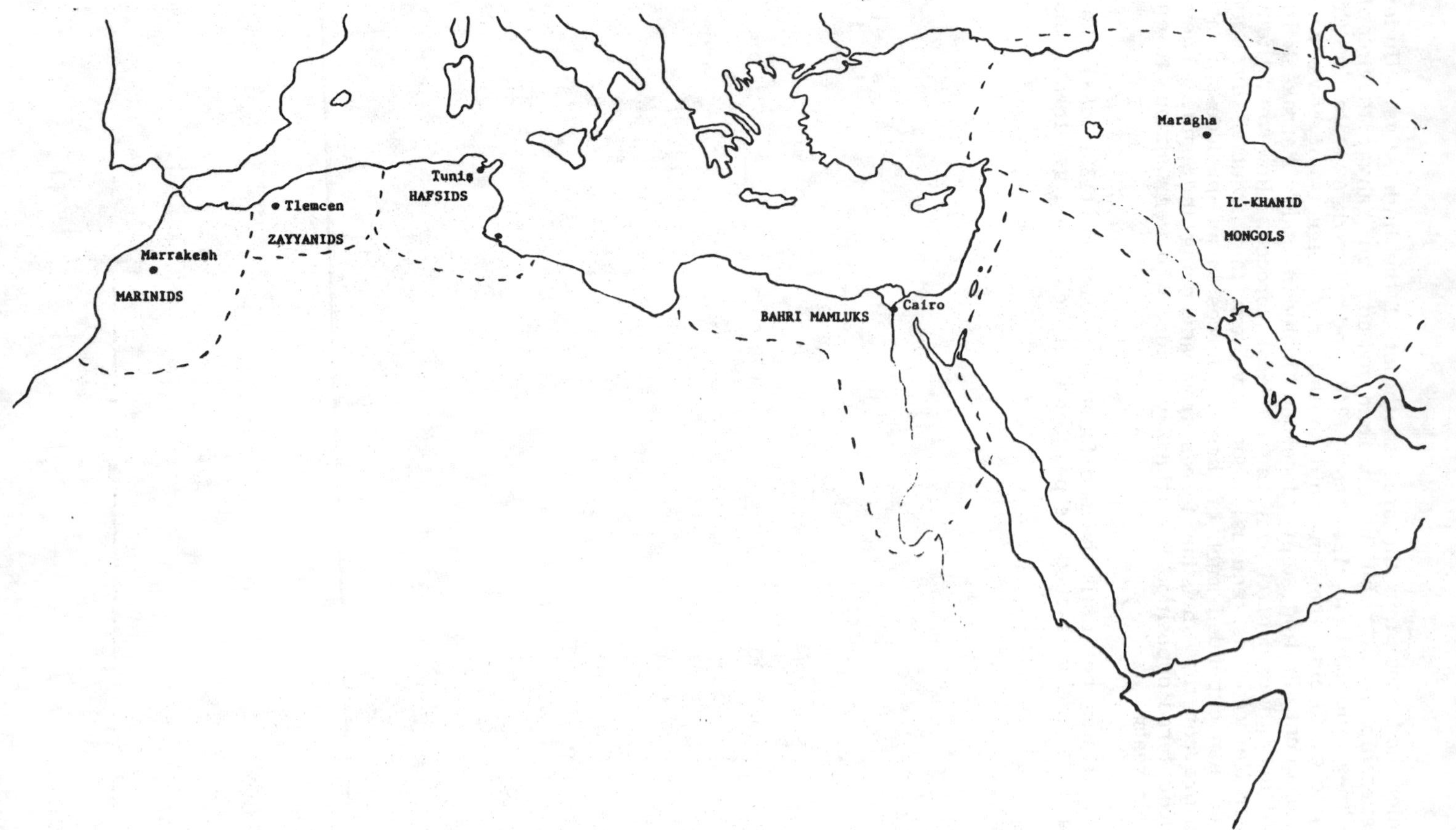

to the capable rule of Abu'l-Hasan ᶜAlī and his son Abū ᶜInān. It was during this period that, owing to turmoil within the Hafsid state, the Marīnids were able to extend their power momentarily on two occasions over Tunisia. After the death of Abū ᶜInān in 1358, the Marīnid state fell victim to circumstances similar to those which had afflicted the Hafsid state: rivalries between great families and intrigues of bedouin tribes. To this must be added the occasional intervention of foreign powers, such as the Christian rulers of Spain, the Muslim ruler of Granada, and the Zayyānids. In 1420, power in Morocco passed into the hands of the Wattasids, who formally put an end to Marīnid rule in 1465.

The Marīnids were zealous promoters of Mālikī orthodoxy. Under their rule, the Mālikī fuqahā' once again enjoyed the pre-eminence which had been denied them by the Muwahhids. Madrasas were built on an unprecedented scale. These madrasas provided lodging for students wishing to engage in full-time study of the religious disciplines. As had been the case in the Islamic countries to the east, the madrasa now became a primary instrument for the inculcation of Sunnī orthodoxy, the form of orthodoxy accepted in Morocco being that of the Mālikī school. This spread of orthodoxy helped to check the influence of Sūfī mysticism, particularly in its more extreme forms. As in the eastern countries, Sūfī mysticism had great appeal among the masses, especially in the countryside where it produced cults of saints. The emotional fervor which these cults aroused stood in sharp contrast to the more disciplined piety of the fuqahā'.

By building mosques and madrasas and by patronizing orthodox religious scholars, the Marīnids compensated for their unspectacular origins. Unlike the Murābits and Muwahhids before them, the Marīnids did not appear on the scene in the first instance as religious reformers. There was no Ibn Yāsīn or Ibn Tūmart among them, no fraternity of religious warriors bound together by an iron-tight discipline and by devotion to a charismatic leader. The original driving force behind the Marīnids had been nomadism pure and simple. However, the Marīnids won for themselves a firm place in the religious history of Morocco by helping the country, through their zealous patronage of Mālikī orthodoxy, to assume the religious character which it was to retain to the present day. They also placed their stamp on popular religions by organizing the cult of Mawlay Idrīs, Morocco's first independent ruler. The annual festival at the shrine of Mawlay Idrīs would take on the character of a Moroccan national holiday.

Under the Marīnids, Fez became the primary city of Morocco, being the capital of the dynasty and the leading religious and intellectual center. The Marīnids erected, adjacent to the ancient city, a center for government offices and military quarters called New Fez (Fās al-Jadid). Old Fez was Morocco's oldest Muslim city, having been founded by Mawlay Idrīs himself. Now under the Marīnids it once again regained the pre-eminence of former times. The great mosque-university of the Qarawiyyīn rivaled the Zaytūna in Tunis as a center of learning.

The origins of the Zayyānid state go back to 1236, when a certain Ibn Zayyān, chieftain of the Berber tribe of the Banū ʿAbd al-Wād, who held power in the region of Tlemcen (Tilimsān), repudiated the authority of the Muwahhid caliph. Ibn Zayyān's descendants were to retain control of this region for three centuries. As the smallest of the three Maghribi states, the Zayyānid state often faced great difficulties, sandwiched as it was between two more powerful rivals. (Tlemcen, it should be noted, is situated some 50 kilometers from the coast of modern Algeria not far from that country's western border.) Despite the fact that the Zayyānid state was placed under the suzerainty of the Marīnids in the fourteenth century and under that of the Hafsids in the fifteenth, it was never abolished and managed to survive until the coming of the Ottomans in the sixteenth century.

CHAPTER EIGHT

THE ARAB LANDS UNDER OTTOMAN RULE, 1517-1600

During the sixteenth century, most Arabic-speaking lands became provinces of the Ottoman Empire. Because this Muslim-Turkish State began its rise to prominence and power more than two hundred years earlier, around 1300, its acquisition of the "Arab lands" belongs to the final stages of its expansion process. But, although entering the Ottoman Empire relatively late, many of the "Arab lands" would continue to be associated with it until the nineteenth century and beyond. Indeed, most of the Fertile Crescent and portions of the Arabian peninsula would remain an integral part of it until the empire's formal dissolution in 1918 following World War I. In order fully to appreciate certain aspects of contemporary Arab society, therefore, it is often necessary to consider its Ottoman background; and the history of the Arabic-speaking peoples during 1516-1918 can neither be told accurately nor understood correctly without placing it in its Ottoman context. Accordingly, this chapter will include, first, an historical narrative of the Ottoman Empire's rise and expansion, and secondly, a reconstruction of the mature empire's important structures and processes. That is, the initial half of the chapter will trace the origin and growth of the Ottoman Empire to 1600, by which time it included most Arabic-speaking territories. The second half will then analyze the major institutions of the Ottoman state and society, focusing upon those which by 1600 the empire's Arabic-speaking subjects shared with its Turkish-speaking rulers.

The Rise and Expansion of the Ottoman Empire

The series of Mongol incursions into the Fertile Crescent during the mid-thirteenth century, among other factors, brought about conditions of uncertainty and disorder throughout the Near East. In Anatolia, the chaotic situation was exacerbated by the continued influx of Muslim-Turkish tribes, which had been entering the peninsula since before the battle of Manzikert (1071). The pace of this Volkerwanderung (mass migration) intensified after 1258, as large numbers of tribes fled westward in search of territories beyond the Mongols' effective control. Many of these newcomers settled at the extreme western end of Anatolia in a region which Ottoman historians have called "the Byzantine march," a disputed borderland area between the long established Greek-Christian population and the recently arrived Turkish-Muslim population. Because of the Mongol destruction of the Seljuk state and the consequent decline of the "Seljuks of Rūm" (whose capital was at Konya), Anatolia lacked an all-encompassing centralized political authority. The power vacuum was filled in part by the immigrant Turkish warlords, many of whom created for themselves petty amirates along the Byzantine march. These Turkish principalities of late thirteenth-century Anatolia have also been called "Ghazi states," because many of them were engaged more or less constantly in a holy war of raids and expansion against the aged and declining Byzantine

Empire. The weak and friendless Seljuks of Rūm were also attacked by neighboring amirates such as Karamān, the largest "Ghazi state," which ultimately seized Konya. When the famous Muslim traveller-geographer Ibn Battūta (d. 1369) visited Anatolia during the early fourteenth century, he counted dozens of these Turkish march amirates. Some of them, like Karamān, were stronger than others; so perhaps it was only a matter of time until one or more strong principalities began to expand at the expense of weaker neighbors.

A principality named Söğüt, initially one of the smaller Ghazi states, was established in the extreme northwest corner of the Byzantine march by a warrior named Osman ("ᶜUthmān" in Arabic, "Ottoman" in Italian and other Western European languages). Although Ottoman subjects would subsequently claim a common descent from a remote and illustrious ancestor, certain modern historians have demonstrated that Osman's original followers consisted not of a single tribe but rather of ghazi warriors from diverse tribal origins. Three main factors help to explain why the Ottoman amirate of Söğüt began and continued to expand. First, of all the ghazi states it was strategically located in the best position to take advantage of Byzantine weakness. Other march amirates either could not expand at Byzantine expense at all or else could do so only to the southern shores of the Aegean Sea; Söğüt could and did expand right into Europe. Secondly, during two and a half centuries the Ottoman state was blessed with a remarkable series of ten outstanding rulers.* Originally a petty dynasty which gradually transformed itself into a powerful sultanate, the House of Osman provided the emerging state and the expanding empire with strong central authority and political unity. Finally, the Ottomans' continuously successful campaigns against the Byzantines attracted other ghazi warriors who steadily added to their military strength. It also attracted, from former Seljuk territories in the Fertile Crescent and further east, a number of ulama, bureaucrats, artisans and merchants who counterbalanced the turbulence and superstitiousness of the ghazi warriors with scripture-based worship and learning, orderly governmental administration, industry, commerce, and other institutions of traditional urban Islamic civilization.

The First Ottoman Empire (1326-1402)

Expanding towards and into Europe was the successful formula for Ottoman growth during its initial stages. Following the death of Osman (1300-26), his son Orhan (1326-60) proceeded to conquer and to annex the remaining Byzantine territory in Anatolia, containing such important cities as Bursa (which became the first imperial capital) and Iznik (formerly Nicaea). Sending its armies directly into Europe, the Ottoman state continued to acquire new territories there throughout the

---

*Osman (1300-26), Orhan (1326-60), Murād I (1360-89), Bayezid I (1389-1402), Mehmed I (1413-21), Murād II (1421-51), Mehmed II (1451-81), Bayezid II (1481-1512), Selīm I (1512-20), Sulaymān (1520-66).

fourteenth century. The bulk of its territorial expansion in Europe came not so much at the expense of Byzantium, now a radically truncated principality whose Balkan provinces had become semi-autonomous, but rather at the expense of the Emperor's Serbian and Bulgarian vassals. Murad I (1360-89) seized Edirne (Adrianopolis), thereby completely encircling Constantinople, and then destroyed the Serbian forces at Kossovo (1389). Bayezid I (1389-1402) defeated a central European "crusade" at Nicopolis (1393) and extended Ottoman rule beyond the Danube. The Ottoman Empire thus arose and established itself during the fourteenth century mainly through a policy of expansion in Europe at the expense of the Byzantines and other Balkan peoples.

Meanwhile, with respect to certain Ottoman institutions there were occurring changes which would eventually alter the empire's character and reverse the direction of its expansion. At first, much of the territory conquered by the Ottomans in Byzantine Anatolia and in Europe was parcelled out, in the form of fiefs called timar-s, to cooperating ghazi warlords. On a basis reminiscent of the Seljuk or Ayyubid iqta[c], the timar-holder was required to pay a token annual tribute to the Ottoman ruler as well as to furnish to him, upon request, a stipulated number of mounted ghazi warriors (called sipahi-s or cavalrymen). The Ottoman rulers learned by experience that the Turkish timar-holders and their sipahi-s were not always loyal and reliable, however, so they began to change their policies with regard to land tenure, provincial administration, and military recruitment. For example, Christian notables in the Balkans, if they submitted peacefully and agreed to switch their allegiance from the Byzantine to the Ottoman sovereign, were allowed to retain their fiefs and to become, in effect, Ottoman vassals having the same financial and military obligations as Muslim-Turkish timar-holders. On the other hand, the domains of those Christian notables who resisted, and which the Ottomans were therefore obliged to conquer by force were confiscated and entrusted to administrators responsible directly to the sultan. The sultans also began to create their own private military force out of young male prisoners of war from the Balkan campaigns. This new palace guard of Islamized Europeans, known as the janissary corps (from Turkish yeniseri or "new corps") consisted of the sultan's personal slaves who were therefore presumed to be more loyal than the sipahi-s.

During the fourteenth century the Ottomans also acquired a certain amount of territory and influence in Turkish Anatolia, chiefly through such peaceful means as state marriages and purchase. After Nicopolis (1393), the sultan's Christian vassals and his ex-Christian slave-soldiers began to act as a sort of "Christian lobby" at the Ottoman court, persuading Bayezid I to seek more lands in Anatolia by military conquest. In doing so, Bayezid shifted the main thrust of expansion from west to east and thereby renounced the Ottoman state's ghazi tradition. This upset the Turkish-Muslim timar-holders and sipahi-s, who consequently refused to participate in Bayezid's Anatolian campaigns against fellow Muslims and Turks. Yet, relying principally upon his Christian vassals and upon the janissary corps, Bayezid proceeded to conquer most of Anatolia, including Karaman, by the end of the fourteenth century. This sudden eastward lurch of the Ottoman

Empire alarmed the imperial heir of the Mongols, Timur Leng (Tamerlane), who mobilized his considerable forces and defeated the Ottomans at Ankara in 1402. Timur restored to their lands the ruler of Karaman and other recently dispossessed Turkish amirs and then split the remaining Ottoman territories between the three sons of Bayezid I. Ottoman historians refer to these actions by Timur as the end of the "First Ottoman Empire."

The "Second Ottoman Empire" (1413 onwards)

There is a certain irony in the fact that, while Timur's state and empire rapidly and completely disintegrated after his death in 1405, one of Bayezid's sons, Mehmed (Muhammad), succeeded by 1413 in reuniting the Ottoman domains and then resumed the process of expansion. Establishing Edirne as the imperial capital, Mehmed I (1413-21) campaigned mainly in Europe. But his successor, Murad II (1421-51), turned eastward and steadily reconquered all, save Karaman, of the central Anatolian Turkish amirates which Timur had restored to independence in 1402. Murad II also regularized the recruitment of slaves for the sultan's military and bureaucracy by instituting the devshirme, a systematic "legal kidnapping" of male children from the Balkan provinces. Mehmed II (1451-81) elaborated the procedure whereby slave boys were trained for the imperial bureaucracy by creating an official school in a wing of his palace in Constantinople, a city which he finally seized in 1453 and which became the third and last Ottoman capital. "Mehmed the Conqueror" also annexed Albania, Bosnia, Wallachia, the Crimea, Trebizon, and Karaman (see map). So by 1481 the Ottoman Empire bordered in Europe on the kingdoms of Hungary, Poland, and Russia. In Asia its southern frontier abutted the Syrian province of the Egypt-based Mamluk empire, while its eastern frontier constituted a "march" zone occupied by Turkish tribal amirates competing to fill the political void brought on by the collapse of the Timuri state.

By the end of the fifteenth century, the Ottoman sultan ruled a polity which had become something more than a ghazi state or a march amirate. Bayezid II (1481-1512) presided over a genuine empire which had completely absorbed and therefore replaced Byzantium. Thus, in some ways the Ottoman Empire represented tradition and continuity. For over a thousand years an imperial state, initially featuring a Greek-Christian ruling elite and now featuring a Turkish-Muslim one, had been centered at Constantinople, uniting portions of Europe and Asia under a single crown. From their Byzantine predecessors, the Ottoman sultans consequently inherited not just territory but also certain imperial traditions and institutions. Yet in other ways the Ottoman Empire represented innovation and discontinuity. For example, to an extent the Ottoman state was typical of several new land-based empires which arose during the fifteenth century in large part through their effective use of gunpowder and artillery--the keys, according to some analysts, of Mehmed II's conquest of Constantinople and his near doubling of his domains during 1451-81. Other "gunpowder empires" that emerged during the fifteenth and early sixteenth centuries included Safavi Iran, Mughal India, and Tsarist Russia. During this same period Egypt's Burji Mamluk sultanate also adopted the use of firearms, although less thoroughly and therefore less effectively than did its neighbors to the north and northeast. At any rate, during the later phases of its expansion after 1500, the Ottoman state was no longer dealing primarily with aging empires and petty tribal amirates but rather with rival "gunpowder empires." Indeed, the Ottoman Empire's acquisition of the "Arab lands" occurred within the context of its confrontation with Safavi Iran and Mamluk Egypt as well as with such maritime powers as Portugal and Spain.

The Rise of Safavi Iran

Although the imperial rivals (Ottoman Sultan) Bayezid II and (Mamluk Sultan) Qait Bey clashed during 1481-85 over a pair of small amirates in southeastern Anatolia, the Ottoman Empire's ultimate showdown with Mamluk Egypt did not come until some thirty years after this so-called "First Ottoman-Mamluk war." It was instead a conflict with Safavi Iran that became the Ottoman Empire's first major confrontation with another "gunpowder empire." The Safavi dynasty originated in Azerbayjan as a Sufi brotherhood, called the Safawiyya after its founder, Shaykh Safī al-Dīn (d. 1334). During the fifteenth century, the Safawiyya made two important transitions, first, from a "Sunni Order" having Alid tendencies to a frankly Shi'i Order and, secondly, from a religious brotherhood with an essentially spiritual raison d'etre to a theocratic state with imperial ambitions. At the beginning of the sixteenth century, the Safavi ruler, Shah Ismail (1502-24), finally solved the problem of the Timuri succession by imposing his family's rule on the whole of Iran and Iraq.

At the same time, Shah Ismail imposed Shi'ism on his Persian-speaking and Arabic-speaking subjects. The adoption of Shi'ism as a state religion may have been a measure of political expediency, for Shah Ismail apparently wanted to differentiate his domain from the Ottoman Empire and other "Sunni" neighbors. The Safavis also exploited the Shi'i sympathies of the Turkish tribesmen of Eastern Anatolia as a means of provoking them to resist the Ottoman Empire's eastward expansion. Bayezid II (1481-1512) was preoccupied during much of his reign with a series of revolts undertaken in Anatolia by tribesmen who were sympathetic to Shi'ism and who looked to Shah Ismail as their spiritual leader and military protector. The rise of the Shi'i Safavi state in Iran thus represented a threat to the Ottomans. When Selīm I (1512-20) came to power, he consequently resolved to eliminate the threat by attacking and destroying the Safavi state. In a confrontation between the two imperial armies on the plains of Chaldiran during the summer and fall of 1514, Selīm defeated the Safavi army but, although discouraging Ismail from engaging in further machinations among the Anatolian tribesmen, could not wreck the Safavi state. The Ottomans consequently came away from their initial confrontation with the Safavis without achieving all of their objectives. By virtue of his victory, Selīm was able to establish his claim to Mosul and the hilly region to the north (which was inhabited by Kurdish tribes), but the Arabic-speaking areas of central and southern Iraq temporarily remained in Safavi hands.

The Ottoman Conquest of Syria and Egypt from the Mamluks

The Ottomans withdrew from Safavi territory after the inconclusive campaign of Chaldiran in part because their southern flank was threatened by the concentration of Mamluk forces in Northern Syria. The Mamluk army returned to Aleppo in the spring of 1516 when Selīm was preparing a second expedition against the Safavis. The Ottoman sultan's sudden decision to attack the Mamluks rather than the Safavis caught the former off guard and even created a schism within their ranks, as the Mamluk governor of Aleppo (Khayr Bey) led a mutiny to join forces with the enemy. This conspiracy, coming on top of normal Ottoman military superiority (both in numbers of troops and in kinds of weapons), turned the confrontation into a rout. The people of Aleppo locked their city gates against the retreating Mamluks, so the latter hastily withdrew into Egypt, abandoning Syria to the Ottomans. Selim divided the newly acquired territory into two directly administered Ottoman provinces, a northern province centered at Aleppo and a southern province centered at Damascus. However, he decided against trying to impose his direct rule on the mountainous region of Lebanon and northern Palestine, an area to which even the Mamluks had permitted a measure of autonomy. He therefore acknowledged, as semi-independent local amirs, a certain number of hereditary chieftains who promised both to pay him an annual tribute and to refrain from raiding the villages on the Syrian plain.

The Ottomans were not necessarily determined, at this point, to proceed with the conquest of Egypt. Selim even offered to (Mamluk Sultan) Tūmān Bey the same vassal status that he had arranged with various amirs in Lebanon. The Mamluks underscored their rejection of Selīm's offer by attempting, unsuccessfully, to retake Gaza. Selīm therefore invaded Egypt in pursuit of the Mamluks, who made another stand in January 1517 at the fortified camp of al-Raydaniyya near Cairo. Although their commanding general Sinān Pasha was killed, the Ottoman forces easily prevailed; and Tūmān Bey withdrew his remaining troops up the Nile. Selīm renewed his offer of semi-autonomous vassalage which Tūmān Bey again refused. Selīm's conquest of Egypt was consolidated at a final battle in April 1517 near Giza, where the Ottomans again routed the Mamluks. Although it had not been his objective when leaving Istanbul, within a year Selīm had thus incorporated into his own domains the entire Mamluk empire--not only Syria but also Egypt and the Hijaz. Khayr Bey, the former Mamluk governor of Aleppo, was made the Ottoman governor of Egypt; and seven janissary garrisons were quartered near Cairo on a permanent basis. The Sharif Barakat of Mecca, who had ruled the Hijaz on the Mamluk's behalf, was confirmed in his position as an Ottoman official. However, while the Mamluk sultanate was suppressed, the Mamluks themselves were not exterminated. Nor did their well established processes of recruiting and training new mamluks stop. Nevertheless, at least of the remainder of the sixteenth century, the defeated Mamluks allowed themselves to be co-opted into the Ottoman administration of Egypt.

The Ottoman Conquest of Iraq

Hostilities between the Ottomans and the Safavis were renewed after the deaths of Selim I (d. 1520) and Shah Ismail (d. 1524). Intending perhaps to forestall the revival of Safavi military strength, Ottoman Sultan Sulayman "the Magnificent" (1520-66) launched a campaign in 1534 against the Safavis and easily took Tabriz. To the Ottoman Empire, the Safavis ceded the city of Baghdad and the surrounding Arabic-speaking districts of central Iraq. An Arabic tribal chieftain named Rashid ibn Mughamis was initially confirmed as an Ottoman vassal in Basra. But he was suppressed by the Ottoman governor of Baghdad in 1547, whereupon Basra became a directly administered province of the empire. On the other hand, a region called al-Ahsa', on the western side of the Gulf, remained a semi-autonomous Ottoman vassal state under Arab tribal leadership. From the territory which they had seized from the Safavis, the Ottomans thus created five separate provinces: Shahrizor (in the mountainous Kurdish region), Mosul, Baghdad, Basra, and al-Ahsa'.

The Ottoman Conquest of Yemen

The Ottomans acquired, along with the vast domains of the Mamluks, a vital interest in the maritime trade routes. This new interest obliged the essentially land-based Ottoman Empire also to become a naval power; for during the sixteenth century it had to meet the challenges of the Portuguese in the Indian Ocean and of the Spaniards in the Mediterranean Sea. The Ottomans' conquest of Yemen, beginning with the seizure of Aden in 1538, was thus a logical extension of their acquisition of Egypt and the Hijaz; it represented the consolidation of their control over the important Red Sea-Indian Ocean trade route to India and the Far East. The Ottomans' penetration into the Yemeni highlands encountered a strong local resistance movement led by the imam of the Zaydi sect, a Shi'i dynasty which had been extending its spiritual and political influence among the mountain tribesmen of Southwest Arabia since the early Abbasid period. In 1567 the imam-led tribal resistance drove the Ottoman troops out of the highlands altogether; but by 1572 the "Turks" had reasserted their control over most of the country, temporarily confining the imam's power base to the northern town of Sa'ada and reducing his authority to its spiritual dimension. The Ottomans installed a governor and a large garrison of janissaries in Sanaa, Yemen's 2,350-meter high capital and a Zaydi stronghold, where in general they were resented by the local population on religious as well as on political grounds. The Ottomans received a better reception in the lowlands and coastal regions of Yemen, where as a rule the inhabitants were Sunni Muslims of the Shafi'i madhhab. In particular, the Shafi'i merchants in such towns as Aden, Taiz, Mokha and Zabid viewed the Ottomans not just as fellow Sunnis but also as protectors of their commercial activities, which included the export of Yemeni (Mokha) coffee.

The Ottoman Conquest of North Africa

The Ottoman acquisition of certain portions of the Maghrib grew out of a Spanish-Muslim conflict that involved both holy warriors and pirates on either side. After the fall of the kingdom of Granada in 1492, Iberian Christians carried their anti-Muslim crusade into North Africa itself. From the aged and declining "Berber kingdoms," the Portuguese and the Spaniards seized certain port cities along, respectively, the Atlantic and Mediterranean coasts. When thus threatened by Christians, the notables of the small town of Algiers appealed to a Muslim pirate named ^{c}Arūj, the eldest of four brothers who had gained both notoriety and a large following of booty-seeking adventurers by successfully attacking European merchant ships as well as by transporting Morisco refugees to North Africa. In 1516 ^{c}Arūj "rescued" Algiers from the Spaniards and then, after ruthlessly eliminating independent-minded local notables, proclaimed himself "sultan" of the port, which he had used as a base for privateering. The death in 1518 of ^{c}Arūj, who was succeeded by his younger brother, Khayr al-Din Barbarossa, coincided with a major Spanish offensive against Algiers. It was at this point that the Ottomans became indirectly involved in North Africa. Khayr al-Din appealed to and acknowledged the sovereignty of Sultan Selīm I (1512-20), who named the adventurer his vassal with the title of *beylerbey* ("bey of the beys"). Selīm also dispatched to Khayr al-Dīn 2,000 janissaries (and the right to raise 4,000 volunteers), which he used to retake and to consolidate his position in Algiers as well as to attack, in theory on behalf of the Ottomans, other Spanish-held ports along the Mediterranean coast.

Under a series of *beylerbeys*, beginning with Khayr al-Din Barbarossa (d. 1544) and ending with ^{c}Ulj ^{c}Ali (d. 1587), the "Ottoman navy" proceeded to capture most of the key Christian-held cities of North Africa's Mediterranean coast, including Tripoli in 1551 and Tunis in 1574. During the mid-sixteenth century, the *beylerbeys* thus established and ruled on Ottoman vassal state centered in Algiers. This represented a new historical role for the central Maghrib, a region which had traditionally lacked important centers of urban civilization. Yet the corsair state of the *beylerbeys* was oriented towards the sea rather than towards its own hinterland. Indeed, while coming to control a moderately wide coastal strip, the Turks proved unwilling or unable to assert their rule on a permanent basis over the tribal areas of the Atlas Mountains and the Sahara. Another division existed for a time *within* the vassal state's capital, as the janissaries resented the political preeminence of the corsair captains and successfully agitated for the right to participate in the election of the *beylerbey*. After the death of ^{c}Ulj ^{c}Ali in 1587, however, the Ottoman sultan moved decisively to bring the Turkish-controlled territories of the Maghrib under his immediate control. Algiers, Tunis, and Tripoli became headquarters for three separate Ottoman provinces, each administered by a governor appointed by and responsible directly to the sultan.

The *beylerbeys* and the Ottomans also tried to "assist" the Moroccans in their efforts to expel the Portuguese from the Atlantic coast. But Morocco's inhabitants as well as its Wattasi rulers

(1420-1548), the last of the country's "Berber dynasties," were not eager to exchange a limited Portuguese occupation for an extensive Turkish one. The liberation and defense of dar al-islām in Morocco, a mountainous region like Lebanon and Yemen, therefore occurred on a regional basis. There arose popular local jihads led in the main by MARABOUTS (holy men in North African "folk Sufism") many of whom claimed to be ashraf (descendants of the Prophet Muhammad). Getting their start as organizers and leaders of such a jihad in the Moroccan Sahara, the SA'DI dyansty used its religious appeal and growing military strength not only against the Portuguese but also against the Wattasis, whom it ultimately replaced in 1548 as the sovereigns of Morocco. The Sa'dis (1548-1641) represented the first of Morocco's SHARIFIAN DYNASTIES--the second and last being the Alawi dynasty (1641-present)--which dislodged the Portuguese and preserved Morocco's independence from the Ottomans. They also used their mountainous kingdom as a power base from which they expanded into Mauretania and West Africa and which they consequently transformed into a "gunpowder empire" of sorts.

Ottoman Institutions

During the course of three centuries, the tiny Turkish ghazi state of Söğüt thus expanded to become the vast Ottoman Empire, whose subjects professed a variety of religions and spoke a variety of languages, including Turkish, Greek (and numerous other Balkan and Eastern European tongues), Armenian, Kurdish, Berber, and Arabic. Indeed, by 1600 most Arabic-speaking peoples acknowledge the Ottoman sultan, directly or indirectly, as their sovereign. They therefore became associated with the empire's major institutions which we shall now attempt to depict in cross section. For a time, following the lead of American historian Albert Lyber, it was the practice of scholars to distinguish only between the Ottoman state's "Ruling Institution" and its "Muslim Institution," a practice and a distinction which has lately become the object of serious criticism.* Perhaps a more fruitful schema for analyzing Ottoman institutions is that observed by traditional Turkish historians, who have conceptualized four principal socio-political structures: the sultanate (the melkiye); the bureaucracy, composed of the secretariat (the kalemiye) and the treasury (the maliye); the military (the seyfiye); and the religious establishment (the ilmiye).

The Sultanate

Originating as a tribal chieftaincy, the Ottoman sultanate evolved by 1600 with Byzantine as well as Turkish influences, into an imperial monarchy. It did retain some of the warlord character of the ghazi

---

*The scheme is set forth in Lyber's The Government of the Ottoman Empire in the Time of Suleiman the Magnificent (Harvard University Press, 1913) has lately been criticized by, among others, Halil Inalcik, Norman Itskowitz, and Stanford J. Shaw.

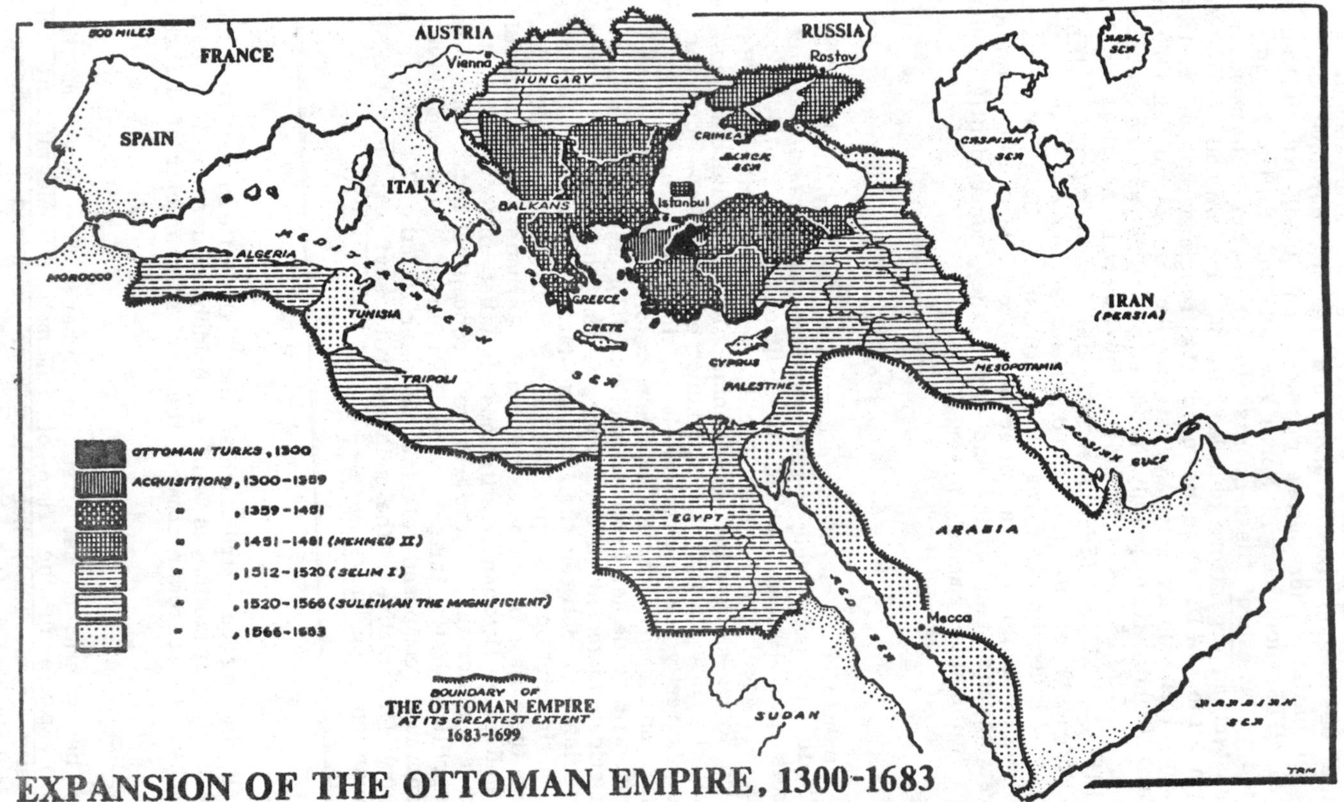

EXPANSION OF THE OTTOMAN EMPIRE, 1300-1683

from S. N. Fisher, The Middle East: A History

tradition. With respect to a fundamental division of Ottoman society, for example, the sultan was considered the head of the askari (military) class, as opposed to the raiya (subject class). Yet the ruling family lived in Byzantine splendor and seclusion in Constantinople's Topkapi Palace. According to Turkish political institutions, government was a family matter. Succession to the sultanate, therefore, occurred exclusively within the Ottoman family, although not necessarily from father to eldest son. If there existed a specific principle of Ottoman succession, it could perhaps be called, not primogeniture, but "survival of the fittest." Young princes were customarily given official responsibilities, frequently as provincial governors. At the death of a sultan, his sons would contend with one another over the vacant throne until one of them, presumably the cleverest and most ruthless, prevailed. Beginning with the seizure of power by Bayezid I in 1389, it even became customary for the new sultan, either during or immediately after the succession contest, to assassinate all of his brothers.

In theory, the sultan was the supreme military commander and the head of state, roles which Ottoman rulers until Sulayman also performed in practice with diligence and even jealousy. They insisted upon their right to lead the important military campaigns, for example, and they presided over the council of state, the diwan (divan in Turkish), which discussed and formulated imperial policy. In addition to the sultan, the diwan included the prime minister (al-sadr al-a^czam) along with the chief financial, administrative, military, and Islamic religious officials. Among the self-appointed tasks of the ulama was to see that scriptural Islam became the only effective and legitimate basis for the Ottoman state and sultanate. Since the Ottoman family arose from a Turco-Mongol tribal milieu that was strongly influenced by popular Sufism and by Shi'ism, the ulama's task was not an easy one. Many of the early sultans, along with their soldiers and bureaucrats, regularly participated in the ceremonies of popular Sufi brotherhoods having pronounced Alid tendencies. By the end of the fifteenth century, however, the Ottoman sultanate had moved away from the Shi'i-oriented folk Islam of its origins and had become associated with the Sunni "orthodoxy" of the Hanafi madhhab, the official Ottoman rite. This development possibly occurred in part because of the rise of a frankly Shi'i state in Iran. On the other hand, the Ottoman sultans never completely abandoned another feature of the Turco-Mongol tradition: the right of the sovereign to rule by decree. Although proclaiming itself to be an "Islamic state," therefore, the Ottoman sultans developed a constitutional tradition resting not exclusively on the shari^ca but also on their own qanun-s (decrees).

The Devshirme System

In order to discuss intelligently the Ottoman bureaucracy and military, it is first necessary to describe the institution of the devshirme, which provided the means whereby qualified persons were recruited and trained for the empire's armed forces and for its governmental administration. To an extent, it represented a continuation of the traditional "slave system" that had arisen during early Abbasi times. As mentioned above, the first Ottoman rulers created the janissary corps from prisoners of war captured during their campaigns of conquest in the Balkans. War prisoners, however, soon proved to be an insufficient and unreliable source of slaves having such desired qualities as youth, strength, and intelligence. Around the year 1400, therefore, the Ottoman ruling elite began systematically to levy a special human tax, called the devshirme, which in essence entailed the periodic confiscation by the state of a certain number of male children between the ages of eight and eighteen. The devshirme tax, which was levied only on Christian villages in the Balkans and (later) in Western Anatolia, was thus able to procure for the state as many slave boys as it needed and at the same time to select those youngsters who showed the most promise of physical and intellectual ability.

In addition to the levy itself, the "devshirme system" referred to the whole elaborate procedure for training the Christian slave boys once they had been selected and taken from their villages by the Ottoman officials. The procedure included gathering the recruits in Edirne or Istanbul where they were circumcized, converted to Islam and subjected to a variety of tests designed to identify the nature and extent of their potential skills. The very best recruits, about the top 10%, immediately began a special educational experience in one of the "palace schools," including the Palace School of Muhammad the Conqueror in Istanbul. A palace school's curriculum, while including traditional Islamic subjects (Qur'an, Hanafi law, etc.), also emphasized classical philosophy, logic, mathematics, history (including Ibn Khaldun), and music. In the tradition of "court schools" which prepared royal princes to assume their official responsibilities, the palace school's function was to train candidates for the imperial bureaucracy. Accordingly, the best graduates were appointed to junior but responsible administrative posts from whence, depending upon their ability and diligence, they would rise through the ranks to the highest positions in the Ottoman state. The other 90% of the devshirme recruits were given some military training and then hired out to Turkish farmers as a means of building up their physical strength and familiarizing them with the beliefs and practices of the Islamic religion. After a certain period, they were brought back to Istanbul and formally inducted into the janissary corps. Unlike those recruited into the "households" of Egypt's Mamluk bosses, the slave boys of the Ottoman devshirme were never manumitted but always remained, at least in theory, the personal property of the sultan.

The Ottoman Bureaucracy

The sultan, along with the dīwān (the state's policy-making council), stood at the top of the huge Ottoman bureaucracy which was concerned, among other things, with correspondence, tax-collecting, and provincial administration. The scribes (kātib-s), each of whom bore the title of "effendi," were frequently drawn from the corps of ulama. Most other Ottoman bureaucrats, particularly those engaged in financial activities or in administration per se, as a rule were products of the devshirme and of the palace schools. Toward the end of the fourteenth century, the imperial treasury was separated from the sultan's personal treasury and was put under the authority of a head treasurer (bash defterdar) who sat on the diwan. The imperial treasury was a financial institution having four major departments: registry, accounting, auditing, and waqf-s. Its principle concern was the collection of taxes. These included traditional Islamic taxes, such as zakat and 'ushr (one-tenth of agricultural produce), collected from Muslims, along with jizya and kharaj collected from non-Muslims. They also included various new taxes, levied by decree of the sultan, such as a special household tax to support military campaigns and a market tax collected by the muhtasib ("market inspector"), a position inherited from the Abbasis via the Seljuks.

Taxes were collected according to two different systems: the timar system and the iltizam system. Timar-s were fiefs which the sultan alienated from conquered territories to members of the Ottoman askari class: Turkish warlords and cooperative Christian notables (most of whom converted to Islam by 1400) at first and, later on, janissary officers and influencial bureaucrats. Timar-holders were the sultan's vasals whose non-hereditary fiefs reverted to the state in the event of the holder's death or the sultan's displeasure. Also, timar-holders could not alienate subdivisions of their fiefs and thereby create their own vassals. Although sometimes described as a "feudal" kind of landownership, the timar system thus differed considerably from European feudalism which was characterized by hereditary fiefs and subinfeudation; and timar-holders were consequently never able to become as independent from the sovereign as were their Western counterparts. Nevertheless, as did European feudal lords, timar-holders had "feudal" military responsibilities in exchange for which they collected, from the peasants and/or townsmen inhabiting their respective domains, the various taxes of which they retained the majority, sending an annual tribute (perhaps 10%) to the imperial treasury.

Whereas the timar system was one of semi-autonomous vassalage, the iltizam system was applied in areas which the Ottoman state theoretically administered more or less directly. Territories not alienated by the sultan in the form of timar-s were thus divided for financial purposes into tax concessions (iltizam-s) and assigned to tax concessionaires (multazim-s), who functioned as employees of the Ottoman bureaucracy. Obliged to remit to the imperial treasury the majority of the taxes they collected, multazim-s were permitted to retain a percentage (perhaps 10%) as their personal salary. While the timar system was a regular feature of Ottoman administration in Anatolia and the Balkans, the iltizam system prevailed in most other provinces, including the "Arab lands" where the multazim became a familiar and, eventually, a feared and hated symbol of the imperial bureaucracy.

Ottoman provinces, known as wilaya-s, were each administered by a governor (wali) who bore the title of "pasha." Sultans tended to be suspicious of the personal ambitions of governors whose authorities they limited in various ways. For example, the typical wali was rotated on an average of every three years as a means of preventing him from transforming his province into a power base for himself. In addition, each province's treasurer (defterdar), who directed the tax-collecting operation with a large squad of multazim-s, did not turn over the revenues to the wali. Rather, the defterdar was appointed separately by the sultan to whom the tax moneys were sent directly, bypassing the governor. Nor did the wali have jurisdiction over the Ottoman military regiments stationed in his province, as the regimental commanders theoretically were, like the defterdar-s, appointed by and responsible to the sultan directly. The two "core" wilaya-s of the Ottoman Empire were Anatolia and Rumelia, which were dotted with hundreds of small timar fiefs. Large timar provinces included the Crimea and, in the Balkans, Wallachia, Moldavia, and Transylvania. Al-Ahsa (on the Gulf) and Lebanon enjoyed roughly similar vassalage status. The remainder of the Ottoman "Arab lands" were divided into wilaya-s which were administered by wali-s or pashas, kept submissive by janissary regiments, and milked for revenues by multazim-s. The following map gives an idea of the basic Ottoman administrative divisions in the "Arab world" in about 1600.

The Ottoman Military

Although not the largest component of the Ottoman military, the janissary corps became the most famous and, perhaps, the most important of the empire's armed forces. Recruited at first exclusively from the devshirme, future janissaries were selected for such qualities as strength, agility, and intelligence. Having received some military training as youthful conscripts, once in the corps they continued to train regularly in order to maintain themselves in a state of combat readiness. For this reason, janissaries were not permitted to marry; rather, they lived together in special barracks, an arrangement which facilitated constant training and rapid mobilization. Although numbering less than 30,000 during the second half of the sixteenth century, the janissaries were thus highly disciplined as well as tightly organized into 101 battalions under the overall command of their supreme commander, the agha, whose seat on the diwan reflected the corps' significance. Thoroughly trained in the use not only of pikes, bows and arrows but also of rifles, artillery and siege engines, the janissaries thus constituted an elite, "crack" military force of a gunpowder empire. When not engaged in actual combat, janissary regiments were frequently stationed as security forces to maintain order in certain troublesome provinces. Indeed, it was ordinarily in this police role of the janissaries that the Sultan's Arabic-speaking subjects knew them.

The largest component of the Ottoman military, the "feudal" or sipahi cavalry, was closely linked to the timar system whose financial and administrative aspects were discussed above. With regard to its military role, the timar-holder enjoyed the right to administer his fief and to collect taxes from its inhabitants in exchange for putting his resources at the sultan's disposal in times of war. In other words, revenue-producing timar-s were given in lieu of salaries to certain officers and notables in payment for their military services. Commensurate with the size of his fief and the amount of his annual revenues, each timar-holder maintained a certain number of cavalrymen which, upon the sultan's request, he had to furnish to the imperial army along with a corresponding supply of horses, weapons, food, and clothing. In contrast to the janissaries, the sipahi warriors could both marry and

The Arab Provinces of the Ottoman Empire

Istanbul
SHAHRIZOR
Aleppo
ALEPPO
Mosul
MOSUL
Beirut
Damascus
DAMASCUS
Baghdad
BAGHDAD
BASRA
Basra
AL-AHSA
Algiers
ALGIERS
Tunis
TUNIS
Tripoli
TRIPOLI
Sultanate of MOROCCO
Cairo
EGYPT
Mecca
HIJAZ
YEMEN
Sanaa
Muscat
Sultanate of OMAN

Arab Province of Ottoman Empire
Provincial Capital
NAME OF PROVINCE
Lebanon; Ottoman Vassal Region
Independent Arab Sultanate

train their own sons for identical military roles. Shortly after 1600 an Ottoman bureaucrat reported that there existed over 44,000 timar-s (of varying sizes) which collectively maintained a cavalry force of about 105,000 men. These included, in addition to regular siphai-s, nearly 10,000 timar-based soldiers who manned fort garrisons throughout the empire. The vast majority of these were located in Europe (63%) or Anatolia (27%); only about 5% of them--chiefly in Iraq, Egypt, Algeria and Syria--could be found in the Arabic-speaking provinces.

Since the Turks were not by custom a sea-going people, the Ottoman navy was initially a rather haphazard service which only gradually acquired an organization comparable to that of the army. Even so, nothing on the order of the devshirme was over devised as a means of recruiting and training sailors. Rather, privateers--as a rule of Greek, Italian, or Arab descent--were simply co-opted into the "Ottoman navy." Their salary at first was simply the right to attack European merchant ships and to keep a portion of the booty. As the empire expanded, Ottoman flotillas were gradually built up in the Mediterranean, Black, and Red Seas in order to protect the newly acquired territories and trade routes. The main imperial shipyard was at Galata near Istanbul, but other port cities--including Sidon, Algiers, Tunis, Alexandria, Damietta, Rosetta, Suez, and Aden--became important Ottoman naval bases. The conqueror of Algiers, Khayr al-Din Barbarossa, was the first Grand Admiral of the Ottoman fleet, a position in which he was succeeded by the series of beylerbey-s. A number of Aegean islands, along with the entire vassal state ruled by the beylerbey-s from Algiers, were constituted as timar-s to reward the Grand Admiral, who sat on the dīwān. In Egypt, urban revenue-producing properties in Alexandria, Damietta, Rosetta, and Suez were also transformed into timar-s to be given, in lieu of salaries, to commanders of local Ottoman flotillas. Eventually gaining a reputation for skill and bravery, the Ottoman navy rivalled Portugal and Spain for control of the seas during the sixteenth and seventeenth centuries.

Ottoman-Islamic Educational and Judicial Institutions

The Ottoman specialists in Islamic learning, the ulama, collectively formed the ilmiye, which was concerned with propagating the Islamic faith and with interpreting and enforcing the Islamic legal tradition (the sharī^ca). Just as the devshirme was the main source of recruits for the bureaucracy and the military, two levels of Ottoman-Islamic schools provided opportunities for candidates to the ilmiye. The lower or introductory level consisted of the thousands of neighborhood or village maktab-s (Qur'an schools) which in small doses and with crude methods dispensed literacy and scripture to the masses. The upper level consisted of the madrasa-s, wherein prospective ulama completed their education. Ottoman madrasa-s, like their Seljuk models, taught all branches of Islamic learning, including the "religious sciences" such as Qur'anic analysis (tafsīr), theology (^cilm al-kalām), law (fiqh), and calligraphy. They also taught such "rational sciences" as logic (mantiq), philosophy (^cilm al-hikma), and astronomy. Orhan (d. 1361) established the first Ottoman madrasa at Iznik in 1331. By 1600 there existed dozens of these facilities in the Ottoman-Islamic system of higher education, which was crowned by the constellation of eight madrasa-s constructed by Muhammad the Conqueror (d. 1481) adjacent to his mosque, the Muhammadiye, in Istanbul. During 1550-59 Sulayman the Magnificent built, around his Sulaymaniye mosque, a complex of four madrasa-s wherein medicine, mathematics, and some of the physical sciences were added to the traditional curriculum.

Madrasa students, who received small stipends as well as free lodging and food, aspired to positions either as teachers (mudarris-es) or judges (qadi-s) in the ilmiye itself or as scribes in the imperial bureaucracy. A madrasa graduate who became a mudarris generally began his career at one of the less prestigious facilities and then tried, vacancies and his own ability permitting, to work his way up through the ranks to an appointment at one of the Muhammadiye or Sulaymaniye madrasa-s. A young mudarris was eligible also to become a qadi in a local mahkama sharʿiya (Islamic law court), while an experienced mudarris could compete for a more lucrative and prestigious post as an official Ottoman shariʿa magistrate (qadi or mufti), perhaps in one of the main provincial capitals or centers of learning: Bursa, Edirne, Mecca, Medina, Jerusalem, Damascus, Aleppo, Cairo, Baghdad, Basra, and Tunis. In such towns the chief qadi and head mufti always represented the Hanafi madhhab, the official Ottoman rite. Qadi-s customarily also assumed certain non-judicial duties, such as certifying tax assessment lists, devising and enforcing building codes, and directing the muhtasib in establishing and implementing regulations and price controls for the merchants and artisans.

The Ottoman Learned Institution--the ilmiye--was formally organized and controlled by the state to an unprecedented degree. Ottoman madrasa-s were arranged hierarchically; and students and teachers alike were expected to move up the ladder as they advanced in their academic careers. Not only did a head qadi and head mufti (bash mufti) represent the Ottoman judicial system in each major town, but two chief qadi-s--the qadiasker-s of Rum and Anatolia--stood at the summit of the state's shariʿa court system. In addition, at the top of the whole ilmiye institution, there was placed during the sixteenth century a supreme head, an Ottoman-Islamic dignitary who bore the title shaykh al-islam. In this regard, from an historical perspective, Sultan Sulayman's appointment of Abu'l-Su'ud Khoja Chelebi (d. 1574) as Shaykh al-Islam in 1545 is seen by many historians as representing the culmination of three related developments that occurred gradually during the 1000-1600 period: (1) the tendency for centralized hierarchies to evolve among the ulama, whose interpersonal relationships had earlier operated on a more informal and decentralized basis; (2) the tendency for the state to absorb the evolving ulama hierarchies into its regular bureaucracy; thereby facilitating (3) the tendency for the state to undermine the "academic freedom" of the Islamic scholarly community. While these developments took place in various forms and to varying degrees in many Islamic countries, they probably advanced faster and further in the Ottoman state than they did anywhere else. By 1600 the extent to which Ottoman-Islamic education and justice were centralized, organized into an elaborate hierarchy, and assimilated into the imperial bureaucracy was greater than at any previous time in Islamic history.

In the "Arab provinces," groups of Arabic-speaking ulama located in traditional centers of Islamic learning--e.g., Mecca, Medina, Cairo, Damascus, and Tunis--were not wholly absorbed into the Ottoman bureaucracy. In Cairo, for example, although a Turkish-speaking Hanafi "chief qadi" was installed along with the Ottoman governor, the native Egyptian qadis of the other madhhab-s remained independent of him in practice if not in theory. Similarly, although Ottomans expanded the teaching of Hanafi law in such mosque-universities as al-Azhar (Cairo) and al-Zaytuna (Tunis), as a rule the various corps of "Arab" ulama retained their informal basis of organization, at least for a time. The emergence during the seventeenth century of the office of Shaykh al-Azhar would subsequently evidence and symbolize the evolution and centralization of an Ottoman-type ulama hierarchy in Egypt.

The Raiya Class and the Millet System

The Sultans, along with janissaries, timar-holders, Sipahi-s, wāli-s and multazim-s, formed the Ottoman State's askari or ruling class. The remainder of the population belonged to the raiya or the subject class. While Ottoman Society was thus divided more or less clearly into two strata, the rulers and the ruled, "classes" per se were not the only or even the most important social groupings. Indeed, it can be said that, among the masses of Ottoman subjects, "class consciousness" was rather low. Instead, religion was the primary object of personal identity and loyalty. The raiya class could thus be subdivided into Muslims and non-Muslims. The differing tax obligations of each of these two groups symbolized the social and political barriers that separated them. Although clearly not the socio-economic or political equals of their fellow Muslims in the askari class (many of whom were converts from Christianity), the Muslims in the subject class considered themselves superior to their non-Muslim fellow raiya. The latter could be subdivided further into a number of religions, rites, and sects. The fact that Ottoman subjects, including Arabic-speakers, tended to focus their identity and loyalty upon their religious grouping served as the basis for the "millet system."

In the Ottoman Empire, millets were quasi-autonomous communities based primarily on religious affiliation. The Ottomans originated neither the practice of dividing subjects into religious communities nor that of giving each religious community the right to handle its own affairs to a considerable extent. In the Near East such practices were old customs that had been followed earlier by a number of imperial states, including the Romans, the Umawis, and the Abbasis. But the Ottomans did institutionalize these practices, thereby making the "millet system" a governmental institution as well as a social one.

One logical imperative of the millet system was that the Sharī^c^a (Islamic law) was not accepted by non-Muslim raiya as the official code for regulating their personal behavior. Nor did they accept it as a basis for resolving legal disputes among them, particularly with regard to such matters of personal status as marriage, divorce, and inheritance. The Ottomans therefore found it appropriate to let each non-Muslim religious community use its own scriptures and traditions as a basis for regulating the behavior of its members and for resolving their legal disputes over personal status.

Another imperative was political expediency. The Ottoman rulers, a majority of whose subjects were Christian until Selīm's conquest of the "Arab lands" during 1514-17, wanted and needed the support of the influential Christian hierarchies; and the sultans were willing to purchase that support by indulging the clergies' desire for increased group autonomy and greater personal authority. It was thus Mehmed II, immediately after Constantinople fell to him in 1453, who more or less inaugurated the Ottoman "millet system" by guaranteeing to the Greek Orthodox clergy not only considerable religious freedom but also broad powers over the internal affairs of the Sultan's Orthodox subjects. Historians frequently observe that the patriarch enjoyed greater authority and more independence under the Ottomans than under the Byzantines. The Greek Orthodox community thus became the first--and remained the largest--of the non-Muslim millets enjoying the official recognition of the Ottoman state. The next (in terms of time) two millets consisted of the Jews (including many refugees from Spain), who were organized under the Chief Rabbi of Istanbul, and the Armenians, who were formally constituted as a millet in 1461 when Mehmed II appointed the Archbishop of Bursa to be the Armenian patriarch.

The Ottoman conquest of the "Arab lands" during the sixteenth century not only swelled the ranks of the Muslim raiya to the point where they now formed a majority of the empire's population but it also extended the authority of the Greek Orthodox and Armenian millets. With the assistance of the Ottoman state, the Greek patriarch re-established his control over the ancient bishoprics of Antioch, Jerusalem, and Alexandria, thereby including Arabic-speaking Orthodox Christians in a millet dominated from Istanbul by Greek-speaking clergy. Because the Armenian church was monophysite in doctrine, the Armenian millet was given jurisdiction over all other monophysite Christian sects, including the Assyrians of Iraq, the Jacobites of Syria, and the Copts of Egypt. The Maronites of Lebanon sought to escape Armenian domination by recognizing the authority of the distant Roman Catholic Pope who, in exchange, permitted them to maintain their Eastern ritual under their own quasi-autonomous patriarch. But the Ottomans did not recognize the Maronites as an official, separate millet.

The three official millets, to which others were later added, shared a number of features which characterized the Ottoman millet system. Each had a leader (a patriarch, chief rabbi, etc.) who was appointed by the Sultan but who possessed important secular responsibilities in addition to his extensive religious duties. One of the religious leader's responsibilities, for example, was to play a direct role in the allocation and collection of taxes from members of his religious community, on behalf of the state. Another feature was that the millet was virtually autonomous in a number of domains. The higher clergy acted as judges when intracommunal legal questions needed to be decided. The religious community in effect operated its own educational system of primary-level schools and graduate seminaries. It also performed services: it financed and staffed hospitals, homes for the poor and the aged, and cemeteries; and it encouraged and facilitated intragroup marriages as a means of perpetuating the religion and its culture. In this regard, the religious community was also the effective cultural unit, as evidenced by the fact that it was the normal subject of histories or chronicles. Each millet thus functioned to a degree as a state within a state. To Ottoman subjects, millets were the main object of their personal identity and loyalty, much as tribes were among the pre-Islamic Arabs.

Technically, the Muslims did not constitute a millet per se. Rather, they belonged to the *umma* (the Islamic community), which enjoyed a privileged status within the Ottoman state. Yet, in many ways, the Ottoman-Islamic community effectively functioned as a millet; and the term *al-milla al-islamiya* (the Islamic Millet) was occasionally employed. The head of the "Islamic millet" was the Shaykh al-Islam, whose office some historians feel was patterned to a degree after that of the Greek Orthodox patriarch. Like other millets, the Muslims had their own courts (*al-mahakim al-shar^{c}iya*), schools (*maktab*-s and *madrasa*-s), charitable institutions, and cemeteries. The normal subject of academic or historical studies by Muslims was the Islamic religion, which accordingly served as the main focus of identity and loyalty for virtually all of the Muslim *raiya*. It thus appears that, in 1600, it was of little significance to Arabic-speaking Muslims that a Turkish-speaking ruling class controlled the Ottoman Empire, for "national" as well as "class" consciousness was very low, and the Islamic character of the Ottoman state was compatible with self-perceptions of Arabic-speaking Muslims, most of whom endowed the term "Arab" (which, in most dialects, meant "bedouin") with pejorative connotations.

Summary

During the sixteenth century, most "Arab lands" (Morocco, the Sahara, the Nilotic Sudan, and Eastern Arabia being the principal exceptions) were conquered by and integrated into the Ottoman Empire. The ruling or *askari* class, which staffed the empire's major institutions, were drawn as a rule from the Ottoman family or from European slave boys who had been "Turkified" and Islamized by the *devshirme*. The Arabic-speaking population, Muslims and Christians alike, were part of the empire's subject class or *raiya*. They thus acknowledged their *wali* as the sultan's representative; they stood in awe of the fearsome jannisaries quartered among them; and they paid their taxes, non-Muslims sometimes via the head of their millet, to their assigned *multazim* or *timar*-holder. In addition, they perceived their own identity largely in terms of their religion; Muslims looked to the ulama and Christians to their clergy not only for spiritual guidance but also for institutionalized legal, educational, and social services. Such were the institutional contacts shared by most Arabic-speakers with other Ottoman subjects in 1600. Thereafter, when the Ottoman Empire began to stagnate and to decline, the historical development of the "Arab lands" would in some ways parallel and in other ways diverge from the experience of the rest of the Ottoman Empire.

CHAPTER NINE

THE ARAB LANDS IN THE AGE OF OTTOMAN DECLINE, 1600-1850: SEMI-AUTONOMOUS STATES AND REVIVALIST MOVEMENTS

The Ottoman Empire reached its peak of power if not of size during the reign of Sulayman (1521-66), after which there followed a lengthy period of general decline--a period in which the Ottomans gradually ceased to be feared and began themselves to fear others. Characterized in 1603 by an English historian as "the present terror of the world," by the nineteenth century the Ottoman Empire became, in the words of Tsar Nicholas II, "the sick man of Europe." This chapter will be subdivided into three sections, each concentrating on a major theme of the 1600-1850 period. In the first section we shall discuss the most significant causes and manifestations of Ottoman decay, including bureaucratic corruption, social upheavals, and territorial fragmentation. During this period the "Arab provinces" suffered through these difficulties along with the rest of the Empire; and, as the Ottoman central government became corrupt and weak, many "Arab lands" became semi-autonomous kingdoms, frequently assuming the approximate geographical shapes of the modern Arab states which we find on today's map. This process of the emergence of semi-independent regimes in the Ottoman Arab provinces is the theme of the second section. Finally, as we shall see in the third section, 1600-1850 was also the period when the peoples of the Middle East came to perceive the state of decline and to perceive the economic, diplomatic and cultural expansion of modern Europe. Among their responses were various movements for religious revival or for technological reform.

Causes and Manifestations of Ottoman Decline

Chief among the internal causes of the Ottoman Empire's decay was an appreciable decline in the quality of its leadership. The Ottoman state was a military machine driven during 1300-1566 by a remarkable series of ten outstanding rulers. The consistently high ability and vigor of the sultans from Osman (d. 1326) to Sulayman (d. 1566) resulted in part from two traditions: giving young Ottoman princes responsible assignments and allowing succession to occur in accordance with the principle of "the survival of the fittest." An equally remarkable series of INCOMPETENT SULTANS accompanied and contributed to the gradual decline of the Ottoman Empire. The regular accession of unfit leaders after the sixteenth century is customarily attributed to modifications of these two traditions. After Ahmed I (d. 1617) the princes were no longer given responsible assignments but were instead confined to the harem, where they were shaped by isolation and luxury rather than by challenging experience. At the same time, the custom of fratricide was abandoned and the principle of succession by "survival of the fittest" was replaced by that of succession by the oldest living male member of the Ottoman family. Sultans thereafter naturally tended to be inexperienced and weak. With the exception of Murād IV (1623-40), there appeared no outstanding

Ottoman ruler after Sulayman until the very end of the eighteenth century.

The regular accession of weak rulers, along with the proliferation of uncles and brothers in the harem, led to numerous palace intrigues, hatched in large part by the leading bureaucrats. Unchecked by the incompetent sultans, the top officials sought greater power and wealth for themselves and their protégés. The once efficient Ottoman slave bureaucracy, wherein promotions used to reward the naturally talented and the hard working, splintered into "households" (political cliques based on patron-client relationships) which contended for the most lucrative offices. These "households" often formed temporary alliances with military leaders and with influential persons in the harem, usually mothers or wives of sitting or potential rulers. During the seventeenth century, two strong-willed and well connected ladies--Kosem, the mother of Sultan Ibrahim (1640-48), and Turhan, the mother of Sultan Muhammad IV (1648-87)--schemed relentlessly to advance their sons and grandsons to the throne. Ottoman historians refer to this period as "the Sultanate of the Women." It was followed by "the Sultanate of the agha-s," a time when the janissary corps began to intervene directly in politics. Sultans thus became mere puppets of the political and the military bosses.[1] Citing a Turkish proverb, "the fish stinks from the head," Ottoman observers of Ottoman decline tended to attribute the increasing corruption and inefficiency of the Empire's bureaucracy and military to the demise of the sultanate as a vital institution.

There were, however, more important causes of Ottoman decline, including external economic developments. During 1300-1566 the Ottoman Empire was not merely powerful but also prosperous, as evidenced and symbolized by the annual surpluses in the treasury. The empire was more or less self-sufficient economically, given its seemingly limitless food supply and the abundant raw materials which domestic artisans used in the manufacture of wares for local consumption and foreign trade. Controlling strategic portions of three continents and of several seas, the empire also earned considerable income from transit, particularly the northwesterly flow through the Middle East of south Asian spices and silks. To an extent, Ottoman economic decline after 1566 was at first only relative--relative mainly to what was going on in Western Europe, where there occurred between the fifteenth and the eighteenth centuries a financial and commercial revolution which fundamentally transformed Europe's feudal economy. Money-lenders and merchants, their activities long restricted by GUILDS which regulated interest rates, fixed prices and kept trade on

---

[1]It is perhaps symbolic that the term "the Sublime Porte" (al-bāb al-ʿālī), which began about this period to mean "the Ottoman Government"--much as "Buckingham Palace" meant to "the British Government" in the time of Queen Elizabeth I (1558-1603)--referred not to the residence of the Ottoman sultans but rather to that of the prime ministers, much as "No. 10 Downing Street" later came to mean "the British government" after the prime minister replaced the monarchy as the effective center of power.

a local basis, began to establish investment banks and joint-stock companies that operated on a world-wide scale. The old craft guilds likewise disappeared in Western Europe with the appearance of entrepreneurs who invested their capital in the bulk purchase of raw materials and in the mass hiring of cheap labor; they then sold their mass-produed textiles and other products at the market price rather than at a regulated price. Like virtually all other "developed" areas of the medieval world, the Ottoman Empire did not experience this capitalistic revolution. Instead, its industrial and commercial institutions did not move beyond handicraft technology and guild organization. Although picturesque, the traditional workshop and bazaar proved to be increasingly archaic and inefficient compared to the modern factory and trading company. The Ottoman economy stood still while capitalism arose in Europe from whence it enveloped the world.

Ottoman economic decline was absolute as well as relative, however. Dynamic Western capitalism not only made the Ottoman economy appear backward, it also disrupted and weakened it. It was not from a position of weakness that Sulayman signed the Treaty of Capitulations in 1535, giving French merchants the right to trade freely in Ottoman domains; but by the following century the Ottoman Empire found itself in an increasingly inferior economic position vis-à-vis the West. As the demand for raw material increased in Europe, prices there rose accordingly and such commodities as wheat, wool, copper, and precious metals were gradually drained out of the Middle East, where prices also rose steadily. Then Western manufacturers exported their mass-produced goods to the Ottoman lands, underselling local handmade products and inaugurating the process that would, during 1750-1850, almost completely destroy Middle Eastern craft industries. Inevitably, into the Ottoman Empire came, in addition to European goods, European inflation which the stagnant Ottoman economy was unable to offset with economic growth. During the same period the Dutch forced their way to the East Indies and blocked the transit trade through the Ottoman lands much more effectively than the Portuguese did earlier. The world's trade shifted decisively to the ocean routes, and the Middle East became an economic back-water. By the mid-seventeenth century the once prosperous Ottoman Empire was financially very hard pressed, as evidenced and symbolized by the annual deficits in the treasury.

The Ottoman Empire failed to keep pace with Western Europe in other ways, too. The rise of a capitalist economic system accompanied and promoted the development of new political institutions, scientific methods, and military techniques. Perhaps the most important political development in Europe during the post-Renaissance period was the rise of the nation state, a political unit which gradually became the focus of popular self-identity and loyalty. By contrast, the Ottoman Empire never became a cohesive politico-cultural unit during 1600-1850 but instead remained a conglomeration of different religious and ethnic groups. The self-identity and loyalty of an Ottoman subject was likely to be focused rather more narrowly--on his extended family or on his millet.

European educational and scientific institutions, revitalized by the Renaissance, gradually surpassed those of the Ottomans which, meanwhile, lapsed into uncritical and imitative routine. Whereas Arabic-Islamic civilization had produced an inordinately large share of the medieval period's great scientists and philosophers, after the fifteenth century (Ibn Khaldun died in 1406) it produced an increasingly smaller percentage of them. Instead, it was in Europe that appeared such ground-breaking scientists as Copernicus (d. 1543), Bacon (d. 1626), Galileo (d. 1642), and Newton (d. 1727). Europe's "scientific revolution" not only led to radically new manufacturing devices, thus paving he way for the Industrial Revolution; it also transformed the weapons and techniques of warfare. A rare few Ottoman intellectuals were able at this point to perceive that their civilization was beginning to lag behind the West with respect to scientific and military innovations if not with respect to economic and political institutions. In the preface to a naval handbook written shortly after the Ottoman fleet was destroyed by the Venetians in 1656, the Ottoman historian Katib Chelebi (d. 1657) lamented the widespread ignorance of geography and mapmaking among Ottoman Muslims: "Sufficient and convincing proof of the necessity for learning this science is the fact that the heathen [i.e., the Europeans], by their application to and their esteem for those branches of learning, have discovered the New World and have overrun the markets of India." Chelebi proceeded to contrast the Muslims' rigorous cultivation of scientific learning during Abbasid times with their neglect of it in his own day. Unless they revive scientific training, he warned, "Henceforth [my] people will be looking at the universe with the eyes of oxen."

The rise of economically and militarily strong states in Europe contributed to an important collateral cause of Ottoman decline. The Empire was essentially a military machine which relied on short, victorious wars to maintain its prosperity. As the Ottomans began to encounter armies financed by booming economies and armed with revolutionary new weapons, the Empire reached its limits of expansion and then started to contract. During the seventeenth century, it began steadily to lose territory to Austria, Russia, and other expansionist European powers. Moreover, territorial losses usually came at the end of long, unsuccessful wars. Thus, the hard pressed Ottoman treasury not only lost major sources of tax revenue but it could no longer benefit from a policy of continuous expansion by a military machine which produced rather than consumed revenue. The now unsuccessful Ottoman army became a major new drain on the Empire's dwindling resources.

We have thus far enumerated at least three major causes of Ottoman decay: the stagnation and disruption of the Empire's economy; the transition from short, successful, revenue-producing wars to long, unsuccessful, revenue-consuming wars; and the drastic decline in the quality of leadership. The condition of decay provoked by these and other factors manifested itself in a number of ways: in the corruption of the armed forces and of the bureaucracy, in the impoverishment and unsettlement of the rural population, and in territorial loss and fragmentation. These <u>effects</u> of decline became in turn <u>causes</u> of further decay and collapse, thereby sustaining a vicious, downward spiral.

One aspect of the decline of the Ottoman armed forces was the abandonment of the timar system as the main source of cavalry, owing partly to inflation as it gradually became too expensive for timar-holders to maintain sipahi horsemen. Meanwhile, the famous JANISSARY CORPS gradually changed from a highly trained fighting force into a HEREDITARY MILITIA. During the latter part of the sixteenth century, the formerly celibate, full-time professional soldiers demanded and won the right to marry, to live outside their barracks, and to supplement their dwindling salaries by engaging in crafts or by acquiring iltizam-s. After securing the right to enroll their own sons in the corps, the janissaries agitated for an end to the devshirme, which last occurred in 1637. Although the janissary corps increased in size from 12,000 at the beginning of the Sulayman's reign to 200,000 by the mid-seventeenth century, it became virtually useless as a fighting force. When wars resulted not in victory and booty but in defeat and territorial loss, the janissaries became demoralized and refused to fight. They also were reluctant to adopt the new weapons and techniques introduced to advantage by the armies of the European nation states, preferring to continue using their outmoded but familiar arms and methods. Yet, although inept militarily, the janissaries became bolder and bolder about intervening in politics in order to prevent any sultan or minister from taking away their privileges.

In light of the palace intrigues regularly fostered by "households" of bureaucrats, the decay of the Ottoman administration can in general be characterized as the gradual replacement of the "merit system" by a SYSTEM OF BRIBES AND PATRONAGE. As inflation, the waging of costly but unsuccessful wars, and the resultant loss of revenue-producing territories transformed the treasury's annual surplus to an annual deficit, sultans and their ministers started to demand "gifts" from office-seekers as a means of raising money. Perhaps at first candidates still needed to possess some ability, but with the end of the devshirme there eventually arose a new system in which nearly every available position of importance was open to the highest bidder, irrespective of his merit. Buyers of iltizam-s and other offices set out to make a profit, among other ways by raising taxes as high as they dared. In the constant rivalry among "household," high officials tried to advance their own fortunes and those of their protégés as well. Thus did nepotism and corruption spread through the Ottoman administration. Corrupt bureaucrats came to form, along with the janissaries, an element which temporarily benefitted from the conditions of decline and which therefore opposed all efforts to arrest or to reform it.

Multazim-s were interested not in the Empire's long-range agricultural production but rather in recovering their investments and maximizing their profits as rapidly as possible. Farmers who could not pay the inflated tax rates were sometimes driven from their lands whereupon they faced three options. Some dispossessed farmers sought employment as hired laborers on large estates, thus forming a new class of landless peasants. Others flocked to the cities, where they swelled the ranks of the unemployed beggars who were responsible for a series of bread riots during the seventeenth century. The third option for dispossessed peasants was to join robber bands, usually led by former sipahi-s. During the seventeenth century such bands became common in mountainous regions of Anatolia and the Balkans, supporting themselves by raiding farms that were still productive. In some cases they even extorted taxes from inhabitants of nearby towns and villages and, in effect, created their own regional governments which replaced and defied that of the sultan.

In this regard, as the Ottoman military and bureaucracy grew increasingly corrupt and weak, the Empire's vast territories could not be controlled effectively by the central government. Neighboring empires like Austria, Russia, and Iran took advantage of Ottoman weakness to sieze as much land as they could. As a result of various unsuccessful wars between 1683 and 1879, the sultan was forced to give up most of his European provinces. Yet even the territories remaining in theory within the Ottoman Empire in practice also escaped control of the central government to varying degrees. In certain districts the powers of government effectively came to be exercised not by representatives of the Ottoman state but rather by local self-appointed bosses or robber chieftains who, often with the help of a European power, typically were able to defy the sultan's authority for decades. Sometimes, if the sultan needed a defiant local notable's military support and tax revenues badly enough, he would simply co-opt him back into the Ottoman provincial administration as the governor (with the title of "pasha"), or the vassal-ruler, of the region already under his control.

Most of these local rulers were merely adventurers seeking power and wealth for themselves. In retrospect, however, a few of them, like the Serbian robber chief, Alexander Karageorge, can be seen as leaders of incipient Balkan Nationalist Movements. The idea of nationalism, as it penetrated the Balkans from Western Europe, did not serve as a force that welded together the various religious and ethnic groupings of the Ottoman Empire; it served instead as a centrifugal force which caused the Empire to disintegrate further and faster, particularly in the Balkans. During the first decade of the nineteenth century, the Greeks and the Serbians (receiving military aid as well as moral support from various European nations) launched national rebellions which resulted in their becoming totally independent from Ottoman rule. The Ottoman sultan was obliged to acknowledge the autonomy of Greece in 1929 and that of Serbia in 1830.

Islam in Ottoman Turkey During the Period of Decline

Scriptural Islam made some positive advances during the period of the Ottoman Empire's rise and expansion. During the period of its decline, however, the now rigidly centralized and bureaucratized Ottoman-Islamic hierarchy seems to have performed a rather negative historical role, at least from the perspective of the reformers who tried to modernize Ottoman institutions. For one thing, the leading Ottoman ulama displayed and imposed a spirit of narrow-minded rigidity. The teaching of logic and of classical philosophy, which had persisted in

Ottoman madrasa-s to a much greater extent than in "Arab" institutions of Islamic learning, came under attack and was almost completely suppressed during the seventeenth century. The influential conservative ulama also successfully opposed and therefore delayed the introduction of such potentially beneficial inventions as the telescope and the printing press. For another thing, the integration of the religious hierarchy into the Ottoman bureaucracy put the leading ulama into close association with the corruption that was becoming so widespread among tax-collectors and other civil servants. More than a few religious dignitaries succumbed to the temptation to amass personal fortunes. They diverted waqf revenues, acquired iltizam-s, and then used their money to live luxuriously and also to buy prestigious and lucrative positions for their sons.

As certain Ottoman ulama families transformed themselves into something of a religious aristocracy, their power came to be more social and economic than moral. During the period of decline the Islamic hierarchy in Ottoman Turkey seems to have relinquished a degree of its moral leadership to popular Sufism or "folk Islam," which continued to expand during 1500-1750. The Shi'a-oriented Bektashi Order became so widespread among the janissaries that the two institutions became identified with each other. Such moderate or "orthodox" orders as the Mevleviya achieved considerable influence among the literate urbanites, including the Ottoman family and the ulama themselves. By the seventeenth century, popular religious concepts like astrology and the cult of saints had become an integral part of regular Islam and were rarely challenged any longer by the doctors of law and theology. Meanwhile, more radical Sufi Orders appealed to the rural population and to the urban lower classes. Many ulama continued to criticize such practices as music, dancing, the drinking of coffee and the smoking of tobacco and hashish--practices which first appeared during the fifteenth and sixteenth centuries within the context of popular Sufi ceremonies. Ulama criticism of "deviant" Sufism was sometimes countered with accusations of "hypocrisy"--i.e., the belief that it is enough simply to perform the required duties, particularly if done in an ostentatious manner. By the eighteenth century, as some high ulama were associated with the corruption and weakness of the Ottoman central government, many elements of the population looked to popular Sufi leaders for moral guidance.

The Emergence of Semi-Independent Regimes in the Arab Lands During the Period of Ottoman Decline

In the Ottoman "Arab provinces" there was evidence of many of the same trends discussed above: economic stagnation and disruption, bureaucratic corruption, social upheavals, decline of the central government's effective control, and the rise of local rulers who furthered their ambitions by dealing directly with European Powers. The relationship between the Ottoman Empire and its "Arab provinces" during 1600-1850 can be approached in two different ways. The first, a chronological approach, focuses upon the nature of the relationship itself. It consists essentially in summarizing the lengthy process during which the Ottoman Empire's ties with its Arab provinces became

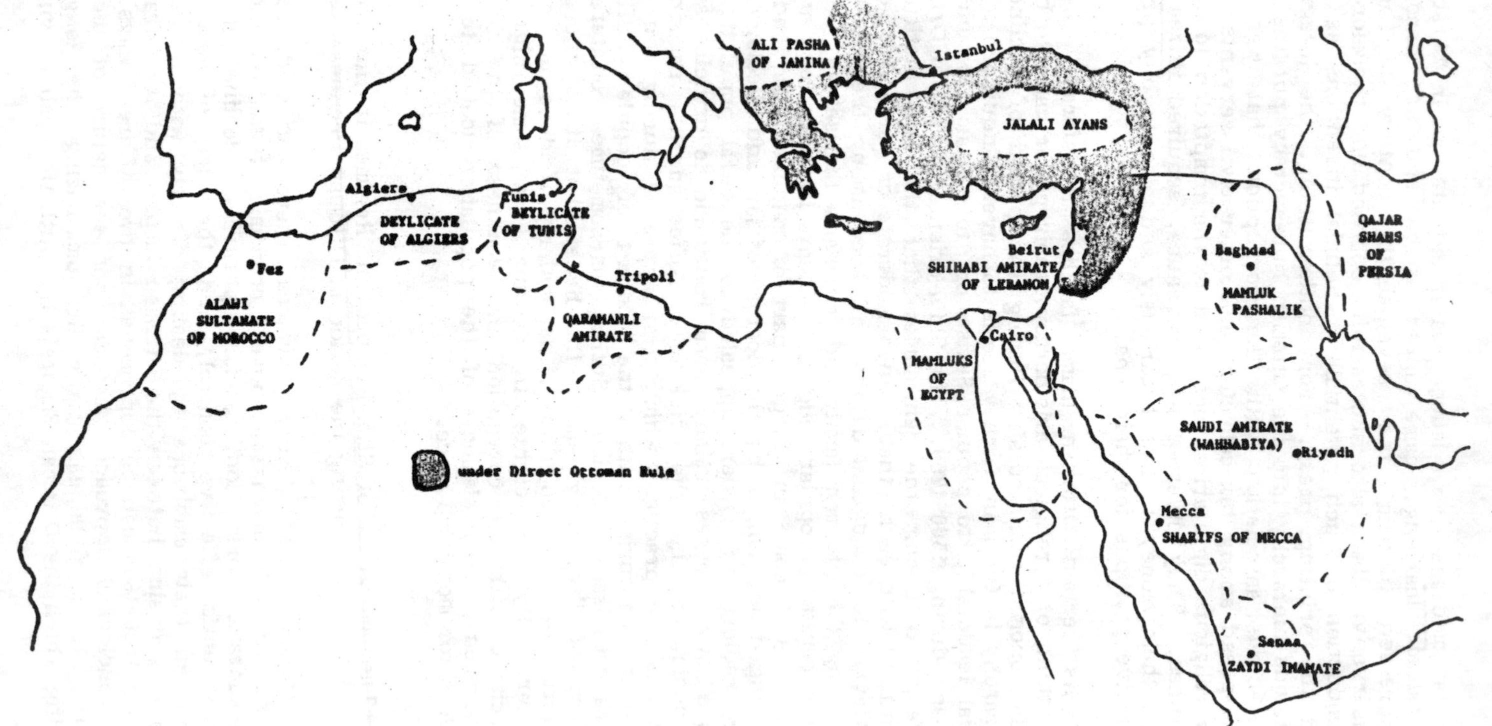

The Ottoman Empire's Fragmentation by 1800
into Local Military & Notable Regimes

The Nature of Political Regimes in 'Arab Lands' during the Period of Ottoman Decline

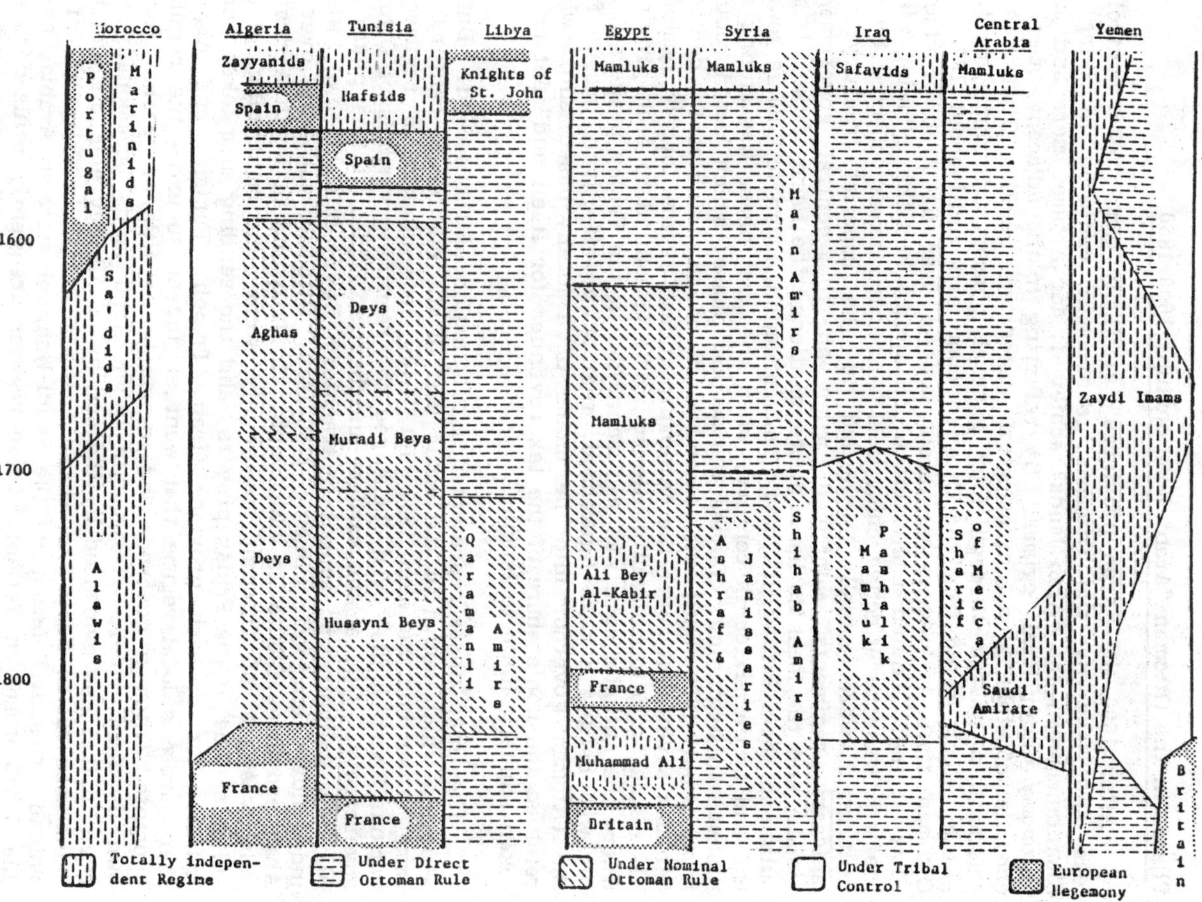

increasingly tenuous and, in come cases at least, finally broke altogether. The second approach is comparative; that is, it seeks to analyze the different kinds of local regimes that emerged in the Arab provinces as they became increasingly independent from Ottoman rule.

Phases in the Ottoman-"Arab" Relationship, 1600-1850

After 1600 the "Arab provinces" gradually came to be controlled less and less by the Ottoman government centered in Istanbul. Simultaneously, the "Arab lands" achieved, for a time, more and more autonomy under local regimes. By referring to the adjacent chart, we can detect that this chronological dimension of the Ottoman-Arab relationship passed through four general phases. During the first phase, which lasted from the Ottoman conquests until about 1600, the Ottoman state exerted rather direct control over its Arab provinces. That is, there existed a situation which approached the following ideal: the wālī was the effective chief local authority; taxes collected by the multazim-s were actually forwarded to the imperial treasury; the janissary regiments maintained order on the central government's behalf; and the local Muslim subjects mentioned the name of the Ottoman sultan in their Friday prayers. This situation began to change toward the end of the sixteenth century, when the first phase was ending and the second beginning. During the second phase, which lasted roughly from about 1600 until the second half of the eighteenth century, Ottoman sovereignty over the "Arab provinces" became largely symbolic. As a rule an Ottoman wālī continued to be appointed to each province, where the sultan's name was still mentioned in the Friday prayers. But the wali became a mere figurehead; real power effectively passed from the Ottoman governor into the hands of a locally-based elite, which retained the lion's share of the tax revenues for itself and sent only a token annual tribute to Istanbul.

The third phase represented a culmination of the second. During a period which began in the latter half of the eighteenth century and came to an end between 1830 and 1840, semi-autonomous regimes in various "Arab lands" even challenged the remaining symbols of Ottoman sovereignty. One of the earliest and best examples of this phase was Alī Bey al-Kabīr who sought to transform Egypt into his own, wholly independent kingdom. During 1750-1830, Ottoman authority over its Arab provinces fell to its lowest ebb. In Iraq and in North Africa the only vestiges of Ottoman sovereignty were the mentioning of the sultan's name in the Friday prayers, and the sending of a token annual tribute; for in each province (Iraq, Tripoli, Tunisia, and Algeria) there arose a local regime that went so far as to expel the regularly appointed Ottoman governor and to usurp the title of "pasha" for its own de facto ruler. Regimes in other Arab lands occasionally went even further, as evidenced by the actions of Alī Bey al-Kabīr and then Muhammad Ali in Egypt, of Ahmad Pasha al-Jazzār in Palestine, of the Shihāb amirs in Lebanon, of the Saudi-Wahhabi state in Arabia, and of the Zaydi imams in Yemen. These regimes frequently refused to send any tribute at all to Istanbul, and then occasionally even undertook military operations against the Ottoman state.

The fourth phase represented the reversal of the decentralization process just described. Intensive efforts to reform the Ottoman military and other institutions during 1826-1839 strengthened the central government and enabled it to reassert a measure of authority over some of the wayward Arab provinces. Iraq (1831), Libya (1835), Syria (1840), the Hijaz (1840), and portions of Yemen (1848) were more or less completely reintegrated into the Ottoman Empire by 1850. By this time, however, Algeria (1830) had been conquered by France and Aden (1839) by Britain; so, in these two areas theoretical Ottoman sovereignty was replaced by direct European rule, heralding the developments of the late nineteenth century (to be discussed in the next chapter). Meanwhile, Egypt, Lebanon, and Tunisia, while retaining a large measure of local autonomy, moved during the mid-nineteenth century back into a closer relationship with the Ottoman state.

Kinds of Regimes in "Arab Lands," 1600-1850

A second approach to the relationship between the Ottoman Empire and its Arab provinces during 1600-1850 focuses not upon the relationship per se but rather upon the kinds of elites that emerged to usurp power from the sultan's representatives. With regard to the ethnic and cultural origins of local ruling cliques, there seems to have been three basic possibilities. One was for Ottoman provincial officials or soldiers to make themselves independent of the Ottoman state but to preserve for their breakaway regime a predominately "Turkish" character. A second possibility was for an indigenous Arabic-speaking notable family to gain effective control over its own and neighboring districts. The third possibility, representing a combination of the first two, was for janissaries or other Turkish-speaking adventurers to transform an Ottoman province into a semi-autonomous vassal state but to bring indigenous notables into association with them to such a degree that the regime became 'naturalized' to a certain extent. Of course, while conforming in some ways to one general pattern or another, every Arabic-speaking country experienced a unique historical development during 1600-1850. To provide a more concrete understanding of these unique developments, in the next few pages we shall analyze, in some detail but in a comparative framework, three specific regions: Algeria, Lebanon, and Egypt.

Algeria

The deylicate of Algiers, which was dominated by janissaries and pirate captains, perhaps furnishes the best example of a breakaway regime that retained a primarily "Turkish" character. From the perspective of urban civilization, Algeria began to assume an historial significance mainly after the expulsion of the Muslims from Spain and after Khayr al-Din Barbarossa's reconquest of Algiers in 1525. It was thus in part under Ottoman influence that Algiers changed from a small town to an important provincial capital. The expanded port of Algiers became the chief haven for Muslim pirates in the Mediterranean as well as the base for subsequent Ottoman conquests along the North African coast. In Algiers, it was the local janissary regiment which, in league with the pirate captains, initially made Algeria independent of the Porte. By the end of the sixteenth century, the agha of the janissaries had become the de facto ruler of Algiers, with the wali continuing as a mere figurehead. In this respect, Algeria was typical of Tunisia, Tripoli, and Baghdad, where janissary cliques usurped effective power from the Ottoman governors who were likewise reduced to symbolic roles. Yet the breakaway elite of Algiers remained more purely Turkish in its orientation than that of Tunis. At any rate, in 1671 the pirate captains, on whom chiefly depended the prosperity of Algiers which derived most of its revenues from privateering, rebelled against and assassinated the reigning agha. The pirate captains then asserted themselves politically by choosing as ruler of Algiers an officer to whom was given the title of "dey," the same title used by the janissary rulers of Tunis after 1591. By 1689 the janissaries had reassumed a role in the selection of the dey, a position which remained elective and never became hereditary. Figurehead governors were still sent every three years from Istanbul until 1710, when the dey expelled the wali and took the title of "pasha" for himself.

Unlike the janissary regime in Tunisia which allied itself with local Arabic-speaking notables and became "Tunisian" to a considerable degree,[2] the regime of the Turkish-speaking deys was "Algerian" only with respect to geography. The dey's authority spread westward and eastward along the North African coast but not southward into the mountains and desert where Berber-speaking and Arabic-speaking tribes alike successfully refused to acknowledge the dey's claims to sovereignty over them. In return for tax-exempt status, certain Arabic-speaking "makhzan tribes" were sometimes employed as military auxiliaries of the Turks whenever the deys tried, usually in vain, to

---

[2]Tunisia differed from Algeria in a number of ways: its terrain is flatter; it had a longer and more important tradition of urban civilization (as symbolized by the Zaytuna Mosque-university); and its farmers, artisans, and merchants conducted economic activities that proved more significant, in terms of revenue, than privateering. As a consequence, Tunisia's path to semi-autonomous status, although resembling that of Algeria in some ways, exhibited several unique features, notably the important role of the notables of Tunis in the drift toward independence and the resultant indigenous "Tunisian" character of the local janissary regimes that emerged. This trend was symbolized by a number of developments. For example, when in 1715 the Porte tried to reassert its authority over Tunis by sending a new wali from Istanbul, the ruling bey (Husayn ibn Ali) referred the matter to a council (diwan) of local ulama and other notables, who resolved to oppose (by force if necessary) the displacement of Husayn by an Ottoman governor. Thereafter, the Husayni dynasty (1705-1881) of beys regularly convened the diwan of ulama and notables, which played an important role in the formulation of policy. A final indication of the "Tunisification" of the Husayni dynasty is that, by the end of the eighteenth century, Arabic rather than Turkish was the "native language" of Tunisia's ruling family.

extend their authority southward. For the most part, in the mountainous and desert interior of the country the functions of government were effectively exercised by tribes and/or popular religious brotherhoods which assumed state-like political and military qualities. The Turkish soldiers were permitted to marry local women, but as a rule their offspring (the kulughli) were not eligible to enter the militia. Instead, new "Turkish" soldiers were acquired as boys in pirate raids or by purchase from Ottoman and Crimean slave markets. Like the Qaramanli dynasty of Tripoli, the regime of the deylicate thus continued both to have a distinctly "Turkish" character and to orient itself toward the Mediterranean rather than toward its own hinterland.

Lebanon

A nearly impenetrable natural fortress, the mountains of Lebanon had been virtually autonomous during the period of Mamluk hegemony over Syria (1300-1516). The highland peasant tribesmen, including Maronite Christians in the north (Kisrawan) and Druzes in the south (Shuf), were just as reluctant to submit to direct Ottoman rule. In this respect, Lebanon resembled several other areas--notably mountainous or desert regions like Morocco, the Sahara, Eastern Arabia, and Yemen--whose terrain was not easily accessible to Ottoman troops. In such regions as these, with the weakening of the Ottoman central government, there consequently tended to emerge autonomous regimes dominated by local Arabic-speaking notables. The Ma'n and Shihab dynasties in Lebanon were typical of these kinds of elites.

Fakhr al-Din I, a Druze notable of the MA'N FAMILY, was granted by Selim I (1512-21) a sort of semi-autonomous vassal status over part of "Lebanon," agreeing in return to pay an annual tribute and to refrain from the mountaineers' practice of raiding the villagers inhabiting the lowland plains. The Ma'n amirs proceeded immediately to consolidate their control over the entire highlands and then also began, after the onset of Ottoman decline, to pillage caravans and lowland villages. An Ottoman punitive expedition in 1584 temporarily broke the Druze dynasty's ascendancy, but this was restored from 1590 onwards by FAKHR AL-DIN II (d. 1635), who recruited mercenaries to build up a 40,000-man army. Fakhr al-Din II also promoted his regime's fortunes by establishing alliances with influential non-Druze "Lebanese" families, such as the Sunni Muslim Shihab clan of Wadi al-Taym, and by trying to create a strong economic base. He encouraged the cultivation of mulberry trees as a means of expanding the fledging SILK INDUSTRY, and he restored the ancient ports of BEIRUT and Sidon in order to facilitate commerce with Europe.

These economic developments were among the factors which inaugurated about this time a MIGRATION OF MARONITE PEASANTS from the northern to the southern mountains (i.e, Beirut and its hinterland), where they either continued to engage in agriculture or else took up commercial activities. For a time the Ottomans attempted to suppress the growing power of Fakhr al-Din II but decided by 1620 to come to terms with him. Fakhr al-Din II's strength peaked during 1624-34 (when he was even able to appoint the amir al-hajj (commander of the annual pilgrimage caravan from Damascus). But in 1634 a dispute between the Ottoman Empire and Safavi Iran led indirectly to a major and successful Ottoman effort to suppress the semi-independent status of the Ma'n amirs of Lebanon.

The vestiges of the Ma'n amirate in Lebanon were inherited by the Sunni Muslim Shihab clan. Through divide and rule tactics, the Ottomans were able during the seventeenth century to contain the SHIHAB AMIRS, but in 1711 the latter consolidated their ascendancy by defeating their main Ottoman-supported rival. Reviving the system of local vassalage used effectively by the Ma'n, the Shihab amirs bought into their association other "Lebanese" notables, like the Maronite Khāzin family in Kisrawan, the Druze Jumblatt family in the Shuf, and the Druze Abu 'l-Lam^c family in al-Matn. The gradual strengthening and expansion of Shihabi power continued throughout the eighteenth century and peaked during the reign of BASHIR SHIHAB II (1790-1841), who allied himself with Muhammad Ali when the latter sent his son to occupy Syria during 1831-40. Other trends in the Lebanese highlands during the eighteenth century included the continuing migration of Maronites from north to south, the steady growth of the local silk industry, the tendency for international commerce to be concentrated in Beirut and to be dominated by the Maronites (whose patriarchs had become affiliated with Roman Catholicism in 1445 and for whose clergy a special college was founded at Rome in 1584). Elements of the Maronite clergy supported the religiously tolerant Shihab amirs but worked simultaneously to strengthen their church's ties with Rome (and, consequently, with France, which regarded itself as the Maronites' protector) as a means of preventing their absorption into a purely Islamic state. The slowly evolving notion that Lebanon's independence from the Ottoman Empire was related to French protection of the Latin Christians apparently began also to impress certain non-Christian notables, for various members of the Druze Abu 'l-Lam^c family and of the Muslim Shihab family (including Bashir II) converted to Christianity.

During 1840-61 the separate status of Lebanon within Syria and within the Ottoman Empire was challenged and then reaffirmed. The events of the last decades of the Shihab amirate strained to the breaking point the old Druze-Maronite alliance. In their reassertion of more or less direct rule over Lebanon, the Ottomans established in 1843 the "DUAL QA'IMAQAMATE" whereby the newly imposed Ottoman governor in Beirut was assisted by a Maronite vice-governor (<u>qa'imaqam</u>) in the north and by a Druze vice-governor in the south. However, there existed by this time in south Lebanon a large number of Maronites who objected to being placed under a Druze administrator. On the other hand, among the relocated Maronites the old lord-peasant relationship gradually broke down and was replaced by more egalitarian structures within the community. This seems to have been a factor in the rise of socio-economic tensions among the Maronites still living in north Lebanon, where the peasants began to express their resentment toward the "feudal" privileges of their own notables. Rebelling in 1858, they drove out such wealthy families as the Khāzin clan whose property they seized. These disorders in the north encouraged the Druzes to attempt to regain their lost supremacy over the whole of Lebanon. The Druze military offensive, which began in April 1860, turned into a general MASSACRE OF CHRISTIANS, which was repeated in Damascus and elsewhere. This anti-Christian episode provided France with the opportunity to intervene, and French troops disembarked at Beirut in August 1860. Supported by Britain, the Ottomans were able to thwart Napoleon III's ambitions to establish a strong French presence in Syria. But in 1861 the dual qa'imaqamate was replaced by a new arrangement--the mutasarrifiyya--whereby Mount Lebanon was constituted as a semi-autonomous Ottoman province under a Christian governor (the mutasarrif), who was advised by a twelve-member council composed of representatives of the various religious communities. The French-imposed settlement of 1861 thus obliged the Ottomans to acknowledge the predominance of Christian leadership within a semi-independent Lebanon.

Egypt

Tunisia was perhaps the most straightforward example of a janissary regime which became naturalized; Egypt represented a more complicated situation, but in several ways, like Tunisia, it was an example of the mixed Turkish-indigenous breakaway regime. As elsewhere, the sixteenth century in Egypt was by and large a period of direct rule by the Ottoman wālī-s. But then the janissary regiments began attempting to seize power for themselves. The soldiers mounted rebellions in 1586, 1589, 1601, and in 1605 when they assassinated the wālī. The suppression of the 1605 revolt by a large expedition from Īstanbul is often called "the second Ottoman conquest of Egypt." Thereafter, to provide a check on the janissaries' political ambitions, the wālī-s were obliged to draw upon the private armies of Egypt's former rulers, the Mamluks, who were therefore permitted to continue their recruiting and training of slave boys within their personal "households." In exchange for the support of their troops, the twenty-four Mamluk Grandees (each of whom bore the title of "bey") were also appointed to district governorships as well as to such positions as qa'imaqam (vice-governor) and amīr al-hajj (commander of the troops accompanying the annual pilgrimage caravan).

Having been co-opted back into important military and political roles, it was then the Mamluks who asserted themselves during the seventeenth century, reducing the Ottoman governor to a mere figurehead and vying with one another for the dominant position. A Circassian mamluk named Ridwān Bey al-Faqārī, who used as his power base the post of amīr al-hajj which he held from 1631 until his death in 1656, became the paramount figure in Egyptian politics during the mid-seventeenth century. His "household," the Faqariyya, tried to perpetuate itself in power after his death, but was soon challenged and displaced by a household of Bosnian mamluks which, however, was unable to consolidate its position, enabling the Ottoman wālī-s, supported by the janissary regiments, temporarily to reassert their authority. Politics in Egypt during 1517-1711 thus consisted of a three-cornered struggle between the Ottoman wālī-s, the janissary regiments, and the Mamluk Grandees. While the latter's ultimate triumph did not, as in Lebanon, entail the emergence of a purely native, Arabic-speaking regime, it did entail the re-emergence of a power clique produced by a system that had been indigenous to Egypt since the early thirteenth century.

In 1711 the three-cornered struggle resulted in a three-month civil war. Within a decade a new Mamluk household, the *Qazdughliyya*, seized power and retained it for the rest of the eighteenth century. During that period a new governor of Egypt was still periodically sent from Istanbul but he now fulfilled a purely symbolic function, real power being in the hands of the paramount Mamluk Grandee who assumed the title of *shaykh al-balad*. Shortly after mid-century, *shaykh al-balad* Ali Bey al-Kabir set out to make himself the absolute ruler of an autonomous empire based in Egypt. His ambitions led him to exterminate ruthlessly his rivals among the Mamluk Beys (including some within his own Qazdughilyya household), to attempt to conquer Syria and the Hijaz from his nominal sovereign the Ottoman sultan, and to seek financial and military assistance from Russia, then at war with the Ottoman Empire. In some ways, the schemes of Ali Bey foreshadowed those of Muhammad Ali a half-century later. But Ali Bey could not outmaneuver the "mamluk system" which had produced him, and in 1773 he was assassinated by a conspiracy of rivals headed by his own client, Muhammad Bey Abu'l-Dhahab (d. 1775), who briefly replaced him as *shaykh al-balad* and was the first mamluk to be recognized as *wali* of Egypt by the Ottomans. During the last quarter of the eighteenth century, the Qazdughilyya household and the Ottoman province of Egypt were ruled by two former clients of Muhammad Bey Abu'l-Dhahab, Ibrahim Bey and Murad Bey. They weathered an attempt in 1786-87 by Sultan Selim III to reassert direct Ottoman control over Egypt but were finally defeated and eliminated from power by the French invasion during 1798-1801.

Egypt's socio-economic structure experienced change as well as continuity during 1600-1800. The local economy was weakened by the discovery of the ocean route to India and by the emigration to the imperial capital, Istanbul, of many of its best artisans. Cairo remained an important center of industry and commerce, but the orientation of its most important trade relationships shifted emphatically from the Red Sea to the Mediterranean. In a pioneering study, Andre Raymond has classified the merchants and artisans of seventeenth-century Cairo into three general strata, the lowest of which included the unskilled workers. The middle stratum was occupied by the skilled artisans and local merchants who were organized according to craft or commodity into guilds. While this level was dominated numerically by Egyptian Muslims, certain of the most lucrative crafts--e.g., jewelry, silk weaving, and watchmaking,--had high concentrations of Copts, Jews, Greeks and Armenians. At the top of the socio-economic pyramid were the international merchants who trafficked in such commodities as coffee, spices, cloth, oil, tobacco, and slaves. While native-born, Arabic-speaking Egyptians (Copts and Jews as well as Muslims) could be found along their ranks, the international merchants tended to be non-Egyptians (Turks, Moroccans, and Levantines) who had the necessary international connections.

This situation was modified by a number of trends during the eighteenth century. The consolidation of the commercial ocean routes in the hands of the Dutch and the English led to a continuing decline of Egypt's participation in the oriental spice and silk trade. New silk industries were established in Lebanon, however, and other kinds of cloth remained commercially important, but less now as exports than as imports--especially the mass-produced fabrics from English, Dutch and French factories, products of the newly invented wide, power-driven loom. The influx of cheap European textiles on the one hand undermined the local weaving industry, whose economic role shrank along with that of the once prosperous spice trade. On the other hand it favored the commercial prospects of those merchants having the best international connections, primarily with Europe and secondarily with Lebanon. This helps to account for the dramatic rise within Egypt's economic elite of the SYRIAN CATHOLICS, who increased numerically from about 3 families in 1730 to about 500 families by 1780 and who came to dominate all aspects of the cloth traffic and of the international trade generally. In chronicling some of these developments, the historian al-Jabarti lamented the loss of economic power by the Cairene Muslims, whom he called awlad al-balad ("sons of the country") in contrast to the atrāk (Turkish-speaking Mamluks and janissaries) and other "foreigners." The concept of IBN AL-BALAD may well represent the germ of the idea of Egyptian national self-identity.

Since access to craft and commerce vocations was governed in the main by heredity, Egyptian Muslims tended to use religious institutions as their own special avenue for upward social mobility. Egypt's educational process began, at the level of rural village or urban quarter, in thousands of Qur'an schools (kuttāb-s); it culminated at the Azhar Mosque-university, where the most learned ulama lectured on Arabic grammar, Qur'anic commentary, law, and theology. Representing the Ottoman effort to control the Islamic establishment in Egypt was the chief qadi, a Hanafi jurist sent from Istanbul and proclaimed head of all sharīᶜa magistrates in the province. But the Hanafi chief qadi became a mere figurehead as did the wālī himself, and the native Egyptian qadis of the other madhhab-s were independent of him in practice if not in theory. Nevertheless, Islamic education in Egypt did become hierarchized and centralized, although to a lesser degree than it did in Istanbul. The Azhar's twenty-five riwāq-s[3] seem to have been organized in accordance with Islam's tradition of decentralization; but the emergence during the seventeenth century of the office of Shaykh al-Azhar evidenced and symbolized the evolution of the Ottoman-type ulama hierarchy in Egypt. Tradition dictated that the Islamic intelligentsia act as spokesmen for the local population, communicating individual or common grievances to the foreign Mamluk rulers, a task which many ulama performed with valor and integrity. In this regard, during the eighteenth century Egypt was a good example of an "amir-ulama regime," wherein power was held by a clique of military bosses (the Mamluks) who received legitimacy from the religious leaders (the ulama) in exchange for economic privileges and control over educa-

---

[3] A riwāq was one of the Azhar's dormitories, which were organized according to madhhab or especially according to place of origin.

tion, justice, and public morals. Indeed, some ulama exhibited a willingness to accept favors and patronage from the Mamluks to the extent of compromising their role of popular advocacy. As in Turkey, certain elements of the Egyptian population consequently turned to the heads of the popular Sufi orders for moral leadership.

In one sense the FRENCH OCCUPATION of Egypt during 1798-1801 wrought significant changes in the country's political institutions, long symbolized by the Mamluks and their "mamluk system," both of which were mortally wounded. The historical causes and personal motives of the invasion commanded by Napoleon Bonaparte sprang partly from the pressures of French domestic politics and the Napoleonic Wars and partly from the desire of French merchants to consolidate their dominant position in Egypt's trade with Europe. The French are often credited with making an intellectual impact on Egyptian society to the extent of inaugurating a cultural renaissance. A number of French scientists accompanied the military expedition. Among other things, they organized an academic society called the Institut d'Egypte; they performed scientific experiments for the benefit of Egyptian scholars; and they undertook extensive anthropological investigations, the results of which were gathered into the multi-volume Description de l'Egypte, now a valuable source of information about Egyptian society of the late eighteenth century. The French are also frequently given credit for introducing "democratic institutions" into Egypt, since Napoleon sought to legitimize his occupation by inviting local notables--mainly ulama--to participate in advisory councils. According to al-Jabarti, however, many ulama refused the invitation outright, giving the excuse that they were accustomed to leaving political matters in the hands of the Turks, and even those who accepted remained skeptical of French motives and ambitions. Indeed, some of the ulama (although not the leading ones) played a role in the anti-French uprising of the populace of Cairo in October 1798, which was provoked by the taxation policies of the French as well as by their destruction of the gates of the city's quarters for "security reasons." First proclaimed at the Azhar, the popular revolt, organized for the most party by the guilds and the Sufi orders, spread throughout the city. While easily quashed by the French artillery, the uprising demonstrated that native Egyptians could be roused to try to exert their own influence on the political process. This influence would again be exerted, this time via the ulama, following the expulsion of the French from Egypt in 1801 by an Anglo-Ottoman expedition.

But, in another sense, Napoleon's invasion and his defeat of the Mamluks merely occasioned the replacement of the Mamluk military caste with another Turkish-speaking military adventurer whose rise to power was in some ways a typical development of the process of Ottoman decay and fragmentation. MUHAMMAD ALI arrived in Egypt with the Anglo-Ottoman expedition as an officer in the Albanian Regiment, of which he assumed command by the end of 1803. The French withdrawal ignited a struggle for the control of Egypt between the newly arrived Ottoman forces and the surviving Mamluks. Rather than using his Albanian troops to support the Ottoman sultan's bid to reassert Istanbul's authority over Egypt, however, Muhammad Ali let the two sides wear each other down and meanwhile promoted his own fortunes.

This he accomplished by presenting himself as the defender of the Egyptian people's interest against the rapacious Ottomans and Mamluks. It was at this point that the ulama of Cairo, apparently convinced that the Albanian Regiment's commander would be preferable either to a restoration of the Mamluks or to direct Ottoman rule, mobilized public opinion in favor of Muhammad Ali. The spokesmen of the ulama, and therefore seemingly of the Egyptian population, was Shaykh Umar Makram. Ottoman Sultan Selim III, salvaging what he could from the situation, bowed to the pressure and in 1805 named Muhammad Ali the Ottoman Governor of Egypt. Like the Husayni dynasty in Tunisia, therefore, the independent regime of Muhammad Ali was established in part because it was able to attract the support of local ulama and other notables.

While theoretically a subordinate of the Ottoman sultan, Muhammad Ali was in all but name the independent ruler of an autonomous state. Perhaps, like similar adventurers in other parts of the fragmenting Empire, he permitted himself to be co-opted back into the Ottoman system in order to consolidate his own position against local rivals: in this case, the Mamluks. Thus, in 1811, when the sultan invited Muhammad Ali Pasha to help him expel the Wahhabis from the Hijaz, he exploited his official position and the occasion to massacre the remaining Mamluk leaders. Muhammad Ali acted to protect the autonomy of his kingdom against English and Ottoman ambitions by entering into a more or less permanent alliance with France, from whom he requested military advisers to assist in the establishment and training of his own armed forces. After successfully consolidating his power about 1811, Muhammad Ali proceeded to move in two directions. First, he moved away from his earlier close reliance on the ulama in order to implement a slate of progressive reforms. Secondly, he indulged his own imperial ambitions which led him, temporarily, to try to destroy the remaining symbols of Ottoman sovereignty over Egypt. Having realized the fundamental weakness of the Ottoman Empire following the Ottoman-Egyptian defeat in a naval battle in 1828 during the Greek war for independence, in 1830-33 Muhammad Ali sent his son to invade Syria and Anatolia where his troops easily defeated those of Sultan Mahmud II. The latter appealed to the European Powers, who pressured Muhammad Ali into withdrawing his army from Anatolia. But the sultan was obliged formally to cede Egypt as an hereditary fief to Muhammad Ali and his descendants as well as to acknowledge the legitimacy of the Pasha's occupation of Syria, which lasted until 1840. Thereafter, although the family of Muhammad Ali ruled Egypt as an hereditary semi-independent fiefdom, theoretical Ottoman sovereignty over Egypt persisted and even increased in some ways.

Pre-Colonial Revivalist and Reformist Movements

The manifestations of Ottoman decline became apparent only gradually. During the seventeenth century the Ottoman Empire acquired as many territories as it lost; only after a severe defeat by Russia, Austria, and Venice in a lengthy series of wars which ended with the Treaty of Karlowitz in 1699 did it begin steadily to shrink in size. Meanwhile, however, many provinces had become the personal fiefs of ambitious janissary officers or of indigenous notables. Also, during the seventeenth century a few individuals among the educated and political elites within the Ottoman Empire began to perceive that Islamic and Ottoman institutions no longer functioned as effectively as they once did. Some of them, like Katib Chelebi, started in effect to pose some disturbing questions: Why is it that Islamic civilization and the Ottoman Empire no longer prevail on the world's battlefields and trade routes? Why is it that the course of Islamic and Ottoman history seems to be going awry? Many of the social and intellectual developments during the 1600-1850 period represent two general categories of responses to such questions. One category includes the responses of the religious leaders, as expressed via a series of Islamic revivalist movements. The other category includes the responses of the political and military leaders, as expressed via a series of movements for technological reform.

Islamic Revivalist Movements

The religious-minded observers of decline posited that Islamic civilization had rendered itself susceptible to internal decay and therefore to external aggression through the Muslims' collective neglect of the true principles and correct practices of their revealed religion. Some went so far as to see the rising European Powers as the agents of divine wrath against the slothful Muslims. Also, to an extent Islamic revivalist movements arose within the context of the traditional tension between the formal or "bookish" Islam of the ulama[4] and the popular or "folk" Islam of the radical Sufi brotherhoods which had become deeply rooted among the rural population and the urban lower classes. This tension was compounded and intensified in such areas as India where, although they constituted the ruling elite, the Muslims represented a minority among the Hindu majority. Radical sufism in India tended, like Hinduism, to be eclectic (a composite of various religious traditions and willing to admit the validity of almost any religious doctrine), and they consequently absorbed a number of Hindu beliefs and practices. In opposition to this tendency for popular Islam to become amalgamated with Hinduism, there developed in India during the early seventeenth century a "neo-orthodox" movement, led by the NAQSHBANDIYYA Sufi order which had traditionally appealed to the ulama and other literate urbanites. While acknowledging the value of mystical experience, such Naqshbandi spokesmen as Ahmad Sirhindi (d. 1624) insisted that mysticism must be kept within certain limits as prescribed by Islamic law (the shari^{c}a). There thus developed in India during the seventeenth century an important movement of sharī^{c}a-minded Islamic revivalism, which was associated at first not with the ulama per se but rather with such "neo-orthodox" Sufi orders as the Naqshbandiyya.

---

[4]Or, as the sociologist-historian Max Weber would say, of the town-based middle classes.

Neo-orthodox Sufism in the Ottoman Mashriq. While not faced with the specific problem of accretions from Hinduism, Islamic society in the Ottoman Empire and in its semi-autonomous "Arab" provinces nevertheless shared the general conditions of internal decay and external pressure that were conducive to the emergence of revivalist movements. These tendencies first appeared, as in India, not among the regular ulama but rather within Sufism itself. The KHALWATIYYA order, associated until the fifteenth century with the Shi'i-oriented "folk Islam" of the Turkish tribes, began after the rise of the Shi'i Safavi dynasty in Iran to become more "orthodox" for political reasons. After Shams al-Din Muhammad Damirdash (d. 1524) introduced it into Egypt, the Khalwatiyya during the early Ottoman period gained the reputation of being at once *Sharī^{c}a*-minded and service-oriented. As such, it even appealed to certain Azhari ulama. Al-Jabarti mentioned that Muhammad al-Hifnawi (d. 1768), a Khalwati shaykh who was also Shaykh al-Azhar, headed a popular movement of Sufi leaders and lesser ulama which protested abuses of Ottoman-Mamluk misrule. Meanwhile, the Naqshbandiyya was introduced into Ottoman and Arabic-speaking Islamic society, where it was favorably received by the well educated men of religion. Ottoman historian Evliya Chelebi (d. 1682) mentioned that many of the learned of Istanbul were affiliating themselves with either the Khalwatiyya or the Naqshbandiyya. These two orders were also welcomed among similar elements in Cairo and in the Hijaz where, by the early eighteenth century, an informal "school" of neo-orthodox Sufism flourished. A relatively unknown but key figure in this development was MUHAMMAD HAYYA AL-SINDI (d. 1750), a Naqshbandi shaykh who encouraged his many pupils in Medina to study *hadith*, not in the manner of *taqlīd* (uncritical imitation) but rather in that of *ijtihād*, and who discouraged them from participating in the various forms of saint-worship. The neo-orthodox Sufi activity of al-Sindi and his colleagues has not been widely noted, in part because it never became politicized; but it nevertheless exerted a considerable impact on a number of Islamic reformers who rose to prominence during the second half of the eighteenth century.

"Wahhabism". Muhammad ibn Abd al-Wahhab (1703-92) was born into a family of ulama in a Najdi village where his father had succeeded his grandfather as the local qadi (of the strict Hanbali *madhhab*). He studied in Medina, under the *hadīth* specialist Shaykh Muhammad Hayya al-Sindi, and then went to Basra in Iraq, where he studied under a famous scholar of *tawhīd* (proofs of the unity/uniqueness of God). It is reported that he was greatly disgusted by the godlessness of Basra, an important commercial center. He also discovered and was profoundly impressed by the writings of the revivalist Ibn Taymiyya (d. 1328). Ibn Abd al-Wahhab soon carried *sharī^{c}a*-minded revivalism beyond the stage of moderate or neo-orthodox Sufism to that of uncompromising anti-Sufism. Expelled from Basra for declaring his ideas there, he returned to his birthplace, where he collected a private circle of disciples and composed a book, *kitāb al-tawhīd*. He probably succeeded his father as the village qadi. In some official capacity, at any rate, Ibn Abd al-Wahhab boldly proclaimed his program by cutting down several trees which the villagers considered sacred, by demolishing the tomb of a local "saint," and by sentencing an adulterous woman to be

stoned to death. As a result of these actions, an opposition to him developed, so in 1745 he transferred to another town, dirᶜiya, with whose amir, Muhammad ibn Saᶜūd, he formed a potent alliance. It was thus the message of al-daᶜwa ila al-tawhīd (the call to [return to] the doctrine of the unity/uniqueness of God) that served as the ideological banner during the rise and expansion of the "First Saudi Empire" (1746-1819). In each newly conquered district the muwahhidūn ("unitarians," or "affirmers of tawhīd"), as the disciples of Ibn ᶜAbd al-Wahhab called themselves, systematically destroyed sacred trees and saint shrines and insisted upon what they held to be the beliefs and practices of the early Muslims, the "pious ancestors" (al-salaf al-sālihīn).

To describe the type of religious movement that "Wahhabism"[5] represented, words like "iconoclastic" and even "puritannical" as well as "revivalistic" are frequently utilized; and to a certain degree they are applicable. In a way reminiscent of some of the Protestant reformers, Ibn Abd al-Wahhab sought to purge his religion of all heretical innovations--particularly those associated with the veneration of living or dead "saints"--and thereby to restore it to its original pure condition. Ibn Abd al-Wahhab believed that after the A.H. third century (A.D. ninth century) the Muslims began to corrupt their revealed religion just as the Jews and the Christians were held to have corrupted theirs by the time of Muhammad. In the eyes of Ibn Abd al-Wahhab, the Sufis were modern counterparts of the pagan sorcerers during the jahiliyya (the time of ignorance/paganism before Islam). Thus an important theme of Wahhabism is that of returning to the pristine purity of original Islam wherein a fundamental concept is tawhīd: belief in a unique transcendent god who is wholly distinct from created objects and beings and who acknowledges no intermediaries between himself and his worshippers.

Aside from providing Saudi expansionism with an ideological banner and a theological justification, the Wahhabi movement and its doctrines also contained important political implications. The call to return to tawhīd and to the sharīᶜa, along with the repudiation of popular religious beliefs and practices, represented to an extent an indictment of, and a declaration of war upon, what we may call the "Ottoman Islamic establishment." The Wahhabis considered themselves justified in waging jihad against those who called themselves Muslims but whose beliefs and actions revealed them to be kuffār (unbelievers) and/or mushrikūn (polytheists). The Ottomans, who in about 1750 banned Wahhabis from performing the pilgrimage, thus became auxiliary targets of the jihad; and Ottoman officials and institutions became symbols of deviation, sinfulness, corruption and decadence. Thus during their occupation of

---

[5]Muslims in Saudi Arabia did not refer to themselves as "Wahhabis," a term first coined by their critics. Rather, they called themselves either "Muwahhidūn" or now more commonly just "Muslims." The term "Wahhabism" is used here, for convenience, to describe the original revivalist movement.

the Hijaz (1803-11), the Wahhabis tried systematically to obliterate all traces of Ottoman culture and authority.

During the apogee of the First Saudi Empire, Wahhabi ulama sent letters proclaiming their message to various parts of the Islamic world. As a rule, the response was nil or even negative. In Tunisia, for example, the ulama of the Zaytuna Mosque-university designated one of their number to compose a refutation of Wahhabi doctrines. The resulting treatise argued that since the time of Muhammad pious ulama had legitimately performed the task of intercession with God (tawassul); and it accused the Wahhabis of killing Muslims and of further dividing the Islamic community. It may be observed in retrospect that conditions in Tunisia, a comparatively integrated society where there existed very little tension between "bookish Islam" and "folk Islam," were not receptive to such an extreme brand of anti-Sufi revivalism. By contrast, conditions in Morocco were receptive to precisely that sort of movement. Thus, Moroccan Sultans Muhammad (1757-90) and Sulayman (1792-1822) welcomed Wahhabi ideas and encouraged the ulama of the Qarawiyin Mosque-university to propagate them. In part their motives were political. Since the dynasty's sphere of authority coincided more or less with that of the Qarawiyin and its "bookish Islam," the sultans saw in Wahhabism a doctrine which could undermine the power of the radical Sufi brotherhoods in dissident tribal areas, thereby enabling the central government to extend its authority over the tribes. Wahhabism also exerted an important impact in less direct ways. Many of its central themes entered the general currents of Islamic thought and contributed to the ideological environment of the nineteenth century which produced such movements as the Sudanese Mahdiyya and such Islamic reformers as Muhammad Abduh and Rashid Rida.

Neo-orthodox Sufism in North Africa. Meanwhile, conditions in certain parts of North Africa were receptive to neo-orthodox Sufism. In this regard, the informal "school" of reformist Naqshbandis and Khalwatis, which flourished in Cairo and the Hijaz during the mid-eighteenth century, was important for its impact not only on Muhammad ibn Abd al-Wahhab but also on a number of Islamic revivalists from the Maghrib. One of these was Muhammad ibn Abd al-Rahman al-Qujtuli (d. 1794), who studied in Cairo under Muhammad al-Hifnawi and then returned to his native Algeria where he founded the Rahmaniyya Order which became widespread among the tribesmen and villagers of Eastern Algeria and Southern Tunisia. Another reformer was AHMAD AL-TIJANI (d. 1815) who studied in both Cairo and Medina and then founded the neo-orthodox TIJANIYYA Order which spread rapidly among the merchants, ulama, and bureaucrats in Fez and Tunis as well as among the tribesmen and villagers of Western Algeria. Shaykh al-Tijani, who was invited by the Moroccan sultan to establish his residence in Fez, forbade his adepts to visit saints and their tombs; he also reportedly told them to examine his sayings in the light of the sharīᶜa, rejecting those which contradicted it. However, al-Tijani's own claims to sainthood and infallibility demonstrate that sharīᶜa-minded revivalism could occasionally backslide into the "errors" of radical Sufism.

Yet the subsequent expressions of neo-orthodox Sufism in the Maghrib--e.g., the Madaniyya and especially the SANUSIYYA (which was created about 1836)--tended to retain only the form of the Sufi brotherhood while essentially representing "bookish Islam" in substance. MUHAMMAD IBN ALI AL-SANUSI (1787-1859) utilized his Sufi order as a missionary organization for teaching Islam's true principles and correct practices to the bedouin of Cyrenaica (Eastern Libya). His revivalist program thus entailed not just the elimination of spiritual intermediaries altogether but also the introduction of scripture-oriented formal education (including advanced studies in law and theology), the training of qadis to administer genuine shari^{c}a law (according to the Maliki madhhab), and practical instruction in agriculture (accompanied by a strong dose of the work ethic). The Sanusiyya thus acted among its bedouin adherents not only as a substitute for central political authority but also as a conveyor of a full array of urban values, including scriptural literacy and sedentary agriculture. It also addressed itself to the question of adapting Islam to "modern" conditions by advocating a return to ijtihad.

Technological Reform Movements

Shari^{c}a-minded Islamic revivalism as a response to internal decay and external pressure, although representing a resurgence of urban middle-class religious institutions and values over popular-rural ones, nevertheless seemed to take root and to flourish in areas where both central governmental authority and cosmopolitan urban civilization were poorly developed. In such urban centers as Istanbul, Cairo, Baghdad, and Tunis, where comparatively strong central governments were able to seize and to retain for themselves the self-strengthening initiative, the "Islamic" response to internal decay and foreign aggression tended to be less "Islamic" in character than it was "technological" or even just "military." Indeed, the bureaucrats and generals of the Ottoman Empire and of certain semi-autonomous "Arab provinces" were interested, as a rule, not so much in calling the believers to repentance as in making their armies powerful in order to deter their enemies and to secure their territories. Even so, there occurred an introductory phase of "backward-looking reforms" before the military officers and technocrats began to advocate the progressive step of borrowing the new weapons and methods of the European nations.

"Traditional" and "Transitional" Ottoman Reforms. Ottoman rulers Osman II (1618-22) and especially Murad IV (1623-40) viewed with concern such trends as the decreasing stature of the sultanate, the growing power of the increasingly corrupt bureaucratic "households," the tendency for sipahi-s and janissaries to interfere in politics while neglecting their military duties, and the appearance of vagabondage in the cities along with the rise of banditry in the countryside. Taking it for granted that Ottoman institutions were inherently superior to any others in theory, seventeenth-century "reformers" like Murad IV and the Albanian KOPRULU FAMILY (four members of which dominated the Grand Vizirate during 1656-91) attributed the Empire's problems to deviations from the procedures followed before the death of Sulayman

Distribution of Islamic Revivalist

Movements, 1750-1890

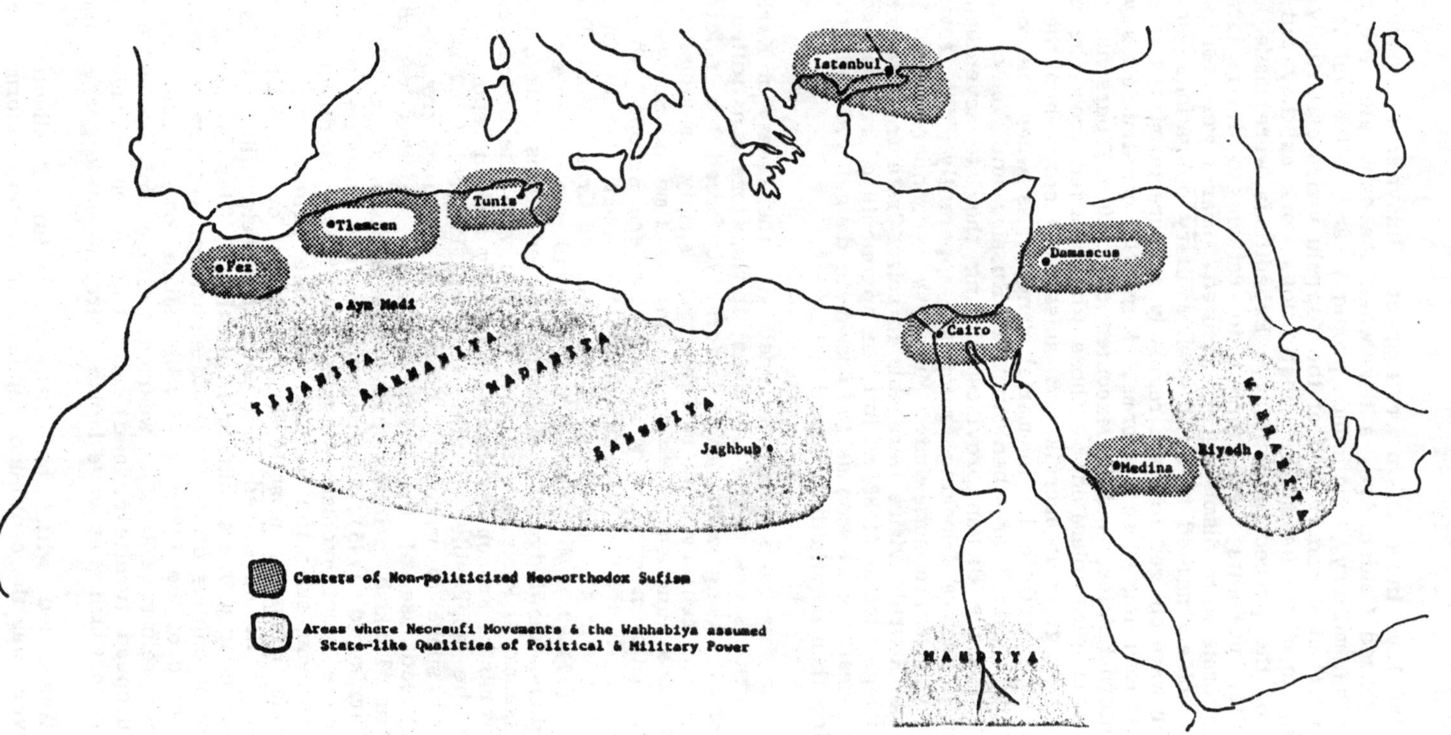

(d. 1566). Indeed, in retrospect Sulayman's epoch became a romanticized Golden Age, a time when the sultanate, the bureaucracy, and the military functioned properly and effectively. Thus, the "reforms" of Murad IV and of the Koprulu vizirs essentially consisted in trying to make the empire's institutions work as they did in the first half of the preceding century. Expeditions were made against rural bandits, peasants were forced to return to their farms, corrupt bureaucrats were dismissed or executed, timar-s were confiscated unless their holders agreed to fulfill their military obligations, and janissaries either were obliged to train regularly or were dismissed from the corps. In implementing these "reforms," Murad IV constructed a vast network of internal spies, and he executed over 20,000 persons. Such harsh measures were tolerated by those who profited from the conditions of decline (e.g., bureaucrats and janissaries) only when the Empire as a whole appeared to be in mortal danger, as when the Safavis seized Baghdad in 1623 or when Austria, Russia, and Venice threatened to overwhelm the Balkan provinces during the late seventeenth century. These "backward-looking reforms" apparently did revive Ottoman military strength somewhat. Murad IV reconquered Baghdad in 1639; and the Koprulu vizirs were able to seize Crete from Venice (1669) and to besiege Vienna (1683). But the opponents of reform overturned the harsh measures as soon as the immediate danger receded; the pattern of decline then inevitably resumed.

The disastrous war that ended with the Treaty of Karlowitz (1699) was a great shock to the Ottomans; it therefore constitutes a watershed of sorts. Along with other factors, it forced the reformers of the eighteenth century to realize that simply making the Empire's institutions function as they did in the time of Sulayman would not restore Ottoman supremacy vis-à-vis modern Europe, which had moved as far or further in the direction of strength as the Ottoman Empire had moved in the direction of weakness. Grand Vizir Damat Ibrahim Pasha (1718-30) was among the first to see the need for obtaining first-hand knowledge of the Western nation states. He sent an Ottoman ambassador to Paris, instructing him "to visit the fortresses, factories, and works of French civilization generally and to report on those which might be applicable [in the Ottoman Empire]." The ambassador's reports spoke of military schools and training grounds and of the widespread use of the printing press. In this regard, the first Ottoman Turkish printing press was introduced in 1715 by Ibrahim Mutefarrika (d. 1745), an Hungarian convert to Islam, who proceeded to publish a twenty-volume encyclopedia as well as numerous translations of European scientific works. He also printed his own book, Usul al-hikam fi nizam al-umam ("Rational Bases for the Policies of Nations"), in which he advocated borrowing the scientific methods of modern Europe along with its military institutions. This Ottoman "discovery" of European culture during the mid-eighteenth century is sometimes called the period of the TULIP REFORMS, since some of the more enthusiastic Ottoman reformers took to wearing Western clothing, importing articles of European furniture, and cultivating formal gardens (with lots of tulips) in which they gave lavish, European-style garden parties.

Associated with this Ottoman cultural-intellectual renaissance, however, was the continued emphasis on military reforms. Such sultans as Mahmud I (1730-54), Abdulhamid I (1774-89), and especially SELIM III (1789-1807) invited European technical advisers to assist them in their efforts to "modernize" the Ottoman military establishment. Each sultan labored to update the old corps of sipahi-s and janissaries, mainly by resorting to the methods of Murad IV--i.e., eliminating soldiers who could not or would not submit to regular discipline. But they also equipped the troops with improved rifles and arranged for them to receive instruction in the tactics of modern warfare from the Western advisers who staffed the officers' training and engineering schools that appeared during the eighteenth century. These schools were periodically closed because of the soldiers' hostility to the reforms, a continuing problem which eventually provoked Selim III to create a wholly new military system: AL-NIZAM AL-JADID (the New Order). Drawn from the Turkish peasantry of Anatolia, the New Corps' recruits were trained and armed in the European style. The officers' school and the engineering school were reopened, and supportive industries--e.g., cannon foundry, rifle works, etc.--were established or expanded. By 1806 the new army had over 24,000 men and officers.

The janissaries perceived the nizām al-jadīd as a threat to their own vested interests, however; and, supported by the ulama and the madrasa students who tended to view the Europe-inspired reforms as heretical innovations, they provoked an uprising which deposed Selim III in May 1807. The nizām al-jadīd corps and most of the other new institutions were abolished. Selim III proved himself a "transitional reformer" (i.e, combining some new ideas with many old ones) not only because he concentrated upon strengthening his military establishment but also because he and his advisors apparently never appreciated the extent to which Europe's technological breakthroughs resulted from the economic and social revolutions which had been going on since the Renaissance. Their piecemeal reforms dealing with the Empire's socio-economic problems thus aimed more at suppressing their symptoms than at changing their root causes. For example, coffeehouses were closed to discourage urban vagrancy, while peasants were compelled to return to their villages; and, in order to balance the rapidly increasing budget, Selim III resorted to such practices as devaluating the currency, confiscating the property of wealthy merchants, and raising taxes.

The Reforms of Muhammad Ali Pasha (1805-48). In the context of the Ottoman Empire's fragmentation into semi-autonomous principalities, Muhammad Ali appeared as a typical military adventurer. In the present context of technological reforms, however, he can be characterized as the most ambitious modernizer to date. In this role he undoubtedly drew inspiration from the efforts of Selim III, but he went beyond them in both military and non-military innovations. Even though many of his projects were abandoned shortly after his death or in some cases even before it, Muhammad Ali richly deserves the title of "the father of modern Egypt." Like the Ottoman "transitional reformers," the Pasha of Egypt fixed as his highest priority the creation of a strong military establishment as a means to the end of securing and expanding his own power base. After attempts to modernize his own Albanian regiment proved unsatisfactory, about 1820 Muhammad Ali decided to establish a completely new military system modeled on Selim III's nizam al-jadid and even called by the same name. In order to train a modern officer corps, he built in Aswan a military academy which he staffed with French advisers. The first group of future officers to receive formal instruction as the ASWAN MILITARY ACADEMY was drawn from Muhammad Ali's own coteri of Turkish-speaking soldiers, in whom he continued to see inherited qualities of combativeness and leadership. The recruitment of ordinary troops proved to be a more difficult problem. Viewing mamluks procured on a large scale in the traditional manner as potentially disloyal and initially disdaining the military abilities of the Egyptian fellahin, Muhammad Ali embarked upon the CONQUEST OF THE SUDAN during 1820-22 in order to conscript for his army some 30,000 Sudanese, many of whom soon died as a result of their being unaccustomed to Egypt's climate and diseases. Although it extended Muhammad Ali's domain up the Nile Valley, the Sudanese adventure thus proved unsuccessful with respect to its main objective of securing a productive source of recruits for the New Army's rank and file. The Pasha was consequently obliged to conscript Egyptian peasants after all.

Muhammad Ali's New Army proved its worth in action during the 1820s on behalf of the Ottoman Sultan against the rebellious Greeks and during the 1830s against the Sultan himself in Anatolia and Syria. Like his predecessor Selim III and his contemporary Mahmud II, Muhammad Ali made the creation of a strong military establishment the basis for most of the other reforms he undertook. For example, the considerable effort to create local industries, or to expand those established by the French during 1798-1801, aimed in large part at fulfilling military needs. Egypt's first heavy industry thus consisted mainly in cannon foundries and shipyards. The textile and tanning factories were greatly expanded in part to produce the uniforms and the boots required by the soldiers. Improved sugar refineries and flour mills were seen as components of a system of military food supply. And even the initial effort in educational reform, the medical school headed by the French physician-historian Clot Bey, was undertaken originally as a means of furnishing the armed forces with doctors and auxiliary medical staff. Most of Muhammad Ali's modernizing schemes can thus be seen as corollaries to his new military establishment.

Yet Muhammad Ali understood better than the Ottoman "transitional reformers" the relationship between an effective military on the one hand and a strong economy and an integrated society on the other. When contrasted with those of Selim III, Muhammad Ali's administrative and socio-economic reforms therefore seem truly revolutionary. In his ADMINISTRATIVE REORGANIZATION OF 1837, for example, he established seven ministries (diwan-s), including Interior, Finance, War, Navy, Education, and Public Works. This European system was adopted not as an end in itself, but rather as a means to the end of strengthening the central government, which had been more or less decentralized during the hegemony of the Mamluk Grandees. Centralization, or monopoly, was also a theme of Muhammad Ali's industrial projects. The massive efforts to develop Egypt's economy during 1811-40 were undertaken not within the context of European notions of free trade but rather within the Pasha's scheme of STATE-CONTROLLED MONOPOLIES. The private textile factories surviving from earlier times were therefore either nationalized or suppressed. Muhammad Ali's monopolistic industrial program also led to the suppression of the traditional craft guilds, as many guild members were absorbed (or coerced) into the new industries. According to some estimates, some 260,000 Egyptians worked in state-controlled industries by 1840. However, industrialization also attracted increasing numbers of European immigrants--mainly Frenchmen, Greeks, and Italians--who tended to perform the skilled labor in addition to dominating such activities as banking and international commerce. Thus, although Muhammad Ali's forced industrialization of Egypt created a new indigenous working class, it perpetuated and consolidated the existing situation wherein the most lucrative entrepreneurial and commercial roles were occupied by non-Egyptians. That situation would not begin to change until the twentieth century.

Muhammad Ali's land and agricultural policies were similarly intended to consolidate the government's authority, to increase its tax revenues, and to enhance its economic self-sufficiency. Having in 1812 taken over all of the properties owned by the defeated Mamluks, the Pasha directed subsequent agrarian reforms against two other groups which between them controlled most of Egypt's agricultural land: _multazim_-s, who had transformed their concessions (_iltizam_-s) into hereditary fiefs, and the ulama, who supervised the extensive agricultural _waqf_-s. By 1820, Muhammad Ali had abolished the _iltizam_-s, confiscated agricultural _waqf_-s, and thereby made himself the country's sole landowner. The tax-farmers and ulama were eliminated as middlemen so that agricultural profits and tax revenues flowed directly into the treasury. At the same time he employed European engineers to repair and to extend the network of irrigation canals in order to bring new land under cultivation. At first, Muhammad Ali redistributed small plots of land to the peasants and to the village headmen. During the 1830s, however, he began to make large-scale land grants to members of his family and to high bureaucratic and military officials. In this respect, the Pasha was merely repeating a traditional procedure whereby the founder of a new dynasty seizes the holdings of the _ancien regime_'s propertied classes and reallocates them to his own supporters. But in Muhammad Ali's case, this traditional procedure was accompanied by the improvement and expansion of irrigation and by the introduction of new crops. Among the new crops introduced by Muhammad Ali was LONG-STAPLE COTTON, which quickly became Egypt's major cash crop. Cotton, along with sugar and other cash crops, became part of Muhammad Ali's system of state monopolies. The government dictated to the farmer the specific crop to be grown each season, purchased it from him at a fixed low price, and then resold it to a foreign exporter at a considerable profit.

The growing need for trained military officers, bureaucrats, and technical experts led Muhammad Ali also to take radical steps in the domain of EDUCATIONAL REFORM. Rather than attempting to modify the existing system of traditional Islamic education (with al-Azhar at the pinnacle) to meet his needs, the Pasha chose to create wholly new educational institutions. In view of the ulama's virtual monopoly over formal learning, the establishment of the Muslim world's first comprehensive, secular, state-controlled educational system was, at least in theory, a revolutionary innovation. One of the first technical institutes was the School of Surveying founded in 1816 to help implement the land reforms. This and other new schools were staffed at first mainly by European teachers but then increasingly by Egyptians educated in Europe. To this end Muhammad Ali sent groups of young Egyptians to Europe for advanced training. Whereas a small group went to Italy about 1813, the EDUCATIONAL MISSIONS PROGRAM began operating on a regular basis in 1826. Between that year and 1847 some 219 Egyptians in nine successive delegations studied in Europe, mainly France.

The imam (prayer-leader) of the first delegation sent to France in 1826 was SHAYKH RIFA^{c}A AL-TAHTAWI, who proved himself a keen student of French history and culture and who came to symbolize the intellectual impact of modern Europe on nineteenth-century Egypt. In this regard, one of the most influential of Muhammad Ali's new educational facilities was the School of Languages, which was established in 1836 under al-Tahtawi's supervision and which offered courses in literature, history, and geography in addition to those in modern languages. In 1841 al-Tahtawi opened a Bureau of Translation attached to his School of Languages, and he personally translated a number of important European philosophical, historical, and scientific works.

Notwithstanding such achievements, Muhammad Ali's new educational system was not, on the whole, an unqualified success. Muslim parents were reluctant to send their children to Europe-inspired schools which they suspected of neglecting religion. Many of the projected facilities--such as a European-style university--were never even created during Muhammad Ali's lifetime; of those which actually did materialize, many were closed shortly after the Pasha's death. Indeed, a number of the industrial projects suffered the same fate. Nevertheless, although falling short of his goals, through his various reforms Muhammad Ali made a profound and lasting impact on Egypt's economy, society, and culture.

Other 19th-century Reform Efforts. During 1816-50 reform-minded rulers also appeared in a couple of other "Arab lands"; meanwhile, at the center of the Ottoman Empire modernizing efforts were resumed and continued for the remainder of the century. A decade or so after he succeeded Selim III in 1808, Ottoman Sultan Mahmud II (1808-39), relying on Prussian assistance, secretly recreated a nizām jadīd army and, in 1826, used it to destroy the janissary corps. The elimination of the chief obstacle to modernization freed the Sultan to introduce additional innovations which he proceeded to do between 1826 and his death in 1839, drawing inspiration from his contemporary Muhammad Ali as well as from his Ottoman predecessors. Like them, Mahmud II emphasized military reforms but also broke some ground in such areas as administration, industry, and education. These areas ultimately displaced military considerations as the chief focus of modernization during the period (1839-70) known as the "Tanzimat reforms," which were directed by Ottoman bureaucrats inspired by their first-hand diplomatic experience in Europe. The government administration was reorganized along Western lines; constitutional measures were introduced to guarantee the equality before the law of all Ottoman subjects, irrespective of religion;[6] new Ottoman penal and commercial law codes were compiled on the model of the Napoleonic and other European legal systems; an economic infrastructure of roads, railway, and telegraph lines were developed; new crops and modern agricultural machinery were introduced; a number of private factories were built with government subsidies; and a modern, state-controlled educational system was established. The avowed purpose of the new schools was to train an elite capable of undertaking more thorough-going reforms in the future. In this regard, although Muhammad Ali was a more successful reformer than Mahmud II, owing in large part to the former's stronger personality and greater ability, cumulative reform efforts in the long run gained a more sustained momentum and ultimately wrought greater transformations in Ottoman Turkey than they did in Egypt. During the 1840s and 1850s, when Muhammad Ali and his successors were backing away from modernization efforts, the men of the Tanzimat kept forging ahead. And they continued to do so for the remainder of the nineteenth century.

Reformers in other breakaway Ottoman provinces included Da'ud Pasha (1816-31) of the Mamluk Pashalik of Baghdad. His modernizing efforts, confined to military considerations, were cut short by the reimposition of direct Ottoman rule. A more extensive reformist movement developed in Tunisia, particularly during the reign of Ahmad Bey (1837-55), who is sometimes depicted as a small-scale counterpart of Mahmud II and Muhammad Ali. Emphasizing military reforms, Ahmad Bey in 1840 established a military academy which he staffed with Italian and French officers. Ancillary industries (e.g., gunpowder factory, rifle works, and cannon foundry) were also created, and the traditional textile and food industries were expanded for military purposes. In addition, Ahmad Bey regularized the administration, faculty and curriculum of the Zaytuna Mosque-university, and in 1846 he issued a decree abolishing slavery. Ahmad Bey's successors were not so enthusiastic about modernization, yet they were pressured by advisors and foreign diplomats into making some significant technological and constitutional changes. For example, a municipal government for the city of Tunis (al-majlis al-baladī) was organized in 1858. Then in 1861 there was promulgated a CONSTITUTION, the first in the "Arab World," guaranteeing religious freedom and legal equality for all citizens as well as in theory transforming Tunisia into a constitutional monarchy complete with a Legislative Assembly and a secular Court of Appeals.

---

[6]These constitutional guarantees were legislated in large part as a result of diplomatic pressure from European powers seeking to improve the condition of Christian communities under Ottoman rule. Particularly as these measures (along with the new secular law codes) were introduced into religiously mixed Syria-Lebanon, they fostered resentment among the Muslims and therefore contributed to the anti-Christian riots of 1850 and 1860.

Although the constitution and the parliamentary institutions created by it were abolished in 1866, they nevertheless contributed to the modernizing efforts which were resumed later in the century by Tunisia's important reformist Prime Minister, Khayr al-Din Pasha.

As the Ottoman Sultans and the semi-autonomous rulers in various Arab provinces undertook the modernization of their military establishments, bureaucracies, educational systems and economies, they forced their societies into increasingly greater contact with Western Europe. By the second half of the nineteenth century, however, Ottoman and "Arab" regimes learned through experience that Europe's interest in the Middle East was not inspired wholly or even primarily by a desire to be of assistance with no strings attached. Rather, it became apparent that the leading European nations, caught up in a fresh wave of empire-building, were eager mainly to further their own economic and strategic interests. This, along with the continued disintegration of the Ottoman Empire, ultimately led to the rise of nationalism among various groups of Ottoman subjects, including the Arabs. European imperialism in Arab lands and nationalist movements among the Arabs are thus the topics of the following two chapters.

CHAPTER TEN

EUROPEAN IMPERIALISM IN THE ARAB LANDS 1830-1914

The major themes discussed in the preceding chapter--the decline and fragmentation of the Ottoman Empire and the various movements for revival and reform--were influenced to a degree by certain developments emanating from Europe. These included, first, the gradual replacement of Europe's medieval economic system of guilds and cottage industries by a modern capitalist system featuring investment banks, large factories, joint stock companies, and world markets; and, secondly, the shifting of the Asian trade from the land routes through the Near East to the deep ocean routes dominated first by Spain and Portugal and then by Holland, England, and France. Thus in Chapter Nine we already encountered, indirectly at least, the question of modern Europe's impact on the Ottoman Empire and the "Arab world." This is a subject deserving more individual attention and closer analysis, however, for the role of modern Europe in the emergence of the contemporary Arab states was just as crucial as was that of Hellenistic civilization in the achievement of the Arab-Islamic synthesis during the Abbasi Golden Age. It is therefore appropriate to devote a full chapter to a discussion of European imperialism in the Arab world. This discussion will include, first, an analysis of the general features and manifestations of modern European imperialism and, secondly, brief accounts of specific examples of European imperialism in North Africa, Egypt, and the Fertile Crescent.

General Features and Manifestations of European Imperialism

Chapter Nine's examples of the European impact on Ottoman decline during 1500-1750 belong to what might be called "the first wave of European imperialism." This first wave was associated with such developments as the voyages of discovery; the slave trade; the establishment by western European countries of colonies in Africa, the Americas, and the Orient; and an economic policy known as mercantilism, which emphasized the importance both of accumulating precious metals and of subordinating individual economic interests to those of the state. This first wave of imperialism ebbed somewhat during the latter half of the eighteenth century, owing to certain events and trends. During the "Great War for the Empire" (1756-1763), for example, France was temporarily knocked out of the shrinking imperialists' club by Great Britain which seized French possessions in North America and the Orient. More importantly, many of the overseas colonies--notably those of England in North America and those of Spain in South America--began to assert their independence from the "mother country," thereby casting doubt on the feasibility of maintaining a worldwide empire over a long period. Finally, industrialists and merchants began to criticize the economic policy of mercantilism which they sought to replace with one inspired by the doctrine of <u>laissez faire</u> or free trade.

Between the publication of Adam Smith's The Wealth of Nations in 1776 and the end of the century, the free trade movement became confident of attaining its objectives: divorcing the economy from the state and allowing entrepreneurs to set the rules of competition without governmental interference.

In this chapter, however, we shall be concerned not with the "first wave of European imperialism" but rather with the "second wave" which began during the nineteenth century and which culminated during 1870-1914 in a period described by some historians as "the age of imperialism." It perhaps needs to be explained why the late nineteenth century was any more "imperial" than earlier periods, in view of the fact that "empires" per se had existed in abundance from the time of ancient Egypt and Rome to the time of the Ottoman state and other "gunpowder empires." European imperialism during the nineteenth century distinguished itself as an historical phenomenon not only quantitatively (i.e., in terms of the sheer number of Europe-centered global empires that emerged and the extent to which these imperial powers dominated world events) but also qualitatively (i.e., in terms of specific institutions and assumptions associated with it). Just as the first wave of European imperialism was symbolized by the voyages of discovery, the slave trade and mercantilism, the second wave had its own institutional and philosophical symbols, including the industrial revolution, monopoly capitalism, and social darwinism. Economic factors were thus central to the second wave of European imperialism, although historians disagree as to whether they were uniquely central. At any rate, the initial section of this chapter will be devoted to a discussion of the economic and non-economic features of the second wave of European imperialism.

Economic and Social Factors

The first of the economic factors associated with nineteenth-century European imperialism was the rapid growth in Europe's demand for raw materials as it became industrialized. Europe's scientific revolution led to important innovations in nearly every aspect of agricultural and industrial technology. Textile manufacturing in England, for example, experienced revolutionary changes and expansion during 1770-1880. Such new spinning devices as the "jenny" and the "mule" vastly increased the supply of yarn, while the flying shuttle and the power loom greatly speeded up the weaving process. The growing use of large and expensive machinery like steam-driven looms made it necessary for weavers and other workers to leave their own "cottage" workshops and to be concentrated in huge textile factories, whose consumption of cotton multiplied twelve times between 1770 and 1880. The transformation and expansion of textile manufacturing influenced and paralleled similar changes in other industries. In transportation, for example, the flood of cheap new products could not be distributed efficiently on the old canals or by other traditional modes of transportation, a problem which was solved by creating a network of railroads using the newly invented steam engine. The need for engines, cars and rails dramatically increased the demand for iron and steel, the production of which was facilitated by the invention of better and larger furnaces. Industrialization thus entailed the need for greater and greater amounts of cotton, iron ore, coal, and other raw materials. Some of these, like iron ore and coal, England and rival industrialized nations possessed in abundance within their own borders. Yet other vital raw materials, like cotton and rubber, had to be purchased abroad from lands with warmer climates. The nearly insatiable demand of their new factories for raw materials was thus one reason why the European powers began during the nineteenth century to look for new colonies and spheres of influence.

Paired with industrial Europe's increased demand for raw materials was her search for new markets. The more abundant and cheaper cloth, along with many other mass-produced manufactured goods, became available not only to the domestic market (i.e., Englishmen, in the case of English goods, or Frenchmen, in the case of French goods), but also to countless foreign customers, including those in such civilized yet non-industrialized areas as the Ottoman empire and its breakaway Arab provinces. Although "opening up" an Asian or African country to their commerce was invariably a major early objective of the imperial states, these states were not always satisfied with just receiving the privilege of selling their goods alongside each other. In each non-industrialized country, every industrialized power would aim and press for the dominant economic and diplomatic position until, as often as not, one achieved it. Thereafter, that particular country was considered to be the more or less exclusive "sphere of influence"--perhaps even the colony--of one European power, which used it both as a source for the raw materials it needed and as an outlet for its manufactured goods. Imperialism thus became resurgent during the nineteenth century in part because overseas colonies held this dual attraction for industrialized states.

The process of acquiring and of using colonies as privileged sources of raw materials and as privileged markets for manufactured goods does not seem entirely consistent with doctrinaire notions of free trade. Indeed, the resurgence of imperialism was accompanied by a gradual but perceptible moving away from the free trade ideal. There was more to this than the tendency for industrialized nations to introduce high tariffs as a means of protecting their own industries against foreign competitors. During the second half of the nineteenth century the state and the economy tended increasingly to use each other for their own purposes. Many entrepreneurs no longer insisted that the government's interest in the economy be restricted, for they recognized that the state was at once their best customer at home and their best protector abroad. Conversely, the governments of imperial states regularly perceived their citizens who engaged in foreign commerce as "advance men," and they frequently employed economic issues as means towards more purely political ends. Nineteenth-century imperialism thus entailed a closer and a more cooperative relationship between the state and the economy than advocated by laissez faire doctrines.

Another symbiosis was occurring within the European economy itself, as banking, industrial and mercantile interests began to form huge conglomerates which effectively controlled whole segments of the world market. A number of historians thus closely associate the "age of imperialism" with the emergence of a system of "monopoly capitalism." In contrast to the earlier "laissez-faire capitalism," which featured more or less free competition, later "monopoly capitalism" was characterized by giant firms and cartels which, often in cooperation with the state, sought to regulate and to dominate certain economic patterns first in the nation and then in the nation's world empire. Some of the best examples of the intimate cooperation between imperialist governments and big businesses can be found in such war-related industries as armaments and shipbuilding. The names of Krupp (Germany) and Vickers-Armstrong (Britain), for example, became economic symbols of the "age of imperialism." During the 1870-1914 period, European monopoly capitalism thus entered into a mutually beneficial relationship with the nation state in order to secure foreign sources of raw materials and foreign outlets for finished products.

To their own colonies and other overseas lands the industrialized states exported more than manufactured goods; they also exported more than capital investments. Since the "home market" could efficiently absorb only so many new railroads and factories, entrepreneurs sought to keep their money active by investing it abroad. By the nineteenth century most European banks had departments or subsidiaries which specialized in foreign investments and whose activities were initially concentrated in America. Between 1840 and the American Civil War (1861-65), however, European investors became increasingly interested in certain Near and Far Eastern countries. Along with this trend there emerged new kinds of investment companies like France's Credit Mobilier, many of which (like the old joint stock company) were open to small investors. In London alone there existed by 1865 nearly fifty finance corporations, two-thirds of which specialized in colonial and foreign enterprise. For their part, too, sovereigns in the Ottoman Empire and in various "Arab lands" were frequently eager to receive European investments in part as a means of rapidly "modernizing" their countries via the development of an infrastructure of roads, railways, canals, and port facilities.

The middle and late nineteenth century, the second wave of imperialism, therefore became an age associated with the quest for and the granting of huge economic concessions. From the borrower's viewpoint, however, the investment boom contained certain risks, and not all of these were purely financial. The loans provided by European banks were frequently guaranteed by the governments of European states, which often approved or even suggested the transactions and then reserved the right of intervention in the event of default. This danger was compounded by the tendency for some European investors to be as unscrupulous as certain Near Eastern or North African sovereigns were naive and hasty. As we shall see, loans and concessions played a major role in the process whereby Egypt, Tunisia, and other "Arab countries" went bankrupt and then fell under direct European domination.

The export of manufactured goods and of capital investments from industrialized European states to foreign lands and colonies was accompanied by a steady outflow of European merchants and settlers. Among the "push factors" of this outburst of European emigration was a rapid population increase at home, as indicated in the following graph:

	Britain	Russia	France	Germany	Italy
1776		29*			
1800-1	10.9		27.3	24.5	18.1
1830-1	16.5		31.9	29.6	
1850-1	20.9		35.8	35.4	23
1858		67			
1870-1	26.2		36.1	40.9	26.6
1897		129			
1900-1	37		39	56.4	32.4
1910-1	40.8		39.2		34.8
1914		142		67.8	

*Millions of inhabitants

Among the "pull factors" was the prospect of cheap land and quick wealth in the boom conditions then existing in imperial colonies or in other foreign countries. A majority of Europe's emigrants, like its capital investments, went to North America but a consistent and increasing amount went elsewhere, including such "Arab" commercial centers as Tangiers, Algiers, Tunis, Alexandria, Cairo, Beirut, and Aden.

More than their counterparts in full-fledged colonies, European merchants and settlers in lands theoretically still under Ottoman sovereignty tended to resort to pressure and subterfuge in order to secure for themselves a privileged economic and legal status. Among their most effective tools in this regard were the Capitulations. Capitulatory privileges--exemption from the jurisdiction of Islamic law and from Ottoman taxes along with fixed low customs duties on imports and exports--had been freely extended by early Ottoman sultans to European merchants as a means of fostering commercial relations with Western kingdoms. When Sulayman the Magnificent (1521-66) signed a treaty of capitulations with French king Francis I (1515-47) in 1536, he was acting from a position of strength rather than of weakness. With regard to legal jurisdiction, moreover, it was entirely consistent with the millet system for litigation between Europeans to be settled in consular courts rather than in sharīʿa courts.

During the nineteenth century, however, the capitulations began to reflect the changed power relationships. On behalf of their merchants, Western governments were now able to demand even lower customs barriers. In 1838, for example, England pressured the Ottoman government into signing a commercial treaty which restricted duties to 5 percent on British goods imported into Ottoman territories and 12 percent on goods exported from it and which also abolished all state monopolies on exports. The Anglo-Ottoman Commercial Convention of 1838 was designed to protect rising British commercial interests, as the value of British goods entering the Ottoman Empire rose from about 500,000 pounds sterling in 1827 to 2,210,000 in 1845. Expectedly, within a year the same privileges were extended to French and Dutch merchants. The capitulations in effect gave European merchants the same rights in the import-export trade as those enjoyed by domestic merchants, although the latter had to pay local taxes while the former did not. That difference, along with other factors, acted to concentrate Ottoman commerce into European hands.

A related trend was for commercially ambitious Ottoman subjects--notably members of religious minority groups that were "protected" by one or another of the great powers--to push their protected status to the point of claiming the nationality of their European patron. Thus did many Greek, Jewish, Armenian and Levantine families, while never leaving the Near East, escape Ottoman taxation and legal jurisdiction and thereby contribute to the abuse of the protégé system. For, as the Ottoman state became weaker and more fearful and the Western nations became stronger and bolder, Europeans and their protégés claimed, with a good deal of success, that only their nations' consuls had effective legal jurisdiction over them.

Political and Cultural Factors

Most political and cultural aspects of the second wave of imperialism were related to the maturing of national consciousness in Europe and to its extension, beyond national boundaries, into international relations. Defined most simply, nationalism entails the strong belief among a large group of people, who usually inhabit a definable homeland and share a common language and historical experience, (a) that they constitute a "nation" distinct from others and (b) that the nation is more deserving of their loyalty than any other institution or concept. Nationalism is often expressed politically in the desire for national self-determination: the insistence upon ending or preventing foreign domination. It is expressed culturally in a feeling of the uniqueness and, frequently, the superiority and/or the purity of the nation's heritage, including its language, history, literature, and customs. Although manifestations of a rudimentary national consciousness can be detected in almost every historical period, before the late eighteenth century nationalism was overshadowed in Europe as elsewhere by other identities and loyalties, notably religious ones. But, beginning in France about the time of the Revolution of 1789, nationalism emerged during the nineteenth century as the dominant ideological force, growing stronger among ordinary people with the spread of popular governmental institutions. In some respects, the second wave of imperialism represented the spilling over of nationalism into the international arena.

Accompanying the maturation of national consciousness in Europe was the emergence of the consolidated nation state as the pre-eminent political unit. Perhaps the best examples of this process of emergence can be found in the birth, during the mid-nineteenth century, of the Italian and the German national states. While these new nations would eventually enter the imperialists' club, the main imperial rivals at mid-century were Great Britain and Russia, shortly to be joined by France which moved to construct a new overseas empire based on possessions in North and West Africa and in Indochina. From a purely political vista, then, the intense quest by the nineteenth-century superpowers for colonial possessions and spheres of influence was, like the arms race of their twentieth-century counterparts, a means to the end of seating themselves at the "top table" in world affairs. Imperial superpowers sought to dominate weaker neighboring countries via "pan" movements and ideologies, each power acting as the chief patron for a group of peoples presumed, on the basis of language affiliation, to be related to each other. Russia was the dominant force in the pan-Slav movement, for example, while France tried to launch and to lead a pan-Latin movement. Yet a more important vehicle for imperial domination than the "pan" movement was the overseas colonial empire, in which an industrialized European nation played the role of a "mother country" to subjugated peoples of Africa and Asia.

European "mother countries" dominated their respective colonies not just economically and politically but also culturally, for the expansion of Europe was supported and fueled not by investors and bureaucrats alone but also by explorers, historians, social scientists, and poets. European geographical societies cooperated closely with the political and economic leaders of imperial states, for example, and nearly every major geographer-explorer of the nineteenth century carried out political assignments as well as scholarly research. The cultural-academic dimension of imperialism can perhaps be summarized by discussing two major sets of attitudes which rivaled each other in the press and in the intellectual circles of late nineteenth-century Europe. One of these has been labelled "social darwinism," for it pictured the relationships between the super powers, as well as between "mother countries" and colonies, within the context of an evolutionary struggle for survival and domination among the various races of men. Social darwinism thus gave birth to such notions as the inherent superiority of white race. Nineteenth-century racism, now popularly associated with such dilettantes as Chamberlain and de Gobineau, was supported at the time by a number of serious pioneering anthropologists and sociologists. Historians too were known to construct their narratives, notably on "national history," around the themes of race and evolution. In The Origins and Destiny of Imperial Britain (London, 1915), for example, Oxford historian J. A. Cramb depicted the British Empire as the "crowning achievement of the Teutonic race." French historians made comparable claims for the French empire as did the German historians for the budding German empire. Conversely, when recounting the past of their colonial subjects, some European historians tended to portray such peoples as the Indians or the "Arabs" as lacking both a significant cultural heritage and an inherent capacity for self-government. The French claimed that their North African subjects possessed a "colonisable" mentality. The social darwinians thus tended to see their own nation not just as a mother country but also as a master race.

Another significant attitude among imperialists, which was not necessarily incompatible with social darwinism but which frequently did criticize its excesses, might be called liberal or humanist imperialism. Humanist imperialists tended to see their nation's colonial subjects not so much as inevitable victims of the evolutionary process but as potential beneficiaries of the advanced civilization possessed and proffered by themselves. Poets like Rudyard Kipling reminded his countrymen that noblesse oblige ("nobility obliges"--i.e., that the fortunate and the well born have certain responsibilities toward the less privileged), which was essentially the message of his famous poem about "The White Man's Burden": "Take up the White Man's Burden, send forth the best ye breed/Go bind your sons to exile, to serve your captive's need." In this regard, Lord Curzon expressed the view, widely held among Englishmen, that history had never produced a better instrument for accomplishing good than the British Empire. French liberal imperialists likewise believed that their nation's culture was the best gift they could offer to the less advanced peoples of the earth. A French slogan equivalent to "the White Man's Burden" was la mission civilisatrice ("the civilizing mission"), frequently used to justify the acquisition of new territories in Africa and Asia.

Related to humanist cultural imperialism was the activity of Christian missionary societies. While missionaries ultimately had different objectives than merchants and politicians and while they often clashed with white colonists (especially those subscribing to social darwinism), they nevertheless appreciated the protection of their powerful governments whose direct intervention they frequently advocated. Indeed, the European states' adoption of Christian groups in non-Christian countries as "protected minorities," a practice begun during the eighteenth century, had established a common interest in overseas expansion between churches or missionary societies on the one hand and governments on the other. The partnership continued during the nineteenth century. Even the anti-clerical French Government of the Second Empire cooperated with the Roman Catholic Church, via such missionary orders as the White Fathers of Cardinal Lavigerie, in spreading Christian and French influence in Africa and the Near East. Cooperation between Protestant churches and governments was even closer. The acquisition of every new colony or sphere of influence by the nation state was seen as advancing the cause of world Protestantism by missionary groups in Britain, America and Germany, where some spoke of an "evangelical empire." As means to the end of preaching the Gospel, missionaries in North Africa and the Near East used education and philanthropy, establishing hundreds of mission schools, health clinics, and orphanages. The souls they attracted were introduced to European culture as well as to Christ.

Priests and missionaries, as well as explorers and merchants, thus frequently acted as "advance men" for imperial states. Indeed, clashes between rival religious groupings often represented one level of the intense competition between expansionist European nations. This is perhaps best illustrated by the Crimean War (1854-56), in which disagreements between Roman Catholic and Eastern Orthodox priests in the Holy Land triggered a military conflict over long standing differences of opinion about the "Eastern Question." According to Russian propaganda, it was the task of the Tsarist Empire to protect and even to liberate the Orthodox Christians suffering under the rule of the weakened and corrupt Ottoman state. (In essence, what the European powers should do with the huge and vulnerable Ottoman Empire constituted the "Eastern Question.") Yet Russia's imperial rivals, understanding that liberating Balkan Christians meant annexing Ottoman territory, in general opposed Russian ambitions to dismember the Ottoman Empire. Britain in particular insisted upon maintaining Ottoman territorial integrity--at least until after 1878 when it began to appear that she could benefit as much as Russia from a partition of the Sultan's domains.

By that time France had rejoined the imperialists' club, by acquiring a fresh slate of overseas colonies (including Algeria in 1830 and Indochina in 1858), and was challenging Britain's influence in Morocco and the Nile Valley. The intense Franco-British imperial rivalry in Africa and the Near East during the last two decades of the nineteenth century was symbolized by the Fashoda Incident in 1898. The emergence of the consolidated nation state of Germany and its rapid ascent as a European and a world power, however, obliged Britain, France and Russia to moderate their traditional rivalries and to effect a mutual rapprochement for their common security. In the Anglo-French "Entente Cordiale" of 1904, by which France agreed to recognize Egypt and the rest of the Nile Valley as a British sphere of influence in return for a free hand in Morocco, the two maritime powers in effect settled their main outstanding differences in order to stand together against the more serious German threat. As a means of advancing her own interests, meanwhile, Germany occupied a position recently abandoned by Great Britain--that of being the ally and patron of Ottoman Turkey, whose government was seized during 1907-09 by the "Young Turks." This pattern of alliances--Britain, France, and Russia against Germany and Turkey--was that which came to the fore in World War I, a culmination of sorts of the age of imperialism.

Specific Examples of European Imperialism in Arabic-Speaking Lands

The French in Algeria

The announced reason for the French occupation of Algeria in 1830 was to put an end to piracy and slavery in the Mediterranean since the Deylicate of Algiers had continued to rely on privateering as a source of revenue well after most other North African and European ports had virtually given up the practice. The more important reasons, however, were not announced at the time. Among these was, first, the attempt by the regime of Charles X, then in power, to divert popular discontent away from itself and onto the Dey of Algiers. The Dey Husayn had recently wounded France's national pride by slapping with a fly swatter the French Consul, who had become a symbol of European bullying as well as of the abuses of the capitulations. (This diversionary tactic failed, since King Charles X was overthrown anyway, shortly after the Algerian expedition landed, by the July Revolution of 1830.) Secondly, the extension of French control over Algeria, an important grain-growing region, was encouraged by the grain importers and bankers of Marseilles in large part as a means of securing French control over an important source of food and commerce.

Although, when occupying Algiers, the French defeated and deposed the Dey and then suppressed the deylicate altogether, they made no attempt to set up a full colonial apparatus right away. The new regime of Louis Philippe, perhaps not sure what to do next with the result of Charles X's diversionary tactic, simply left matters in the hands of the military commanders. France's official Algerian policy, at least for a few years, was that of "limited occupation." That is, the French instituted direct (military) rule only in the coastal region already secured and meanwhile tried to set up, in the mountainous and desert hinterland, cooperative local amirs who would govern more or less on France's behalf. One local sovereign who with French support came to power in Western Algeria was the Amir Abd al-Qadir, who soon emerged as the leader of an important native movement to resist the French occupation. Abd al-Qadir's twelve-year struggle did not represent fully mature "Algerian nationalism" but rather what some scholars have called "primary resistance." His followers consisted mainly of tribesmen and/or ikhwān (members of popular religious brotherhoods), who, having little or no sense of an "Algerian nation," considered themselves defenders of their tribal lands and of their religion. During 1834-42 the French military commander sought to defeat Abd al-Qadir by destroying the crops and seizing the land of his supporters and sympathizers. Onto the confiscated lands were then introduced a number of French settlers (colons). By the time of Abd al-Qadir's defeat in 1847, France had thus abandoned the "limited occupation" policy for one entailing a more thorough and more permanent dominion over the entire country. To this end, the confiscation of native property continued; and in 1846 the French minister of war adopted as a formal policy the practice of "pushing back the Arabs" from the best agricultural lands.

The emergence of "French Algeria," however, was accompanied by a fierce debate between the liberal politicians based in Paris and the French colons (settlers) resident in Algeria. The debate focused on such issues as land ownership, education for Muslims, and the status of Algeria vis-à-vis France. Among the agencies controlled by the liberals, who wanted the military government to restrain the colons in their quest for land, were the bureaux arabes ("Arab Offices"). These were staffed by French officers who combined the functions of anthropology with that of local administration and who frequently exhibited an attitude of benevolent despotism. That is, many of them, although sometimes resorting to brutal methods, saw it as their task to "civilize" the inhabitants of Algeria, whom they typically considered to be backward and fanatical, by introducing them to literacy, modern hygiene, and more efficient agricultural methods. The liberals, who tended to be "humanist imperialists," encouraged a policy known as "assimilation": the integration of the Muslim Algerians into the mainstream of French life and culture. For a time, the best champion of the assimilation policy and of the liberals' "civilizing mission" was Napoleon III, Emperor of France during 1852-70. Proclaiming Algeria not a mere colony but his royaume arabe ("Arab kingdom"), he said that "the natives, like the colons, have a right to my protection" and "I am just as much Emperor of the Arabs as I am Emperor of the French." He instructed French officials in Algeria to convince the Arabs that "we are not here to despoil them, but to bring them the benefits of civilization." Napoleon III encouraged Roman Catholic missionary societies as well as his own government to establish educational facilities by means of which Algerian Muslims could assimilate, and become assimilated by, French culture; and his land policy for a time equated the collective use of land by tribes with tribal ownership.

The land and education policies advocated for Algeria by the Paris-based liberals were resented and opposed by the French settlers actually residing there. In 1870-71 the German invasion of France swept Napoleon III off the throne and emboldened Eastern Algerian villagers and tribesmen, egged on by agents of the Rahmaniyya brotherhood, to launch an anti-French "rebellion." These two developments eventually played into the hands of the growing body of French colons, who first pointed out that some of the rebellion's leaders had been trained in French schools and then gradually consolidated their influence over French policy in Algeria. Liberals in Paris warned that a civilian regime dominated by colons, who tended to be social darwinians, would be even worse than the old military government. As early as 1863 a liberal deputy compained "Already their [the colons'] newspapers in Algeria were filled with pseudo-scientific nonsense which urged the extermination of what they regarded as inferior races." Yet between 1870 and the end of the century, the colons successfully repudiated the liberals' policy of assimilation and began to implement a program of their own. The essence of this program consisted of accelerating the acquisition of Algeria's best agricultural land and of "pushing back the Arabs" to make room for increasing numbers of settlers arriving from France. But it also included a sort of apartheid relationship between colons and indigènes (natives). Schools became strictly segregated; the regular primary and secondary schools as a rule were restricted to European children, while a few vocational schools were opened for Algerians.

It was also in 1870 that Algeria was formally annexed to France; and, by the end of the nineteenth century, a fully developed colonial apparatus had come into existence there. To give the appearance of local participation in and support for the French regime, certain Algerian elites were indulged and co-opted, most notably the fils des grades tentes (notables' sons) in the Kabyle (Berber-speaking) region of Eastern Algeria and the Tijaniyya brotherhood which had opposed Abd al-Qadir. Given better than average opportunities in education and employment, these sons of notables tended to embrace French culture and then to occupy such positions as clerks, translators, school monitors, and foremen. The French referred to them as évolués (those who have evolved or progressed); much later, Algerians would refer to them as beni oui oui (roughly, "yes-men"). Indeed, the colonial regime treated the vast majority of Algerians as second-class citizens in their own country. On the political level, although a few évolués were appointed to the deliberative assemblies, all police, taxation, budgetary and decision-making powers were firmly in the hands of the colons. Economically, Frenchmen owned and profited from the many great agricultural plantations and the few large factories. It was mainly as domestics or manual laborers that Algerians participated in the colonial economic system, which was characterized by the expression "French heads, Arab hands." Denied official support and economic resources, the indigenous Islamic and Arabo-Berber culture could not thrive, and many personally ambitious Algerians began to feel that adopting the language and civilization of France was the only route to a successful life.

France's conquest and colonization of Algeria was only the beginning of imperialism in North Africa, all of which fell under European rule by the outbreak of World War I. While the Italians invaded Libya in 1911, the French conquered Tunisia in 1881 and then Morocco in 1912. These last two countries became "protectorates" rather than full-fledged "colonies." That is, unlike the deylicate of Algiers, the Husayni beylicate of Tunis and the Alawi sultanate of Morocco were maintained under the power of France which preferred to avoid the constant friction of "direct rule" by governing their new subjects _through_ the traditional monarchies. France's initial Resident General in Tunis thus indicated in a private correspondence that "in the Tunisian Government the French Government has, for ruling the _indigènes_, an instrument at once strong and meek with which, when it is necessary, we can strike without giving rise to Muslim fanatacism." Otherwise, there emerged in the other Maghribi countries, as in Algeria, a "colonial system": a power structure and an economy controlled by Europeans and a Europe-oriented "official" cultural life. It is true that the French and Italians carried out in North Africa a large number of such costly and complicated engineering projects as roads, railways, and hydro-electric dams and that they introduced a good deal of modern technology, all of which could potentially benefit the indigenous population. Yet, aside from a restricted number of évolués, few North Africans felt that they occupied a meaningful and respectable role in the colonial economy and society.

The British in Egypt

The European occupation of Egypt occurred much later than that of Algeria which, according to the general pattern of nineteenth-century imperialism, was in some respects premature. The Egyptian case, like those of Tunisia and Morocco, was more typical in that it followed a long period of European economic penetration. In this regard, the first European power to stake a claim to Egypt was not Great Britain, whose imperial policy was guided on the one hand by the desire to consolidate her rule over India, the jewel of her empire by the early nineteenth century, and on the other hand by the need for strategically located port facilities to serve the British navy which "ruled the waves." In large part it was this concern to protect the sea route to India which led Britain to seize Aden in 1838 and then to cultivate treaty relationships with the Arab amirs of the Gulf. During the early nineteenth century, however, Britain's concern for the Eastern Mediterranean was minimal. So it was France, stripped of its Atlantic and Oriental possession by Britain in the mid-eighteenth century and thereafter obliged to seek less distant "spheres of influence," which first expressed an acquisitive interest in Egypt. In exchange for woolen cloth and manufactured items, France regularly imported grain from Egypt as it did from Algeria and other

Mediterranean lands. In 1784 a French consul reported that "the French carry on four-eighths of the [Levant] trade, the Dutch two-eighths, and the English and Venetians one-eighth each." It was partly to consolidate France's dominant position in the Levant trade, and not merely to seize a vantage point from which an attack could theoretically be launched against British India, that Napoleon invaded Egypt in 1798. France's paramount economic role in Egypt survived Napoleon's occupation of 1798-1801; and Muhammad Ali turned primarily to France for military and technical assistance.

Yet to an extent it was Muhammad Ali who inadvertently hastened the exposure of Egypt to British imperial interests. Seeking to create a modern and powerful military establishment that required vastly increased government revenues, Muhammad Ali undertook to revolutionize Egypt's essentially agricultural subsistence economy. As detailed in the preceding chapter (see Chapter Ten), he did so by centralizing the systems of landownership and taxation; by embarking on a program of forced industrialization to reduce imports, which entailed the imposition of high tariffs on foreign goods to protect his own fledging industries; by extending the network of canals to bring more land under cultivation; by introducing new cash crops, notably long-staple cotton, to raise much needed hard currency; and by extending the old system of state monopolies, a system which now obliged farmers to plant specified crops to be sold at fixed prices to the government and which confined European merchants to Alexandria where they had to buy at fixed prices from the government. According to economic historian Charles Issawi, these ambitious projects represented an attempt by Muhammad Ali to leap from an agricultural subsistence economy directly to a diversified industrial economy, bypassing the normal intermediate stage of an "export economy" which produces raw materials (frequently a single cash crop) for the world market.

Muhammad Ali's economic revolution proved too ambitious, however; and internal and external factors contributed to its failure. Internally, the state-sponsored programs were seriously mismanaged, in part because their rapid pace and complex character overstrained Egypt's rudimentary and ill-trained bureaucracy. Externally, the pressures of the world (i.e., European) market also worked against the successful creation of a diversified industrial economy in Egypt. These pressures culminated in the Anglo-Ottoman Commercial Treaty of 1838, which applied specifically to Egypt as a consequence of Muhammad Ali's invasion of Syria and Anatolia and the subsequent intervention by the European powers. The 1838 treaty forced tariffs down to token levels, thereby exposing Egypt's new industries to devastating European competition; and it outlawed state monopolies, thereby forcing Muhammad Ali's government out of its middleman's role and permitting European commercial agents to negotiate directly with Egyptian farmers. After 1838 Egypt's industrial revolution went into a condition of retreat. Moreover, although by no means a 100 percent failure, Muhammad Ali's attempted transformation of the old subsistence economy, together with the provisions of the 1838 treaty, in effect "softened up" Egypt for a more speedy and more thorough transition to an "export economy" producing a single cash crop for the world market.

This crucial transition now attracted Great Britain, whose share of the Levant trade was growing steadily. "From the year 1827 to 1830," observed an Englishman in 1833, "our exports have increased from Ŀ531,704 to Ŀ1,139,616." So, as Egypt was effectively "opened" to the world market by Muhammad Ali's reforms and then by the 1838 treaty, Britain came around to buy the major export--long-staple cotton. This revolutionary crop, introduced by a French expert in 1821 had quickly become central to Muhammad Ali's economic revolution. By 1828, Egypt was exporting 225,000 qantars (a qantar = 99.05 lbs) of cotton which generated about Ŀ500,000 in precious hard currency to finance other reforms. The costly extension of the canal system was undertaken by Muhammad Ali largely for the purpose of growing more cotton. The shift from planting subsistence food crops to cotton as a cash crop was a trend that survived the failure of Muhammad Ali's economic revolution, since Egyptian farmers (especially the large landowners) knew of cotton's profitability and were eager to sell directly to European merchants at the high market price rather than to the government at the low fixed price. In this regard, the post-1838 practice of farmers in the Delta borrowing money from European merchants for cotton seed and other expenses represented the first major avenue of European capital investment in Egypt. Multiplying three times during 1840-60, cotton exports grew until constituting nearly one-half of Egypt's total exports. The "cotton famine" created in Britain by the American Civil War (1861-65) accelerated this trend, as Egypt exported over 1,000,000 qantars of cotton in 1863 and 2,000,000 in 1865. The emergence of cotton as the country's major export brought Egypt into an increasingly close relationship with the economy of Britain, the crop's main buyer. By 1860 Egypt had become Britain's sixth most important source of raw materials and its twelfth largest market for manufactured goods. So, by 1865, Egypt was well on its way to being thoroughly integrated into the European economic system as a supplier of raw cotton to England and as a market for British and French products.

As this process of integration advanced, Britain's economic stake and political interest in Egypt grew considerably. In 1838 Egypt's import-export traffic consisted of goods worth LE 3.5 million. This figure rose to LE 5.1 million in 1860 and then leaped to LE 21.8 million in 1880, when cotton sales (mainly to Britain) accounted for 90 percent of the country's exports. Meanwhile, the 1854 land law ended restrictions on the foreign ownership of land; and British capital began to flow into Egypt in the form of mortgages. Egypt's rulers, Said (1854-63) and Ismail (1863-79), welcomed the foreign capital as a means to the same ends pursued by Muhammad Ali: creating a modern state with a diversified economy and making Egypt politically and economically independent from Europe and the Ottoman Empire. Yet, according to economic historian Roger Owen, these efforts "to use European capital to build up a state and an economy strong enough to withstand European pressures only led to increasing dependence on Europe." This happened, first, because the 1838 treaty denied to Egypt any sovereignty over her own tariffs; so Egypt could not effectively shield her economy from that of Europe. Secondly, economic diversification was hampered by the increasing importance of cotton; the strong pressures of the world market simply wouldn't let Egypt move beyond the cotton-producer's role. Thirdly, the "development projects" undertaken by Said and Ismail (e.g., creating a railway system and enlarging the port of Alexandria) were not producers of revenue in their own right but ultimately just facilitated the planting and sale of more cotton. As Issawi noted, "Cotton was the main beneficiary of the government's investment on public works and the magnet drawing private foreign capital to Egypt. All the other sectors of the economy, such as transport, commerce, and finance, had as their main function the moving of the cotton crop." In other words, the attempt by Said and Ismail to modernize and to diversify Egypt's economy via foreign private investments could not swim against the tide of the world market any better than Muhammad Ali's state-controlled effort. Indeed, the 1854-79 period saw Egypt becoming increasingly subordinated to British economic interests.

As if a steady increase in the output of cotton were not enough to bind Egypt's fate to the needs of the British economy, there occurred during 1854-75 two other developments which heightened Britain's acquisitive interest in Egypt. Each new development was related to the ambitious program of public works undertaken by Said and Ismail in order to modernize Egypt with the assistance of European capital and technology. The reigns of Said and Ismail thus became the golden age of loans and concessions. The great public works concessions included some truly colossal projects: enlarging the port of Alexandria, building the Alexandria-Cairo and Cairo-Suez railways and linking Egypt by undersea cable to both Europe and India. Whereas most of these undertakings were financed with British capital, the undisputed queen of the great concessions, the Suez Canal, was not. The idea of a waterway connecting the Red Sea with the Mediterranean was pushed by the French engineer and diplomat Ferdinand de Lesseps, who in 1854 was granted the concession by his friend, Said Pasha. Forming a public company, de Lesseps appealed to small investors, mainly in France. So at first the Suez Canal was not associated with Britain who, indeed, disdained and opposed the scheme. Egypt contributed more than her fair share, however. Much of the canal was dug by slave labor furnished by Said. The concession also obliged Ismail to buy the remaining shares of stock (44 percent of the total) not purchased by the European public. Once the canal was completed, in 1869, Britain could not ignore this short sea route to India. Consequently, when in 1875 the financially hard pressed Ismail put on sale his large block of Suez shares, it was the British Government that brought them. The acquisition of a sizable interest in the Suez Canal Co. increased Britain's already large economic stake in Egypt and added to it a new strategic dimension.

The second development, the purely financial aspect of the loans-and-concessions period, has been succinctly described by Roger Owen:

> Increasing trade with Europe was followed by a rapid growth in the import of capital. During the 1850s the first European banks were established in Alexandria. At the same time the construction of more public works, further modernization of the army and of the bureaucracy, and, above all, the need to finance the great part of de Lessep's Suez

project meant that Government expenditure rapidly began to outstrip current receipts. Said began to borrow heavily from local bankers and merchants, then (perhaps at de Lessep's suggestion) to issue treasury bonds. Finally, in 1862, he obtained his first foreign loan. This was followed by many others until by 1875 Egypt had borrowed a nominal sum of nearly Ŀ100 million from Europe, of which the Treasury had actually obtained no more than Ŀ68 million.

By 1875, in other words, the Egyptian treasury was virtually bankrupt, a situation which threatened the economic interests of the European powers. These now intervened by imposing on Ismail's government two "controllers" (an Englishman, Evelyn Buring, and a Frenchman). This "Dual Control," exercising more or less absolute authority over Egypt's revenues and expenditures, sought to repay the country's foreign loans among other ways by slashing the amount of funds spent on public works and the military. Ismail, angry and frustrated with the impotent role to which he had been reduced by the European powers, tried to lessen the Dual Control's influence by appealing for sympathy and support to the Assembly of Delegates (an Egyptian "parliament" established in 1866) and to the Egyptian people. Britain and France countered by persuading the Ottoman Sultan (technically, still the Egyptian Khedive's sovereign) to depose Ismail and to replace him by his son, Muhammad Tawfiq (1852-95). This effectively took place in July 1879.

Ismail's luckless maneuvers suggest that there occurred during 1875-82 a confrontation between the European powers (notably Great Britain) having economic interests in Egypt and certain elements inside Egypt who were concerned about the foreign influence increasing within their country. In addition to Ismail's own Turco-Circassian ruling class (which was slowly becoming "Egyptianized" during the late nineteenth century), several specific groups participated in this confrontation known as "the First Egyptian National Movement." One grouping consisted of the ulama, Egypt's traditional educated elite, who typically objected to the exercise of authority by non-Muslims in their Islamic society. Other groupings, having emerged to prominence in Egyptian society more recently than the ulama, included (a) the large landowners (especially the cotton-growers), (b) the Egyptian civil servants or "effendi class" (who resented the growing numbers of Europeans being appointed to high positions in the bureaucracy), and (c) the military officers (many of whom the Dual Control had either retired prematurely or put on half pay). Early in 1881 a coalition of these elements, under the leadership of Col. Urabi Pasha, began to exert pressure on Tawfiq to reduce the European influence within his government. Bowing to this campaign of pressure mounted by the nationalists, during the winter of 1881-2 Tawfiq dismissed the British and French controllers and appointed a new "national government" that included Col. Urabi himself as the Under-Secretary for War. These developments alarmed the governments of Britain and France, who were determined to reaffirm both the nominal authority of Tawfiq and the Dual Control's jurisdiction over the Egyptian economy. It was to this end that British warships bombarded Alexandria on 11 July 1882. This show of strength impressed Tawfiq, who quickly accepted asylum on one of the British warships and who then, no doubt with British concurrence, proclaimed Col. Urabi a rebel. For a couple of months, Urabi's "national government" continued to defy Tawfiq as well as the European powers; but the British invasion during August and September 1882 ended Egypt's "First National Movement" and inaugurated seventy-two years of British occupation.

The British invasion in 1882 thus represented the culmination rather than the beginning of the impact exerted on Egypt by the second wave of European imperialism. In a sense the British occupation merely put the final touches on a "colonial system" that had been emerging in Egypt for a long time--through grain exports to France and cotton exports to Britain, through the Anglo-Ottoman Commercial Treaty of 1838 and the Land Law of 1854, through the Suez Canal and other public works projects, and through the massive borrowing of money and technology from Europe. After 1882, power in Egypt was firmly in British hands. Although Egypt was not annexed (like Algeria) or even formally made a protectorate (like Tunisia and Morocco), the British Ambassador (the first being Evelyn Baring, later known as Lord Cromer) was the country's effective chief executive. "Tawfiq rules Egypt," Cromer was fond of saying, "and I rule Tawfiq." Britain imposed on Egypt what some observes have called a "veiled protectorate." Economically, for all intents and purposes, Egypt was a British colony. Not only because Egypt served as an exclusive source of raw materials (mainly cotton) for British industry and as an exclusive market for British manufactured goods but also because Englishmen (or other Europeans or "protected" non-Muslim minorities) monopolized the upper echelons of Egyptian private enterprise and public affairs. The phrase "British heads, Egyptian hands" was commonly employed to describe the situation in Egypt after 1882.

The Zionists in Palestine

The major European powers expressed more than a casual interest in the Fertile Crescent. By the eighteenth century, for example, France had adopted the Syrian Catholics in general (the Maronites of Lebanon in particular) as their special "protected minority." French patronage of the Maronite-dominated silk and banking industries, which emerged during the nineteenth century in the new port of Beirut, represented just the beginning of France's involvement in Syria in modern times. This involvement, expressed eventually on political and cultural levels as well as on an economic one, would culminate in the proclamation of a French "mandate" over Syria from which Lebanon would then be separated out as a predominately Christian, Europe-oriented state. Prior to these developments which reached their climax after World War I, however, potentially the most significant European penetration of the Fertile Crescent consisted of the settlements established during 1881-1914 in Ottoman Palestine by Zionist Jews coming primarily from Russia.

Some may object to our putting a discussion of Zionist activity in Palestine into a chapter on "European imperialism." As we shall see, the Zionists themselves never perceived their movement as belonging to the pattern of industrialized European nations expanding overseas mainly for the purpose of economic exploitation. Rather, they consistently regarded it as a means to the ends first of liberating themselves from their own oppressed condition and then of finding safety in their "ancient homeland" from subsequent persecution. From the latter point of view, it might be more appropriate to put our discussion of Zionism in the next chapter, which deals with the rise of national consciousness and national liberation movements in the Arab world. Depending on whether one's perspective originates among Europeans or among the "Arabs," however, Zionism can represent a two-sided phenomenon. From the European perspective, it is indeed a national movement--some observers have even referred to it as "European Jewish nationalism"--aiming to solve the problems of identity and status of Jews--ultimately all Jews but primarily at first those residing in Europe. From the Arab perspective, however, Zionist settlers were not perceptibly different from the many others who came to the Levant from Europe. Of course, the Zionists did differ from them in some rather fundamental ways. Yet in some other ways their objectives and tactics resembled those of the British or the French imperialists. Although a work on "Arab history" must necessarily view Zionism from the second perspective, it perhaps ought not to lose sight altogether of the first.

Upheavals like the Crusades, the Inquisition, the Protestant Reformation and the rise of the national monarchies were among the factors which caused the Jews to be distributed very unevenly throughout Europe by the end of the eighteenth century. Virtually non-existent in Spain and Portugal, Jews were scarce in France and Britain and were only moderately numerous in certain German and Italian principalities. It was in Russia, particularly in the provinces which Russia had seized from Poland, where about 90 percent of Europe's Jews resided. There as elsewhere in Europe, however, the condition of Jews was extremely precarious: feudal institutions and values had barred them from owning property and from practicing certain vocations or professions; ordinarily they were permitted to live only in a specified quarter (the ghetto in Western or Central Europe) or region (the Pale in Eastern Europe); and frequently they served as targets for gratuitous popular ridicule and even violence. To some extent the differences separating Jews from the rest of the population were carefully nurtured by themselves as a means of perpetuating their religious identity. Their habits of dress, their peculiar language (Yiddish, derived from Old German with Slavic influences), and strictly endogomous marriage customs were observed nearly as religiously as their religion itself, with its zeal for studying the Torah and the Talmud, its prayers for Zion (signifying that the Jews were in a condition of "exile" from the land which God had given their fathers and to which He would one day restore their children), and its other ancient rituals. Realizing that tolerance often leads to assimilation and the loss of identity, some Jewish leaders saw persecution as a blessing in disguise. For Europe's Jews, the nineteenth century would bring fresh instances of both tolerance and persecution.

Tolerance was offered to them initially and most liberally in France where the Revolution of 1789 both unleashed a powerful current of egalitarianism and raised French national consciousness to the level where it overwhelmed religious distinctions. Now Protestants as well as Catholics could be loyal French citizens. Eventually, French citizenship was also extended to the Jews. Somewhat reluctantly they accepted it and, in the bargain, gave up a good deal of their separate identity, including their prayers for Zion. That is, the small community of French Jews tried to solve the problems stemming from their condition of differentness and of "exile" by voluntarily assimilating to French culture and nationality. For them Judaism henceforth would merely be the religion they observed on the same basis that French Catholics and Protestants observed their respective religions; politically and culturally, the Jews would regard themselves as true Frenchmen.

This development among the few French Jews had a profound influence among the more numerous German Jews, some of whom now resolved to demonstrate their ability to be "good Germans" as a means to the end of winning social acceptance as well as political and legal rights. The German Jews split bitterly over the issue of assimilating to German culture and nationality, however. Many of them (i.e., the "Orthodox") preferred to retain their traditional customs and their peculiarity rather than giving up their identity as Jews on the slim hope of being treated with justice and respect by the Germans. Others (e.g., the "Reformed" Jews) were willing to take the risk. They made an effort to dress and to talk like other Germans; they even modified their worship service, deleting the prayers for Zion and introducing (on the model of the Protestant Church) sermons, organ music, and congregational singing. The German Reformed Jews succeeded neither as rapidly nor as fully as they had hoped. But they won enough acceptance and enough legal rights to encourage them to keep trying (and to blame their failures on the intransigence of the "Orthodox").

More importantly, the German Reformed Jews achieved enough success to spark a similar reform movement among the huge Jewish population of Russia. Reform-minded Russian Jews made an effort to learn Russian, to dress in the Russian style, and in general to behave like "good Russians" in order to assimilate to Russian culture and nationality. Yet whereas assimilation had proven relatively easy for all French Jews and difficult but possible for many German Jews, it proved virtually impossible for any Russian Jews. Idealogues of Russian nationalism accused Jews of introducing such "foreign" ideas as democracy and socialism, which undermined important Russian institutions like the monarchy and the Orthodox Church. Thus they were identified as undesirable aliens. Jews in Russia not only were barred from assimilating but they began to be persecuted with greater frequency and intensity. As a means of directing popular discontent away from itself, the Czarist government encouraged "pogroms" (mass attacks) against the Jews. The already precarious Jewish situation in Russia thus became even worse during the mid-nineteenth century. In the face of this increasingly intolerable situation the Jews of Russia tended to choose between three different solutions. The quickest solution was to leave Russia and go to more tolerant countries in Western Europe or North America. During 1881-1900, for example, more than 600,000 Russian Jews emigrated to the United States alone. A second, long-range solution entailed acting on the assumption that

Russia's feudal society and monarchy, not the Russian people as such, were responsible for the unjust treatment of Jews and of other disadvantaged elements as well. Many Jews who accepted that assumption tended to become involved in one of the socialist reform movements that were beginning to call for the overthrow of the Czarist regime and the establishment of a new social order.

The third solution available to the Russian Jews was for them to fall back with renewed emphasis on their Jewish identity and to make that heightened identity the basis for a political movement of national liberation. Ironically, it was mainly the reform-minded Jews, those once showing themselves most willing to expunge from Russian Judaism all references to "Zion," who now tended to become "Lovers of Zion," the name taken by these early "Jewish nationalists" or "Zionists." In this regard, unlike Jewish liberation movements in previous centuries which tended to be "messianic," modern Zionism was essentially a secular phenomenon advocating self-deliverance. Among the early spokesmen for the Lovers of Zion was Moses Hess who wrote a book called Rome and Jerusalem (1862) which advocated that, since the Italians were successfully struggling against the tyranny of the Austrians and of the Pope in order to forge themselves into an "Italian nation," the Jews ought to follow their example. Of course, the Jews, unlike the Italians, did not reside together in a "national homeland." Their task, according to the Lovers of Zion, was therefore not that of expelling alien tyrants from their current residence but rather that of "returning" to their ancient home, the land of Israel. Beginning about 1882, therefore, small groups of Zionist "pioneers" started to emigrate from Russia to Palestine with the objective of escaping their unbearable situation in Russia and of creating model settlements in Palestine, which they hoped to make "blossom as the rose." Those who arrived during 1882-1905 were said to have participated in the "First Aliyah" (the first wave of immigration). By the end of the nineteenth century, about twenty Zionist settlements had been established, some in former malaria marshes. Subsidized by the French Jewish banker Edmond de Rothschild, like other European settlers these early Zionists tended to acquire property and to engage in farming, often hiring local "Arabs" to perform some of the routine labor.

In spite of Rothschild's subsidies, the early Zionist settlers in Palestine were irregularly financed; they also lacked a coherent organization and leadership. These would emerge, however, in the wake of France's notorious Dreyfus Affair. On the basis of a forged document, Captain Alfred Dreyfus (an "assimilated" French Jew) had been pronounced guilty by a military court of betraying the French army during the Franco-Prussian War and had been sentenced in 1894 to a life sentence at hard labor. It leaked out that the evidence against Dreyfus had been fabricated, however, and for months the Dreyfus Affair made headlines in French newspapers. As a rule, liberals and socialists argued that Dreyfus had been framed while conservatives (including social darwinians) argued not only that he was guilty but that any Jew, by definition, could not be a true Frenchman and was therefore incapable of being loyal to France. A second trial was held in 1899 and, in spite of overwhelming evidence of Dreyfus' innocence, the military court found him guilty a second time. The President of the

French Republic had to step in and issue a pardon. The scandal of the Dreyfus Affair, along with the accompanying wave of anti-Jewish sentiment, raised serious questions as to whether assimilation had solved--or could ever solve--Europe's "Jewish problem." That at least was the doubt created in the mind of Theodor Herzl, an assimilated German Jew assigned to cover the Dreyfus Affair by his Vienna newspaper. The outpouring of European racism in "enlightened France" soon led Herzl independently to the same conclusion reached earlier by the Russian Zionists--that a sovereign Jewish state was the best solution to the "Jewish problem." This conclusion, along with plans for realizing his ambitious new objective, Herzl proclaimed in his book, The Jewish State: An Attempt at a Modern Solution of the Jewish Question (Vienna, 1896). Herzl then proceeded to organize a series of World Zionist Congresses, the first being held in Basel in 1897. Thereafter, Zionism had a world-wide organization and an international leadership.

However, the Zionist leadership (dominated by Western Jews, like Herzl) soon disagreed with the rank and file Zionists (overwhelmingly from Eastern Europe) as to whether their objective should be pursued mainly through "political" or "practical" means. Herzl and other "political Zionists" insisted that, before proceeding with Jewish immigration into Palestine on a large scale, it was necessary to win both the permission of the Ottoman sultan and the support of the great powers. So Herzl tried to talk to Abdulhamid II and various European statesmen into creating in Palestine for the European Jews a status roughly analogous to that which France had pressured the Sultan into creating for the indigenous Christians in Lebanon. A German by culture, Herzl initially hoped that Germany would sponsor the idea. "The suzerainty of the Porte and the protectorate under Germany surely ought to be adequate legal underpinning," he wrote in The Jewish State. When Germany showed no interest, however, the political Zionists began increasingly to pin their hopes on Britain, which had already advanced its claim to protect the Jews of Palestine, since France was the patron of the Syrian Catholics and Russia the patron of the Greek Orthodox Christians. Future Zionist leader Chaim Weizmann went to England, he later wrote, because he considered it "the one country which seemed likely to show a genuine sympathy for a movement like ours. . . ." Herzl therefore initiated discussions with British Colonial Secretary Joseph Chamberlain about guarantees for Jewish settlement in Palestine or elsewhere. That is, Herzl designated Palestine as the Zionists' overwhelming first choice, but--especially after a new wave of pogroms in Russia during 1903--he and other "political Zionists" were willing to consider other British-held territories, such as Cypress, the Sinai (the "El Arish Plan"), and Uganda. Until his death in 1904, Herzl thus labored to win the backing of one or more of the European powers for a large-scale program of Jewish colonization, preferably in Palestine.

Meanwhile, even though lacking a legal basis, the "practical Zionists" urged the continuation and increase of Jewish immigration to Palestine, which they insisted could be the only acceptable site for their "national homeland." Those arriving after 1905, the year of an abortive socialist revolution in Russia, constituted the Second Aliyah (the second wave of immigration) and tended to be "labor Zionists."

Critical of their predecessors for relying on Arab workers, the labor Zionists pledged to avoid exploiting the labor of others by working on the land themselves. The socialist tendencies of labor Zionism would later be cited by those eager to distinguish Zionism from European imperialism, on the assumption that socialism and imperialism were mutually incompatible in every respect. Yet the practical Zionists (including the socialists) relied heavily on the financial resources raised by the World Zionist Organization's Jewish National Fund, primarily from "bourgeois Jews" in Western Europe and America. They also utilized the Organization's banking and land-purchasing agencies--the Jewish Colonial Trust, the Anglo-Palestine Bank, and the Palestine Jewish Colonization Association--which made no effort to hide their "colonial" character. Indeed, the Hebrew word yishuv, used by the Zionists to refer to the Jewish community in Palestine, literally means "colony." By 1914 the yishuv included about 12,000 Zionists settlers out of a total Jewish population of between 60,000 and 85,000 (the Arab population of Palestine was then approximately 644,000). Consistent with the policy of the "practical Zionists," the yishuv forged ahead not only with immigration and land purchase but also with organizing itself along the lines of a potential state.

Although Palestine was the object of their national aspirations, the Zionist Jews of Europe as a rule had only vague or romanticized conceptions of it. Many of them characterized it as an "empty" wasteland. Before he actually went there, Herzl was fond of describing Palestine as "a land without a people for a people without a land." Not many Jews realized then that Herzl's slogan was only half true--i.e., that Palestine did have a people. One of Herzl's first converts to Zionism, Max Nordau, arrived there in 1897. "But there are Arabs in Palestine," he exclaimed. "I did not know that!" Nor, once making Nordau's discovery, did many Zionists realize that this situation posed any real problems. It is true that a few Western Jews, such as Judge Mayer Sulzburger of the United States, criticized Zionism about this time on grounds that "its intent is to overslaugh [overlook, ignore the claims of] the people who are in Palestine and to deprive them of the rights of self-government. . . ." And even Max Nordau had second thoughts, telling Herzl, "We are committing an injustice!" Yet, on the one hand, most political Zionists were less concerned about the attitudes of the local Arabs than they were about those of the Ottoman Turks, who enjoyed the coveted, internationally recognized title of sovereignty over Palestine. In a purely political sense, they still considered Palestine "empty" in that no "civilized" European people was occupying it. As Herzl proposed in The Jewish State, "We should there form a portion of the rampart of Europe against Asia, an outpost of civilization as opposed to barbarism. . . ."

The practical Zionists, on the other hand, tended to think that a program of massive Jewish colonization in Palestine would benefit the indigenous Arabs economically, through the introduction of capital investments and modern technology, and also culturally. In this regard, a Zionist historian subsequently wrote: "The Jews, by race and origin an eastern people and by experience and skills a part of the west, were exceptionally qualified to bring the stagnant east into the orbit of western civilization . . ." Herzl too, after visiting Palestine and seeing that Arabs did indeed live there in great numbers, assured Nordau and others that the Zionists' program would be implemented in cooperation with the local population who would themselves prosper as a result of their participation and support. It is now easy to see the naiveté in Herzl's expectation that this would occur at all--much less that it would occur peacefully! Yet such an idea was, at the time, perfectly consistent with the thinking of most Europeans, including those harboring feelings of sympathy and benevolence for the native subjects of their nation's overseas colonies. In this regard, insofar as they even acknowledged the existence of the Arabic-speaking inhabitants of Palestine, the Zionists' attitudes toward them resembled those exhibited toward the Algerians by the French liberal or "humanist" imperialists who expected the process of European colonization to bring economic prosperity and cultural advancement for the colonized peoples.

Seen in its best light and from a European perspective, Zionism thus appears as a movement for the national liberation of Europe's Jews, some of whom were influenced by socialism and were initially hopeful of benefitting the "backward" inhabitants of the ancient homeland to which they expected to "return" after centuries of "exile." Seen from the perspective of the Arabic-speaking residents of Palestine, however, it appears as a peculiar variety of European imperialism which, defined most simply, consisted of colonization for the purpose of economic and political domination. It is true that the Zionist refugees from Russia, unlike the French colons in Algeria, did not represent an extension per se of a European mother country/nation state that furnished political and military backing along with economic and cultural sustenance. Yet Zionism was essentially European in its cultural orientation; Zionist settlers did receive economic aid from a Europe-centered organization supported by the contributions of Western Jews; and Britain did begin to play a mother country's political role for the Jewish settlers in Palestine (a rule that soon culminated in the Balfour Declaration during World War I and the Mandate following it). The economic benefit that some Arabs may have derived from Zionist colonization could in no way compensate for the sentiments felt by a people upon observing their homeland being acquired and dominated by another people coming from outside. These were sentiments which, before and after World War I, the residents of Palestine began to feel along with the populations of other Arabic-speaking countries. With the breakdown of the Ottoman Empire and the aggressive penetration of the Arab lands by varieties of European imperialism, groups of "Arabs" started to become conscious of the subjugated or threatened condition of their territories. They then proceeded to organize themselves into national movements intent upon self-liberation.

European Imperialism in Arab Lands, 1830-1936

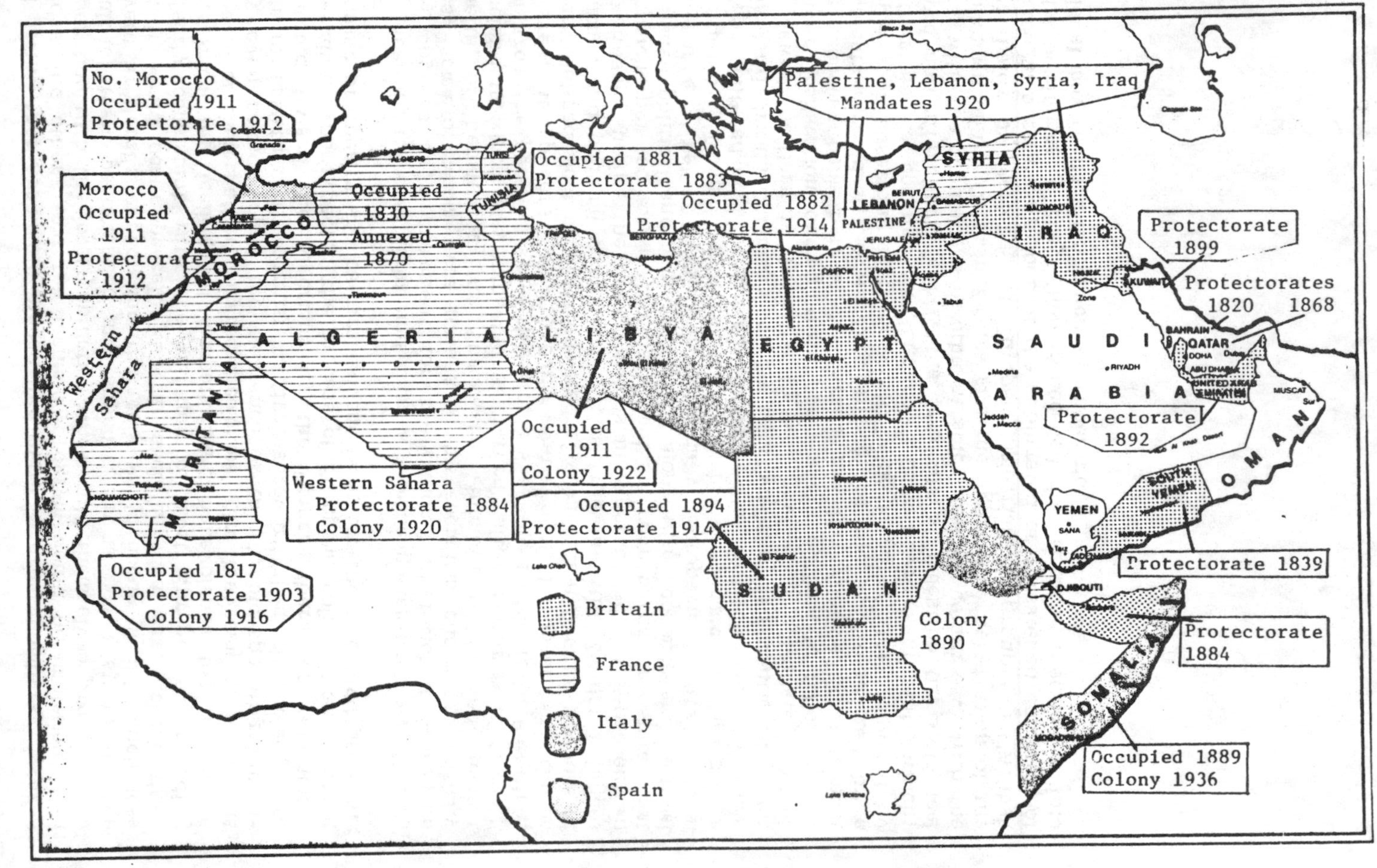

CHAPTER ELEVEN

THE RISE OF NATIONAL CONSCIOUSNESS AND NATIONALIST MOVEMENTS IN ARAB LANDS

The disintegration of the Ottoman Empire and the expansion of European empires were among the factors that prepared the ground for the rise of national sentiments and the appearance of nation-states in the Arab lands. Since national consciousness legitimizes--perhaps even necessitates--such concepts as "Arab people" and "Arab history," it behooves us to consider not only "Arab nationalism" in particular but also nationalism in general. The introductory section of this chapter will thus seek to define the concept of "nation" mainly by delineating some of its most common ingredients as well as some of the major stages in its emergence. Thereafter, in the body of the chapter, we shall trace the rise of national consciousness and the development of national movements in the Arab lands until the 1930s.

Nationalism: Ingredients and Patterns

It is no easy matter to compose a universally acceptable definition of "nation" or "nationalism." The many writers on this elusive topic have frequently quarrelled with each other's statements and analyses. Most agree, however, that nationalism has a lot to do with the focus of identity and loyalty among relatively large groups of individuals. With regard to identity, one of the most common definitions of "nation" is that it consists of an agglomeration of persons who feel that the set of experiences, customs, interests and expectations they share binds them all into one people. They are conscious, in other words, that they belong to a single nation distinct from others. There consequently exists a broad and deep sense of community--even a vague sense of kinship--that draws individuals together and fosters among them a "national identity." If such an identity exists to a significant degree, then the nation will have first call on the loyalty of its sons and daughters. There may exist other loyalties--e.g., to one's immediate or extended family, religion, employing institution, profession, or social class--but ideally the loyalty to one's nation takes precedence, especially in times of crisis such as war.

It is often said that national identity is rooted in and focused upon certain specific features sometimes called the ingredients of nationalism. Disagreements also exist among scholars as to which, if any, of these features a "nation" <u>must</u> have; and exceptions can usually be found to any criterion pronounced indispensable. But several features are nearly always present, and nearly always play a prominent role, in the life of a given nation. Among these are: territory, language, history and culture, the state, and the desire to be free of alien control or influence. The ideal situation is for the nation to be living in its own well-defined territory, sometimes referred to as the "fatherland" or as the "national homeland." An island homeland like that of Ireland is more easily defined than one abutting territory claimed by neighboring peoples, in which case there is a tendency to speak of "natural borders." Of course, conflicting claims over boundary lines between nations frequently cause tension and even war. If, like the Zionist Jews of Russia, a group of persons lacks a homeland yet believes that it constitutes a nation, then it is likely that such a group will make a zealous effort to acquire a territory and to gain exclusive possession of it.

To an extent, language is the most obvious badge of nationality; on the assumption that those who speak alike also think and behave alike, "nation" is sometimes defined simply as a people speaking the same language. Despite the negative example of Switzerland, in most cases there is a single "national language," which is one of the most powerful sources of national identity--so much so that the Zionists revived Hebrew as their national language and some Irish even tried to revive Gaelic. Closely related to language are history and culture. A "national culture" is the result of generations of a shared historical experience that endows a people with the same heroes, holidays, customs, habits, and tastes. An Irish nationalist explained: "I stand for an Irish civilization based on the people and embodying and maintaining the things--their habits, ways of thought, customs--that makes them different--the sort of life I was brought up in. . . ." Another nearly essential feature of a nation is a state (i.e., political sovereignty over persons living within a specific territory). Indeed, there appears to be an almost instinctive impulse to bring about a coincidence between state and nation. As one scholar put it, "the nation seeks to take over the state as the political instrument through which it can protect and assert itself."

There are other, less central ingredients of nationalism, including race and religion. A half-cynical definition of "nation" is that it is a group of persons united by a common error about their ancestry and a common dislike of their neighbors. That is, nowadays a people's belief in its collective descent from a single ancestor is usually considered to be no more than a national myth. Yet even myths and prejudices, if they are commonly shared, can figure in a national identity. Religion has not proven itself to be an important factor in modern nationalism--at least not in Europe where only in Ireland and Poland has it played a significant role in the national identity. Indeed, in modern times nationalism has ordinarily assumed a secular posture.

Another, not so concrete but very important, ingredient of nationalism has to do with the ideals of autonomy and integrity. Nations more or less instinctively seek to attain and to preserve freedom from alien control or influence not only for the nation-state, its territory and its citizens, but also for the nation's cultural institutions. For example, a nation often exhibits a jealous and protective attitude toward its national language lest it be subordinated to another tongue or corrupted by foreign loan words. Nations are likely to insist upon a particular version of their own history, a version which dwells upon events having to do with the nation's emergence or self-defense and which glorifies its national heroes and promotes a sense of national pride among its school children. Nationalism's insistence upon autonomy and integrity suggests that its most visible and most powerful manifestations occur when the nation believes itself either oppressed or threatened with oppression. One scholar has defined nationalism as a "movement depending on a feeling of collective grievance against foreigners," adding that "the national grievance must be collective. And the collectivity must be a nation."

This suggests that the "nation" has not always been mankind's principal focus of identity. Prior to the nineteenth century, persons tended to identify themselves not so much in terms of their nationality as in terms of their family or tribe, their immediate locality (town or district), their religion, their allegiance to a ruler, their occupation, or their social estate or class. When threats were perceived or grievances felt, they were usually perceived and responded to on behalf of some grouping other than a nation. In pre-modern times nationalism was not ordinarily the most prominent banner that rallied individuals to join the great historical movements. This is not to suggest that national consciousness did not exist at all prior to the nineteenth century. Some historians of medieval Europe, for example, find evidence of national sentiment in such events as the Hundred Years' War (1339-1453) between England and France or the periodic rivalry between speakers of French and Italian over the election of Roman Catholic popes. As we shall see, in Arabic-speaking lands on occasions there also appeared manifestations of a rudimentary national consciousness. Yet until the French Revolution of 1789, in which Frenchmen exhibited a strong awareness of both class and nation, national consciousness was everywhere relatively low. During the nineteenth century, however, nationalism asserted itself in certain regions as <u>the</u> major ideological force. There exists, in other words, an historical dimension to nationalism, which can therefore be analyzed not only in terms of its ingredients but also in terms of its sequential phases and its patterns of emergence in time and space.

In the birth and maturation of a nation, three or perhaps four stages are discernable. The initial phase is one during which, although visible manifestations of national consciousness may remain low, there occur certain developments that will ultimately facilitate, at an appropriate historical moment, the rise of both a national identity and a national movement. Perhaps the most crucial development is the decline of a feudal (or decentralized) socio-economic and political order and its replacement by a centralized one having integrative and homogenizing tendencies. This often lengthy process gradually weakens the local attachments of individuals and induces them to refocus their identity and loyalty on the emerging larger community. Related to this process of integration are most of the other developments that can prepare the ground for the actual rise of nationalism: the growth of population, much of it migrating from villages to towns (urbanization) and shifting into non-agricultural occupations; the spread of a money economy and of a wage-labor system; the growth of a bourgeoisie and of an intelligentsia, urban elites which characteristically provide the model for correct speech and "high culture"; the spread of literacy and of means for mass communication; and the growth of popular (democratic) governmental ideas and institutions. These developments tend to estrange persons from local circumstances of isolation, ignorance and apathy and to place them into those where awareness and activity are more possible.

The second stage, usually called something like "the growth of national consciousness," is the time when the nation becomes aware--or more fully aware--of its own existence. At the beginning of this phase, there are usually present at least two factors, one of which is that the potential nation be in an oppressed condition or that it face an external threat or that it has some kind of collective grievance against foreigners. The grievance of oppression is often directed against an alien ruling elite. Of course, to be ruled by foreigners was, prior to the nineteenth century, the normal condition of the majority of mankind. So the very expression of grave concern about it represents an upsurge of national consciousness, since nationalism teaches in effect that alien rule as such offends human dignity. A related factor, often present at the beginning of nationalism's second phase, might be called "the crisis of the intellectuals." This refers to the process whereby a few innovative thinkers gradually reach the conclusion that the unit (e.g., religion or village), which previously served as the chief focus of their identity and loyalty, is not up to the task of defending the community or of alleviating its grievance. This realization constitutes a crisis for the intellectuals, who proceed to cast about for another unit having the ability to command loyalty and to coordinate self-defense. Sooner or later it is the concept of the nation which the urban elite acknowledges and then promotes among the more provincial elements of the population. It is thus during the period of "the growth of national consciousness" that the idea of the nation acquires greater breadth and depth within the society. It is also the time when the intellectuals begin to define their national culture, reviving or purifying the national language and writing histories to provide the nation with roots, heroes, and even myths. The second phase often begins gradually, with a barely perceptible "stirring" of national consciousness, but then quickens its pace as the idea of the nation influences the society more widely and deeply.

The second phase accelerates its pace until it culminates in the third, the most easily recognized and perhaps the most crucial stage of nationalism, which is the period of the "struggle for independence." Whereas during the previous phase the elite may have been preoccupied with cultural issues like history, language and literature, it now turns its attention increasingly to politics. This is thus the time when nationalism becomes an organized "movement," perhaps even a political party, acquiring an authoritative leadership, a structure, and means for communicating with and mobilizing the masses. In these developments as a rule the initiative is taken and the central role is played by an urban elite, which simultaneously pursues two objectives. The primary one is, of course, the independence of the nation from any sort of foreign domination or influence--cultural or economic but especially political and military. The importance of this goal is such that the nationalists often justify the use of almost any "means" toward the "ends" of freedom and integrity, including such means as secret societies, armed rebellion, and even terrorism. The secondary objective is to speed up the process of cultural integration, which began on an involuntary basis during the first phase and which continued on a voluntary basis during the second, in effect by imposing the standards of the urban elite on the rest of the population. One of the aims of the French Revolution of 1789, for example, was to diffuse the language and culture of Paris throughout the country. If or when the primary objective of self-government is achieved, however, it can be said that the third phase ends whether or not the secondary objective of cultural homogeneity is also attained.

If the third phase represents the climax of nationalism then the fourth (often called "consolidation") is usually anticlimactic. Sometimes it is even missing altogether if all elements of the society have been fully integrated into the nation. "Consolidation" becomes necessary only in cases where little progress was made toward cultural homogeneity during the first three phases, thereby leaving important social or regional groupings which retain other, earlier foci of identity and which therefore harbor little or no loyalty toward the "nation." The new national ruling elite usually then declares that independence does not terminate the national struggle but merely ends one phase of it and inaugurates another--that of consolidating the nation. In other words, this phase consists of a final effort to diffuse throughout the country, or to impose upon it, the culture and values of the nationalist elite. The remaining older identities and subcultures thus in effect are viewed as unworthy relics and may disappear if "consolidation" is successfully achieved. This is perhaps what one scholar had in mind when observing that "the essence of a nation is that all the individuals have many things in common, and also that all have forgotten a good many things." Total cultural integration within the nation is, of course, by no means bound to succeed. Social or regional subcultures indeed frequently remain or reappear, rendering a given nation incomplete or unconsolidated and acting as sources of tension within it.

In addition to delimiting the "phases" of nationalism, scholars have occasionally attempted to describe the various general "patterns" to which specific national movements may conform. The model of France, Germany and Italy, for example, suggests an integrative pattern whereby separate principalities (and subcultures) are knit into a larger unit. The model of Portugal could be called a secessionist pattern whereby the nation detaches itself from a larger political and cultural unit. The Polish model suggests a revivalist pattern, whereby a nation recreates an earlier policy and culture that had partially disappeared. Most nationalisms of Asia and Africa are said to belong to a general anti-colonial pattern entailing the overturning of European imperialism. The case of Greece suggests that a given nationalism can at the same time be secessionist (detaching itself from the Ottoman Empire) and revivalist (to some extent recreating Byzantium). As we shall see, the national movements arising in the Arab lands also frequently typified more than one pattern.

The Rise of Nationalism in Arab Lands

Chapters 9 and 10 describe some of the impersonal developments which prepared the ground for the growth of national identity among the Arabs. The reforms carried out by the Ottoman "men of the tanzimat" and by Muhammad Ali, among others, had the effect of weakening the decentralized "feudal order" of the eighteenth century, which was also seriously undermined by the impact of European trade, and of bringing about much more centralized states and societies. Throughout the Arab land the population growth that began toward the end of the eighteenth century continued and accelerated during the nineteenth. Many urban areas--particularly such commercial centers as Cairo, Alexandria, Beirut, and Tunis--doubled or even tripled in size between 1800 and 1860. In addition to being an important catalyst of urbanization, trade with Europe also figured in the emergence and expansion of local, Arabic-speaking bourgeoisies. This, along with educational reforms, facilitated the appearance of a new Arabic-speaking intelligentsia (distinct, in most cases, from the traditional ulama). Educational reforms also helped to spread literacy among more elements of society. In time, this made it possible, via official gazettes and other sorts of newspapers, for central governments and/or intellectual elites to communicate their ideas to other segments of the population. By the mid-nineteenth century, many of the conditions conducive to the rise of nationalism had thus materialized in the Arab lands.

Chapters 9 and 10 also suggest that the "Arabs" had good reasons for harboring collective grievances against foreigners. Indeed, there existed among them the potential for feeling resentment about two different sources of alien domination. One potential object of the grievance of "Arabs" was the Ottoman Empire, whose decline had led to widespread corruption and misrule. During the first half of the nineteenth century, a number of Christian minorities in the Balkans, the Serbs and the Greeks being the most prominent examples, acquired national identities and, with the support of certain European powers, successfully launched national movements against "Ottoman tyranny." The status of an independent nation was achieved by Serbia in 1830 and by Greece in 1832. In this regard, the Ottoman tanzimat reforms of the mid-nineteenth century attempted to end corruption and in general to reverse the process of decline in part to encourage other minority groups, who might come to regard themselves as separate nations, to remain loyal to the Ottoman Empire. The tanzimat reforms did indeed help to bring about a temporary Ottoman revival and a slowing of the Empire's disintegration, but there remained at least the potential for non-Turkish Ottoman subjects to consider themselves oppressed by the Ottoman Turks. Meanwhile, by the end of the nineteenth century, European imperialism had resulted in France's occupation of Algeria (1830) and Tunisia (1881) and in Britain's occupation of Aden (1838) and Egypt (1882). Each of these two powers, moreover, was asserting its claim to additional "spheres of influence," France in Syria and Morocco and Britain in Iraq, Palestine, and the Egyptian Sudan. Even the new nation of Italy began to claim "historic rights" in Libya, which it proceeded to occupy in 1911, the year before France declared a protectorate over Morocco. And of course the Palestinian Arabs also perceived Zionist immigration within the context of European imperial domination.

During the course of the nineteenth century, the inhabitants of the Arab lands consequently became vaguely aware that they harbored collective grievances against foreigners. However, it was not initially on behalf of an "Arab nation" that the grievances were felt but rather on behalf of more traditional (mainly religious) groupings. Yet, with the passage of time, the inherited objects of group identity like the millets came to be perceived by a few intellectuals as inadequate for the purposes of self-strengthening and self-defense and, ultimately, the concept of "nation" was perceived as an alternative. Slowly at first but then more rapidly during and after World War I, national consciousness arose in the Arab lands. National consciousness did not, however, begin to assert itself as the same moment in all Arabic-speaking lands; nor, in each region, did it accelerate at the same pace. Moreover, national identity in various Arabic-speaking territories did not always have precisely the same "ingredients." Islam became a more important factor in some instances than in others, for example. In certain cases, as we shall see, an Arabic-speaking elite conceptualized a nation which it did not even consider to be "Arab." Two of the most significant examples of the growth of national consciousness in Arab lands occurred in the Fertile Crescent, the birthplace of modern "Arab nationalism," and in Egypt, where nationalism experienced a separate development and acquired a different focus.

The Rise of Arab Nationalism in the Fertile Crescent

It is possible, perhaps even likely, that before the nineteenth century there existed vague notions of Arab consciousness among certain elements of the population dwelling in the Fertile Crescent. For this was the scene of many pride-inspiring moments in Arab history, including the seventh-century Arab conquests, the Arab Kingdom of the Umayyads, and the flowering of an Arab high culture within Islam during the early Abbasi Caliphate. Some recent Arab writers on Arab nationalism have tended also to depict movements like the Wahhabiyya as early manifestations of Arab nationalism; while it is difficult to isolate specific examples of Arab national identity in it, the Wahhabiyya's hostility toward the Ottoman Turks possibly suggested a kind of subconscious "national grievance" on the part of certain Arab Muslims. In this regard, however, the conscious or explicit grievance--and therefore the main identity--expressed by participants in the Wahhabiyya was overwhelmingly Islamic rather than Arab. Similarly, urban or sedentary inhabitants of the Fertile Crescent in the eighteenth century not only identified themselves primarily in terms of their religion but, as did the majority of Arabic-speakers elsewhere, they popularly associated the term "Arabs" with "bedouin." Indeed, the term "Arabs" usually carried a pejorative or negative connotation among town-dwellers, who frequently employed it to describe a social grouping they considered to be illiterate, uncouth, and predatory.

So, while the identity and loyalty of tribesmen was focused more or less exclusively on their extended family, that of the rest of the population was also focused on their millet or, in the Muslims' case, on the Ottoman Empire as well as the Islamic religion. In this regard, one of the most perceptive writers on Arab nationalism, Sāti^{c} al-Husri, has described, first, how the Muslim and Christian Arabs of the Fertile Crescent held differing attitudes toward the Ottoman state and, secondly, how Arab nationalism therefore developed differently within the Muslim and Christian communities. For the Muslims focused their identity and loyalty not only on Islam generally, remembering "Islamic history" and being concerned for the territorial integrity of dar al-islam (the sphere of Islam). They also held positive feelings toward the Ottoman Empire, which they viewed as an Islamic state--indeed, as the strongest Islamic state. More easily than their Christian counterparts, the Muslim Arabs of the Fertile Crescent could participate in such Ottoman institutions as the imperial army and the bureaucracy. And they regularly heard the name of the Ottoman sultan mentioned in the Friday prayer.

The Christian Arabs, on the other hand, were constitutionally less privileged and less willing Ottoman subjects whose identity was focused not on the Sultan or his Islamic state but rather on their own respective millets. This religious identity was reinforced in sermons and in millet schools, which taught the history of Christianity in general and the history of the denomination or sect in particular. To an extent, the Christian Arabs' version of their own history nourished collective grievances against the Muslims and the Ottoman Turks for having subjugated them. Thus conditioned, the Christian Arabs were receptive to contacts with European Christian nations, who promised to look out for their interests. Yet relations with fellow Christians were also subject to strain. For example, in the Greek Orthodox patriarchate of Antioch (centered in Damascus), it had long been the tradition for the lower clergy to be drawn from local Arabic-speakers but for the upper clergy to consist of Greeks appointed from Constantinople, the seat of the Patriarch himself. In 1899, however, the Arab membership of the patriarchate of Antioch demanded the appointment of a native Arabic-speaking bishop. Upon succeeding in that objective, they then proceeded to insist upon the "Arabization" of all the important ecclesiastical positions in the patriarchate. Sati^c al-Husri describes this movement as one of the first manifestations of genuine Arab national consciousness.

This incident, however, represented the culmination of a long, gradual process of "consciousness-raising" among the Christian Arabs. In that process, Western missionary societies and such educational institutions as the Syrian Protestant College (opened in 1866 and later called the American University in Beirut) played a certain role by emphasizing Arabic literature and Arab history. There thus emerged during the mid-nineteenth century a generation of Christian Arab intellectuals who formed Arabic literary societies and who, in their "intellectual crisis" during 1860-1914, formulated the concept of an Arab nation. One of the most prominent of these Syrian Christian intellectuals was Butrus al-Bustani (1819-83). After helping Western missionaries to translate the Bible into Arabic, he served as secretary of Beirut's first Arabic literary society (majma^c al-tahdhib, created in 1845-46) and then founded his own school, al-madrasa al-wataniyya, in order to teach modern sciences in Arabic. Bustani was one of several dynamic thinkers of the mid-nineteenth century whose interest in the Arabic language contributed to a renaissance of Arabic literature. He personally compiled ah Arabic dictionary, wrote a multi-volume encyclopedia in Arabic, and edited an influential Arabic literary journal, al-Jinan. Via such media, Bustani praised the greatness of the Arabs' past, called for constitutional reforms to permit "Arabs" a greater role in the Ottoman provincial administration, advocated making Arabic an official language in schools and courts, and in general encouraged "Arabs" to be proud of their language, their past, and their watan (homeland or fatherland). The motto of al-Jinan was a saying attributed to the Prophet Muhammad: hubb al-watan min al-iman ("love of country is an article of faith"). Bustani's pioneering nationalist ideas were not without some ambivalence. Although he joined a short-lived secret society that in 1875 mounted posters calling for the autonomy of Syria, he occasionally affirmed in print that his watan was the Ottoman Empire; and, while he maintained that all Arabic-speakers were Arabs, his own identity and loyalty seem to have been focused upon Syria rather than upon a larger "Arab" territory.

At any rate, although having once negatively associated the term "Arabs" with uncouth bedouin and with the Islamic conquest, a few Christian Arab thinkers like Bustani, via their interest in Arabic language and literature, gradually formulated positive concepts of an "Arab people," with which Christian Arabs could identify, and of an "Arab history," in which Christian Arabs could take pride. In their reconstruction of Arab history, they emphasized the multi-religious character of early Arab civilization, pointing out that one of the first Arab states, that of the Banu Ghassan, was Christian and that Christian scholars like Hunayn ibn Ishaq (d. 873 A.D.) contributed substantially to the great intellectual flowering of Abbasi times. At the same time, however, the Christian Arab intellectuals were obliged to come to terms with the predominant role of Islam in the Arab culture and history they were seeking to define. Some, confronting this issue head on, concluded that Christian Arabs must learn to regard the Prophet Muhammad as an "Arab hero" and the Qur'an as a masterpiece of Arabic literature. Yet most of the pioneering nationalists among the Christian Arabs tended to minimize the role of religion in Arab nationalism. They called for an Arab renaissance (nahda), a national awakening that would transcend religious differences. As reformers, Christian Arab nationalists as a rule advocated the separation of religion and politics. There was, in other words, a pronounced secular flavor to the "Arab nation" conceptualized by Christian Arabs in the decade or so prior to World War I.

Meanwhile, a few Muslim Arab intellectuals were also beginning to feel proud and protective of their Arabness. Muslim Arabs as a rule were attracted to the idea of Arab nationalism more slowly than their Christian counterparts, however. This occurred in part because their traditional foci of identity--Islam and the Ottoman Empire--seriously undertook the tasks of strengthening and of defending the community and therefore also continued to command their loyalties. In this regard, during the late nineteenth century there developed two ideological movements which appealed with some success to thinkers and activists among the Muslim Arabs and which consequently retarded the rise of a genuine Arab national consciousness among them. One of these ideologies was Pan-Islam which taught, in effect, that the Islamic religion was fully equal to the task of protecting its adherents and subjects against external threats, particularly that of European imperialism. A leading ideologue of Pan-Islam was Jamal al-Din "al-Afghani" (1839-97), an Iranian-born scholar-activist who in 1857 witnessed both the Muslim-led "mutiny" of the Indian troops against their British officers and the British administration's subsequent repression of India's Muslim community. Thereafter, Jamal al-Din became greatly concerned with the need to protect dar al-islam from the rapacity of European (particularly British) imperialism. At first he sought merely to convince individual Muslim sovereigns to adopt an anti-British policy, but gradually--especially during the 1880s--he formulated the notion of ittihad al-islam (Pan-Islam), which envisioned a more structured movement of Muslims acting collectively in their self-defense.

Jamal al-Din and other advocates of Pan-Islam naturally looked to the Ottoman Empire, the largest and strongest Islamic state, to take the lead in uniting Muslims for purposes of self-strengthening and self-protection. The idea of Islamic unity under Ottoman leadership appealed to Ottoman Sultan Abdulhamid II (1876-1909), for it greatly enhanced his claim to be "Caliph of all Muslims." It was not until the end of the eighteenth century that the title of "caliph" was assumed by the Ottoman sultan and that there began to be circulated the legend about the transfer of the caliphate in 1517 from the "shadow Abbasids" of Mamluk Egypt to the Ottomans. And it was not until the reigns of Abd al-Aziz (1861-76) and especially Abdulhamid II that the claim and the legend started to be taken seriously by large numbers of Muslims. The ideology and movement of Pan-Islam, conceptualized by Afghani and others and led by Sultan-Caliph Abdulhamid II, thus kept the identity and loyalty of many Muslim Arabs focused upon Islam and the Ottoman Empire, thereby delaying their susceptibility to the Arab nationalism being formulated by a few Christian Arab intellectuals.

The second ideological movement, Ottomanism, was conceptualized by a group of Abdulhamid II's opponents known as the "Young Ottomans." Having earlier criticized the autocratic tendencies of the tanzimat reforms, the Young Ottomans regarded Abdulhamid II as a tyrannical dictator, in large part because he had suspended the constitution of 1876. Although European newspapers referred to them as the "Young Turks," the Young Ottomans did not consider themselves "Turks," a term they associated with Anatolian tribesmen and peasants who spoke a crass dialect and who possessed only a rude folk culture. Rather, they considered themselves to be "Osmanlis" or Ottomans. They spoke a court language known as Osmanli/Ottoman, drawn from literary Arabic and Persian as well as from Turkish; and they participated in the high culture of the Ottoman elite. Eager to liberalize the Ottoman state by introducing constitutional reforms, the Young Ottomans invited other discontented elements of the empire to join them. They sought at once to restore the constitution in order to curb the unlimited powers of the sultan and to create, in effect, an "Ottoman nation" based on the Osmanli language and culture. Ottomanism was not necessarily incompatible with Islam, but the Young Ottomans spoke of guaranteeing the civil rights of non-Islamic minorities. In brief, Ottomanism was an attempt to transform what remained of the Ottoman Empire into a sort of Ottoman nation. While the attempt ultimately failed, Ottomanism temporarily attracted a certain allegiance from many reform-minded Arab intellectuals who therefore delayed the moment of their espousing Arab nationalism proper.

While Hamidian Pan-Islam and reform-minded Ottomanism attracted many Muslim intellectuals in the Fertile Crescent and slowed the growth of Arab nationalism among them, these two movements also contained issues that figured in the gradual emergence of an Arab national consciousness among the Muslim Arabs still under Ottoman rule. In the case of Pan-Islam, it was the issue of the Caliphate. As the title of "caliph" became more prominently associated with the name of Abdulhamid II, certain Arab ulama began to point out that, according to the authoritative classical scholars, one of the caliphate's main prerequisites was that its occupant be a descendant of the Arab tribe of Quraysh. This observation was picked up and expanded by a few activist Muslim-Arab intellectuals--most notably by Abd al-Rahman al-Kawakibi (1849-1903), one of the many Syrians who sought refuge in Egypt to avoid the authoritarian rule of Abdulhamid II. In his book, Umm al-Qura (Cairo, 1900), al-Kawakibi accused the Ottoman sultans of having usurped the caliphate from the Arabs and called for the designation of an "Arab caliph."

Al-Kawakibi and other Muslim intellectuals--including the Egyptian Muhammad Abduh and his disciple Rashid Rida (another Syrian refugee in Egypt)--also began to distinguish between "Arab" and "Turkish" periods in Islamic history. That is, they elaborated the notion (expressed before somewhat vaguely in Wahhabi doctrines) that the most exemplary age of Islam was its first three centuries when it was still close to its Arabic sources and still guided by Arab politico-intellectual leaders and before it fell under the influence of such non-Arab peoples as the Turks who corrupted and weakened Islam through their superstitiousness on the one hand and their rigidity on the other. What was needed, according to these few Arab-Muslim intellectuals, was a renaissance among the Arab elements within Islam to restore it to its original pure condition and thereby to strengthen it.

This position, as defined by the likes of al-Kawakibi and Rashid Rida, was more "Islamic" than it was "Arab" and therefore cannot be called fully mature Arab nationalism. Al-Kawakibi never advocated the independence of the Arabs from Ottoman rule, and Rida continued to regard Islam as the most important unit of identity and self-defense for Muslim Arabs. Yet the debate over such issues as an "Arab caliphate" and an "Arab age of Islamic history" represented the growth of the idea among certain Muslim intellectuals of the Fertile Crescent that they too harbored grievances, on behalf of the Arabs, against the Ottoman Empire.

It thus remained for the Fertile Crescent's reform-minded Muslim-Arab intellectuals, those who were cooperating with the Young Ottomans, to move gradually but steadily all the way to an unequivocal position of Arab nationalism. In the Ottomanism movement the problematic issue was that of centralization. The Young Ottomans, while criticizing the authoritarian rule of Abdulhamid II and while advocating a constitutional regime, nevertheless resented the centrifugal tendencies of certain ethnic groups still under Ottoman rule (e.g.,

Albanians, Bulgarians, Armenians, Kurds, and Arabs). They consequently tried to resist these tendencies, which they perceived as constituting a threat to the strength and territorial integrity of the Ottoman Empire. Although they were progressive constitutionalists, the Young Ottomans thus advocated a policy of centralization (markaziya). In other words, the Young Ottomans in effect were beginning to formulate and to insist upon the concept of an "Ottoman nation" to which any regional subcultures (Arabism, for example) would have to be subordinated if the new (Ottoman) nation was to emerge and survive.

The issue dominated and, ultimately frustrated two "Ottoman Liberal Congresses" held in Paris, the first in 1902 and the second in 1907. Along with Albanian and Armenian delegates, a number of reform-minded Arab intellectuals, including a few Muslims, participated in the congresses which were sponsored by the Young Ottomans. Other issues arose and were also discussed at length. All concurred, for example, that the autocratic regime of Abdulhamid II would have to be transformed or overthrown. Most Arab participants further agreed on the necessity of transcending religious differences, an issue considered particularly urgent by Arab intellectuals seeking to define Arab culture. In this regard, each of the Ottoman Liberal Congresses eventually divided and collapsed over the issue of centralization. The Arab and other non-Turkish "Ottomanists" wanted the reformed Ottoman state to be decentralized into several quasi-autonomous provinces each controlled by a major ethnic group which, via a strong local administration and educational system, could promote and protect its own language and culture. Fearing that the Ottoman minorities would exploit a weak federal government to transform their semi-autonomous provinces into wholly independent principalities, however, most of the Young Ottomans insisted that the reformed Ottoman state must have both a strong central government as well as a homogeneous "Ottoman" culture.

In the decade following the collapse of the first Ottoman Liberal Congress, the Young Ottomans and the Arab reformers moved further and further away from a relationship based on shared objectives and mutual cooperation to one that increasingly entailed disparate goals and mutual hostility. Concluding that Abdulhamid II remained unaffected by their agitation from abroad, the most activist of the Young Ottomans formed a secret society, the Committee of Union and Progress (CUP), and then returned to Ottoman Turkey where they recruited supporters and infiltrated key Ottoman institutions, especially the army. In 1907 the CUP led the "Young Turk Revolution" which first reduced Abdulhamid to a constitutional monarch and then, after an unsuccessful counter-revolution, deposed him altogether in favor of a figurehead sultan-caliph. During these difficulties, the Albanian nationalists launched a successful revolt and the Greeks seized Crete, developments which caused the "Young Turks" to suspect and to resent the growing separatist tendencies of the Arabs and the Armenians. In 1909 a new clique, headed by Enver Pasha, came to power within the CUP leadership. As evidenced by the ideology and policy of this clique, the orientation of the Young Ottomans (who now unashamedly called themselves "Young Turks") had moved from "Ottomanism" to "Turkish nationalism" proper. Turkish nationalism, as defined by its chief architect, Ziya Gokalp, considered its culture to be "European" rather than "Oriental" (the Ottomans had ruled portions of Europe for six centuries). To some extent, therefore, Turkish nationalists tried to purify their nation's language and culture from alien, including Arabic, influences. More importantly, the new Young Turk regime, in part to counter Arab and Armenian separatists movements, inaugurated a policy of "Turkification" in the Fertile Crescent. That is, among other things, Turkish was to be the only official language used in administration, justice, and education. Needless to say, the successful implementation of this policy would entail the supression of Arab culture and Arab consciousness.

After the failure of the 1902 Congress, Ottoman Arab reformers also began to pursue their own objectives independently of the Young Ottomans, with whom they clashed more and more. While a rare few Arab exiles began calling for Arab independence from Ottoman rule as early as 1905, most of the Arab nationalists in the Fertile Crescent preferred for the moment to continue working within the (Ottoman) system. They did so by joining either of two new reformist parties: The Party of Freedom and Concord, whose very active "Beirut Committee" drafted a seminal manifesto calling for limited Arab home rule, or the Ottoman Decentralization Party (hizb al-lāmarkazīya al-ᶜuthmānī), composed mainly of Syrian exiles in Egypt. In 1913 these groups held in Paris an "Arab Congress" attended by twenty-odd Muslim and Christian Arab reformers. Among the titles of their speeches were: "Reform on the Basis of Decentralization," "Our Educational Policy," "Rights of the Arabs in the Ottoman Kingdom," and "The National Life in the Ottoman Arab Countries." Complaining about the use of Turkish in "Arab" schools and about the selection of Turks to represent Arab districts in the Ottoman parliament, the "Arab Congress" more or less adopted the Beirut Committee's reform program. They reaffirmed that Arabness (ᶜurūba) transcended religious differences; and the Muslim Arabs seem not to have objected to the Christians' tendency to look to France and other European countries for support. The conference's discussions and resolutions centered on the demand for reforms both to guarantee the political rights of Arabs within a decentralized Ottoman state and to safeguard the language and culture of the newly defined Arab nation (al-umma al-ᶜarabīya).

The small size of the "Arab Congress" indicates that by 1913 only a few of the Fertile Crescent's intellectual elite had espoused Arab nationalism. The great mass of the region's Arabic-speaking population maintained parochial ties and identities; and even the majority of the elite, bureaucrats in particular, still had a stake in the Ottoman establishment and therefore clung to "Ottomanism" and/or to Pan-Islam. Advocates of Arab nationalism tended to be military officers or members of new professions like journalism. This is born out by the composition of the secret societies which from 1911 onward began to denounce the policy of working only for limited Arab home rule within the (Ottoman) system. Instead, they planned to adopt the Albanian and Bulgarian tactics for dealing with "Ottoman tyranny" by asserting Arab independence, if necessary by violence and terrorism. Among the first of the Arab nationalists secret societies was al-Fatāt (the Young Arab

Society), founded in Europe in 1911 by a group of exiles. Copying the tactic of the Young Turks, members of al-Fatat returned to Syria in order to seek recruits and to organize their clandestine movement. Another secret Arab nationalist organization was al-cAhd (the Covenant Society), founded in 1913 by Major Aziz Ali al-Misri and other Arab officers (mostly Iraqis) in the Ottoman army. The propaganda of these societies was frankly anti-Turkish, accusing the Turks of oppressing the Arabs and of hindering progress among them. During this period the Young Turk regime did become increasingly repressive toward the budding Arab nationalist movement. Aziz Ali al-Misri was arrested for treason in 1914 and probably would have been executed had not Britain intervened. At the outbreak of World War I the Young Turk regime appointed to the governorship of Syria a hardline advocate of the policy of Turkification. He tried to crush Arab nationalism by arresting and executing outspoken Arabists, which proved to be a self-defeating policy in the long run because it embittered more and more Arabs towards the Turks and, in effect, promoted Arab nationalism.

From 1914 onward, therefore, Arab nationalism spread rapidly among the intellectuals and activists of the Fertile Crescent. In part because of its predominantly anti-Turkish character at this stage, Arab nationalism was encouraged during World War I by the British, who were eager to undermine Ottoman Turkey's ability to aid Germany, its ally and Britain's enemy. Indeed, Britain's war preparations included plans to encourage an Arab insurrection against the Turks. The British High Commissioner of Egypt, Sir Henry MacMahon, contacted the Ottoman Governor of the Hijaz, Sharif Husayn of Mecca, and asked him to provide leadership for such a movement. Husayn, who during 1904-11 had cooperated with the Young Turks' efforts to suppress an anti-Ottoman uprising in Yemen, seems now to have become receptive to Arab nationalism in order to enlarge and to consolidate his own potentially independent domain. The Husayn-MacMahon correspondence reveals that Britain gave vague promises to support Husayn's ambition to head a sovereign Arab state that would include most of the Arabic-speaking districts still under Ottoman rule. Suspicious of MacMahon's ambiguous assurances, Husayn delayed for more than two years but finally, in June 1916, appointed his son Faysal to lead the "Arab revolt" against the Ottoman forces in the Hijaz and Syria. Among the British officers assigned to advise Faysal was Col. T. E. Lawrence. Faysal's "Arab army" effectively raided Ottoman supply lines and, just ahead of the British army under General Allenby, entered Damascus in October 1918, shortly before the surrender of Germany and Ottoman Turkey. The Arab nationalists of Syria proclaimed Faysal as their ruler, organized an Arab national congress, and looked forward to the ratification of their newly won independence by Britain and her allies who were soon to begin their negotiations at the Versailles Peace Conference.

In their aspirations for an independent state, the Arab nationalists had been encouraged by the U.S. President's wartime announcement (the Fourteen Points) committing the Allies to dispose of the defeated Ottoman Empire's possessions in accordance with the principle of self-determination. Rumors of other wartime agreements, however, disturbed them. After the 1917 Revolution, for example, Lenin's Russia accused the overthrown Czarist regime of having plotted with Britain and France to divide the Ottoman territories among themselves. According to this secret "Sykes-Picot agreement," Russia was to seize Constantinople, France was to obtain Syria (including Lebanon) and northern Iraq, and Britain was to take southern Iraq, Palestine, and Transjordan (see map). No less disturbing to the Arab nationalists was the Balfour Declaration (made public in late 1917), in which it was announced that the British Government "views with favour the establishment in Palestine of a national home for the Jewish people. . . ." To the dismay of the Arab nationalists, the promises contained in the Husayn-MacMahon correspondence and in the idealistic Fourteen Points were set aside during the peace negotiations in favor of those contained in the Sykes-Picot agreement and in the Balfour Declaration. Meeting at San Remo in 1920 to create the League of Nations, the European Powers thus divided the Fertile Crescent into French and British spheres. France was awarded a "mandate" over Syria, which it proceeded to occupy, suppressing Faysal's fledgling government in the process. Britain was awarded mandates over Iraq, where Faysal was installed as king, and over Palestine, where the Balfour Declaration initially became the controlling document. The territory of mandatory Palestine included Transjordan, which in 1928 was instituted as a separate state over which Britain made Abd Allah (Faysal's elder brother) king. The outcome of World War I's peace conferences thus constituted a humiliating setback for the Arab nationalists. Whereas the Ottoman Empire's most backward Arab provinces (Yemen and Hijaz) had become totally independent under, respectively, (the Zaydi) Imam Yahya and Sharif Husayn, its most advanced provinces in the Fertile Crescent were subjected to European rule on grounds that they were not ready for self-government.

Until World War I, the ideology and movement of Arab nationalism was actively supported by relatively few intellectuals whose grievances were directed primarily against the Ottoman Turks. Pre-1918 Arab nationalism can therefore be described as "secessionist" in that its main objective was to withdraw Arab territory and Arab culture from the jurisdiction of the increasingly "Turkish" Ottoman Empire. It was also "revivalist" to the extent that Arabism (ʿurūba) defined itself in terms of an Arab culture from an earlier historical period. World War I destroyed the Ottoman Empire; but, in the place of Turkish rule, the peace settlements substituted European rule over the Fertile Crescent by incorporating certain Ottoman Arab provinces into the British and French world empires. Britain and France henceforth became the main targets of the Arabs' grievances. They were in effect accused of having betrayed the Arabs with the unkept wartime promises and thereafter of oppressing them in various ways. The French bombardment of Damascus in 1925 to suppress a Syrian uprising, France's transfer of Arabic-speaking Alexandretta to Turkish sovereignty, France's definitive reconstitution of Lebanon as a separate state, and Britain's sponsorship of Zionist immigration into Arab Palestine, among other incidents, became symbols for European wrongs against the Arab nation. After 1920, in other words, Arab nationalism became essentially "anti-colonial." Moreover, since Britain and France were accused of using divide-and-rule tactics in order to fragment and

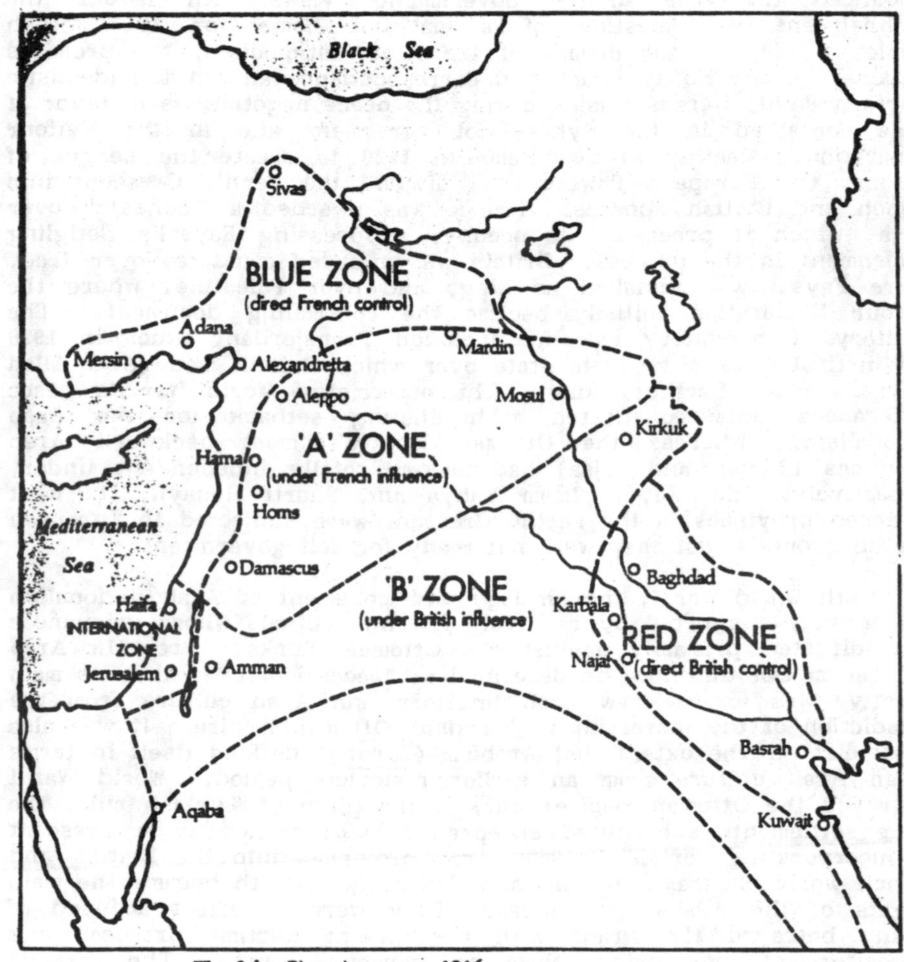

The Sykes-Picot Agreement, 1916

from A. Goldschmidt, <u>A Concise History of the Middle East</u>

to weaken the Arab nation, many Arab nationalists began to assert unity as a major goal along with independence. That is, although some Arab nationalists focused their identity on regional subcultures (in Lebanon, for example), most now became "integrationist." In time, this main current would be called "pan-Arab nationalism."

Most of the Arab intellectuals who until World War I had clung to "Ottomanism" embraced Arab nationalism following the peace settlements. This trend, along with the rise of secular pan-Arabism, can be traced during the 1920s in the career of Sati^{c} al-Husri (1880-1968), one of the most devoted and most articulate Arab nationalists. The son of a Syrian-born Ottoman official, Sati^{c} al-Husri was educated at Istanbul's best secular school and then followed his father into the Ottoman bureaucracy. Speaking Ottoman Turkish and considering himself part of the Ottoman elite, he supported "Ottomanism" and, perhaps in part because of his assignments during 1900-14 kept him in the Balkans or in Istanbul, had virtually nothing to do with "Arabism." After the peace settlements, however, he moved swiftly to a position of Arab nationalism. When the briefly independent Arab government at Damascus was suppressed by the French, along with many other old and new Arab nationalists Sati^{c} al-Husri followed Faysal to Iraq where he entered the Ministry of Education. Thereafter he and others formulated and preached modern, secular pan-Arab nationalism.

According to Sati^{c} al-Husri, the two most powerful determinants of the Arab nation were a shared historical experience and especially the Arabic language. All Arabic-speakers, he asserted, were "Arabs" whether they acknowledged it or not. On these grounds, in a memorable debate with Taha Husayn in 1925, he attempted to convince Egyptian intellectuals that they too were Arabs. Sati^{c} al-Husri viewed the Arab nation on the whole as a secular entity. Welcoming Ataturk's suppression of the caliphate in 1924 because it obliged Muslim Arabs to acknowledge their own Arabness, he argued that an Arab people and history as well as the Arabic language all preceded the appearance of Islam. Since many Christians spoke Arabic and shared the culture produced by Arab history, he insisted that the Arab nation was essentially non-religious rather than essentially Islamic, although he conceded that Islam had made important contributions to Arab history. Perhaps most importantly, since he considered the main enemies of the Arab nation to be regional particularism as well as Western imperialism, Sati^{c} al-Husri consistently advocated the unity of the Arabs as well as their complete political and cultural freedom from alien domination.

Not all inhabitants of the Fertile Crescent shared Sati^{c} al-Husri's vision of a secular, pan-Arab nation. Muslim intellectuals--ulama and those trained at Islamic educational institutions in particular--tended to reject secularism and to insist upon a close association between Arabism and Islam. Guided by such thinkers as Rashid Rida (1865-1935), the Islam-oriented Arab nationalists sponsored a number of Caliphate and general Islamic conferences during the 1920s in such cities as Cairo and Jerusalem. Pointing out that it was within Islam that the Arabs first became a unified people and achieved greatness, they argued that *al-umma al-^{c}arabīya* (the Arab nation) formed an irrevocable part--indeed, the most vital part--of *al-umma al-islamīya* (the Islamic umma). Meanwhile, certain regional subcultures in the Fertile Crescent, reacting against both Islamic and pan-Arabism, formulated purely local nationalisms that, in effect, seceded from the larger Arab nation. Of these the most extreme example was Lebanese nationalism whose Maronite Christian nucleus initially tolerated French tutelage as a means to the end of conclusively detaching Lebanon from the Arab-Muslim Fertile Crescent. To the extent that Lebanese nationalism was "revivalist" as well as "secessionist," it fastened its historical identity on neither classical Islamic civilization nor early Arab culture but rather on the memory of the Phoenicians. To a degree, the Phoenician symbols of Lebanese nationalism represented a national orientation away from the Arab-Islamic heartland and towards the Mediterranean and therefore towards modern France. Lebanese particularism and Islam-oriented Arab nationalism were thus among the side currents which diverged from the main channel of secular pan-Arabism.

Yet pan-Arabism represented a fully mature national ideology and movement which had come a long way from the first tentative ideas of intellectuals like Bustani and Kawakibi. By 1930 many thinkers had a rather well-defined conception of an Arab nation, with its heartland in the Fertile Crescent and the Arabian Peninsula, and with its identity rooted in the Arabic language and in an Arab culture resulting from an Arab history. Of course they continued to feel frustrated and resentful about the divided and subjugated condition of Arab territory. Not only was there no general coincidence between state and nation, but the best part of the nation was not free and Zionist immigration was increasing. These factors constituted grievances of considerable magnitude which still needed to be alleviated and which still found regular expression. Indeed, to an extent the internal bickering over such problematic issues as Arab unity and the relationship between Arabism and Islam became intensified because of the failure to solve the larger and more crucial issue of national independence from alien rule. A hostile attitude toward the circumstances of foreign domination eventually manifested itself even in Lebanon. During the 1930s, therefore, nationalists in the Fertile Crescent continued to organize themselves, within the constraints of their fragmented condition, into national movements devoted to their liberation from French or British imperialism.

The Rise of Nationalism in Egypt

In Egypt the development of nationalism went through a series of more or less distinct phases, beginning with a period of socio-economic and political integration that overlapped with the reign of Muhammad Ali (1805-48). During a second phase, national consciousness first "stirred" in the time of al-Tahtawi's greatest intellectual activity and then culminated in the "first Egyptian nationalist movement": the Urabi "rebellion" of 1880-81. The succeeding phase, during the initial two decades of the British occupation, represented an era when nationalism became quiescent and when introspective thinkers like Muhammad Abduh emphasized the need for educational and social reforms. The decade and a half preceding World War I saw the re-emergence of nationalism in the "second Egyptian nationalist movement" which expressed itself through Egypt's first two political parties, one associated with Ahmad Lutfi al-Sayyid and the other with Mustafa Kamil. Finally, after World War I the mature stage of Egyptian nationalism was bound up with the political leadership of Sa^{c}d Zaghlul and the Wafd Party and with the intellectual activity of Taha Husayn.

Although Muhammad Ali's subjects tended to identify themselves primarily in terms of their religion, their extended family and/or their village or quarter, something of a national consciousness existed in Egypt well before the mid-nineteenth century. This incipient nationalism seems to have been stronger in Egypt than in the Fertile Crescent, moreover, perhaps because the narrowness of the Nile Valley produced a society at once comparatively integrated and metropolitan. Pre-modern Egypt's national identity was expressed through the idea of awlād al-balad (literally, "the children of the community"). The historian al-Jabarti used this term in such a way as to signify an awareness among certain native Egyptians that they constituted a group distinct from such foreigners as the European Christian merchants, the Turkish military and political elite, and even some Egyptians (called awlād al-dhawat) who, along with many of the Syrian immigrants, adopted European manners. In their dress, etiquette and dialect, awlād al-balad proudly adhered to the local culture and attitudes. The notion of ibn al-balad fell short of being mature nationalism not only because other identities as a rule took precedence over it but also because its focus was somewhat parochial and not truly "national." That is, in al-Jabarti's time the concept of ibn al-balad excluded many categories of "Egyptians," including the indigenous Christians (the Copts) and the numerous fallāhīn (farmers/peasants). Indeed, the concept centered mainly on Cairene Muslims. Important changes would thus have to occur before a genuinely national consciousness would arise in Egypt.

In this regard, as a stage in the emergence of nationalism in Egypt the 1800-60 period's main significance lay in the occurrence of socio-economic and political changes that produced conditions favorable to the growth of nationalism. The policies of Muhammad Ali resulted in at least two important political developments which affected the subsequent appearance and character of Egyptian nationalism. One of these was the more or less definitive separation of Egypt from the Ottoman Empire. This meant that, in contrast to Arab nationalism in the Fertile Crescent, Egyptian nationalism would not need to regard seceding from the Ottoman polity and culture as its only major objective. Secondly, Muhammad Ali destroyed the decentralized administrative institutions of the Mamluks and created a rather highly integrated state with a bureaucracy staffed increasingly by native Egyptians. His economic reforms likewise tended to centralize Egyptian society as well as to accelerate the movement of peasants out of subsistence agriculture either into a state-controlled money economy or else away from the village altogether into non-agricultural occupations in an urban setting. Muhammad Ali also spread literacy by establishing schools and by sending young Egyptians on educational missions to Europe; and he enhanced the central government's ability to communicate with the people by creating such official organs as al-Waqā'i^{c} al-misrīya (the Egyptian Gazette). Thus, while Muhammad Alī was not himself an

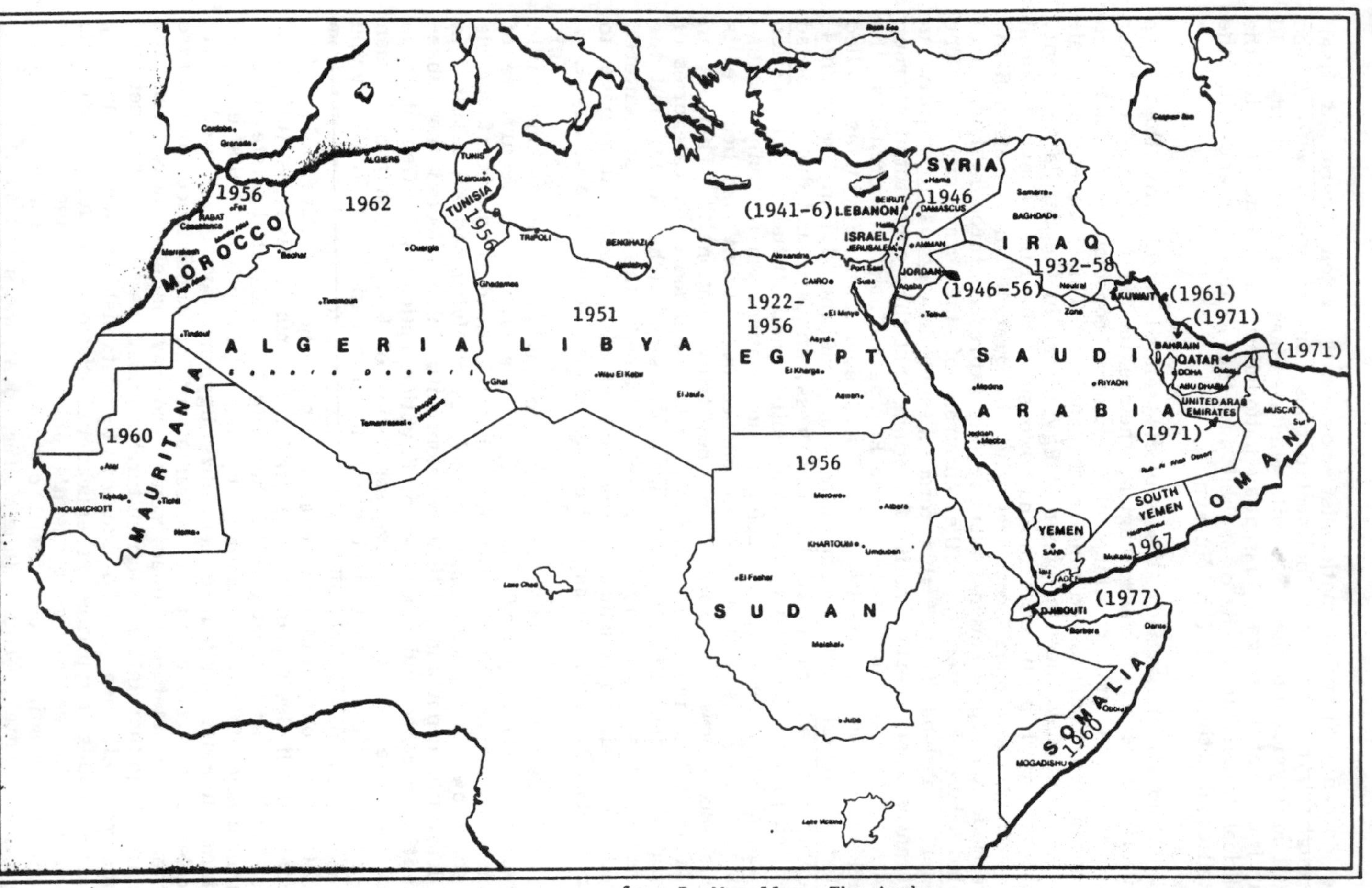

from B. Musallam, <u>The Arabs</u>

The Emergence of Independent Arab Nations

Egyptian nationalist by any stretch of the imagination, his policies played a crucial role in bringing about the necessary preconditions to the rise of a truly national consciousness.

That such a consciousness soon did begin to stir can be seen in the life and works of Rifa'a al-Tahtawi (1801-73), whose period of greatest intellectual activity (1837-69) preceded yet overlapped with that of Butrus al-Bustani. Particularly in his book Manāhij al-albāb al-misriyya fī mabāhij al-ādāb al-ᶜasriyya (Cairo, 1869), wherein he frequently used the word watan and the phrase hubb al-watan, Tahtawi articulated the general concept of an Egyptian nation. In Egypt, as in the Fertile Crescent, by tradition "Arabs" popularly meant "bedouin"; but in Egypt, unlike the Fertile Crescent, this essentially negative connotation did not change with the stirring of national consciousness. For Egypt's embryonic national identity did not acquire an explicitly "Arab" orientation. Rather, the symbol of Tahtawi's Egyptian nation was the ancient civilization of the pharoahs, whose cultural and economic vitality he held up as a model for modern Egypt to emulate. Tahtawi's nationalism was still vague as well as embryonic in a number of respects. For example, although he blamed Egypt's decline on "foreign rulers," Tahtawi apparently did not include in that category Muhammad Ali and his successors whom he personally served. Nor did he clearly define the distinction between the Egyptian nation and the Islamic umma when arguing that "there is a national brotherhood between [Egyptian Muslims] over and above the brotherhood in religion"; and that "Egypt is part of the Islamic umma, but she has also been a separate umma, in ancient and modern times alike, and as such is a distinct object of historical thought." Albert Hourani has pointed out that "in his thought there is no sense of Europe's being a political danger." Perhaps this absence of a clear and immediate foreign threat, usually a prerequisite to the rise of nationalism, accounts for the fact that Tahtawi's pioneering conception of an Egyptian nation was somewhat shadowy.

By the mid-1870s, however, a number of Egyptians had begun to perceive Europe as a danger to their country's sovereignty and well being. It was about this time that the nascent ideology of Pan-Islam attracted several Egyptian Muslim intellectuals. Jamal al-Din al-Afghani spent the 1871-79 period in Egypt teaching his local disciples--including Muhammad Abduh, Saᶜd Zaghlul, and other young activitists of an Azharite background--that Egyptian Muslims should energetically resist European (especially British) imperialism. Yet other, more recently emerged groupings in Egypt--large landowners, bureaucrats (the "efendi class"), and military officers, for example--also grew concerned that Egypt was becoming increasingly subordinated to foreign domination. A small group of native Egyptian military officers even formed a semi-secret society, al-hizb al-watanī. Initially directing their resentment against the Turco-Circassian elite which controlled Egypt's army as well as its government, the native officers also expressed their disapproval of the growing European presence. They accordingly constituted the most active element in Egypt's "First National Movement"--the "rebellion" led by Colonel Ahmad Urabi against the regime of the Khedive Tawfiq (1879-1892) that included two European ministers having full power over the Egyptian government's revenues and expenditures. In effect, it was in order to protect and to consolidate that power that in 1882 Britain occupied Egypt, crushed the nationalist "rebellion" of Col. Urabi, and imposed a "veiled protectorate."

"Egypt for the Egyptians" was a prominent slogan of the Urabi revolt which, however, ended in a situation entailing a more extensive form of alien domination than did the situation it was seeking to end. The humiliating failure of the "First National Movement" to protect and to liberate Egypt from foreign control seems for a time to have turned Egyptian intellectuals away from militant tactics and nationalist ideologies. The last two decades of the nineteenth century thus represented, for Egyptian nationalism, a period of quiescence. One of the country's most profound and most articulate thinkers of that era, Shaykh Muhammad Abduh (1849-1905), advocated a policy of educational, legal and social reforms rather than one of anti-foreign agitation and overt resistance. In other words, Abduh in effect acknowledged that Egyptians would not likely be successful in an armed struggle against the British occupation and that their energies could be utilized more efficiently and more productively in an effort to strengthen the institutions of Egyptian society by implementing needed reforms. Although he cautioned that modernizing reforms ought to be kept within Islamic guidelines, Abduh inspired a number of thinkers who began to call for fundamental changes in Egyptian society. One of the most prominent of these was Qasim Amin (1865-1908), whose advocacy of socialism and of the emancipation of Muslim women reflected Abduh's concern for domestic reform but ultimately went beyond Abduh's Islamic guidelines.

While during the 1880s and 1890s such thinkers as Muhammad Abduh and Qasim Amin more or less ignored the British occupation per se in order to concentrate on domestic social problems, about 1900 certain other intellectuals started once again to refer publicly to the humiliation and the injustice of alien rule and to call for Egypt's independence. This resurgence of Egyptian nationalism was promoted by a number of factors. First, impersonal developments--like population growth, urbanization, the formation of a centralized national economy, political and social integration, and the spread of literacy--continued and accelerated during the second half of the nineteenth century. The material conditions in Egypt thus became increasingly favorable to the rise of a national consciousness. So, secondly, did the political and psychological conditions. By 1900 the generation-old British occupation appeared to be growing more permanent and more oppressive, as the upper and middle levels of Egypt's bureaucracy became thoroughly Anglicized and as Lord Cromer sought to smother every hint of opposition with a show of force. This policy of "teaching the Egyptians a lesson"--by dealing harshly with any challenge to British authority--resulted during June 1906 in the famous Dinshaway incident,* which became a symbol of Egyptian resistance to foreign oppression. Finally, Egypt's ruler, the Khedive Abbas Hilmi II (1892-1914), secretly yet actively encouraged the development and the expression of Egyptian nationalism, in part for reasons of personal ambition. Although he ultimately failed to obtain the strong, independent authority he was seeking, Abbas Hilmi II did contribute to a renaissance of nationalist activity through his confidential subsidies to anti-British Egyptian newspapers and through his clandestine promotion of secret societies.

Egypt's "Second Nationalist Movement" expressed itself through two loosely structured political parties. Al-hizb al-watanī (the Nationalist or Patriotic Party), which revived the name of Ahmad Urabi's secret society but which had no direct connection with the movement of 1881-82, was founded in October 1907 by Mustafa Kamel (1874-1908). A lawyer educated in France, Mustafa Kamel had since 1900 been publicizing his nationalist views in al-Liwā, a newspaper subsidized by the Khedive. Drawing its leadership primarily from Cairo's urban, professional intelligentsia, al-hizb al-watanī insisted on an immediate British withdrawal. Strongly anti-British, it first looked to France and then to Ottoman Turkey for external support. Although his personal correspondence suggests that Mustafa Kamel privately harbored a more or less secular world view, in public his party frequently sounded pan-Islamic themes as a means of strengthening an Ottoman-Egyptian alliance against Britain. This popular association of al-hizb al-watanī with pan-Islam to some extent alienated form it Egypt's Christian (Coptic) intellectuals, but won for it considerable sympathy (although not a large membership) among urban Muslims of all social categories.

The other political party, hizb al-umma (the Party of the Nation) which was organized in 1907 by Ahmad Lutfī al-Sayyid (1872-1963) and which publicized its views through al-Jarīda, on the one hand differed in some respects from al-hizb al-watanī. Drawing its leadership from wealthy rural landowners (including cottongrowers), it was more anti-Ottoman than anti-British. Indeed, exhibiting liberal, gradualist attitudes, hizb al-umma seemed willing to tolerate a period of British tutelage in order to facilitate domestic reform and in order definitively to sever Egypt's residual relationship with the Ottoman Empire. Lutfi al-Sayyid's views were explicitly secular in public as well as in private; as editor of al-Jarīda, he identified as the constituents of the Egyptian nation all those having a common interest in the welfare and destiny of

---

*A party of British officers, while shooting pigeons near Minufiyya in the Delta, were attacked by villagers from Dinshaway after a local woman was accidentally wounded by gunshot. One of the officers, who opened fire at the villagers, was struck in the head by a rock and later died of the wound. Fifty-two inhabitants of the village were quickly arrested and tried by a court dominated by British officials. The sentences--four Egyptians to be hanged and most of the others to be flogged and then imprisoned at hard labor--were carried out swiftly and publicly at Dinshaway.

Egypt, regardless of ethnic origin or of religion. On the other hand, notwithstanding the differences, hizb al-umma had a number of features in common with al-hizb al-watani. For example, both parties held that Egypt was a nation which needed to progress and which deserved to be free (although one party advocated an Ottoman alliance as a means to the end of independence from the British occupation, while the other tolerated the British presence as a means to the end of terminating nominal Ottoman sovereignty). Typical of embryonic nationalist movements, both also had a relatively small membership, limited as a rule to the well-to-do, literate and articulate urban population.

The principal activities of these two parties during 1907-14 was to publicize their respective programs via newspapers. By the early 1920s, however, Egyptian nationalism had moved beyond a journalistic phase into one that was more political and even constitutional. Eldon Gorst, who replaced Lord Cromer in 1907 as British Agent and Consul-General in Egypt, initiated a policy of making concessions to Egyptian nationalism in order to stem the rising tide of anti-British feeling. But this policy was reversed at the outbreak of World War I when the British (a) deposed Abbas Hilmi II, (b) formally proclaimed a protectorate over Egypt, and (c) greatly increased the number of its troops there. By the war's end in 1918, when the Ottoman Empire ceased to exist, Britain thus loomed larger than ever as the main object of the Egyptian people's resentment at foreign domination. By then, also, the death of the charismatic Mustafa Kamel had rendered al-hizb al-watani somewhat ineffective and the more or less pro-British stance of hizb al-umma had been discredited. A number of new leaders consequently came forward as spokesmen for the Egyptian nation, some having been moderates of the Umma Party who were "radicalized" during the war and the post-war settlements. Among these was Sa^{c}d Zaghlul (1857-1927), who as an Azhar student during the 1870s was a disciple of al-Afghani, who as a disciple of Lutfi al-Sayyid served as Egypt's Minister of Education (1906-10) and Minister of Justice (1910-13), and who emerged during 1918-23 as the leading advocate of Egypt's independence from British rule.

To some extent during 1918-23, one fundamental question ("how soon and to what degree will Egypt become independent from British rule?") became entangled with another ("who will speak for the Egyptian people: the traditional sovereign or a self-appointed nationalist elite?"). When the British authorities forbade Zaghlul and his delegation (wafd) to leave Egypt in order to bring the nationalists' demands to the attention of world leaders, there began to occur anti-British demonstrations in Cairo and other large cities. Then, when the British attempted to suppress the demonstrations by arresting and exiling Sa^{c}d Zaghlul, there occurred the Revolution of 1919, an anti-British uprising involving all regions and levels of Egyptian society. These events served both as evidences and catalysts for Zaghlul's acquisition of a good deal of popular support. His residence in Cairo came to be called bayt al-umma ("home of the nation"), and Zaghlul himself was called za^{c}im al-umma ("leader of the nation"). Nevertheless, King Fuad I (1917-36) and the British authorities were resolved both to keep their dealings with Zaghlul to the barest minimum and to retain as much authority as possible in their own hands. The result was a three-cornered power struggle between the British, the Egyptian monarchy, and the Egyptian nationalist elite whose chief spokesman was Sa^{c}d Zaghlul.

The main symbol of Britain's desire to continue ruling Egypt was the "Declaration of the British Government to Egypt" (February 1922)*, which proclaimed Egypt to be a sovereign independent state but which preserved British jurisdiction over four crucial areas: British communications in and through Egypt (including security for the Suez Canal), Egypt's defense needs and policies (requiring the continued presence in Egypt of large numbers of British troops), the economic and legal interests of foreigners and of non-Islamic minorities in Egypt, and Sudanese affairs. The chief symbol of the King's bid for power was the Egyptian Constitution, which was drafted in 1923 by an appointed commission (rather than by a popularly elected commission as demanded by Zaghlul, who was rearrested during this period) and which gave the balance of power to the monarchy--including unconditional jurisdiction over such Islamic institutions as *waqf* properties and al-Azhar as well as the authority to appoint the prime minister and to dismiss parliament. The new parliament, along with public demonstrations and some terrorist activity, became the principal medium through which the nationalists could express themselves. Zaghlul organized the Wafd Party, Egypt's first genuine political party, which consistently won a majority of the elected seats in the parliament where Zaghlul consistently served as Speaker until his death in 1927.

However, throughout the 1920s, sometimes called the "era of Egypt's liberal experiment," the nationalists failed to advance through parliamentary methods toward their primary objectives: fully liberating Egypt from the British occupation and seizing effective political power from the monarchy. In retrospect, the failure became apparent as early as Sa^{c}d Zaghlul's disastrous term as prime minister, an office he won by virtue of the Wafd Party's overwhelming victory in the 1924 parliamentary elections. Since Britain stood adamant against making additional concessions to Egyptian independence, Zaghlul more or less ignored that fundamental issues to engage in a fruitless power struggle not only with the King but also with the Wafd's rival political parties, which he did not hesitate to shackle by applying to them the hated press censorship law. When in November 1924 the British Governor-General of the Sudan, Sir Lee Stack, was assassinated by Egyptian terrorists, Zaghlul's Wafdist government fell as British reinstituted a "get tough" policy toward Egypt. A new election law, entailing a two-step election procedure designed to minimize the impact of the Wafd's popularity, was implemented and in effect enabled King Fuad to rule through coalition governments composed of minor parties. The Wafd, further weakened in 1927 by the death of Zaghlul, remained the dominant party in a legislature rendered ineffectual by the first "royal coup against parliamentary life." Additional "royal coups"

---

*This document is also referred to as the Anglo-Egyptian Treaty ("of Independence") of 1922.

occurred in 1928, when the King dismissed parliament and postponed elections for three years, and in 1930, when he promulgated a new constitution and a new electoral law which concentrated even greater authority in his own hands. By the early 1930s, when the world-wide economic depression was beginning to affect them, Egyptians were becoming disillusioned with parliamentary liberalism as an effective means to the end of national independence.

The world-wide depression, along with continued foreign domination of Egypt's economy, also led during the 1930s to the faltering of a bold effort in the sphere of economic nationalism. In 1922 a committee that included future prime minister Ismail Sidqi and industrialist Tal^{c}at Harb published its report, which concluded among other things that Egypt's economy was bound up too closely with the export of cotton and was overdependent on imported manufactured goods. In other words, the report recommended ending the neglect of industrialization that had been the pattern in Egypt since Muhammad Ali's factories were closed during the 1840s. Although called the "Sidqi Report," this recommendation to promote Egypt's economic independence through industrialization was closely associated with the ideas of Tal^{c}at harb, who in 1920 had created Bank Misr as a purely national bank drawing exclusively on Egyptian capital investments and relying on a board of directors composed entirely of Egyptian citizens. Under the presidency of Tal^{c}at Harb, Bank Misr used its profits to establish a number of "Misr Companies"--such as Misr Spinning and Weaving Company, Misr Printing Company, and Misr Travel. When the depression produced a crisis at Bank Misr, however, the foreign-owned banks were persuaded to come to its aid only on the conditions that Tal^{c}at Harb resign as the bank's president and that Bank Misr mitigate its policy of economic nationalism. Thus, although many of the institutions founded by Tal^{c}at Harb survived, these institutions ultimately did not produce the result for which he had created them: Egypt's economic independence.

The 1930s witnessed not only the impotence of parliamentary democracy and the failure of economic nationalism; about that time secular liberalism also began to lose the popularity it had temporarily enjoyed among Egyptian intellectuals as a major component of their national identity. The decade of the 1920s represented a culmination of the Egyptian intelligentsia's fascination with European culture, a fascination that had already advanced during the late nineteenth century to the point where the Khedive Ismail could designate Egypt as "part of Europe" and where Qasim Amin could in effect advocate European models for Egyptian social institutions. As a continuation of this trend, the worldview of Ahmad Lutfi al-Sayyid, perhaps Egypt's major intellectual force during the first two decades of the twentieth century, can be described as being essential "liberal rationalism."* By the 1920s, when Egypt's nationalist elite was dominated by graduates of modern and/or European schools, secular liberalism served as the dominant philosophical theme of Egyptian nationalism and influenced the legal and cultural orientation of the national identity.

In a legal expression of secular liberalism, Wafdist and nationalist representatives of other parties sought consistently to create secular national institutions, like the King Fuad University (now Cairo University), and to enact secular legislation, like a proposed divorce law inspired by European civil codes. In many cases, as in Turkey during the 1920s, the new institutions and laws advocated by the Egyptian nationalists were intended to provide alternatives to or even replacements for traditional Islamic institutions. In this regard, the popularity of secular liberalism also attracted a number of Azhar-trained intellectuals, including two who made important contributions to the political-cultural debates of the "era of Egypt's liberal experiment." As a consequence of the abolition of the Caliphate by Kemal Ataturk (President of the new Turkish Republic), an Azhar teacher named Ali Abd al-Raziq wrote and published Islām wa usūl al-hukm ("Islam and the sources of political power," Cairo, 1925). In this much refuted and much defended book, Abd al-Raziq supported Ataturk's action with the argument that the religion of Islam had been revealed prior to the establishment of an "Islamic state" and therefore could be distinguished from it. He then proceeded in effect to advocate the separation of state and religion in twentieth-century Egypt. Similarly, the great blind teacher (at the Azhar) and man of letters, Taha Husayn, elaborated Tahtawi's theme of "pharaonism" and defined Egypt's national culture largely in terms of its "Mediterranean" past during the pharaonic and Greco-Roman periods. Suggesting that Egypt had thrived in the past by participating in a "Mediterranean civilization," he observed with satisfaction that such a Mediterranean-oriented culture was re-emerging in Egypt. In part it was this cultural vision for their country and its people which provoked Taha Husayn and other intellectuals during the 1920s to reject Sati^c al-Husri's argument that Egyptians were "Arabs" who formed an integral part of a pan-Arab nation.

By the mid-1930s, however, among Egyptian intellectuals secular liberalism was losing its popularity with respect to culture as well as with respect to politics. One symbol of this trend's political aspect was the Anglo-Egyptian Treaty of 1936, a document replacing the 1922 "Treaty of Independence" the revision of which the Wafd Party and other nationalist groups had demanded for more than a decade. The

---

*By "liberal" is meant a basic attitude of openmindedness and tolerance as well as an inclination toward parliamentary methods for bringing about needed reforms. By "rationalism" is meant the acceptance of human reason, rather than revelation or some other dogmatic source of authority, as the best guide in the formulation of opinions and policies.

new treaty arrangement, negotiated by a Wafd government, fell way short of popular expectations. While clearing the way to transfer to Egyptian courts legal jurisdiction over foreigners and minorities(in effect ending the Capitulations) and while facilitating the training of some young Egyptians for officerships in the Egyptian army, the 1936 Treaty reaffirmed Britain's right to quarter troops in Egypt to protect its own interests (particularly the Suez Canal) and it preserved Britain's jurisdiction over Sudanese affairs. Immensely unpopular, the 1936 Treaty became a symbol of national humiliation. It underscored the fact that, like the "Arab nation" in the Fertile Crescent, the Egyptian nation was not yet free, that its long-standing grievance against a foreign military occupation was still unresolved. During the 1930s Egyptian intellectuals thus began to lose faith in liberal parliamentary methods generally and in the Wafd Party specifically as effective means for relieving the national grievance. For Egypt this period consequently represented something of a new "crisis of the intellectuals," who began to search for other, more successful formulas. Some would become supporters of the popular new young king, Farouk (1936-52). Others would resolve to revitalize Islam, which was on the defensive during the 1920s but which, via such groups as al-Ikhwān al-muslimīn (the Muslim Brethren), would soon begin to mount a popular offensive against secularism and foreign influence. Finally, the few young Egyptians, admitted as officers into the army after 1936, would first become politicized over such issues as Palestine and internal corruption and would then plan a military solution to Egypt's problems of a decadent monarchy and of an alien occupation.

Index